*Martin Erdmann*

# BUILDING THE KINGDOM OF GOD ON EARTH

The Churches' Contribution to Marshal Public
Support for World Order and Peace, 1919-1945

*Wipf and Stock Publishers*
Eugene, Oregon

2005

Wipf and Stock Publishers
199 W. 8th Ave, Suite 3 • Eugene, OR 97401


Building the Kingdom of God on Earth
The Churches' Contribution to Marshal Public Support
for World Order and Peace, 1919-1945
Copyright ©: 2005 by Martin Erdmann
ISBN:1-59752-135-3
Publication Date: April 2005

# DEDICATION

This book is dedicated to those I love most

Joy E. Erdmann,
Estelle Chérie Erdmann, Johannes Luc Erdmann,
Edgar & Alide Erdmann,
and Beate L. Gsell

# ACKNOWLEDGEMENTS

It is a pleasure to acknowledge my indebtedness to those who have contributed to the completion of this book – a pleasure muted only by the knowledge that it is impossible to express fully the extent of my appreciation.

Dr Peter Cotterell and Dr Meic Pearse of London School of Theology, an associated institution of Brunel University, have given the entire manuscript careful, critical, and helpful readings. I am indebted also to Professor Edgar H. Andrews of the University of London for his constant encouragement throughout all stages of the research and for his continuing interest in the study. To him and his wife, Thelma, I am indebted for financial support and other arrangements and kindnesses without which this study could not have been completed at this time.

The library staffs at the British Library, London, at Bodleian Library (Rhodes House), Oxford, at Ohio State University, Columbus, Ohio, and at Henderson County Public Library will be remembered for their careful, courteous, and efficient assistance.

The love and care of my parents, Edgar and Alide Erdmann, and my sister, Beate L. Gsell, were constantly present with me in all my studies. This present book would not have been written were it not for their many prayers (and much more besides).

It is also most fitting to be appreciative of the many expressions of love which were freely given to me by my in-laws, Dr Gorden and Othella Elliott, who graciously agreed to let us live in their home for several months. As a family, we enjoyed their company greatly and look back with fond memories on the many wonderful times we were able to spend with them.

To acknowledge adequately the debt which I owe to my wife, Joy, is most difficult of all. No mere words can convey the appreciation for various types of direct and indirect assistance over a period of several years. More than that she put up with sometimes strenuous circumstances in order for me to pursue my academic work. Her love and understanding will be etched in my memory for ever.

Our most adorable daughter, Estelle Chérie, who was born in

Stevenage, Hertfordshire, on November 29, 1994, will be a constant reminder of God's boundless goodness to us while living in Knebworth, England. On March 30, 1998 we were again abundantly blessed by the arrival of Johannes Luc, our son, who has been a constant ray of sunshine while we were residing in Hendersonville, North Carolina.

# FOREWORD

## Dr. Meic Pearse
London School of Theology, an Associated Institution of Brunel University

The twentieth century has been the age of ever expanding technocracy, a feature which neither that century's passing nor the shift from a modernist paradigm to postmodernity has diminished. Rather, the drift towards rule by technocrats, allegedly impartial souls, undriven by dogma and supposedly free of the partisan concerns that motivate the rest of us, has intensified. Neither has religious life, avowedly the realm of the spirit and private communion with God, been free of this propensity. Instead, the twentieth century witnessed the rise of the ecumenical movement, an attempt to unify the disparate churches on a global basis – a sort of ecclesiastical counterpart to the League of Nations and, later, the U.N.. Indeed, as this book shows, churchly pressure played a role in the birth of the U.N. itself.

Perhaps to the embarrassment of conservative Christians today, the ecumenical enterprise began its public career in largely evangelical soil, at the Edinburgh Missionary Conference of 1910. But its subsequent history was driven, not by a missionary passion to convert eternal souls, nor by theology or ideology, nor even by great leaders. It was advanced rather by committees, agreements and conferences. Its theology was designedly minimalist, for its underlying conviction was that the values of management and omnicompetent government were one with those of the Sermon on the Mount; the former was but the latter writ large and transposed into the public arena.

The ironical conclusion was that the age that was in full retreat from Christian orthodoxy and supernaturalism witnessed a paradoxical confidence that the Kingdom of God – established, of course, by human management skills – was just around the corner.

Dr. Erdmann, in Building the Kingdom of God on Earth, ably traces the story from 1919 to 1945. The results are illuminating. Scrutinising the documentary evidence (including a very large amount of private correspondence) in impressive detail, he demonstrates how key, highly placed individuals in both Britain and America attempted to harness the churches for a secular technocratic programme to build a new

ix

world order – and ultimately a world government – that would rest upon the minimalist theology of a vague Christian ethic. The easy assumptions inherent in such aspirations, namely the superiority of 'Western Christian civilisation' and the ability of the West to impose its will upon the non West, are unlikely to recommend themselves today, even to so conservative a commentator as S. P. Huntington – or, for that matter, to Martin Erdmann or myself.

Nevertheless, the consequences of the story told here live on, both in the ongoing technocratic trajectory as a whole and in the ecumenical movement. As these pages show, the individuals like John Foster Dulles who come together to make 'big plans' for us lesser mortals are not dispassionately benevolent intelligences. Like all people, they are affected by their peer group: that is, by one another. Beginning by representing their churches to the various ecumenical bodies, they swiftly moved to its reverse; that is, a position of representing ecumenism (i.e. their technocratic peers) to the churches to which they still (nominally) belonged.

It was a privilege to be involved in the long, arduous process of seeing this writing come to fruition in its initial form as a doctoral thesis, and is a delight to see it now published for a wider readership. It is devoutly to be hoped that it will secure the attention – and provoke the debate – which so important a topic and study demands.

# PREFACE

Charles H. Spurgeon (1834-1892), the famous Baptist pastor of the Metropolitan Tabernacle in London, preached a sermon once on Ps. 2: 8,9: 'Ask of Me, and I shall give Thee the heathen for Thine inheritance, and the uttermost parts of the earth for thy possession. Thou shalt break them with a rod of iron; Thou shalt dash them in pieces like a potter's vessel.'

The title he gave to the sermon, Christ's Universal Kingdom, And How It Cometh, pointed to the establishment of the millennial kingdom of God on earth. In his introductory remarks Spurgeon voiced comforting words to his congregation concerning the ultimate triumph of God, in installing his Son Jesus Christ as supreme ruler of all nations.

Godless kings and potentates have always tried (and are still trying) to thwart the eternal decree of God in exalting his anointed Son to the highest place in heaven and earth, for the display of his own glory and majesty (cf. Phil. 2:9-11). But the more they try, the less they will, finally, succeed.

Taking to heart Spurgeon's thoughts on Ps. 2 (quoted below), it seems presumptuous for anyone to set himself up in opposition to the Almighty. Yet, strange and incomprehensible as it seems, men have frequently pursued such futile schemes to rule the nations without regard for God's revealed purpose in Jesus Christ. They have done so following the extravagant vision of building 'the Kingdom of God' on earth, and in the name, and for the glory, of humankind. The historical record is there to prove it.

World empires

World empires have come and gone, but none were able to subjugate the whole world under one rule. Perhaps the closest approach occurred in the late 1800s, when the immense expansion of the British Empire seemed to succeed in uniting peoples on all continents under its colors.

The centuries-old humanistic dream of establishing a world government inspired idealistic and wealthy individuals such as Cecil Rhodes, Lord Alfred Milner and their successors to do whatever was in their power to transform the British Empire into an imperial federation, expressly including the 'lost colonies' of North America.

In his Confession of Faith of 1877, Rhodes wrote:

> The idea gleaming and dancing before ones eyes like a will-of-the-wisp at last frames itself into a plan. Why should we not form a secret society with but one object the furtherance of the British Empire and the bringing of the whole uncivilised world under British rule for the recovery of the United States for the making the Anglo-Saxon race but one Empire. What a dream, but yet it is probable, it is possible.[1]

William T. Stead, a member of the inner circle of Rhodes' confidants, added the elucidating remarks in his commentary on this and similar statements:

> Fancy the charm of young America, just coming on and dissatisfied − for they have filled up their own country and do not know what to tackle next − to share in a scheme to take the government of the world![2]

Internationalism

In the early 20th century it became painfully apparent that the nationalistic and fiercely independent sentiments of the American people prevented any foreseeable reunification of their nation with Great Britain. At the same time, the British Empire drifted apart politically and transmuted gradually into a more or less loosely associated Commonwealth of Nations. The establishment of the League of Nations on 10 January 1920, one of the final acts of the Versailles Peace Conference, rekindled the hopes of internationalists everywhere that a relentless march towards global governance could be sustained. Yet shortly thereafter, those high aspirations were ruthlessly dashed to pieces once again by the refusal of the United States Senate to ratify the Peace Treaty and become a full member of the League.

Even prior to this devastating blow to the idea of a one-world state, many of the politicians, academicians, financiers and industrialists who had come to Paris in 1919, had seen the need to regain a sure footing on the shifting ground of international politics.

Amid the growing realisation that the Conference would not bring about the desired results, a handful of these internationalists met at the Hotel Majestic on 30 May 1919 to devise a strategy. They sought a way to make internationalism attractive to the common masses, especially in Great Britain and the United States of America.

In order to overcome the enormous barrier of rampant nationalism, exhibited even among the victorious Allied nations at Versailles, only one way seemed to promise success. It had to be made clear to everyone that only the establishment of a new world order could end for all time the waging of devastating wars.

These high-minded diplomats put their confidence in a steady stream of internationalist propaganda. Public opinion would be persuaded to clamour for a voluntary abrogation of national sovereignty. To this end, the Institute of International Affairs was formed. It later received a royal charter and united more or less informally with the American Council on Foreign Relations.


Ecumenical Movement

As time went on, it seemed more and more expeditious to use the Protestant churches, and especially the nascent ecumenical movement, as a vehicle to condition the person on the street to abandon isolationist sentiments in favour of world government.

The internationalist message began to resound from the pulpits of the English-speaking world. It prepared the ground for the establishment of a better (though still less than perfect) successor to the dismally ineffective League of Nations, by then dismantled.

The new organisation was to be a powerful guarantor of peace and prosperity. The opportune moment for its genesis came at the end of the Second World War, when the Allies, who had called themselves 'the United Nations', met in San Francisco. Their aim was to transform their military coalition into a political organisation, inviting other nations to join them.

For the liberal Church establishment and its associated Christian laity, the ratification of the United Nations Charter presented the best possible opportunity to realise their aspiration of building a secularised version of a postmillennial kingdom of God on earth.

Others, especially those who were cognisant of the prophetic meaning of Psalm 2, saw things differently.


God is Sovereign

These Christians sympathised with the introductory remarks of Spurgeon's sermon on Ps 2:8-9 to which we now turn:

> Observe, dear Friends, the wonderful contrast between the violent excitement of the enemies of the Lord, and the sublime serenity of God Himself. He is not disturbed though the heathen so furiously rage, and their kings and mighty ones set themselves in battle array. He smiles at them: He hath them in derision. You and I are often downcast and depressed, and our forebodings are dark and dismal, but God sits in His eternal peacefulness, and serenely overrules tumult and rebellion. The Lord reigneth, and His throne is not moved, nor His rest broken, whatever may be the noise and turmoil down below.

Notice the sublimity of this divine calm. While the heathen and their princes are plotting and planning from them, He has already defeated their devices, and He says to them, 'Yet have I set My king upon My holy hill of Zion.' 'You will not have My Son to reign over you, but nevertheless He reigns. While you have been raging I have crowned Him. Your imaginations are indeed vain, for I have forestalled you, and established Him upon His throne. Hear Him as He proclaims My decree, and asserts His filial sovereignty.' God is ever beforehand with His adversaries: they find their scheming frustrated, and their craft baffled, even before they begun to execute their plans. By God's decree the ever-blessed Son of the Highest is placed in power, and exalted to His throne. The rulers cannot snatch from His hand the sceptre, nor dash from His head the crown: Jesus reigns and must reign till all enemies are put under His feet. God has set Him firmly upon Zion's sacred hill, and raging nations cannot cast Him down: the very idea of their so doing excites the derision of Jehovah, He disturbs not His great soul because of their blustering. As if it were a banquet rather than a conflict, the Lord God, as Himself a king, speaks to the King's Son, even to His Anointed on His right hand, and having owned His royal rank, confers upon Him the highest honours. At great feasts many a monarch has been known to say to his favourite, 'Ask what I shall give thee, and nothing shall be denied thee this day.' Even thus doth the great Father say to His glorious Son the Prince of Peace, 'Ask of Me, and I will give thee the heathen, Thine inheritance, and the uttermost parts of the earth, Thy possession.' He bids Him open His mouth wide, and request a boundless dominion. He will give Him distant nations, yea, and the whole round earth to be His kingdom. There is an air of regal festivity and peaceful joy about all this which strangely contrasts with the uproar of the adversaries. Brethren, I wish we could enter in some measure into this sublime quiet. We may well be confident since God is so. If the Captain be assured of victory it behooves the common soldier to be bravely hopeful. The battle is the Lord's, and since He is the Lord God omnipotent, fear about the issue of the conflict is foolish and wicked. All events are in His hand — His hand who can dash whole worlds to dust, or make them when it pleases Him. What can stand against the almighty will? Who shall say unto Jehovah, 'What doest Thou?' In this eternal all-sufficiency is our rest, and we may therefore cease from anxiety. Stand thou still my weary brother, and see the salvation of God. Put not forth thy timorous hand to stay the trembling ark, but know that Jehovah can protect His own. Lay thy Martha cares aside; sit at thy Saviour's feet, and listen to His voice. He will tell thee that God reigneth yet, and that His Anointed shall reign also. Things are not as they seem: all is well when all looks ill. If the heavens are clouded the sun is not put out: if the evening hath darkened, even to midnight, yet the morning cometh; to the moment shall it break, nor can all the powers of darkness hinder the dawning day. Jehovah's fixed decrees remain engraved as in eternal brass, nor can the craft of hell efface a single line nor stay the execution of a single purpose. Despite all opposition the sacred purpose will blossom into the actual providence, and the providence will ripen into salvation. God's plan will be carried out without failure in any point, and there is no cause for alarm.

# Notes

[1] See Cecil Rhodes, 'Confession of Faith of 1877' in: John Flint, *Cecil Rhodes* (London: Hutchinson & Co., [1974] 1976) 248-252. The original manuscript is in Mss. Afr. t. 1 (17), Rhodes House, Oxford.

[2] William T. Stead, ed., *The Last Will and Testament of Cecil John Rhodes. With Elucidatory Notes* (London: Review of Reviews Office, 1902) 70. Writing in 1946 Frank Aydelotte, the American Secretary to the Rhodes Trustees, was confident in being able to project the realisation of Rhodes' vision by contemplating the achievements of Rhodes Scholars, especially in the United States, since the turn of the century: 'Meanwhile during the forty odd years since Rhodes' death greater forces than any that he could set in motion are bringing about the unity of the English speaking people of the world. In the two world wars soldiers from the United States, Great Britain and the British Dominions have fought side by side in defence of the basic ideals of democracy. They have twice been united in war and it is only sober truth to say that the greatest question before the world today is whether they can remain united in the maintenance of peace. Not merely Rhodes Scholars but all forward looking men are today working and praying for the continuance of that union ... If all the far flung nations of the English speaking world remain united in support of a new international order in which force will be the servant of law, they will bring to reality, in ways which he could not have foreseen, the Vision of Cecil Rhodes.' Frank Aydelotte, *The American Rhodes Scholarship. A Review of The First Forty Years* (Princeton: Princeton University Press, 1946) 120, 121.

# TABLE OF CONTENTS

# 1

# THE PRETENSIONS OF IDEALISM

## 1.1    Introduction

In tracing the development of the idea of world federation from 1919 to 1945, it is our purpose to demonstrate that the ascendancy of internationalism as a political movement during the interwar years, and especially during the Second World War, can be credited in part to the efforts of John Foster Dulles, the chairman of the Commission on a Just and Durable Peace. Following his lead, the Federal Council of Churches conducted a successful campaign in support of world order and peace. Their strategy to focus on informing public opinion about international co-operation proved effective in drawing the United States away from the isolationism that had rejected Wilson's League of Nations and towards participation in the United Nations Organisation. The willing acceptance of America to play a leading role in the community of nations was deemed by many Church leaders an indispensable step towards the future realisation of the Kingdom of God on earth.

Of particular concern to us will be the influences of the Round Table Group on representatives of the churches in formulating a common socio-political and internationalist agenda. The Round Table Group was formed in Britain, and its dominions, at around 1910. Its principal leaders, Lionel G. Curtis and Philip Kerr, became outstanding proponents of the imperial federation movement and later of a federal 'world commonwealth'. To further their objectives, Curtis and Kerr played an instrumental role in establishing the Institute of International Affairs at the Paris Peace Conference in 1919. Members of the American delegation, such as John Foster Dulles and Whitney H. Shepardson, joined them in the endeavour. Disillusioned about the outcome of the Peace Conference, they decided to promote, in their respective countries, the ideal of a unified world. The American branch of the Institute of International Affairs eventually merged with the Council on Foreign Relations.

1

The British branch became known as the Royal Institute of International Affairs. The founding of the United Nations Organisation in 1945, in which the United States were firmly integrated, was the crowning achievement of their concerted efforts.


## 1.2 John Foster Dulles: Corporate Lawyer

When President Wilson went to the Versailles Peace Conference at the end of 1918, he appointed both Bernard M. Baruch and Vance McCormick as his principal aides. Some thirty members of the Inquiry[1] also accompanied Wilson to Paris.[2] According to the President's previous arrangement, the Inquiry had been formed by Colonel House, the President's personal advisor, in September 1916.[3] Sidney Mezes, the president of the College of the City of New York, was appointed director of the organisation. The secretarial post[4] was given to the former Rhodes Scholar Walter Lippmann, a journalist of the liberal magazine *New Republic*. All members were specially selected and consisted of approximately 150 economists, lawyers, university professors, graduate students, and journalists.[5] The Inquiry's primary task was to formulate specific war aims and to determine the American contribution to the peace settlement. Moreover, this group of intellectuals outlined the long-term foreign policy of the United States, including the drafting of a charter for an international organization.[6] It compiled nearly 2,000 separate reports and documents and at least 1,200 maps.

During his service as chairman of the War Industries Board, Bernard Baruch frequently came in contact with members of the Inquiry, especially with a young lawyer and representative of the War Trade Board by the name of John Foster Dulles. Dulles' efficiency in handling difficult legal procedures left a favourable impression on Baruch, who eventually secured the assistance of this brilliant lawyer at the Peace Conference.


## 1.2.1 At Sullivan & Cromwell

Following his graduation from Princeton, Dulles was employed as a clerk at the prestigious law firm of Sullivan & Cromwell. On numerous occasions he demonstrated his outstanding abilities in managing intricate legal affairs, and was soon promoted to a junior partnership. Although Dulles was fully occupied with the daily routine of his chosen profession, he soon desired to expand his sphere of influence beyond that of a successful corporate lawyer on Wall Street. He saw himself continuing a proud family tradition of distinguished public service. Perhaps he anticipated that one day he would become a Secretary of State, like his grandfather, Colonel John Watson Foster, who had served under President Harrison, and his uncle, Robert Lansing.[7]

After practising law for five years he embarked on a new, and more

2

exciting, venture in his professional career. Robert Lansing, who had succeeded William Jennings Bryan as Secretary of State, sent him on an important mission to South America, involving the most delicate matters of diplomacy. In anticipation of America's direct participation in the war, the U.S. government decided in early 1917 to take precautionary measures to secure its political and commercial interests in Central America. Through intelligence channels it became known that German agents were operating in Panama, Costa Rica, and Nicaragua, and Wilson feared that Germany might possibly attack the Panama Canal if the United States should join the Allies on the European battlefields. In such an event the American government wanted to make sure that most, if not all, of its neighbouring countries would simultaneously enter the war on its side. Secretary Lansing chose Dulles to discuss these matters with the Central American governments.[8] Although family connections might have played a part in Dulles' selection, his appointment was probably more a choice of expediency. Lansing was certainly aware of the diplomatic and political risks involved in this precarious mission. The pretended neutrality of the United States would have suffered a serious blow had it become known that Wilson pressured other neutral countries into a future alliance with the Allied Powers. Besides, a public disclosure of the real purpose of Dulles' mission would have suggested to the American voters that the President intended to lead the United States into war. Any such revelation would have jeopardized Wilson's chances of being re-elected for a second term in office, since it contradicted the pacifist overtones of his campaign slogan 'He kept us out of the War'. The opportune time would come when the American people could safely be told that it might be their destiny to have a part in the struggle. This is, at least, the way the President explained himself later in a public announcement, shortly after it was confirmed that he had won the election. But for the moment, it was important to cater to the isolationist mood in the country.

The Secretary of State acted shrewdly on behalf of his superior in sending a representative of Sullivan & Cromwell as his personal envoy to the Central American governments[9], because this law firm had been the official legal counsel of the Panamanian government for several years.[10] Dulles could thus discharge his duties for the State Department under the pretext of doing normal business. Apart from these considerations, Dulles was superbly qualified to lead the delicate negotiations. In the event, he secured the promise of most Central American countries to co-operate with the American government. This assurance put Wilson's fears to rest and might have strengthened his resolve to enter the military struggle against the Central Powers at the earliest possible moment. Years later Robert Lansing recorded in his *War Memoirs* that the success of his twenty-nine-year-old nephew was of strategic importance in tilting the scales in favour of America's entry into the war.[11] The day after the United States joined the Allies in the conflict, both Panama and Cuba proclaimed a state of war with the German Empire.

### 1.2.2    At the War Trade Board

Being exempted from active military service in 1918 because of his impaired eyesight[12], Dulles became an army captain working with Military Intelligence, and later a lawyer on the War Trade Board in Washington. His assignment at the War Trade Board[13] was to assure that neutral countries like Sweden and the Netherlands would strictly adhere to the foreign trade agreements with the United States. Government regulations prohibited any exports of American goods to Germany, even if they were imported and traded by neutral countries.[14] In time, Vance McCormick, the chairman of the War Trade Board[15], promoted Dulles to the position of personal assistant, and entrusted to the young lawyer many of his own duties on the Board.[16] Dulles also served as a liaison officer between different government agencies. In this capacity he was responsible for the efficient co-operation between the War Trade Board, the Army General Staff, and the War and Navy Departments, thus gaining valuable insights into the mechanism of central planning in a wartime economy.[17] In addition to his regular duties, he gave legal advice to Bernard Baruch at the War Industries Board. To work with Bernard Baruch must have been a valuable experience for John F. Dulles, as it provided him with a chance to observe firsthand the nature and purpose of wartime regimentation. He prepared, for example, the draft of an executive order to confiscate eighty-seven merchant ships of neutral Holland, then anchored in American ports. Since initial lease negotiations with the Dutch government had broken down, the seizure of these ships was seen as the next best alternative for quickly adding another 354,478 tons of shipping capacity to the U.S. Navy.[18] John R. Beal states 'that there was considerable outcry over the order, which some held to be unconstitutional, but it was not formally challenged.'[19]

### 1.2.3    At Versailles

In the fall of 1918, Dulles was promoted to the rank of major, a gesture of gratitude extended to him by Vance McCormick. McCormick had come to admire his extraordinary proficiency. Bernard M. Baruch, the chairman of the War Industries Board, had equally observed Dulles' competence and subsequently chose him as his legal counsel, while serving as head of the American Delegation to the Reparations Commission at Versailles.[20] Inspired by Wilson's idealism, Dulles was exceedingly pleased to be part of the American delegation which set out to reconstruct the world on the basis of the Fourteen Points.[21] Versailles promised to become the much anticipated culmination of the Allied policy to construct a new world order on the ruins of the old. In April 1917 Dulles had already stated that he believed 'it to be of the utmost importance that the nations at war with Germany should unite in a new statement of their purposes, which should be asserted to be the creation of a world of new international relationships.'[22] The Peace Conference would surely fulfil the dreams of the ages and inaugurate the dawn of a new era of international co-operation. The jubilant crowd which praised Wilson as 'the angel of peace' at his triumphant arrival in Paris were convinced that the American President would bring to life the vivid pictures his high sounding rhetoric had painted in their hearts and minds of a world united under the banner of peace and justice. Yet, experience was to prove, and nowhere clearer than at Versailles, nationalistic ambitions and greed swept the pretensions of idealism into the depths of compromised morality.

1.3     Breach of Contract

The story of the Versailles Peace Conference actually began on October 5, 1918, when Prince Max of Baden, communicated his desire to negotiate a peace settlement with President Wilson based on the Fourteen Points. Three days later the President requested from the German Government a definite statement to the effect that it would agree with his points as the basis for an armistice. After receiving this statement on October 12, Wilson replied with a list of additional conditions two days later.[23] He would not be prepared to sign any armistice which did not guarantee 'absolutely satisfactory safeguards for the maintenance of the present military supremacy of the Allied and Associated armies.' The Kaiser would also be required to abdicate and permit the establishment of a democratic and representative government in Berlin. The German Government accepted these conditions. Whereupon the President told Prince Max on October 23 that he would approach the Associated governments with the proposed conditions for an armistice. Its terms would still be contingent on their general approval of his Fourteen Points. The Associated governments were agreeable to Wilson's proposals with the understanding that the 'freedom of the seas' means 'complete freedom' and that the reparation payments would be made 'by Germany for all damage done to the civilian population of the Allies, and their property, by the aggression of Germany by land, by sea, and from the air.' On November 5 the German Government agreed to these terms. Six days later, on November 11, an armistice was signed in the Forest of Compiègne.

    In the ensuing negotiations the German Government counted on the integrity of Wilson to comply with his promise in making the Fourteen Points the basis of a peace settlement, a promise which had been formally, though reluctantly, extended to its representatives by all heads of state of the Allied Powers. That the British and French governments never intended to keep this promise, marred the proceedings at the Peace Conference in Paris from its very beginnings. At the London Conference, on December 1-3, 1918, Lloyd George openly declared his intention to make the Pre-Armistice Agreement a mere scrap of paper. He proposed a resolution, which was later adopted, to form an inter-Allied Commission endowed with powers to 'examine and report on the amount enemy countries are able to pay for reparation and indemnity.' The

5

word 'indemnity' could easily be interpreted as an obligation of Germany to reimburse the Allied Governments for all 'costs of the war'. Although such an interpretation did not conform with the intent of the Pre-Armistice Agreement, Lloyd George showed an 'apparent nonchalance about principle and contract'.[24]

During the December election the British Prime Minister assured his national constituency that he did not intend to honour his pledge to Colonel House in accepting the principles set forth in the Fourteen Points. In a speech at Bristol on December 11, 1918 he told his jubilant audience that 'we propose to demand the whole cost of the war [from Germany]'[25], and thereby he effectively discarded the Pre-Armistice contract.[26] Speaking to a large crowd in the Cambridge Guildhall, Eric Geddes captured the spirit of the election campaign by expressing his approval of Lloyd George's intentions: 'We shall squeeze the orange until the pips squeak.'[27]

At the Paris Peace Conference, Lloyd George (January 22, 1919) suggested the appointment of a commission to study 'reparation and indemnity'. In an attempt to follow the guidelines of the Pre-Armistice Agreement, President Wilson managed to have the word 'indemnity' removed from the commission's purpose statement. On February 24, then returning to the United States on the S.S. *George Washington*, President Wilson unequivocally stated that America was 'bound in honor to decline to agree to the inclusion of war costs in the reparation demanded ... It is clearly inconsistent with what we deliberately led the enemy to expect ... We should dissent and dissent publicly if necessary.'[28] This gesture of good faith by the American President, however, proved to be ineffectual against the joint efforts of the British and French governments to follow through with their schemes for the economic dismemberment of Germany.[29] Lloyd George and Clemenceau demanded that Germany must accept the obligation for all 'war costs'.[30]

This concerted attempt to circumvent the Pre-Armistice Agreement was primarily challenged on legal and moral grounds by John Foster Dulles, the American members on the Reparation Commission.[31] Dulles emphasised the fact that the Pre-Armistice Agreement on reparations was essentially a legal contract: 'We have not before us a blank page ... but one which is already filled with writing, and at the bottom are the signatures of Mr. Wilson, of Mr. Orlando, of Mr. Clemenceau and of Mr. Lloyd George. It is the agreed basis of peace with Germany.'[32] Only by this expedient had the Associated governments succeeded in persuading the Germans to sign the armistice. The American lawyer simply reminded the Allies that they had given their word to the Kaiser that they would live up to this arrangement.

In a letter to Arnold J. Toynbee on 10 August 1919[33], and again years later in his book, *Spiritual Values and World Affairs*, Alfred E. Zimmern, the Montague Burton Professor of International Relations at the University of Oxford, reflected on the intricacies of the controversy at Versailles and cast his vote squarely in favour of Dulles' position concerning the binding force of the Pre-Armistice Agreement:

One such issue – a very plain issue – arose within a few weeks of the signing of the Armistice. The Prime Minister had embarked on an election campaign with a programme, one of the main planks of which was in violation of an international engagement on which the ink was hardly dry – the reparations clause of the pre-Armistice agreement ... But that did not alter the fact that it was a binding agreement – as binding as the Belgian Treaty of 1839 with the violation of which our action in August 1914 had so much to do. In other words, the Prime Minster was committing the British people, within a few weeks of the Armistice, to a policy which involved an offence against international morality (to use the language of the Versailles treaty) of the same kind as that which we later imputed to the Kaiser. Here surely was a moral issue of the plainest and most unmistakable kind -- and an issue which, as was evident to any student of international affairs, was pregnant with momentous consequences for the future of Europe and of the world.[34]

Dulles further noted that Germany's capacity to pay reparations was limited and that the Allies would sow the bitter seeds of a new war if they pressed their claims beyond those limits. This brought him into direct confrontation with W. M. Hughes, the Prime Minister of Australia. Hughes had persistently argued for an open-ended solution to the reparation question allowing Britain and France to make the most exacting demands from Germany. Since these two countries were obligated by treaty to defend the integrity of Belgium's territory, Hughes contended, they were, like policemen, fulfilling their duty to uphold the law. The other countries engaged in war with Germany were comparable to private citizens on a city street, who could not remain by-standers while the 'policemen' rushed to Belgium's defence and, having participated in the struggle, should also receive full payment to recover their expenses. In his rebuttal, Dulles challenged the Australian Prime Minister's logic by asking: 'Does the policeman receive his hire from the wrongdoer whom he arrests? No; in making the arrest the policeman has performed his duty nobly, gallantly, at great sacrifice, if you will; but still his duty. And the reparation paid by the wrongdoer is made to the victim not to the guardian of the law.'[35] By applying this principle Dulles established the case that only Belgium (because her territory alone had been attacked) had the right to press its claim for full recompense of war damages. The other countries should be content with payments covering any damages sustained by the destruction of property and by physical injury to civilians. Yet Dulles soon realised that, in the matter of reparations, it was useless to remind his principal disputants that their integrity and honour as statesmen were at stake. His moral appeals quickly evaporated in the hot atmosphere of the Peace Conference.[36] In a private memorandum, he later wrote that 'there was not one of them who recognized the binding force of this provision [the Pre-Armistice Agreement].'[37]

Dulles was not prepared, however, to lower his flag so soon. Fearing the grave consequences which might follow such flagrant breach of contract by the Allies, he tried tenaciously to hold his position and embarked on a more

7

casuistic course of action. By pretending to accommodate the demands of his disputants, he tried to persuade them to fix the reparations payments to a mutually agreeable amount. On February 21, 1919 he declared in a draft statement that 'the German Government shall ... make reparation for the entire cost of the war', but added that 'the ability of the German Government ... to make reparation is limited'. The Associated Governments could now prudently 'renounce' their right to payment beyond a specified level.[38] Colonel House supported him in this tactical manoeuvre.[39]

Lloyd George remained unconvinced and, on Lord Sumner's recommendation, demanded that both war pensions and separation allowances should be included in the reparations.[40] Clemenceau scrupulously agreed with him, although both of them knew that by stipulating these items as 'war cost' they violated the expressed terms of the Pre-Armistice Agreement. In response Dulles maintained that the United States and the Allies had committed themselves to a legal agreement with Germany on November 5, 1918, which explicitly excluded pensions and separation allowances from claims of compensation. 'If the Allies expected Germany to understand that she was to repay the costs of these items,' he wrote, 'I, personally, do not see how the Allies could have chosen words less apt to convey that meaning.'[41]

To disperse any lingering doubts about his determination to exact all 'war costs' from Germany, the British Prime Minister instructed his private secretary, Philip Kerr, to draft the position of the Associated Powers on reparations.[42] Kerr later admitted that his note, especially the phrase, 'the aggression of Germany', was used in formulating the famous 'war guilt clause' (Article 231 of the Treaty of Versailles).[43] Reflecting on the consequences of this particular clause, Dulles stated in 1938, at a time when the worst features of Hitler's tyranny had become general knowledge, that 'it was the revulsion of the German people from this article of the Treaty which, above all else, laid the foundation for the Germany which we see today.'[44] On May 29, 1919, Lloyd George introduced a revised version of Kerr's draft to the Council of Four. Describing in vivid pictures the immense destruction of war caused 'by the aggression of the enemy states', he continued to emphasise 'the indisputable claim of the Allies and Associated Governments to full compensation.'[45] Dulles expected that President Wilson would resolutely oppose this obvious attempt to break the Pre-Armistice Agreement and constrain the Allies to abide by the assurances they had extended to the Kaiser. But when the President's financial advisers pointed out to him that Lloyd George's proposals were devoid of any logical foundation[46], Wilson deeply shocked the American delegation by bursting out in petulant tones: 'Logic! Logic! I don't give a damn for logic. I am going to include pensions.'[47] Due to the President's surprising volte-face in regard to the reparations issue, Dulles, again, failed to reach a reasonable agreement with the Associated governments.[48] In a last, desperate attempt, Dulles proposed on June 3, 1919, that, whatever the formula used for determining 'war costs', at least a clearly defined limit of reparations payments should be established.[49] The financial experts at Versailles, however, postponed the decision to settle for any particular amount of reparation payments. In 1921 the Reparation Commission remedied this omission by demanding from Germany to pay the astronomical sum of approximately $33,000,000,000.[50] One third of this sum represented damages to Allied property, 'and one-half to two thirds, pensions and similar allowances. In short, Wilson's decision doubled and perhaps tripled the bill.'[51] Germany might have been able to pay a bill of not more than ten billion dollars, but when Wilson consented to the British and French position, he pointed the way to the financial chaos that eventually overwhelmed Germany and Europe. In the dark soil of this breach of contract the seeds of another world war were sown.[52]

John Foster was present when the punitive terms of the Peace Treaty were finally set down, signed by the victors and presented to the Germans.[53] His vivid impression of the Peace Conference was that, beyond injustice, its outcome would lead to a course of self-destruction. The realisation that Wilson's plan to erect an international order of peace at Versailles foundered on the rock of senatorial opposition at home left an indelible impression on his mind. From the collapse of Wilson's idealism he concluded that statesmen should not prematurely attempt to alter political realities before they are assured of a strong political base as a platform on which lasting diplomatic victories can be achieved. In the final analysis it was not that Wilson had failed in reaching his goal of establishing a world government (although the President could be faulted for his poor handling of the negotiations in Paris and his deplorable inconsistency); it was more the lack of public support behind his efforts that had contributed to the downfall of an international system of collective security. Subsequently, Dulles would always use the historical lessons he had learnt at Versailles as the touchstone against which he measured his own performance as an expert of foreign affairs. He became convinced that the use of propaganda was essential in shifting public opinion in America from its traditional isolationist stance to a new policy of interdependence. In a published response to Keynes' criticism of President Wilson's diplomatic blunders at the Peace Conference, Dulles concurred with the British scholar's own conclusion in *The Economic Consequences of the Peace* (chapter 'Remedies'): 'A great change is necessary in public opinion before the proposals of this chapter can enter the region of practical politics.'[54] In the same article Dulles also asserted that, while the 'balance of power structure' was subject to limitations imposed by political realities, the restraints forced upon the politicians by public temperament and conceptions, as expressed in congressional resolutions, could be overcome in time.[55] As it turned out, only a month later, on March 19, 1920, the first part of Dulles' prescient remarks came true. On that day the U.S. Senate rejected America's participation in a League of Nations. The tragedy of the First World War was destined to be repeated in a much more devastating world conflict twenty years later. John F. Dulles noted that, at Paris, democratic Europe had proved unworthy of a world order which was based on the principle of a community of nations. It still seemed unable to rise above petty nationalistic ambitions. The day would come, however, when the second part of his response to Keynes would also find its fulfilment. In 1949, at a Church conference, Dulles announced that internationalism had finally triumphed over isolationism. He took great pride in the churches' accomplishment of convincing the American public to accept membership in the United Nations Organisation.

> If our nation has abandoned political isolation, it is largely because our Christian people took the lead in developing the public opinion that not only permitted but that compelled our Government to work to establish a world organization and to work with it.[56]

Years later, Richard M. Fagley, the executive secretary of the Commission of the Churches on International Affairs, essentially confirmed Dulles' assessment. Fagley maintained that the failure of the League of Nations served a pedagogical purpose ('the major teacher') in revealing the fragile nature of a collective security system which did not rest on a broad base of public support. Fortunately, Dulles' chairmanship of the Commission on a Just and Durable Peace during the war years 'had a part in helping to awaken the American people to their need for a more responsible role in the post-war world.'[57]

To understand Dulles' purpose in using the churches to proclaim his message of peaceful change in the international community, we need to examine first the events which led to the founding of the Institute of International Affairs at the Peace Conference. Later we will consider the Institute's connection to the British Round Table Group.

1.4     The Institute of International Affairs

In 1917 an unsigned article was published in *The Round Table*, entitled 'Windows of Freedom', which netted its author, Lionel G. Curtis, an invitation from Lord Robert Cecil to attend the Paris Peace Conference.[58] The article challenged the United States to shoulder its responsibility in securing 'the world's future freedom from war'. As a first step America was urged to occupy either Palestine, Armenia, Tanganyika, or Cameroon.[59]

At Versailles Curtis served as a British delegate to the League of Nations Section. There he rubbed shoulders with an impressive array of bankers, lawyers, and academicians. They had come to Paris as counsellors of their respective governments and cherished the opportunity to write a new chapter in human history. The task they faced was monumental. The British delegates, for example, soon discovered how difficult, expensive, and time-consuming it was to obtain current information about foreign affairs.[60] This predicament was compounded by another problem. On occasions when the political theorists put forth sensible recommendations the career diplomats bungled them up in notorious flawed decisions, a situation which became all too familiar to Curtis.[61] He collaborated closely with members of Colonel House's 'Inquiry', primarily George L. Beer, the American expert on colonial matters, and Whitney H. Shepardson[62], in lobbying the French to accept his 'Freedom' proposal. On 30 January 1919 Wilson declared America's interest in accepting a mandate for one of the German colonies. Curtis and Beer, who had spoken with the President about this matter two days earlier, were exuberant. Their high hopes, however, were dashed to pieces in the following weeks. The Anglo-French agreement that partitioned Africa exclusively among the European powers left America standing in the cold. Wilson's aspirations to gain territorial advantages as a participant of war came to naught. Put under pressure he again surrendered to the Europeans. This experience upset Curtis. Suffering under the impression of having failed in his mission to overcome 'the old pernicious idea of imperialism', he had to leave Paris for a while to regain his emotional balance.[63]

The lesson Curtis learned at Versailles was that the outbreak of another war could only be prevented if foreign policy experts rather than politicians would be in charge of creating a new world order. He persuaded his American colleagues Beer and Shepardson to undertake an ambitious project, namely to establish an Anglo-American research institute of international affairs.

On the evening of May 30, 1919, some thirty members of the American and British delegation followed Curtis' invitation to a dinner meeting at Hotel Majestic in Paris.[64] Clement Jones, the Assistant Secretary to the British Empire Delegation, later described Curtis' aptitude for convincing others to do his bidding:

> Under his own rules because he [Curtis] had known me as a schoolboy he had a perfect right, in later life, to ask me to do anything he wanted. With him a request was a command and for those of us who "served under him" it was great fun. There can be few men who ever "roped in" more friends and casual acquaintances in support of his projects ... Chatham House was one of his major round-ups.[65]

At the suggestion of Lord Robert Cecil, the chair was given to General Tasker Bliss of the American delegation.[66] It was a shrewd move, as it was known that Bliss held Curtis in the highest regard and could be expected to endorse any British scheme. '[Curtis] is the most intelligent man', Bliss once stated, 'and evidently deeply informed on world affairs of great importance.'[67] During the dinner Thomas W. Lamont and Robert Cecil gave two spirited speeches, echoing Lord Grey's opening remarks in praising the mutual bonds between the United States and Great Britain.[68]

John Foster Dulles was delighted by what he saw and heard at the dinner meeting. Almost immediately an intimate intellectual and personal bond began to develop between him and Curtis which time only deepened.[69] Dulles also established a lasting friendship with Philip Kerr.[70] The close relationships he maintained with these two Englishmen over the years proved highly significant in the unfolding of future events.

Intimately involved in the proceedings at the conference, most of the dinner guests at the Hotel Majestic had become disenchanted with the high expectations placed upon the conference of bringing about a new world order. They had lost faith in the peace settlement to create an international arrangement which would be better than the one that had only a few years ago culminated in a devastating world war.[71] 'The reigning notion among those present was,' writes William McNeill, 'that an informed public opinion about international affairs was the only way to make sure that future wars would not break out because of secret diplomacy and the irresponsibility of officials dealing with matters about which ordinary persons before the war knew next to nothing.'[72] Many agreed with Lionel Curtis' position, that the imperfect provisions of the Peace Treaty were reflecting the current state of public opinion. In his speech, Curtis asserted that future agreements would equally mirror the consensus of the people in the streets. The only effective solution would be to lead public opinion 'along the right path'. Thinking primarily of those present at the dinner meeting, Curtis maintained that this is the task of 'a small number of people in real contact with the facts who had thought out the issues involved.'[73] He warned the assembled diplomats that they would lose their influence on the public mind unless they kept in touch and continued the work they had set out to do after the Peace Conference. Harold G. Nicolson thought Curtis' speech was 'really admirable'.[74]

The group gathered at the Hotel Majestic resolved to find an arrangement which would provide a suitable platform for an ongoing and constructive discussion of international affairs. It was suggested to establish an Anglo-American institute, which would operate across national boundaries and offer its members the opportunity of exchanging ideas about foreign policy.[75] Curtis' outlined the institute's two primary functions. First, the new organisation would shape national policy in conformity with the interests of society at large, and secondly, it would bring public opinion in accord with expert knowledge in each of the countries.[76] Only Eyre Crowe expressed doubts about the practicality of this approach, fearing that 'official responsibility and independent comment' would clash rather than complement each other.[77] The proposal was nevertheless enthusiastically received by the other dinner guests. They agreed to set up 'The Institute of International Affairs', which would be modelled after the Royal Geographic Society, and serve as a congenial meeting place for statesmen and intellectuals.[78]

To prevent any criticism about the Anglo-American character of the institute, it was divided into two separate organisations, which would work out their own constitutions and operate independently in Great Britain and the United States, for 'it seemed unwise to set up a single institute with branches.'[79] It was feared that an organisation jointly operated by British and American diplomats would soon arouse suspicion among the general public. A united front would be preserved by encouraging a lively interchange of ideas and personnel across the Atlantic, and, as Curtis put it, 'to keep alive the spirit of cooperation begun at Paris'. This arrangement gave both organisations the freedom to develop autonomously along national lines, and yet allow enough room for a broad international co-operation, without being bound by undue considerations of national concerns. To symbolize the common origin of both organisations, George L. Beer and Harold W. Temperley, a well-known British historian, were commissioned to edit a comprehensive history of the Peace Conference.[80] The American banker Thomas Lamont gave £2,000 to fund the project. It was also decided to co-publish an annual survey of international affairs, 'a publication which no speaker or writer would dare to leave unconsulted.' The sales profits of the successive surveys would be used to pay for specialist monographs edited by the directors of research on both sides of the Atlantic, but prepared for the Institute as a whole.[81]

A committee of six was appointed to carry the proposal for the Institute of International Affairs forward. It consisted of international lawyer and State Department official James Brown Scott, the historians Archibald Cary Coolidge (Harvard) and James T. Shotwell (Columbia), and three British representatives. On June 17, 1919, the Institute of International Affairs was officially established as a private, bilateral organisation, which would provide a stage to express internationalist views detached from particular national issues. Lionel G. Curtis and Whitney H. Shepardson were appointed as joint secretaries of the British and American organisations respectively.[82] They would be responsible 'to keep its members in touch with the international situation and enable them to study the relation between national policies and the interests of society as a whole.'[83] In accord with Curtis' proposal the preamble to its founding document announced that, in establishing the League of Nations, the Allied Powers declared their agreement and determination to pursue their foreign policies henceforth with a concern for 'the welfare of Society at large'.[84] To that internationalist ideal the members of the Institute would pledge their allegiance.

The Institute would concentrate its activities on five main areas: (1) meetings, (2) research, (3) information and library, (4) publications, and (5) conferences.[85] Thus the organisation would operate primarily as a research centre to 'provide the material from which those who are most influential and who have the greatest amount of knowledge, comprehension and perspective in foreign affairs can form public opinion.'[86]

Opposition from the British Foreign Office was quickly overcome after Curtis convinced Lord Curzon, the Lord President of the Council, of the Institute's useful purpose. The only requirement which Curzon imposed was that its membership had to be chosen carefully.[87] Thereupon Lord Cecil was put in charge of an election committee which recruited new members for the Institute from the American, British and Dominion representatives gathered at Paris. At once Curtis and Jones began to prey on their 'victims' during meal times at the Majestic. It was 'a happy hunting-ground where Curtis would stalk and bag his game.'[88] On one evening alone, Jones hauled in a catch of eight new members - Seton-Watson (a Balkans expert), Allen Lepper (Romania), Felix Frankfurter (Poland), F. W. Bourdillon (Boundary Commission), Alfred

E. Zimmern, E. H. Carr, Charles Webster, and the son of J. H. Thomas.[89] Curtis was not to be outdone, however, and doubled his efforts to boost the Institute's membership roster, especially among the American delegates.

> In this way Curtis met for the first time members of the American East Coast establishment - the financiers, businessmen, and lawyers who constituted an important internationalist lobby in the inter-war years. They were naturally interested in trade and investment opportunities when European capital was in short supply, but they also regarded their wealth as a trust for the welfare of all and for the promotion of world peace. They provided the transatlantic foreign policy-making élite whose significance has been analysed by D.C. Watt and others.[90]

More than a year later the British *Saturday Review* noted that the Institute of International Affairs brought together 'the young men in Paris [who] thought more, knew more, and learned more than the old men who actually signed the treaty.' This gathering represented, 'the revolt of the Peace makers against the Peace [Treaty].' The Institute would become known for its accomplishments in three areas: (1) the study of international affairs, (2) the publication of information about foreign relations, and (3) above all, the provision of a medium of interchange between its officials and publicists.[91]

### 1.4.1    The Royal Institute of International Affairs

On 5 July 1920 the British section of the Institute of International Affairs rented two rooms in Malet Street, London from the Institute of Historical Research, vacating the cramped quarters of *The Round Table* offices. The Astors opened their mansion in St. James's Square for the inaugural ceremony which was presided over by Arthur Balfour; Lords Grey and Clynes were in attendance as representatives of the other parties. Briefed by Curtis, who stage-choreographed the entire program for maximum publicity effect, the British press described the event as one of the most magnificent of recent years.

Institutes are usually composed of men presumably too old ever to know better, but the British Institute of International Affairs is surprisingly low in the average of its years per member. The internationalism for which this Institute stands is, in fact, something almost entirely new in politics. It is not the old internationalism of the working classes, which aimed at a horizontal division of Europe ... It is not the internationalism of cosmopolitan trade and banking, which regards a frontier as an inconvenience when it does not happen to be an opportunity. It is an internationalism which respects frontiers, values the principles of nationality, and seeks to comprehend and sympathise with the various countries of the world in their national aims and activities.[92]

Lord Robert Cecil was selected chairman of the organisation, while Lionel G. Curtis and G. M. Gathorne-Hardy became the two honorary secretaries. At

14

once Curtis showed off his talents as a quintessential organiser, 'who rounded up a glittering array of political grandees as Presidents, recruited an executive committee, raised the initial donation from A. B. Bailey to sustain the first activities, and recruited the first generation of staff.'[93] The 1926 *Report of the Council* paid tribute to Curtis and Gathorne-Hardy for being primarily responsible for running the Institute: 'It is not too much to say that the very existence of the Institute is due to those who have served as Honorary Officers.'

In 1923, Colonel R. W. Leonard, a long-standing member of the Canadian Round Table, President of Conigas Mines, and Chairman of the Canadian National Trans-continental Railway Commission, bought Lord Kinnaird's house at 19 St. James Square as a home for the Institute. Since Prime Minister William Pitt, the Earl of Chatham, had once lived in the building, it was named 'Chatham House'.[94] A devoted Anglophile, Leonard had deeply imbibed the doctrine of Commonwealth while accompanying Curtis on his Canadian tour in 1916, and hoped, though largely in vain, that his generosity would counteract the American influence on the Institute.[95]

In 1926 the Duke of Devonshire, the Colonial Secretary, procured a royal charter for the Institute, 'which was all-important because it meant that no charter would in future be granted to any other Institute for similar purposes.'[96] Not leaving anything to chance, Curtis had actually written the royal petition to which the Duke of Devonshire appended his signature. Subsequently, the Institute became known as the Royal Institute of International Affairs (RIIA). The charter and the patronage of the Prince of Wales as a 'Visitor' added immensely to the Institute's standing and prestige. It also guaranteed Leonard's continued financial support.[97]

As a non-profit organisation, the Institute was financed entirely by membership fees and donations. A few affluent patrons, most notably the South African mining magnate Abe Bailey and the American industrialist John D. Rockefeller Sr., contributed some funds initially to cover operational expenses. These resources proved insufficient, however, and Curtis was forced reluctantly to take out a loan against future membership fees. He was immediately subjected to personal criticism, but in the end his optimism prevailed: 'Again and again, in my experience, I have had to face these difficulties and someone has always come forward with the necessary advance.'[98] Over the years the Institute forged close ties with the British and American financial establishment and the various branches of the Carnegie Trust. As part of a fundraising drive in 1929, important banks, corporations and wealthy individuals contributed generously to set up a well-financed endowment for the Institute.[99] The largest single gift of £100,000 came from Abe Bailey, as a token of his admiration and gratitude for Lionel Curtis.[100] He also decided to give £5,000 per year in perpetuity. From then on the organisation's financial independence was guaranteed.[101]

The by-laws were drawn up by G. M. Gathorne-Hardy and Lionel G. Curtis, while the other members wrote the constitution and proposed individuals who might be suitable to join the Institute.[102] Soon the Institute attracted illustrious members, such as Geoffrey Dawson, George W. Prothero, Harold Temperley, A. L. Smith, J. A. C. (later Sir John) Tilley, Philip Noel-Baker, and Lord Eustace Percy.[103] In 1920 there were about 300 of them. Two years later this number increased to 714; in 1929 it spiralled to 1707, and in 1936 to 2414.[104]

The active governing body of the Institute was the council, originally called the executive committee.[105] It generally had twenty-five to thirty members. In 1924, Philip Kerr was elected to the council for the first time. In 1936, the council included among others Lord Astor (chairman), Lionel G. Curtis, G. M. Gathorne-Hardy, Lord Hailey, H.D. Henderson, Stephen King-Hall, Mrs Alfred Lyttelton, Sir Neill Malcolm, Lord Meston, Sir Arthur Salter, J. W. Wheeler-Bennet, E. L. Woodward, and Sir Alfred E. Zimmern. Others who were on the council's roster at various times were E. H. Carr, Harold Butler, G. N. Clark, Geoffrey Crowther, H. V. Hodson, Hugh Wyndham, G. W. A. Ormsby-Gore, Walter Layton, Austen Chamberlain, and Malcolm MacDonald.

With the completion of the six and final volume of Temperley's *The History of the Peace Conference* in sight, the Institute decided to publish an annual 'Survey of International Affairs' and a Yearbook of International Law. In January of 1924 James Headlam-Morley, then Chairman of the Institute's Publication Sub-Committee, invited Arnold J. Toynbee for lunch to 'discuss a matter of some importance'.[106] Headlam-Morley wanted to know if Toynbee was interested in writing a survey of international affairs for the year 1924 (among some other research assignments). The salary would be set at £1000 including secretarial assistance. Toynbee, whose appointment to the Koraes Chair at the University of London was soon to expire (30 June 1924), accepted the offer after securing an additional £200 for compensation of lost income as a journalist. Engaging Arnold J. Toynbee as Director of Studies and editor of the 'Survey' (at first temporarily) was arguably the most fortuitous decision in the history of the Institute. Toynbee's extraordinary abilities which brought him fame and fortune added lustre to the organisation's reputation and broadened its influence far beyond the original scope, both intellectually and geographically.

Headlam-Morley had already known Toynbee from their days at the Department of Political Intelligence (P.I.D.) in 1918-1919 when they wrote war propaganda pieces for the British government. In 1918 Alfred E. Zimmern had joined them at Headlam-Morley's behest. Others working at the P.I.D. were Lewis Namier, Eustace Percy, Edwyn Bevan, George Saunders, and the Leeper brothers, most of whom were to become members of the RIIA.

The Institute eventually added its own quarterly journal, *International Affairs*, to its popular array of publications. The journal's articles were mainly based on material collected by Clemens Jones at the Institute's monthly meetings. The first editor was G. M. Gathorne-Hardy. In January 1932 an editorial board was placed in charge of the publication. It consisted of Sir

Alfred E. Zimmern, Lord Meston, and G. M. Gathorne-Hardy. This same board remained in control until it was temporarily forced to suspend publication at the end of 1939.

During the early years of the Institute Curtis worked indefatigably as a fund raiser, garnering the endorsements of Dominion premiers and other prominent political figures.[107] When Toynbee came on staff at Chatham House on 15 February 1924,[108] Lionel began to parade him before potential patrons of the Institute.[109] Impressed by Toynbee's scholarship, Sir Daniel Stevenson, Lord Provost of Glasgow and president of a coal-importing company, endowed the Stevenson Chair of International Relations in the University of London in 1925 and also financed the research and publication of the Survey.[110] Curtis persuaded Sir William Beveridge, the Vice-Chancellor of the University, to locate the Chair at the Royal Institute of International Affairs. In *Acquaintances* Toynbee amusingly described Curtis as 'a master of the sales man's fine art of making the maximum display with the minimum outfit,' and added the following narrative of an incident which he had witnessed:

> Lionel made an urgent appeal to me for stage properties. All that I had to give him were a few clutches of the galley-proofs of the first volume of the Survey; and I was depressed at the thought of his having to go into action so poorly equipped. Peeping round the door of Lionel's room, I saw him waving my galley-proofs, like a hypnotist, in front of the visitor's face, while the visitor stood open-mouthed, listening spellbound, to Lionel's earnest allocutions. I realized that, in Lionel's hands, those galleys were ample material, it was Lionel's personality that was producing the desired effect.[111]

Curtis was well-versed in the art of making friends in high places to further the causes he espoused.[112] His unique power of persuasion served him well in his 'Kindergarten'[113] days in South Africa when he and his partners determined to canvass the political public for closer union among the four colonies.[114] Information, communication, and persuasion were the tools which he had successfully employed in the making of the Union of South Africa and later in the forging of the British Commonwealth. In his time he was perhaps the most traveled and knowledgeable expert about Dominion affairs. The large number of personal contacts he had made on all continents testified to his growing influence in world politics. Curtis' friendship to the Astor family, for example, opened up new opportunities to expand his activities across the Atlantic. He was especially keen on fostering friendly Anglo-American relations which he perceived as the most promising avenue to further Britain's international interests. On occasion, while lecturing in the United States, Curtis was introduced by Whitney H. Shepardson as a speaker. Shepardson never failed to inform the American audiences of his friend's peculiar way of thinking. 'Curtis believes in his heart that the United States is a temporarily lost section of the British Commonwealth which some day, like the prodigal son, will come back within the fold. I do not think he realises to any important degree that we have grown along lines of our own.'[115] Curtis replied to Whitney on his return to England, 'I'm more than ever convinced that God's in his heaven looking after "his Englishmen" in which Miltonic term I include my American brothers. Don't get mad. You're bigger than me I know but I can afford to make you mad with the Atlantic between us and old Page [Walter Page[116]] smiles benignly from Paradise.'[117]


1.4.2    Council on Foreign Relations

After the Peace Conference the American section of the Institute of International Affairs encountered some problems in getting the organisation started in the United States. A certain apathy had spread among its members. They seemed to have lost interest in studying international relations, as it became increasingly clear that the Peace Treaty would not be ratified by the U.S. Senate. None of its twenty-three members took the initiative to work out a suitable structure and purpose for the Institute. To solve this problem, Bowman and Shepardson proposed to join a dinner club of New York bankers and lawyers, known as the Council on Foreign Relations.

The original Council on Foreign Relations was founded on June 10, 1918, by some thirty gentlemen who had accepted the invitation of Elihu Root, a Wall Street lawyer and former Secretary of State and Secretary of War[118], to a special dinner meeting. Root wanted to form a club of wealthy and influential patrons who would be interested in the discussion of foreign affairs.[119] His idea met with much acclamation and it was decided to arrange similar meetings at regular intervals.[120] Three years later, in 1921, the Council had shown signs of disintegration. Few of its members regularly participated at the Club's social events, even though distinguished foreign visitors frequently were invited to deliver speeches.

Elihu Root accepted the proposal to merge the Council with the American Institute of International Affairs.[121] He agreed to select a committee on policy to work out the details. George W. Wickersham, Wall Street lawyer and former Attorney General under President Taft, assumed the committee's chairmanship and Whitney H. Shepardson became executive secretary. This committee wrote up the statutes of the new organisation which was eventually incorporated as the Council on Foreign Relations (CFR) under New York State law on July 29, 1921.[122] Root was elected Honorary Chairman of the joint organisation. Lindsay Russell, a New York lawyer, became chairman of the Council and Alexander Hemphill, a banker at Guaranty Trust Company, presided over the Finance Committee. Edwin F. Gay, the editor of the *New York Evening Post*,[123] became secretary and treasurer.[124] John W. Davis[125] and Paul Cravath accepted the presidency and vice-presidency respectively.

The Council on Foreign Relations attracted many influential members, among them many 'high-ranking officers of banking, manufacturing, trading and finance companies, together with many lawyers.'[126] In most cases these

18

members were directly aligned with the financial network of J.P. Morgan & Co. To offset the monolithic character of the membership roster, a steering committee was commissioned to ask thirty journalists and academicians to join the new organisation.

The CFR scheduled monthly dinner meeting at the Harvard Club on East 43rd Street. At first its members were 'concerned primarily with the effect that the war and the treaty of peace might have on post-war business.'[127] They would be briefed on the current state of international affairs by government officials and foreign diplomats at the Council's headquarters in New York City.[128] In its 1922 statement of purpose, the fifteen-man board reaffirmed the goals of the organisation:

> The Council on Foreign Relations aims to provide a continuous conference on the international aspects of America's political, economic and financial problems ... It simply is a group of men concerned in spreading a knowledge of international relations, and, in particular, in developing a reasoned American foreign policy.[129]

In their attempt to establish the Council as a prestigious research institute of international affairs, the founding members decided early on that it ought to publish a journal. The prime instigator of this venture was Edwin F. Gay, who thought that the Council's future would be put on the line if it did not publish a journal. He persuaded Professor Archibald Cary Coolidge of Harvard to assume the editorship of the new quarterly, which bore the title *Foreign Affairs*. After Coolidge's death in 1928, Hamilton Fish Armstrong, a young Princetonian who had acted as European reporter and managing editor of the journal, became senior editor and remained in this position until 1972. *Foreign Affairs* established itself quickly as the leading journal in its field.[130] Its first publication in September 1922 carried articles by André Tardieu, Clemenceau's closest confidant; Eduard Benes, Prime Minister of Czechoslovakia; Elihu Root; Charles Eliot; and John Foster Dulles. In December 1922, *Foreign Affairs* published Philip Kerr's article 'From Empire to Commonwealth', in which the future secretary of the Rhodes Trust and British Ambassador to the United States detailed vital aspects of his political creed:

> There is going to be no steady progress in civilization or self-government among the more backward peoples until some kind of international system is created which will put an end to the diplomatic struggles incident to the attempt of every nation to make itself secure ... The real problem today is that of world government.[131]

While the idea for the Institute of International Affairs and its successor organisations was conceived in Paris, as part of the Conference proceedings, it was, as Gordon Martel points out, part of a larger historical movement which had been set in motion several years earlier.

> The most interesting thing about the Royal Institute of International Affairs
> is its central location at the intersection of ideas, institutions and interests in
> twentieth century Britain. It is most properly seen as the logical culmination
> of the Edwardian imperial and social reform movement, particularly as this
> centred on the "Round Table" in which Lionel Curtis and Philip Kerr were
> such outstanding characters, and as transformed by the experience of the
> First World War ... there seems to be a fairly clear line of continuity running
> from the foundation of the Round Table to the creation of the British (later
> Royal) Institute of International Affairs. In this, of course, Lionel Curtis was
> the central character, as the idea of an Anglo-American institution was his
> brainchild.[132]

About nine years prior to the Peace Conference, Curtis had begun to organise a network of study groups in the British Dominions.[133] Acting on the instructions of Lord Milner and primarily financed by the Rhodes Trust, Curtis (first secretary) and Kerr (first editor of the journal *The Round Table*), consolidated this network into one organisation, the so-called Round Table Group. According to Alan C. Johnson, they intended to use this organisation, which eventually led to the founding of the Institute of International Affairs, as a meeting place for promising young imperial administrators and scholars who would share their federal ideas:

> If federation could knit together the British Commonwealth it could do the
> same for the world at large; perhaps the federal formula was the only
> solution to the diplomatic anomaly of political and economic nationalism.
> Curtis and other members of the [Round Table] group gave impetus to the
> founding of the Royal Institute of International Affairs, which was designed
> to be a fact-finding treasure-house for the architects of the new world
> order.[134]

The story of the Round Table Group actually begins nearly 50 years earlier with John Ruskin's famous inaugural lecture of 1870 at the University of Oxford. This is where we turn our attention now.

Notes

---

[1] Some of the distinguished members of the 'Inquiry' who participated at the Paris Peace Conference were: David Huntley Miller, lawyer; Walter Lippmann, journalist; Dr Sidney E. Mezes of CCNY; Dr Charles Hoskins of Harvard; Dr R.N. Lord of Harvard; Dr W.E. Lunt of Haverford; Dr Clive Day of Yale; Dr W.E. Westermann of Wisconsin University; Capt. S.K. Hornbeck, later professor at Harvard; A.A. Young of Cornell University; Maj. Douglas Johnson of Columbia; Mark Jefferson, State Normal College, Ypsilanti, Mich.; James Brown Scott; Dr James T. Shotwell of Columbia

University; Norman Thomas; Tasker Boward Bliss; Allen Dulles, John Foster Dulles; Christian Archibald Herter; Manley O. Hudson; Frank L. Polk; Elihu Root, Prof. A.C. Coolidge; see Lawrence Gelfand, *The Inquiry. American Preparations for Peace, 1917-1919* (New Haven: Yale University Press, 1963) 53-67,154-180; and also Joseph Kraft, 'School for Statesmen,' *Harper's* (July 1958) 217:64-68; Zygmunt Nagorski, 'A Member of the CFR Talks Back,' *National Review*, December 9, 1977, 1419.

[2] See Edward M. House & Charles Seymour, eds., *What Really Happened at Paris. The Story of the Peace Conference, 1918-1919* (New York: Charles Scribners' Sons, 1921) 1; James T. Shotwell, *At the Paris Peace Conference* (New York: Macmillan, 1937) 3-15.

[3] Secretary of State Robert Lansing acquiesced in Wilson's choice of House as the organiser of the Inquiry; see Charles Seymour, ed., *The Intimate Papers of Colonel House*, Vol. III (London: Ernest Benn, 1926-1928) 174.

[4] *Ibid.*

[5] See Lawrence E. Gelfand, *The Inquiry*, x.

[6] See *ibid*, 312: 'Throughout the Inquiry's papers dealing with trade, finance, and international law, the theme of international organization could be distinguished. World peace involved not solely the construction of just boundaries. A lasting peace in 1917-19 seemed possible only when such matters as commercial competition among nations, labor conditions, financial arrangements among nations, and the availability of raw materials to all nations were regulated for the benefit of the world community. The Inquiry members working on these topics were hopeful that a method for accomplishing these ends would be provided in the establishment of an international organization.'

[7] A personal friend, Clarence Dillon, believed that Dulles 'always had in the back of his head ... the hope that someday he might be Secretary of State ... It may not always have been his conscious wish to be Secretary of State, but I wouldn't be surprised if it was.' See Clarence Dillon, *Oral History Collection*, 1964, 10. One of Dulles' partners at Sullivan and Cromwell, David R. Hawkins, states that 'he prepared himself, undoubtedly, all his life to be Secretary of State.' See David R. Hawkins, *Oral History Collection*, 1965, 8. The *Oral History Collection* comprises about three hundred tape-recorded interviews with personal acquaintances of Dulles. All of the interviews have been reduced to manuscript. They are located with the *John Foster Dulles Papers* at the Princeton University Library, Princeton, New Jersey. See also Richard D. Challener and John M. Fenton, 'Recent Past Come Alive in Dulles "Oral History,"' University: A Princeton Quarterly (Spring 1967), 3-34.

[8] See letter, John F. Dulles to Helen Bramble, October 24, 1928, *JFD Papers*.

[9] In his memoirs, Lansing wrote later, 'It seemed ... expedient to send a special emissary on a secret mission to Panama to urge the principal officials of that government to declare war on Germany as soon as the American congress acted.' Robert Lansing, *The War Memoirs of Robert Lansing* (London: Rich & Cowan, 1935) 314; additional details are given in Forrest Davis, 'The G.O.P.'s Mr. Hull,' *The Saturday Evening Post*, CCXVII (September 9, 1944) 48. Davis attributes Dulles' high standing in President Wilson's esteem to the former's success on this mission. It might be noted, however, that an additional part of his mission involved an appraisal of the situation in Costa Rica where General Federico Tinoco (1883-1919) had unleashed a communist revolt and overthrew the government. Dulles recommended recognition of Tinoco's government. Wilson, however, refused to grant it to Tinoco's revolutionary

party; see John F. Dulles, 'Conceptions and Misconceptions Regarding Intervention,' *The Annals of the American Academy of Political and Social Science*, CXLIV (July, 1929) 103.

[10] See Townsend Hoopes, *The Devil and John Foster Dulles* (Boston: Little, Brown, and Company, 1973) 25, 26.

[11] Robert Lansing, *The War Memoirs of Robert Lansing*, 314.

[12] After contracting malaria Dulles damaged his optic nerve by taking an overdose of quinine; see Townsend Hoopes, *The Devil and John Foster Dulles*, 26.

[13] Bernard M. Baruch made some interesting remarks about the relationship between the War Industries Board and the War Trade Board: 'The President gave direction on the war effort and co-ordinated the work of the war agencies through his "War Cabinet", which consisted of the Secretaries of War, Navy, and the Treasury, and the heads of special agencies, including Herbert Hoover, the Food Administrator; Harry Garfield, Fuel; Edward N. Hurley, Shipping, Vance McCormick, War Trade Board; and myself ... The Shipping Board was never as closely integrated with WIB as was the War Trade Board, which was administered by the indefatigable Vance McCormick. Bernard M. Baruch, *The Public Years* (London: Odhams Press Ltd., [1960] 1961) 87, 89.

[14] Vance McCormick summarised the 'trading with the enemy' act thus: 'The important object which the United States and the Allied Governments had in mind in placing the embargo on exports to the border [of] neutrals and in negotiating agreements with them was the restriction or prohibition of exports from these countries to Germany of essential war materials, including foodstuffs and military supplies.' Vance McCormick, *Report of the War Trade Board*, 20-21; see also letter, John Biddle (Secretary of War) to Vance McCormick, 12 March 1918, *John Foster Dulles Papers*, Seeley G. Mudd Library, Princeton University, Princeton, New Jersey (hereafter cited as *JFD Papers*).

[15] McCormick was also chairman of the Democratic National Committee.

[16] Letter, John F. Dulles to Chief of Staff, July 23, 1918, *JFD Papers*.

[17] See *War Trade Board Journal*, November, 1917-July, 1919, U.S. War Trade Board, *Report of the War Trade Board* (Washington, D. C.: Government Printing Office, 1920) 425. For additional details, see John Chamberlain, 'John Foster Dulles. A Wilsonian at Versailles. This famous Lawyer may be Dewey's Secretary of State,' *Life*, XVII (August 21, 1944) 90; Forrest Davis, 'The G.O.P.'s Mr. Hull,' 48; and Dulles' testimony in U.S. Congress, Senate Hearings before the Committee on Foreign Relations, *United States Assistance to European Recovery Program*, Part 2, 80th Congress, 2nd Session (Washington, D. C.: Government Printing Office, 1948) 598.

[18] John F. Dulles, Draft statement of March 21, 1918; see also 'Eleven Documents relating to Work with the War Trade Board, 1918-1919,' *JFD Papers*.

[19] John R. Beal, *John Foster Dulles. 1888-1959* (New York: Harper & Brothers) 62: 'This particular draft was one on which Wilson did no more than pencil in a few minor changes before signing. Dulles kept the original copy with Wilson's emendations.'

[20] See the Acting Secretary of State to the Commission to Negotiate Peace, December 19, 1919, in U.S. Department of State, *Papers Relating to the Foreign Relations of the United States. The Paris Peace Conference, 1919*, Vol. I, 207; Bernard M. Baruch, *The Making of the Reparation and Economic Sections of the Treaty* (New York: Harper and Brothers, 1920) 18; idem, *The Public Years*, 102.

[21] Charles Seymour summarised the importance of the Fourteen Points in bringing about peace and a 'new political order' based on a League of Nations: '... it [Wilson's speech of the 'The Fourteen Points'] became for liberals all over the world something of a Magna Charta of international relations of the future. "An evident principle," said Mr. Wilson in the concluding paragraph of his speech, "runs through the whole programme I have outlined. It is the principle of justice to all peoples and nationalities, and their right to live on equal terms of liberty and safety with one another, whether they be strong or weak. Unless this principle be made its foundation no part of the structure of international justice can stand. The people of the United States could act upon no other principle; and to the vindication of this principle they are ready to devote their lives, their honour, and everything that they possess. The moral climax of this the culminating and final war for human liberty has come, and they are ready to put their own strength, their own highest purpose, their own integrity and devotion to the test." It was the spirit of this paragraph that persuaded liberals in the Entente countries to regard President Wilson as the apostle of the new political order, and the smaller nations to hail him as their champion. It was this same spirit that compelled the Germans to ask whether they might not better accept the guarantees of security offered by Wilson than continue the devastating struggle. In the end it was to Wilson that the German Government turned offering to make peace, and it was upon the distinct understanding that his principles would prevail that they laid down their arms. The speech of the Fourteen Points was important also because of the position which it gave to the proposal for a League of Nations. Mr. Lloyd George, in his statement, approved the project of a League ...' Charles Seymour, *The Intimate Papers of Colonel House*, Vol. III, 357.

[22] Dulles memorandum, August 1917, *JFD Papers*.

[23] Prince Max assured Wilson that the purpose of 'entering into discussions would be only to agree upon practical details of the application' of the Fourteen Points to the terms of the treaty of peace. The correspondence dealing with the Pre-Armistice agreement is printed in full in *Foreign Relations, 1918*, Supplement, Vol. I, The World War, 1 (Washington, D. C.: 1933) 337-338, 343, 357-358, 379-381, 382-383, 425, 468-469.

[24] Paul Birdsall, *Versailles Twenty Years After* (London: G. Allen & Unwin, 1941) 35-36.

[25] David Lloyd George, *Memoirs of the Peace Conference* (New Haven: Yale University Press, 1939, Vol. I) 306-9.

[26] After arriving in Paris, Lloyd George described his election campaign as follows: 'Heaven only knows what I would have had to promise them [the British voters] if the campaign had lasted a week longer.' Thomas A. Bailey, *Woodrow Wilson and the Lost Peace* (New York: Quadrangle Books, 1963) 238-251; see also Arno Mayer, *Politics and Diplomacy of Peacemaking. Containment and Counterrevolution at Versailles, 1918-1919* (New York: Alfred A. Knopf, 1967) 152-158, 623-652; and Seth P. Tillman, *Anglo-American Relations at the Paris Peace Conference of 1919* (Princeton: Princeton University Press, 1961) 229-259.

[27] Harold G. Nicolson, *Peacemaking 1919* (London: Constable & Co., 1933) 18.

[28] Philip M. Burnett, *Reparation at the Paris Peace Conference. From the Standpoint of the American Delegation* (New York: Columbia University, 1940, Vol. I) 27, 613-614; see also Charles Seymour, *The Intimate Papers of Colonel* House, Vol. IV, 343. Burnett's work is an excellent source to study the reparations negotiations in

1919. His two volumes basically consist of *verbatim* documents loaned to the author by various individuals. His primary source (and Burnett admitted to a great debt in 1940) was the materials he received from John Foster Dulles. Dulles had collected numerous documents from the Paris Peace Conference. The originals are now available in the *John Foster Dulles Papers*, at Princeton Library, but Burnett's volumes provide a readily available version of a great number of items.

[29] After it was brought to his attention that the British government demanded about $ 90 billion and the French $ 200 billion in reparations from Germany, Colonel House confided to his diary that 'I thought the British were as crazy as the French but they seem only half as crazy which still leaves them a good heavy margin of lunacy.' *House Diary*, Yale University Library; as cited in Philip M. Burnett, *Reparation at the Paris Peace Conference*, Vol. I, 600; see also Charles Seymour, *Intimate Papers of Colonel House*, Vol. IV, 343-344.

[30] See Ronald W. Pruessen, *John Foster Dulles*, 33; see also Philip M. Burnett, *Reparation at the Paris Peace Conference*, Vol. II, 294-307.

[31] For his bold defence of the Pre-Armistice agreement, Dulles received high praise from some of his associates at Paris. See for example: André Tardieu, *The Truth About the Treaty* (Indianapolis: The Bobbs-Merrill Co., 1921) 287; Thomas W. Lamont, 'Reparations,' in Edward M. House & Charles Seymour, eds., *What Really Happened at Paris*, 270; and John Maynard Keynes, *A Revision of the Treaty* (New York: Harcourt, Brace and Co., 1922) 156.

[32] John F. Dulles, Address on Principles of Reparations, in 'Commission on Reparation of Damages', February 7, 1919, quoted in Philip M. Burnett, *Reparation at the Paris Peace Conference*, Vol. I, 536-543; see also John F. Dulles, 'Comment on French Project of Principles Governing Reparations for Damages', February 4, 1919, as cited in *ibid.*, Vol. I, 522; 'Address on Behalf of the American Delegates by John Foster Dulles, Esq., on February 13, 1919,' as cited in Bernard M. Baruch, *The Making of the Reparation and Economic Sections of the Treaty*, 295; John R. Beal, *John Foster Dulles*, 65.

[33] See Gordon Martel, 'From Round Table to New Europe. Some intellectual Origins of the Institute of International Affairs,' in Andrea Bosco and Cornelia Navari, eds., *Chatham House and British Foreign Policy 1919-1945: The Royal Institute of International Affairs during the Inter-War Period* (London: Lothian Foundation Press, 1994), 33: 'The country ought to be told in plain language "that the breach of the armistice of Nov. 5 1918 is as great a crime against the law of nations as the breach of the Belgian Treaty, and far less excusable"' (Letter, Zimmern to Toynbee, 10 August 1919, *Toynbee Papers*).

[34] Sir Alfred E. Zimmern, *Spiritual Values and World Affairs* (Oxford: Clarendon Press, 1939) 89-91. Zimmern also criticised the leadership of the Church of England for its acquiescence in Lloyd George's tactics: 'Did the leaders of the Churches raise their voices in protest? Some few of them did, to their lasting credit [Bishops Gore and Henson]. But the most representative voices were silent.'

[35] John R. Beal, *John Foster Dulles*, 67.

[36] See Edward M. House & Charles Seymour, eds., *What Really Happened at Paris*, 269-270.

[37] John F. Dulles, Private memorandum, December 19, 1922, *JFD Papers*.

[38] Dulles' draft of February 21, 1919, reads in part as follows: 'Certain of the governments at war with Germany, believing that it is just and within the

24

contemplation of the principles agreed to as governing the peace settlement, that the German Government shall, in addition to the reparation above specified for, make reparation for the entire cost of the war to the governments with which Germany has been at war and the indirect damage flowing therefrom, in order that these nations should be put back in as nearly the same position as may be to the condition which they would have been in had war not occurred by the aggression of Germany, the Government of Germany recognizes its liability in the premises. It is agreed, however, that the ability of the German Government and nation to make reparation is limited to such an extent as will render the making of such complete reparation impracticable, and accordingly, the governments at war with Germany renounce the right to insist upon reparation other than is expressly specified for herein.' As cited in Philip M. Burnett, *Reparation at the Paris Peace Conference*, 600-604; see also Michael A. Guhin, *John Foster Dulles*, 30.

[39] See Charles Seymour, *The Intimate Papers of Colonel House*, Vol. IV, 396-397.

[40] See Ronald W. Pruessen, *John Foster Dulles*, 39, 40: 'At the end of March, for example, the British put forth a proposal that deeply disturbed American negotiators. On March 27, Lord Sumner recommended that Germany's obligation included the costs of Allied expenses for *pensions and separation allowances*. Fully supported by Lloyd George, the proposal was based on the argument that without such an inclusion, Great Britain's share of reparations would be smaller than was just.' In a footnote Pruessen refers to the Memorandum of Lord Sumner, March 27, 1919, quoted in Philip M. Burnett, *Reparation at the Paris Peace Conference*, 719-725, and explains: '"Pensions" were defined as payment to wounded or maimed war veterans and payments to the orphans or widows of soldiers killed in the war; "separation allowances" were those payments made by governments to the families of men who were called to military service to compensate those families for the income they would be deprived of for the length of service.'

[41] Dulles' memorandum, March 29, 1919, in Philip M. Burnett, *Reparation at the Paris Peace Conference*, 758-762.

[42] J.R.M. Butler, the biographer of Philip Kerr (Lord Lothian), states that it was Kerr who drafted the note concerning the British understanding of the reparation issue, and which was later incorporated in the war guilt clause; see J.R.M. Butler, *Lord Lothian (Philip Kerr) 1882-1940* (London: Macmillan, 1960) 72.

[43] Article 231 of the Treaty of Versailles, signed on June 28, 1919, read as follows: 'The Allied and Associated Governments affirm and Germany accepts the responsibility of Germany and her allies for causing all the loss and damage to which the Allied and Associated Governments and their nationals have been subjected as a consequence of the war imposed upon them by the aggression of Germany and her allies.' As cited in Frederick C. Hicks, *The New World Order* (New York: Doubleday, Page & Co., 1920) 330; see also Harry Elmer Barnes, *The Genesis of the World War* (New York: A.A. Knopf, 1929) 34, 35.

[44] John F. Dulles, 'Foreword', in Philip M. Burnett, *Reparation at the Paris Peace Conference*, Vol. I., xi.

[45] Lloyd George draft, May 29, 1919; as cited in Philip M. Burnett, *Reparation at the Paris Peace Conference*, Vol. I., 754-756; see also *ibid.*, 66-70.

[46] See Ronald W. Pruessen, *John Foster Dulles*, 40.

[47] Philip M. Burnett, *Reparation at the Paris Peace Conference*, Vol. 1, 63-64; see also Dulles and Lamont memoranda of April 1, 1919; as cited in *ibid.*, 775-777.

[48] Dulles later singled out Wilson's illogical decision to give in to Lloyd George's inflated demands as the cause of the whole reparations debacle. See *New York Times*, December 20, 1922, 2.

[49] See John F. Dulles, 'Memorandum on the Desirability of a Fixed Sum,' June 3, 1919; as cited in Philip M. Burnett, *Reparation at the Paris Peace*, Vol. II, 109. Dulles took the opportunity provided by the German counter-proposals to urge that a fixed sum for reparations be written into the treaty. His advice, however, was not heeded.

[50] See Harry Elmer Barnes, *The Genesis of the World War*, 708, 709.

[51] Philip M. Burnett, *Reparation at the Paris Peace Conference*, Vol. 1, 240. In writing his history of the Paris Peace Conference, Harold Temperley wrote to Headlam-Morley on 18 February 1920, 'I notice also Dulles, in his letter to *The Times* of 16th February, says that the Commission which proposed the Pension Scheme was the result of a report made by General Smuts as this has been published might we mention it? It is the only argument in favour of that point which I have ever heard.' The chapter on reparations was already written however, and Temperley sent it to Shotwell, remarking, 'I notice ... that as a result of the correspondence between Dulles and Keynes it appears that the President's legal advisers were against Pensions as not arising out of the Armistice ... we ought to quote it but the whole is a very delicate matter ... we are not justified, of course, as it has now been published in not alluding to it.' Shotwell advised against changing the text and Temperley agreed, 'I will just make quotations in a note from what Dulles says ... We cannot, of course, tell the whole truth, but what we do tell should not be misleading.' See letter, Temperley to Headlam-Morley, 18 February 1920, *Headlam-Morley Papers* 43; letter, Temperley to Shotwell, 19 February 1920 and 26 February 1920, PPC16/2a, as cited in Andrea Bosco & Cornelia Navari, eds., *Chatham House and British Foreign Policy, 1919-1945: The Royal Institute of International Affairs During the Inter-War Period* (London: Lothian Foundation Press, 1994) 108.

[52] See Charles C. Tansill, *Back Door To War. The Roosevelt Foreign Policy 1933-1941* (Chicago: Regnery, 1952) 10, 11: 'It should be kept in mind that Woodrow Wilson acquiesced in this violation of contract. His ardent admirers have contended that he was tricked into this unsavory arrangement by Lloyd George and Clemenceau who were masters of the craft sinister. Ben Hecht, in his *Erik Dorn*, accepts this viewpoint and pungently refers to Wilson in Paris as a 'long-faced virgin trapped in a bawdy house and calling in valiant tones for a glass of lemonade' (Oscar Cargill, *Intellectual America. Ideas on the March,* New York, 1941, 504). In truth, Wilson ordered his glass of lemonade heavily spiked with the hard liquor of deceit, and the whole world has paid for the extended binge of a so-called statesman who promised peace while weaving a web of war ... When President Wilson surrendered [his position of honouring the Pre-Armistice Agreement] he thereby extended a favor to Adolf Hitler who warmly welcomed illustrations of Allied duplicity as one of the best means of promoting the Nazi movement.'

[53] John Foster's brother, Allen, remembered that, 'the German delegate couldn't stand up, he was so affected with emotion. Everybody attributed it to insolence. Poor fellow, he wasn't insolent that day ... I was sitting there not more than thirty, forty feet from him. The fellow couldn't get up under the weight of the Treaty.' Allen W. Dulles, *Oral History Collection*, 1965, 29.

[54] John F. Dulles, *The London Times* (February 16, 1920), 10.

[55] *Ibid.*

[56] Henry P. Van Dusen, *The Spiritual Legacy of John Foster Dulles* (Philadelphia: The Westminster Press, 1960) 199.

[57] Richard M. Fagley, *Oral History Collection*, 1964, 9.

[58] [Lionel G. Curtis], 'Windows of Freedom,' *The Round Table*, Volume IX, No. 33, December 1918, 1-47.

[59] See W.R. Louis, 'Great Britain and the African Peace Settlement,' *Journal of American History*, 72 (1966), 857-892.

[60] See Deborah Lavin, *From Empire To International Commonwealth. A Biography of Lionel Curtis* (Oxford: Clarendon Press, 1995) 164.

[61] See [Lionel G. Curtis], *Report of the Provisional Committee appointed to prepare a Constitution, and select the original members of the British Branch of the Institute of International Affairs*, Chatham House 2/1/2; as cited in F. Whyte, 'The British Institute of International Affairs,' *The New Europe*, July 1920, 308-309.

[62] Whitney H. Shepardson, a former Rhodes Scholar and close friend of Lionel G. Curtis, was to become one of the key figures in the Council on Foreign Relations. The only biography of Curtis which was authorised by him and written during his life time, was an unpublished M.A. thesis of J.W. Shepardson, the son of Whitney, entitled 'Lionel Curtis, Commonwealth Builder' (Cambridge, Mass.: Harvard University, 1949).

[63] See Deborah Lavin, *From Empire To International Commonwealth*, 163.

[64] See, e.g., Royal Institute of International Affairs, *Annual Report* (London: 1942-1943). Charles Seymour, a member of the American delegation at Paris, was invited by Lord Robert Cecil to the meeting in the Hotel Majestic, but was prevented by a cold from attending. In his book, *Letters From The Paris Peace Conference*, Seymour recalled that Lord Cecil wanted to present 'a scheme for an international institute for the study of international relations and publications of documents.' He further states that Lionel G. Curtis was the originator of the Institute, citing Harold Nicolson as his source; see Charles Seymour, *Letters From The Paris Peace Conference* (New Haven: Yale University Press, 1965) 251; and also Harold G. Nicolson, *Peacemaking 1919*, 352; Arnold J. Toynbee, 'Was Britain's Abdication Folly?,' *The Round Table* 60 (November 1970), London, 227.

[65] Clement Jones, 'The Origin of Chatham House,' Bodl. MSS Eng. Hist. c. 869, also Chatham House 4/JONE; as cited in Deborah Lavin, *From Empire To International Commonwealth*, 164. Chatham House became the headquarters of the Royal Institute of International Affairs and was used as an alternative name of the Institute.

[66] The historian of the Royal Institute of International Affairs, Stephen King-Hall, writing in 1937, stated: 'The decision to found an Institute of International Affairs was taken at a joint conference between Americans and British on May 30th, 1919, at the Hotel Majestic, under the presidency of General Tasker Bliss. The British group included Mr. Lionel Curtis, Lord Robert Cecil, Lord Eustace Percy, the late Sir Eyre Crowe, Sir Cecil Hurst, and Mr. J.W. Headlam-Morley, afterwards Historical Adviser to the Foreign Office.' Stephen King-Hall, *Chatham House. A Brief Account of the Origins, Purposes, and Methods of the Royal Institute of International Affairs* (London: Oxford University Press, 1937) 11.

[67] See 22 December 1918, Diaries, 1917-1919, *Bliss Papers* Ac 5069 Box 65 (transcription in Bodl. MSS Eng. Hist. c. 869); as cited in Deborah Lavin, *From Empire To International Commonwealth*, 162.

[68] In July 1958 Joseph Kraft, a journalist who was closely associated with the officials of the Council on Foreign Relations, published an article in *Harper's* magazine about the history of the Council. Although he erroneously believed that the meeting was held on May 19, 1919, his historical account contains useful information; see Joseph Kraft, 'School for Statesmen,' *Harper's* magazine (July 1958) 217: 64-68.

[69] See Mark G. Toulouse, *The Transformation of John Foster Dulles, From Prophet of Realism to Priest of Nationalism* (Macon, GA.: Mercer University Press, 1985) xxvii.

[70] See Ronald W. Pruessen, *John Foster Dulles. The Road to Power* (New York: The Free Press, 1982) 519, 520.

[71] Eighteen years later an official publication of the Council on Foreign Relations stated: 'Under the pressure of a public opinion which was impatient to be done with war-making and peace-making, decisions had to be taken in haste; and the minds of diplomats, generals, admirals, financiers, lawyers and technical experts were not sufficiently well furnished to enable them to function satisfactorily on critical issues at top speed. Realizing their own shortcomings, some of these men found themselves talking with others about a way of providing against such a state of things in the future.'

[72] William H. McNeill, *Arnold J. Toynbee. A Life* (New York: Oxford University Press, 1989) 121.

[73] Memorandum by Lionel Curtis and Whitney H. Shepardson, Chatham House 2/1/2; as cited in Deborah Lavin, 'Lionel Curtis and the Idea of Commonwealth,' in Frederick Madden & D.K. Fieldhouse, eds., *Oxford and the Ideal of Commonwealth* (London: Croom Helm, 1982) 112; see also Deborah Lavin, 'Lionel Curtis and the Founding of Chatham House,' in Andrea Bosco and Cornelia Navari, eds., *Chatham House and British Foreign Policy 1919-1945: The Royal Institute of International Affairs during the Inter-War Period* (London: Lothian Foundation Press, 1994) 64.

[74] Harold G. Nicolson, *Peacemaking 1919*, 353-353.

[75] In a published lecture, entitled *The Way To Peace*, Lionel G. Curtis stated that 'at the Conference of Paris in 1919 American and British delegates agreed to create laboratories for the scientific study of international questions, that is to say of questions which determine the issues of peace and war. For this purpose our American colleagues organized the Council of Foreign Relations in New York. The British delegates established the Royal Institute of International Affairs, which is now commonly know as Chatham House.' Lionel G. Curtis, *The Way To Peace* (London: Oxford University Press, 1944) 11.

[76] Speech by Lionel G. Curtis, Chatham House 2/1/2; as cited in Deborah Lavin, 'Lionel Curtis and the Founding of Chatham House,' 63.

[77] Lionel G. Curtis, 'Record of interview with Sir Austen Chamberlain on 18 June 1929,' Chatham House 4/BAIL; as cited in Deborah Lavin, 'Lionel Curtis and the Founding of Chatham House,' 64.

[78] See Minutes of a meeting at the Hotel Majestic on 30 May 1919 to consider a project for forming an institute of international affairs, Chatham House 2/1/6; as cited in Deborah Lavin, *From Empire To International Commonwealth*, 164. A German Institute of International Affairs was later established by Dr Albrecht Mendelssohn-Bartholdy, which was closely modelled after its Anglo-American counterpart. 'On the other side of the fence, so to speak, the late Dr. Albrecht Mendelssohn-Bartholdy, who was attached to the German Delegation [at the Peace Conference], conceived the idea

of, and later founded, the Institut für Auswärtige Politik at Hamburg.' Stephen King-Hall, *Chatham House*, 11.

[79] Council on Foreign Relations, *Annual Report* (New York: Council on Foreign Relation, 1924). The 25th *Annual Report* of the Council on Foreign Relations is less precise in its description of the Institute's organisational structure than that in Stephen King-Hall's book, *Chatham House*, 12, 14.

[80] H. W. V. Temperley, ed., *A History of the Peace Conference of Paris* (London: Hodder & Stoughton, 1920).

[81] See Deborah Lavin, *From Empire To International Commonwealth*, 167.

[82] See James T. Shotwell, *At the Paris Peace Conference*, 118.

[83] Whitney H. Shepardson, *Early History of the Council on Foreign Relations* (Stanford, CA: Stanford University Press, 1960) 3.

[84] The preamble of the founding document begins as follows: 'Until recent years it was usual to assume that in foreign affairs each government must think mainly, if not entirely, of the interests of its own people. In founding the League of Nations, the Allied Powers have now recognized that national policies ought to be framed with an eye to the welfare of Society at large ....' Report of the Provisional Committee appointed to prepare a Constitution, and select the original members of the British Branch of the Institute of International Affairs, 1; as cited in Gordon Martel, 'From Round Table to New Europe. Some intellectual Origins of the Institute of International Affairs,' in Andrea Bosco and Cornelia Navari, eds., *Chatham House and British Foreign Policy 1919-1945*, 19.

[85] See Stephen King-Hall, *Chatham House*, 30, 31.

[86] British Institute of International Affairs, *Rules and List of Members* (1920), 13, Royal Institute of International Affairs Archives (henceforth cited as RIIA Archives), Chatham House, London.

[87] See Sir James Headlam-Morley, diary; transcript of entry for 31 May 1919, Chatham House 2/1/2A; and M. Dockrill, 'The Foreign Office and the Creation of Chatham House,' 79-81; as cited in Deborah Lavin, *From Empire To International Commonwealth*, 166.

[88] See Deborah Lavin, *From Empire To International Commonwealth*, 166.

[89] See *ibid.*; Lavin refers to 'Clement Jones, Diary, 17 June 1919.'

[90] *Ibid.*; see also P. M. Roberts, 'The American "Eastern Establishment" and World War I: The Emergence of a Foreign Policy Tradition,' 2 vols. (Cambridge University Ph.D. thesis, 1981); and H. C. Allen, *Great Britain and the United States: A History of Anglo-American Relations, 1783-1952* (London, 1954).

[91] *Saturday Review* (London), July 10, 1920. See also Minutes of Meeting, May 30, 1919, 2/1/6, RIIA Archives; and Harold Temperley, ed., *History of the Paris Peace Conference* (London: Oxford University Press, Vol.1) xx.

[92] *Saturday Review* (London), July 10, 1920; as cited in Deborah Lavin, *From Empire To International Commonwealth*, 168.

[93] Deborah Lavin, 'Lionel Curtis and the Founding of Chatham House,' 65.

[94] Gladstone had also lived there.

[95] See Deborah Lavin, *From Empire To International Commonwealth*, 173. Lavin refers to the following sources: Letter, Curtis to Leonard, 19 July 1923; letter, Leonard to Curtis, 13 Aug. 1923, Chatham House 4/LEON.

[96] See Stephen King-Hall, *Chatham House*, 19.

[97] Curtis' draft of Devonshire to Leonard, 21 June 1923, Chatham House 4/LEON;

letters, Curtis to Leonard, 19 July, 26 July, 13 August, 15 August 1923, *ibid.*; letter, Curtis to Shepardson, 3 January 1924, MSS Eng. Hist. C. 872; as cited in Deborah Lavin, 'Lionel Curtis and the Founding of Chatham House,' 66, 67.

[98] Letter, Lionel Curtis to Lord Cecil, 15 January 1920, Chatham House 2/1/2; as cited in Deborah Lavin, 'Lionel Curtis and the Founding of Chatham House,' 65.

[99] See letter, Curtis to Bailey, 24 May 1929, Chatham House, Endowment 2768; Interview with Austen Chamberlain, 18 June 1929; and letter, Curtis to Grey, 20 June 1929, Chatham House 4/MEST; as referred to by Deborah Lavin, *From Empire To International Commonwealth*, 176.

[100] Letter, Bailey to Curtis, 14 July [1929], Chatham House 4/BAIL; as referred to by Deborah Lavin, *From Empire To International Commonwealth*, 176.

[101] See Stephen King-Hall, *Chatham House*, 140, 141. The companies King-Hall listed are the following: Anglo-Iranian Oil Company, the Bank of England, Barclay's Bank, Baring Brothers, Erlangers, Ltd, Lazard Brothers, Lever Brothers, Lloyd's Bank, Midland Bank, Ltd., Reuters, N.M. Rothschild & Sons, J.H. Schroder & Company, and the Westminster Bank, Anglo-Saxon Petroleum Company, Ltd., A.W. Bain & Sons, Ltd., the British American Tobacco Company, the British South Africa Company, Central Mining and Investment Corporation, Brandeis, Goldschmidt & Company, Chartered Bank of India, Australia, and China, Ford Motor Company, Hambros' Bank, Imperial Chemical Industries, The Honourable Company of Clothworkers, Deloitte, Plender, Griffiths & Company, District Bank, Ltd., Foy, Morgan & Company, Ltd., Furness, Withy & Company, Ltd., Glyn, Mills & Company, The Honourable Company of Goldsmiths, Guinness, Mahon & Company, Harrisons & Crosfield, Ltd., Helbert, Wagg & Company, Ltd., Imperial Chemical Industries, Ltd., Kleinwort, Sons & Company, Matheson & Company, Ltd., Mercantile & General Insurance Company, Ltd., National Provincial Bank, Ltd., Prudential Assurance Company, Ltd., Slaughter & May, John Swire & Sons, Thomson McLintock & Company, Stern Brothers, Vickers-Armstrong, Willis, Faber & Dumas, Ltd., and Whitehall Securities Corporation.

[102] See *ibid.*, 14-15.

[103] See *ibid.*, 13-14.

[104] See *ibid.*, 22-23.

[105] See *ibid.*, 27-30.

[106] Letter, J. W. Headlam-Morley to Arnold J. Toynbee, 16 January 1924, Bodleian Library, Toynbee Papers, as cited in William H. McNeill, *Arnold J. Toynbee. A Life*, 121.

[107] In a letter to Ivison Macadam, Whitney H. Shepardson used a biblical analogy to describe Curtis' gift in raising funds: 'He's like the Hound of Heaven. Or Jacob wrestling with the angel. There was some talk at Council [on Foreign Relations] Directors' meeting today about Chatham House and its resources. Cravath said that Chatham House had been lucky in having one or two "angels" to give it money. I said, "Yes, but what's more important they had a Jacob in the shape of Lionel Curtis to wrestle with these angels saying "I will not let thee go until thou bless me!"' Letter, Shepardson to Macadam, 3 Nov. 1932, Bodl. Mss Eng. Hist. c. 872; as cited in Deborah Lavin, *From Empire To International Commonwealth*, 176.

[108] See letter, Arnold J. Toynbee to Gilbert Murray (Toynbee's father-in-law), 15 February, *Toynbee Papers*, Bodleian Library. The reference is found in William H. McNeill, *Arnold Toynbee. A Life*, 123.

[109] See Deborah Lavin, 'Lionel Curtis and the Founding of Chatham House,' 67.

[110] See Deborah Lavin, *From Empire To International Commonwealth*, 174. Lavin refers to the following source: Letter, Stevenson to I. Macadam, 23 Oct. 1932, Chatham House 4TEV.

[111] Arnold J. Toynbee, *Acquaintances* (London: Oxford University Press, 1967) 140-141.

[112] See Deborah Lavin, 'Lionel Curtis and the Founding of Chatham House,' 63: 'His American friends, his wide acquaintance among officials and politicians throughout the British empire, and the fact that his influence derived from personal relationships rather than official position or control of any of the more usual levers of power, gave Curtis a great advantage in assembling the small Anglo-American gathering on 30 May 1919 described by Toynbee, where the Chatham House idea took shape.'

[113] See chapter 2: 'Milner's Kindergarten'.

[114] See Walter Nimocks, *Milner's Young Men: The 'Kindergarten' in Edwardian Imperial Affairs* (London: Hodder and Stoughton, [1968] 1970).

[115] Letter, Whitney H. Shepardson to Judge Brandeis, 26 Sept. 1925, Bodl. MSS Eng. Hist. c. 872; as cited in Deborah Lavin, *From Empire To International Commonwealth*, 171.

[116] Walter Page was a former American ambassador to Great Britain whose sympathies for the British Empire were legendary.

[117] Letter, Lionel Curtis to Whitney H. Shepardson, 1 January 1923, Bodl. MSS Eng. Hist. c. 872; as cited in Deborah Lavin, *From Empire To International Commonwealth*, 171-172.

[118] Elihu Root was an early leader in America's imperial expansion, being responsible for organising the administration of the overseas territories won by the United States in the Spanish-American War. He acted as counsel for several leading American corporations and banks of the time. In addition he advised Andrew Carnegie on his philanthropies, and served as first president of the Carnegie Endowment For International Peace.

[119] See Herbert Heaton, *A Scholar in Action. Edwin F. Gay* (Cambridge: Harvard University Press, Mass., 1952) 203. The Council's handbook for 1919 relates the following: 'In the late spring of 1918 a few gentlemen came together at a conference at the Metropolitan Club, New York, to discuss the most interesting and vital subjects concerned with the United States and its relations with the rest of the world. Two or three meetings were held, which showed that much could be learned and much good could be accomplished by such conferences, made up of people who were concerned in the world's affairs in a large way ... The object of the Council on Foreign Relations is to afford a continuous conference on foreign affairs, bringing together at each meeting international thinkers so that in the course of a year several hundred expert minds in finance, industry, education, statecraft and science will have been brought to bear on international problems. It is a Board of Initiation - a Board of Invention. It plans to cooperate with the Government and all existing international agencies and to bring all of them into constructive accord.' Council on Foreign Relations, *Handbook* (New York: Council on Foreign Relations, 1919) 3, 5.

[120] See Minutes of American Institute of International Affairs, November 18, 1920; Letters, Herbert Houston to Lionel G. Curtis, November 24, 1920; Whitney H. Shepardson to members of CFR, December 2, 1920, Whitney H. Shepardson to Lionel G. Curtis, December 17, 1920; all reference material in 3/6/COU, RIIA Archives.

[121] See Whitney H. Shepardson, *Early History of the Council on Foreign Relations*, 4. Letter, William R. Shepard to George W. Wickersham, August 5, 1921, Box 6, *John W. Davis Papers*, Yale University Library. *In Peace and Counterpeace* Hamilton Fish Armstrong listed most of the members of the American Institute of International Affairs who joined the Council on Foreign Relations in 1921. He omitted to mention the Dulles brothers. Hamilton Fish Armstrong, George Barr Baker, Ray Stannard Baker, Tasker H. Bliss, Archibald C. Cookidge, F. Trubee Davison, Clive Day, Martin Egan, Raymond B. Fosdick, Edwin F. Gay, Louis H. Gray, Jerome Green, Charles H. Haskins, Gerard C. Henderson, Christian A. Herter, Herbert Hoover, Stanley K. Hornbeck, Edward M. House, Charles P. Howland, Manley O. Hudson, Douglas Jonson, T.B. Kitteredge, Thomas W. Lamont, Robert H. Lord, George Rublee, James Brown Scott, Charles Seymour, Whitney H. Shepardson, James T. Shotwell, Alonzo E. Taylor, Vanderbilt Webb; see Hamilton Fish Armstrong, *Peace and Counterpeace* (New York: Harper & Row, 1971) 565.

[122] Council on Foreign Relations, 'Annual Report of the Executive Director, 1922-1923,' 5, in CFR Archives. Council on Foreign Relations, 'Statement of Incorporation,' July 25, 1921, Box 6, *John W. Davis Papers*, Yale University Library. Letter, Walter H. Mallory to Margaret Cleeve (Secretary of Chatham House preparing a history), February 16, 1937, 3/6/COU, RIIA Archives.

[123] Edwin F. Gay was a historian and the first dean of the Harvard Business School. During the war he was employed by the Shipping Board as director of planning and statistics. At the end of the war he became editor of the *New York Evening Post*, owned by Thomas W. Lamont. Lamont had recommended Gay to Shepardson, because he thought he would be a good member for the Institute of International Affairs. Gay became a member in October 1920, subsequently joining the original committee on policy as well.

[124] Besides John W. Davis, William K. Shepherd, Paul Cravath, Frank L. Polk, Paul M. Warburg, Stephen P. Duggan, and Edwin F. Gay, the board of directors consisted of the following men: Isaiah Bowman, director of the American Geographical Society; Archibald Cary Coolidge, Harvard historian; Norman H. Davis, New York banker and former Undersecretary of State; John H. Finley of the *New York Times*; David F. Houston, former Secretary of Treasury; Otto H. Kahn, New York banker; Whitney H. Shepardson; and George W. Wickersham. In all, there were sixteen men (including Root). Eight - Cravath, both Davises, Finley, Kahn, Polk, Root, and Wickersham - were listed in the 1920 *New York Social Register* (Social Register Association, 1920, 159, 175, 243, 379, 556, 604, 771). Warburg and Gay were corporate executives and Coolidge came from a wealthy Boston family.

[125] John W. Davis was a Democratic congressman from West Virginia. President Wilson first chose him as Solicitor General and then as ambassador to Great Britain. After the war and the peace conference, he established himself as a corporate lawyer in New York, and became chief counsel for J.P. Morgan and Company. In 1924 he was the Democratic presidential candidate, but lost the election to the Republican Calvin Coolidge.

[126] Whitney H. Shepardson, *Early History of the Council on Foreign Relations*, 11.

[127] *Ibid.*

[128] See *ibid.*, 6. Letters, George Wickersham to John W. Davis, June 27, 1921; Davis to Wickersham, July 7, 1929; William R. Grace to Davis, August 10, 1921, Box

6, in *John W. Davis Papers*, Yale University Library.

[129] Council on Foreign Relations, *By-Laws with List of Officers and Members* (New York: Harold Pratt House, 1922) 1.

[130] The Council stated in 1924 that '*Foreign Affairs* has established itself as the most authoritative American review dealing with international relations.' CFR, *By-Laws with List of Officers and Members*, 1. In 1937, the success of *Foreign Affairs* was even more extraordinary: 'In the fifteen years since its first number appeared, *Foreign Affairs* has won wide recognition because of the authoritative character of its contributed articles and the judicious temper of its editorial direction. Leading statesmen, economists, publicists and scholars of all nationalities representing a great variety of points of view are numbered among its contributors, and it is now regarded as the most authoritative publication of its character in any country. CFR, *The Council on Foreign Relations. A Record of Fifteen Years* (New York: Harold Pratt House, 1937) 17.

[131] Philip Kerr (Lord Lothian), 'From Empire to Commonwealth,' *Foreign Affairs* (New York: Harold Pratt House, December 1922) 97-98.

[132] Gordon Martel, 'From Round Table to New Europe. Some intellectual Origins of the Institute of International Affairs,' 13-14.

[133] David Watt, 'The Foundation of the Round Table,' *The Round Table* 60 (November 1970) 425; see also Walter Nimocks, *Milner's Young Men*, 158-196.

[134] Alan C. Johnson, *Viscount Halifax. A Biography* (London: Robert Hale, 1941) 58.

# 2

# THE PURSUIT OF A WORLD FEDERATION

2.1    Ruskin - The Prophet of Imperialism

R uskin was Slade Professor of Fine Art at Oxford from 1869 to 1879 and again from 1883 to 1884. In earlier years his lectures were well attended by students and his influence on the University was great.

John Ruskin (1819-1900) was born in London, the son of a wealthy wine merchant from whom he inherited a substantial fortune. His education was in art, literature, architecture, mathematics, Latin and Greek. After having travelled extensively, he settled in Oxford, to lecture about art and a number of other subjects.

2.1.1    Ruskin's Social Utopia

Ruskin believed in the dignity of manual labour. He was strongly repelled by what he perceived as the dissipation of an economy based on free enterprise. An outspoken opponent of the Manchester School, he saw the anarchism of modern society as a by-product of self-seeking individuals concerned only about their own personal advantage. His social ideal was a community of people living in harmony with one another, as each member tries to meet the needs of his neighbour. Although he was opposed to the abolition of the English class system, affirming the rights of the landed aristocracy to establish and govern an ordered society, he campaigned for a national education policy, old age pensions and council houses.

In 1874, he encouraged a group of undergraduate students to construct a road in the swampy region between North and South Hinksey. A remarkable variety of men participated; among them were Alfred Milner, Arnold Toynbee, George R. Parkin[1], Oscar Wilde and E.B. Poulton. In practical terms the project was a total failure - the street was mostly crooked and humped, and never finished - but the hard-working road builders were amply rewarded for their toil of two months by being allowed to eat their breakfast in the presence of the Master.[2]

Ruskin established the 'St. George's Guild' which was designed to set up a model industrial and social movement, to buy lands, mills and factories, and to start a model co-operative. The Guild failed, but the ideas of Ruskin were planted in the fertile minds of his students who were the scions of the British aristocracy. In his famous inaugural lecture of 1870, Ruskin, like a prophet of old, declared:

> ... Will you youths of England make your country again a royal throne of kings, a sceptred isle, for all the world a source of light, a centre of peace; a mistress of learning and of the Arts, faithful guardian of time-tried principles? And this is what she [England] must do or perish: she must found colonies as fast and as far as she is able, formed of her most energetic and worthiest men; – seizing every piece of fruitful waste ground she can get her foot on, and there teaching these her colonists that their chief virtue is to be fidelity to their country, and that their first aim is to be to advance the power of England by land and sea: and that, though they live in a distant plot of land, they are no more to consider themselves therefore disenfranchised from their native land than the sailors of her fleet do ... You think that an impossible ideal. Be it so; refuse to accept it, if you will: but see that you form your own in its stead. All that I ask of you is to have a fixed purpose of some kind for your country and for yourselves, no matter how restricted, so that it be fixed and unselfish.

According to Ruskin, Plato's *Republic* was the pattern of a perfect society, a community of people ruled by an elite class, which would serve as the blueprint of the social structure of the British Empire.[3]

### 2.1.2    Ruskin's 'Impossible Ideal'

Ruskin's inaugural lecture left an indelible impression on a generation of undergraduates.[4] His message that Englishmen should go out and colonise every piece of fruitful land on which they could set foot became the guiding star of many aspiring colonial administrators.[5] It was, indeed, an 'impossible ideal' that Ruskin had proposed, but it was one with a strong emotional appeal to romantic, idealistic youths.

Ruskin also expressed his admiration for the authoritarian style of the rulers of the dependent Empire. In *A Knight's Faith* (1885) he praised the heroes of the Punjab, Havelock, Lawrence and Edwardes. Their success, he proclaimed, was not owed to Parliamentary or any kind of collective wisdom. 'It is not by a majority of votes that Bunnoochees throw down their forts ... in every vital matter the right opinion is in the majority of one.'[6]

Ruskin's mystical ideas made themselves felt in the Empire in a variety of other ways. Though by no means uncritically accepted by Milner, Parkin and Toynbee, they contributed to their belief in a more positive role for the state in the development of the Empire than was prevalent either in Conservative or Liberal contemporary thinking. Ruskin's teaching on the dignity of manual labour and on the revival of handicrafts such as spinning was to become an important element in the philosophy of M.K. Gandhi. J.A. Hobson of Lincoln College, whose attacks on imperialism Lenin was to admire, said that his own economic theories owed more to Ruskin than to anyone who taught him at Oxford, and he wrote a book on Ruskin as a social reformer.[7]

Most important of all, Ruskin's dream, with its promise of the kingdom of heaven on earth, came at a time when the teachings of Darwin and others had undermined, to some degree, the foundations of orthodox Christianity as a personal faith, leaving many among the educated classes groping for some belief that could infuse existence with a sense of purpose and direction.

The loss of faith among the educated British scions is vividly described in one of the many accounts which survive of undergraduate life at Jowett's[8] Balliol College, the memoirs of John MacMillan Brown[9], who came up to Balliol in 1871 and later went out to teach in New Zealand. Most of his contemporaries at Balliol, he recalled, had broken loose from their religious moorings and were adrift on a great ocean of belief in search, as a rule hopelessly, of some fixed point from which they could take their bearings. Like spiritual dynamite, he said, was the problem of evolution which Darwin had flung into contemporary debate with the *Descent of Man.* All the undergraduates in Brown's circle were reading ethnological books and had been struck by the implication that the fundamental doctrines of the Christian creed were rooted in the customs and beliefs of primitive peoples. This seemed to dispose of the idea that Christianity was a revelation from heaven.

Most damaging to the Christian faith, at least in its immediate effect, was William Winwoode Reade's *The Martyrdom of Man,* published in 1872. Reade, an obscure novel writer, had twice left his native Oxford to travel to the African continent in the 1860s, on a quest to refute the theory of evolution. A personal study of the habits of gorillas convinced him, however, that the human race and its civilisation evolved, as Darwin had postulated, from West African apes.

Despite many critical reviews, Reade's book was widely circulated and found ready acceptance among the general public. Quite apart from its passages about the universal history of mankind, it blatantly propagated atheistic views: 'Christianity is false. God worship is idolatry. Prayer is useless. The soul is not immortal. There are no rewards and punishments in a future state.' Instead, the rewards of man were in continuing and improving the human race. According to Reade, 'To develop to the utmost our genius and our love, that is the only true religion.'[10]

For a number of Oxford men of this generation the stoicism of the classics and the mysticism of an imperial creed were to replace the lost faith in Christianity. From Brown's memoirs it seems that he never regained his faith. Fascinated by the story of Greek expansion in the Mediterranean and by Alexander's conquests, as well as by the accounts in Livy and Tacitus of the expansion of the Roman Empire, he determined to work in the British Empire; and after considering teaching posts in India and Canada, he obtained through Jowett's influence a professorship in the new University College of Canterbury, New Zealand.

## 2.2    The Classics and the British Empire

In the late nineteenth-century British imperialism was in its full bloom. From 1874 until 1880, Benjamin Disraeli was Prime Minister of Great Britain. These were the triumphant years of the British Empire. British regiments opened the way to mastery of Egypt and the Far East. Queen Victoria was proclaimed Empress of India. The annexation of the Transvaal Republic was looked upon as a first step towards a great Confederation of South Africa; Disraeli achieved a major diplomatic coup at the Congress of Berlin by bringing home his famous 'Peace with Honour'. This new blend of national and territorial aggrandizement was an ideal cherished in the hearts of many a young man in Victorian England.

It was also the era in which a privileged group of Englishmen could enter the colonial civil service, after completing their classical education at Oxford or Cambridge. Both class and racial distinctions were observed in the selection of colonial administrators. Sir Charles Lucas, a Fellow of All Souls and senior official in the Colonial Office, compared in his historical study, *Greater Rome and Greater Britain* (1912), the imperial governance of the Romans with that of British colonial administrators. To Lucas it seemed that the distinctive feature of the Roman Empire was its class system, separating freemen and slaves; in contrast, the distinguishing mark of the British Empire was its emphasis on racial distinctions. He noted that in Rome anyone, regardless of his background and racial descent, could become a provincial administrator and even rise to imperial honours. But the posts in the British Colonial Service were reserved for individuals of British descent. Lucas suggested liberalising the recruitment regulations to offer men from the Dominions the same opportunities as in Rome of old.[11] In the colonies, however, Leopold S. Amery, a close associate of Lord Milner, could not be persuaded to change the qualifications of employment in the civil service. He chose his administrators along racial lines, accentuating further the distinction between white rulers and coloured subjects.

Professors of Classics would periodically recite the fate of the glorious,

38

but short-lived, Athenian Empire.[12] To some the loose connection between the Greek city state and its overseas settlements provided a blue-print to be used by the developing British Empire. To others it represented a perverted form of democracy.

The famous Oxford professor Gilbert Murray regarded England's culture to be Greek at home, but Roman in the Empire.[13] His close associate, Alfred E. Zimmern, however, warned his compatriots in *The Third British Empire* (1926) that 'if Oxford ever became a self-conscious intellectual metropolis, inculcating an Imperial culture, she would very quickly degenerate and stiffen into a cold and pedantic conceit, as Athens stiffened under the Romans, when men flocked thither for culture and Greece herself was dying.'[14]

The favourite pastime of Sir Arthur Hertzel, Permanent Under Secretary for India, was to edit the poems of Virgil at his desk in the India Office. Like him, most colonial administrators in the latter part of the nineteenth century would distinguish themselves by emulating the Platonic virtues of loyalty, courage, responsibility and truthfulness; but they also adopted Plato's belief that intelligence alone was the best qualification for the highest posts in the imperial administration. In Greek philosophy they found ample encouragement for autocratic rule by an elite of modern day 'philosopher kings'.

Frequently, the colonial administrators of the British Empire would assume the roles of their favourite heroes of ancient Greece. Philip Woodruff, in his history of the Indian Civil Service, compared its members to Plato's Guardians.[15] Assuming his duties as High Commissioner of South Africa, Lord Milner saw himself as a character in a Greek tragedy, forced by circumstances into precipitating the Boer War. John Buchan, a close associate if not actually a member of his 'Kindergarten',[16] admired him as 'Plato's philosopher-turned-king'.[17] To Elinor Glyn he appeared in the posture of a new Socrates, as they talked incessantly about Greek poets and philosophers, while walking through the woodlands of a German resort.

If the classical education at Oxford left its indelible mark on the intellectual and philosophical outlook of Milner, he was equally influenced by the idealism of his friend at Balliol College, Arnold Toynbee.[18] Toynbee's ideas eventually shaped the philosophical and political orientation of the Round Table Group as a whole, although individual members were known for their assorted views.


2.3    Arnold Toynbee's Idealism

Twenty-one years after his first encounter with Toynbee, Alfred Milner still lived under the impression of that memorable moment which took place at Oxford University in 1873: 'I fell at once under his spell and have always remained under it.'[19] When Milner published his *Reminiscence of Arnold Toynbee*, it was reprinted in subsequent editions of the *Industrial Revolution*, as a more pertinent introduction than Jowett's.[20] In spite of Toynbee's early death in 1883, his ideas became a constant source of inspiration for Milner and his associates. 'There are many men now active in public life,' Milner wrote in 1894, 'and some whose best work is probably yet to come, who are simply working out ideas inspired by him [Arnold Toynbee].'[21]

Principally, Toynbee's idealism can be divided into two parts: (1) the most excellent and refined qualities of humankind are exhibited in the British way of life; and (2) British imperialism and the spread of social welfare were fundamental to the continued existence of the British way of life.

There were three ideas of Toynbee, in particular, which shaped the philosophy of Milner: (a) to mitigate by social service work (especially educational work) the abject misery of the working classes of English society and of the underdeveloped nations around the world; (b) to discharge the duty and obligation to the state as an act of complete devotion; and (c) to regard the history of the British Empire as the unfolding of a great moral idea - the idea of freedom. Only in adhering to that idea would it be possible to preserve the unity of the Empire.[22]

Toynbee can also be regarded as the founder of the method used first by the Round Table Group and then by the Royal Institute of International Affairs. As described by Benjamin Jowett, Master of Balliol, in his preface to the 1884 edition of Toynbee's *Lectures on the Industrial Revolution* this method was as follows: 'He would gather his friends around him; they would form an organisation; they would work on quietly for a time, some at Oxford, some in London; they would prepare themselves in different parts of the subject until they were ready to strike in public.'[23] In the preface to this same edition, Charlotte M. Toynbee wrote: 'The whole has been revised by the friend who shared my husband's entire intellectual life, Mr. Alfred Milner, without whose help the volume would have been far more imperfect than it is.' Ramsay MacDonald later described the Round Table movement's mode of operation as 'the Chatham House technique', a three-pronged approach of staying informed about international affairs, discussing them in private study groups, and publicizing the findings.

2.4     The Virtues of Guild Socialism

Arnold Toynbee was an articulate proponent of socialist ideas and opposed the ideology of liberal capitalism as proclaimed by the economists of the Manchester School. Both Toynbee and Milner were early sceptics on the advantages of free trade.[24]

As revealed in his book, *Questions of the Hour* (1923), Milner favoured guild socialism and objected vigorously to the orthodox financial policy of deflation, balanced budget, gold standard, and free international exchange. He insisted on the subservience of financial considerations to economic calculations and economic calculations to political expediencies; and urged the British government to abandon its deflationary policy based on financial reasons to abate injurious economic and political consequences.

In 1906, when Leopold Amery made his first attempt to be elected to Parliament[25], Milner worked actively in support of his candidacy. Amery might have unwisely counted on Milner's personal prestige to boost his political fortunes, for Milner made no efforts to hide his highly controversial economic and social ideas. On 17 December 1906, he spoke at Wolverhampton as follows:

> I am unable to join in the hue and cry against Socialism. That there is an odious form of Socialism I admit, a Socialism which attacks wealth simply because it is wealth, and lives on the cultivation of class hatred. But that is not the whole story; most assuredly not. There is a nobler Socialism, which so far from springing from envy, hatred, and uncharitableness, is born of genuine sympathy and a lofty and wise conception of what is meant by national life.[26]

Although still unpopular among the general public, Milner's idealistic notion of 'a nobler Socialism', was largely, but not uncritically, shared by Amery. Consequently, the latter's association with Milner grew steadily closer until it became possibly the most intimate within the Group.[27]

In 1882 Milner had already given six lectures on socialism in Toynbee Hall.[28] Even a cursory reading of these lectures reveals that the author advocated an undemocratic kind of socialism, willing to make many sacrifices for the well-being of the masses, but reluctant to share with these masses the political power that might allow them to seek their own well-being. To Milner, democracy was deficient as a political system to the degree that it impeded the autocratic rule of highly qualified administrators. These sentiments were not entirely shared by some members of the Round Table Group. Curtis expressed only the highest admiration of the parliamentary system and Kerr saw imperial federation as a way to democratise the Empire.

Milner's antipathy to democracy as practised in the existing party and parliamentary system surfaces occasionally in his letters and public statements. Writing to his old friend Sir Clinton Dawkins, who had been, with Milner, a member of the Toynbee group in 1879-1884, he noted in 1902: 'Two things constantly strike me. One is the soundness of the British nation as a whole, contrasted with the rottenness of party politics.'[29] His friend Edmund Garrett, who described Milner's preferred method of influencing the political process by advising the men in power, wrote in 1905:

> Rhodes and Milner both number themselves of that great unformed party which is neither the ins nor the outs, which touches here the foreign politics of the one, here the home politics of the other; a party to which Imperialism and Carlyle's Condition of the People Question are one and the same business of fitly rearing, housing, distributing, coordinating, and training for war and peace the people of this commonwealth; a party which seems to have no name, no official leader, no paper even, but which I believe, when it

comes by a soul and a voice, will prove to include a majority of the British in Britain and a still greater majority of the British overseas.[30]

There is no reason to doubt that Garrett represented Milner's sentiments accurately.[31] Milner efficiently advanced his own political ambitions by bestowing upon that unformed party 'a soul and a voice', and he intended to do this outside the confines of party politics. Milner applied this principle rigorously, if he felt that his immediate access to the corridors of power would be jeopardised by one or the other position which was offered to him. He refused, for example, to become president of the imperial federalist organisation, not so much because he disagreed with the objectives of this organisation, but because he would be chained to a group of men with limited influence to accomplish their laudable goal. He explained himself to the secretary, Mr. F. H. Congdon, as follows:

> Personally I have no political interest worth mentioning, except the maintenance of the Imperial connection, and I look upon the future with alarm. The party system at home and in the Colonies seems to me to work for the severance of ties, and that contrary to the desire of our people on both sides. It is a melancholy instance of the manner in which bad political arrangements, lauded to the skies from year's end to year's end and as the best in the world, may not only injure the interests, but actually frustrate the desires of the people. I can see no remedy or protection, under the present circumstances, except a powerful body of men - and it would have to be very powerful - determined at all times and under all circumstances to vote and work, regardless of every other circumstance, against the man or party who played fast and loose with the cause of National Unity. You can be sure that for my own part I shall always do that ...[32]

Milner, in his distaste for party politics, and in his emphasis on administration for social welfare, national unity, and imperial federation, gave meaning to James Burnham's description of a 'managerial revolution' - that is the growth of a group of managers, operating outsides the confines of public opinion, who seek efficiently to obtain what they regard as good for the people. To a considerable extent this point of view, as A. M. Gollin points out, became part of the ideology of the Round Table Group:

> Like Milner, however, most of them [the Round Table Group members] sought to obtain power and influence by 'non-party' means; that is, they preferred to exercise their great abilities elsewhere than in Parliament or in the familiar controversies between parties. Their chief had affected them with his dislike of the ordinary methods of English political life. It was more congenial for them to achieve their aims by influencing the Press; by acting behind-the-scenes; by demonstrating the sagacity of their opinions in private conversations with the statesmen, who possessed the visible trappings and the formal authority of office. They tried to act on a plane above that of the

politicians.[33]

When David Lloyd George replaced Herbert Asquith as Prime Minister in 1916, Milner had already established his position in the War Cabinet and was, after Lloyd George, one of the most important figures in the government.[34] While Minister without Portfolio he was chiefly interested in food policy, war trade regulations, and postwar settlements.[35] In early 1917 he went with Lloyd George to a meeting of the Allied War Council in Rome and from there on a mission to Russia, which was already in the throe of revolution. In April of the same year he became Secretary of State for War.[36] After the election of December 1918, he became Colonial Secretary and was one of the signatories of the Treaty of Versailles.

During his distinguished political career, Milner was always interested in shaping the destiny of the British Empire through some young, energetic Oxonians, notably Philip Kerr and Lionel Curtis, who had come to South Africa in the late 1890s to join a group of colonial administrators, generally known as Milner's Kindergarten. Discharging their duty of reconstructing a war-torn land under the tutelage of the High Commissioner, they were to leave an indelible mark on the political landscape of the Republic of South Africa.

2.5    Milner's Kindergarten

The term 'Milner's Kindergarten' was first used derisively by Sir William Marriott in a newspaper article,[37] but the group had no objections to this name. Indeed, they took great pride in it.[38] Of the eleven colonial administrators who were originally part of the Kindergarten, nine had graduated from New College at Oxford University, of which Milner was a Fellow, and four were Fellows of All Souls.[39]

Their method of selection from among the many applicants who wished to work with Milner in the reconstruction of South Africa provides some insights into Oxford's informal network of influence at the time. Lionel G. Curtis of New College, for example, had participated in the Boer War and was made Town Clerk of Johannesburg by Milner on the basis of a letter of introduction from the Chairman of the London County Council, with which he had briefly served. Patrick Duncan of Balliol, who was the oldest member of the Kindergarten, had worked with Milner in the Inland Revenue Department and was appointed Colonial Secretary. John Frederick Perry of New College and All Souls, who was put in charge of Swaziland, Basutoland, Bechuanaland and Rhodesia, came from the Colonial Office.[40] Geoffrey Robinson (later Dawson, the 'perennial' editor of The Times)[41], of Magdalen and All Souls, who was also formerly employed at the Colonial Office, became Milner's Private Secretary and closest confidant.[42] Perry brought in his New College contemporary, the Hon. R. H. Brand, another Fellow of All Souls, who became Secretary of the Intercolonial Council[43]; Brand in turn engaged as his assistant

Philip Kerr of New College who had come out to South Africa as Secretary to the Lieutenant Governor of the Transvaal, a former member of his father's regiment.[44]

Most of the members of the Kindergarten were bachelors,[45] as was Lord Milner himself (at least for most of his life). They lived in close quarters in or around the 'Moot House' built for them by Herbert Baker. They held fortnightly meetings modelled on those of New College Essay Society. From their study of Aristotle they believed that the work of a public servant was the noblest form of activity. The philosophic idealism of T. H. Green caused them to view the State as a positive moral good and to see social improvement and reform as a duty. From Stubbs and Freeman came the concept of the progression of self-government from the Anglo-Saxon Moot through to the English Parliamentary system. From the constitutional lawyer, A. V. Dicey, came the belief that religion and politics are inseparable.[46] Later, in one of his Williamstown lectures, Lionel G. Curtis stated that 'religion and politics are but two aspects of life; to ignore one is to miss the meaning of the other. The Principle of the Commonwealth is love in the sense of duty to each other which love inspires in men.'[47]

In April, 1905, Milner resigned as High Commissioner for South Africa and returned to England a broken and bitter man. After the Boer War he had initiated a reconstruction program which had ended in failure at the time of his retirement. Milner's plan presupposed that a quickly restored prosperity in the war-torn South African colonies would attract sufficient numbers of British colonists. Instead, drought and a slowly rebounding mining industry precipitated a postwar depression which had a dampening effect on the rate of immigration. Although these economic convulsions severely curtailed Milner's policies, they may have only temporarily halted the advance of his reconstruction program had it not been for the ruling Liberals' decision in England to grant political self-government to the Boer republics. In Milner's view this was the height of folly, being perpetrated by spineless politicians less than five years after the war had ended. It precluded the permanent British dominance of the Boers and barred the way to create a united South African state within the British Empire. The spoils of war had been carelessly squandered and Milner lost faith in a British future for South Africa.[48]

After Milner's departure, the situation appeared bleak, but not entirely beyond redemption to that small band of young colonial administrators who were put in charge of the reconstruction program. They continued their duties under Milner's successor, Lord Selborne, abandoned the unworkable Milnerian policies and opted instead for a program of co-operation with the Afrikaners. Unlike Milner, they viewed the liberal concessions made to the Boers as a positive development, promising to accelerate the unification process of South Africa.

Curtis later claimed that a chance reading of Frederick Scott Oliver's biography of Alexander Hamilton provided the inspiration which he and his associates needed to come to a positive assessment of the situation.[49] As an enthusiastic imperial federalist, Oliver had devoted a large part of his book to the description of Hamilton's efforts of gaining support for the United States constitution which conceded broad powers to the central government.[50] According to the historian Basil Williams, it was agreed among the members of the Kindergarten that 'somebody ought to get busy preparing a memorandum stating clearly, by means of facts and statistics, the dangers of disunion in South Africa and indicating Union as the only remedy.'[51] In a long letter Curtis communicated this decision of the Kindergarten to Milner, mentioning the proposed draft of a memorandum on South African government.[52] The memorandum was to consist of a detailed analysis of the relationship among the South Africa colonies, a petition for unification, and a draft constitution outlining the specific form which such unification might assume. The Kindergarten appointed a committee which authorised Curtis to travel extensively and collect material for the study of conditions in the various colonies. Additionally, he was asked to write a number of reports on each stage of his work and submit them to the committee for critical analysis and discussion. These reports would later comprise the core of the memorandum. As soon as the committee had agreed on its content, Curtis planned on visiting Canada, the United States, and Australia 'to review the draft in the light of experience gained in those countries.'[53] Any further insights from these trips were to be included in the revised draft which would then be passed on to the governor general, Lord Selborne. It was hoped that the memorandum would be published as the official policy of the British government and its recommendations implemented in the various South African colonies.

During June and July, 1906, the Kindergarten set out to put their ideas to work.[54] In his letter Curtis asked Milner to approve of their plans. It was also a thinly veiled plea for financial assistance of the project from individuals and groups in Great Britain who held a stake in the political union of South Africa. On August 21, 1906, Milner expressed his skepticism about the plan. He agreed, however, to present the proposal to the trustees of the Rhodes estate at their next meeting.[55] One month later Milner wrote in a second letter that the Rhodes Trust had decided to underwrite the Kindergarten's study project with a grant of £1,000 for one year. The Rhodes Trustees would refrain from influencing the committee findings of the memorandum, but impose a number of procedural stipulations. In the event, a few South African patrons stepped forward and defrayed the entire cost of the study project, leaving the funds from the Rhodes Trust unspent. According to Dawson (aka Robinson), it was 'banked in the joint names of Feetham & myself & [is] still untouched.'

The Kindergarten, sensing a unique opportunity to accomplish South African unification, did not wait until Milner's second letter arrived to begin their work on the memorandum. They completed it with the active assistance of Lord Selborne himself by the end of 1906.[56] Milner, who appears to have first learned of the specific recommendations of the Selborne Memorandum, as it came to be known, after it had been sent to the various colonial governments, was informed by Dawson that the members of the Kindergarten were intent on translating their conceptual framework for closer union into political reality. In order to squelch any opposition to their scheme by the reactionary leaders of South Africa, the young administrators saw the need to organise a popular movement in support of the unification proposal. To the Kindergarten, the recently finished memorandum constituted only an incomplete draft of their plans to create a new South African Union. They perceived its inadequacy to serve as the basis of concrete legislation and proposed a second study. 'The idea,' wrote Dawson, 'is to form a small private committee in each colony to help Curtis in collecting materials & to postpone any public propaganda, the formation of a league etc. till he has done so.'[57] Since the original grant from the Rhodes Trust had not been spent, Dawson asked Milner if the trustees would permit the Kindergarten to use the money for the new project. At once Milner obtained the permission.[58] Soon it became obvious that more funds were needed. On January 21, 1907, Sir Abe Bailey gave a subscription dinner to which he invited leading South African businessmen and politicians who sided with the British. As expected, the banquet was a rousing success and resulted, according to Dawson, in 'a largish subscription on the spot to cover preliminary expenses ...' of the project.[59] The Kindergarten set out at once to work for South African unification. The second study project was an exact replica of that which had produced the Selborne Memorandum, except that it was more detailed. Curtis was again commissioned to travel and obtain pertinent information for the draft report. After it was examined and revised by his colleagues, the resulting study was published in two volumes in mid-1908, entitled *The Government of South Africa*.[60]

Even before the report was published, it was decided that the cause of unification would best be served by setting up an association of closer union societies. The local groups would be furnished with information and propaganda to arouse public enthusiasm for a South African federation.[61] In January, 1909 the first issue of *The State*, a monthly journal of the Association of Closer Union Societies, was published. Philip Kerr assumed the editorship and described its purpose as a rallying point of federalists.[62] The popular movement gained momentum rapidly when Curtis was employed as a full-time organizer. The other members of the Kindergarten assisted him in his task as much as they could. By March, 1909, sixty local groups supported the closer union activities.[63]

Milner was kept informed about the developments in South Africa by those of the Kindergarten who happened to visit him in London on occasion. Despite his valuable help in raising funds to finance their political activities, he counselled his young disciples that they should not expend their efforts needlessly. He maintained that the unification of South Africa was hopeless from the start. No amount of political manipulation and propaganda would suffice to turn the tide. In a letter in late 1907, Milner advised the Kindergarten to assess the situation in South Africa realistically, admit defeat and move on: 'The fight is no longer for predominance,' noted Milner.

That is settled ... My view is that the policy to which we devoted years of labour, & which was worth it ... must be regarded as a thing of the past. I never had any doubt about it from the first moment that the election of January 1906 began to come in, although the disaster has been more rapid and more complete than I imagined.[64]

In spite of Milner's advice to the contrary, the members of the Kindergarten kept up their work for South African unification. When in October 1908 the constitutional assembly convened, Curtis noted that the task he and his colleagues had set out to accomplish was nearly completed. In a letter to Milner he expressed his eagerness to embark on a new venture. He wanted to use his talents and experience now on solving the problems of the Empire. 'It becomes more and more apparent every day to my mind,' wrote Curtis, 'that the various countries included in the Empire must come to some definite business arrangement for the support and control of Imperial defence and foreign policy or the Empire must break up.'[65] The preservation of the integrity of the British Empire, which was threatened by a rising colonial nationalism and a deficient constitutional apparatus, was to become his new field of activity. The solution which he wanted to apply to reverse the trend of imperial disintegration was the education of opinion throughout the dominions on the need for closer union. In a federated Empire the responsibility for imperial defence and foreign affairs would be transferred to the whole family of self-governing nations within its domain and not remain the prerogative of Great Britain alone. Although the idea of promoting imperial federation was first mentioned in the letter to Milner, it was not a new concept within the Kindergarten. The plan to federate the empire evolved concurrently with the program to unite the South African colonies.[66] 'It has always been our idea,' Curtis explained to Richard Jeff, 'to unite South Africa & then try to make some scheme for closer Imperial Union grow out of it.'[67]

In the early part of 1909, Curtis, still residing in Johannesburg, sent a detailed description of the Kindergarten plan to Leopold Amery, stating that his primary concern was to promote closer imperial union.[68] At the time Amery stood in the employment of the Rhodes Trust and was deeply involved in the activities of diverse imperialist groups. According to Curtis, the closer union movement in South Africa was only a first milestone on the road to accomplish a much grander scheme of the Kindergarten, namely the federation of the British Empire. In a letter to Lord Selborne on 18 October 1907, he had already expressed himself as follows:

> It begins to dawn on one that South Africa is a microcosm and much that we thought peculiar to it is equally true of the Empire itself. We want some clear and coherent scheme before men's minds of what the Empire can be and should be. When we have done all we can do and should do for South Africa it may be we shall have the time and training to begin some work of the same kind in respect of Imperial Relations.[69]

In creating and directing the fortunes of the association of closer union societies, the members of the Kindergarten had gained experience in developing techniques for political manipulation which they intended to teach their associates in England. Curtis stressed the importance of working out a detailed plan - 'agreed upon amongst ourselves'[70] - before embarking on any political activities. The best approach would be to draft a memorandum on 'the Imperial Problem'. A document of this kind, 'we have found, is an excellent plan for arriving at a common policy and for getting a number of minds to move automatically in the same direction.'[71]

Curtis offered his services in gathering intelligence from Canada, Australia, and New Zealand in order to draft the memorandum. On his visits he would also organise local groups, similar to the closer union societies in South Africa, which would criticize the memorandum from a dominion perspective. Once the problem had been defined, these groups would become catalysts of constitutional change. To counter potential opposition, the members of the Kindergarten decided to represent themselves and their organisation as of South African origin. They intended to explain that their experiences in creating the Union of South Africa taught them to avoid the dangers inherent in disunity. Consequently, they saw the need to raise the awareness of the other self-governing colonies about the need of organic unity of the empire.

Curtis pointed out to Amery that to succeed in this venture it was essential to establish a central bureau which would co-ordinate the activities of travelling agents. In order to keep a common purpose, it would also be vital to publish 'a monthly magazine like "The State" in all the self-governing countries of the Empire.'

> The importance of a monthly in the Colonies is that journalists read and take their opinions out of it. It acts as an ammunition column to the batteries of the press ... Then everyone concerned in the movement from Lord Milner downwards will have at their disposal a medium through which the same train of thought can be set in motion through all the self-governing colonies of the Empire at the same time.[72]

Curtis suggested to employ a 'well paid first rate editor' in each of the dominions to publish the local journal. In addition, a central office would be set up in London under the supervision of Philip Kerr to collect articles and produce the magazine. Once these steps had been taken, the Kindergarten would call on political leaders to convince them that only organic union would arrest the disintegration of the British Empire.

Curtis' plan as outlined in the letter to Amery remained the focal point of the Kindergarten, even after most of its members had returned to England and entered again the orbit of Lord Milner. At later organisational meetings of the Round Table Group almost every point of the ideas presented by Curtis to Amery were adopted, except for the proposal to publish a separate imperial review in each of the dominions. This idea was dropped in favour of a quarterly magazine, called *The Round Table*, which featured a section in each issue devoted to dominion interests.


## 2.6    The Round Table Group

On January 23, 1910, a small group of liberal imperialists, including Lionel Curtis, Philip Kerr, Patrick Duncan, and others[73] met with Lord Milner at Manchester Square, London. Two days later another meeting followed at the offices of the Rhodes Trust. After eight hours of intense deliberations it was decided that a political movement should be launched which had been the object of discussions for several months previously. Philip Kerr summarised the salient points of the resolution in a memorandum. The main objective of the Round Table Group was to bring about 'an organic union ... by the establishment of an Imperial Government constitutionally responsible to all the electors of the Empire and with power to act directly on the individual citizen.'[74] The realisation of this goal would call for 'the preparation and eventual publication of a scheme of union - if possible a constitution'. In the meantime the gradual change of the political realities would be sought 'by the encouragement of intermediate steps, by the promotion of public measures contributing towards the consolidation of the Empire, and the education of public opinion in the truth about Imperial affairs; and the necessity for Union.'[75] Milner and his associates were thus interested in stimulating discussion about the creation of an Imperial Parliament, which would be directly elected by the peoples of Britain and the Dominions, with responsibility for defence and foreign policy and power to levy taxes.

After the Round Table Group had officially been instituted, Lionel G. Curtis and Philip Kerr followed Lord Milner's directives to work out the details of the proposal which had first been discussed at a colloquium on Lord Anglesey's estate at Plas Newydd in early September 1909.[76] According to Curtis' biographer, Deborah Lavin, 'the Round Table thus proposed to recentralize the Empire against disintegration in an organic union where colonial nationalisms would be fully realized and then transcended in a new international commonality with shared controls which they called a Commonwealth of nations.'[77] In the period from 1910 to 1919 the Round Table Group expanded its influence throughout the British Empire. The plan of operation was to establish local groups of influential men in South Africa, Australia, New Zealand, Canada, and later in India, to agitate for imperial federation. The project was so extensive that almost all members of 'Milner's Kindergarten' participated in it at one time or another.

The Round Table Group had unrestricted access to several colleges at Oxford University, most significantly All Souls. Committee meetings of the principal members were held there at regular intervals. Customarily, political sympathizers of the Group, such as Lord Selborne, R.H. Brand, and Edward Grigg, were invited to attend numerous gatherings convened in London, primarily at 175 Piccadilly (offices of the journal *The Round Table*)[78], as well as at many English country houses such as Blickling Hall, Cliveden, Tring Park, and others.

Kerr became the secretary of the office in London, sharing his duties with Robert H. Brand, while Curtis, Dove and others travelled to the British Dominions to set up a network of Round Table groups.[79] These groups were kept in contact with each other by regular visits from representatives of the London office, personal correspondence and a quarterly journal, called *The Round Table*,[80] a magazine which set out to study 'the relation of principle to practical political questions relating to the future of the British Empire.'[81] This journal was funded by wealthy sponsors, of whom Sir Abe Bailey was the most generous.[82] Its main purpose was to influence opinion makers and not the general public. Thus it never developed into a financially independent and widely circulated magazine. Curtis wrote in 1920,

> A large quarterly like The Round Table is not intended so much for the average reader, as for those who write for the average reader. It is meant to be a storehouse of information of all kinds upon which publicists can draw. Its articles must be taken on their merits and as representing nothing beyond the minds and information of the individual writer of each.[83]

An announcement by the *Round Table* editor in July 1910,[84] four months before the first issue was published, stated that the paper would be 'severely detached from the domestic party issues of the day, and written anonymously, with the sole aim of exchanging information and ideas about the imperial problem among people interested, in all parts of the British dominions'.[85] Its anonymity would provide a platform for prominent public figures to state candidly their opinions on important issues of international relations. The journal would differ from all other political magazines in that it had been founded, and would be produced, by individuals residing in different parts of the British Dominions. This arrangement would assure that its content would mirror a broad spectrum of views untainted by parochialism.

From 1910-1920, *The Round Table* was edited and written by Milner's associates,[86] chiefly by Brand, Dawson, Dove, Grigg, Hichens, and Kerr.[87] Curtis was too busy as travelling secretary of the Round Table Group to devote much time to the journal until after the war. But in 1919 he became chief editor for nearly three years. By that time a variety of individuals of high standing had supported the objectives of the Group, chiefly as writers of occasional articles; they included Sir Reginald Coupland, G. M. Gathorne-Hardy, Sir Alfred E. Zimmern, Dr Arnold J. Toynbee, Arthur Salter, Sir Maurice Hankey, and several others.

The author of Hichens' obituary refers to Milner as the leader of the Round Table Group: 'Often at its head sat the old masters of the Kindergarten, Lord Milner and his successor, Lord Selborne, close friends and allies of Hichens to the end.' In the obituary of Lord Milner in *The Round Table* for

June 1925, we find the following significant passage:

> The founders and the editors of The Round Table mourn in a very special sense the death of Lord Milner. For with him they have lost not only a much beloved friend, but one whom they have always regarded as their leader. Most of them had the great good fortune to serve under him in South Africa during or after the South African war, and to learn at first hand from him something of the great ideals which inspired him. From those days at the very beginning of this century right up to the present time, through the days of Crown Colony Government in the Transvaal and Orange Free State, of the making of the South African constitution, and through all the varied and momentous history of the British Empire in the succeeding fifteen years, they have had the advantage of Lord Milner's counsel and guidance, and they are grateful to think that, though at times he disagreed with them, he never ceased to regard himself as the leader to whom, above everyone else, they looked. It is of melancholy interest to recall that Lord Milner had undertaken to come on May 13, the very day of his death, to a meeting specially to discuss with them South African problems.[88]

Under Milner's guidance the Round Table Group became an influential organisation in the British Dominions[89] and not a few imperial policies can be traced back to articles published in the journal *The Round Table*.[90]

### 2.6.1    The Principle of Commonwealth

The Round Table Group, especially Sir Alfred E. Zimmern and Lionel G. Curtis, perceived history as a perennial conflict between the principles of autocracy and the principles of commonwealth, between the powers of darkness and the forces of light, between Asiatic theocracy and European freedom. The antithetic nature of these two principles manifested itself in different concepts of law. The powers of darkness considered law as divine and eternal, yet subordinated to the authority of kings, while the forces of light regarded law as man-made and changeable, but holding sovereign sway over the affairs of humankind. The first brought forth ignorance, monotony, and slavery, while the second engendered growth, diversity, and freedom. The battle between these two forces was already being waged during the Persian Wars and the Punic Wars, possibly even much earlier, and continued unabated in the struggle of England with the army of Spain (Philip II), and Britain's wars with France (Louis XIV, Napoleon) and Germany (Wilhelm II). As defender of all that was cultured in the modern world, Britain was the only country which persistently fought for the principle of light, that is the principle of commonwealth.[91] Thus it became the rightful successor of Athens which had embraced the same values under Pericles.

The Round Table Group considered the political systems of Great Britain as the most efficient, since it included the idea of 'supremacy of law', which had found expression in A. V. Dicey's *The Law and Custom of the Constitution* (1885). According to this view, most of the world's nations, especially Germany[92] and France, were still groping in the darkness of a theocratic system, supporting an autocratic form of government.

While being confident of the ultimate triumph of the forces of light, the Group was still apprehensive that the British Empire might not succeed in its historic mission of federalising the world under its benign rule. Sir Alfred E. Zimmern, in *The Greek Commonwealth* (1911), feared that the British Empire, in failing to contemplate the tragic fate of the Athenian empire, might repeat the decline of Athens' political culture from the idealism of Pericles's funeral oration to the tyranny of the Athenian empire.[93] In describing these historical events, he inferred that British idealism and liberties might be ruined in a vain attempt to rule the Empire by tyranny. Again, taking his lesson from Greek culture and civilisation in the fourth century B.C., Zimmern thought that the incompetence of its rulers to build some kind of political unit larger than the city-state was the reason for Athens' final disintegration.

This tragic spectacle of the Athenian Empire motivated the Round Table Group to do whatever lay in their power to keep the British Empire from succumbing to a similar fate. It was this fear that animated them to transform the British Empire into a Commonwealth of Nations. They believed that all culture and civilisation would be lifted to a higher plane, if some kind of political unit could be established which transcended the nation-state. In his *Letter to the People of India* (1917), Curtis placed the two alternative scenarios of world order before his readers:

> The world is in throes which precede creation or death. Our whole race has outgrown the merely national state, and as surely as day follows night or night the day, will pass either to a Commonwealth of Nations or else an empire of slaves. And the issue of these agonies rests with us.

To create an international society, Curtis, Zimmern and their associates decided to reform the diplomatic process in foreign affairs by making it responsive to an informed public opinion. Nothing seemed to be more important to them than to devise the structural modifications that would make a democratic foreign policy possible. In order to do this they saw the need to educate society about the ideals of liberal progressivism. The mobilisation of the working class to support the war effort during the Great War was regarded as crucial but not sufficient. The espousal of liberal war aims was just as vital. Thus they began to call for a just peace settlement whenever they got a chance. In a letter to his uncle, for example, Arnold J. Toynbee wrote the following:

> I suppose I want to get the best of both worlds - to draw enough of Germany's claws to make her harmless, without embittering her so much that she will use any weapon she retains on the first opportunity. ... My general scheme is to weaken Germany by breaking up her allies, and

conciliate her (perhaps a hopeless idea) by leaving her the maximum of elbow-room in the colonial areas.[94]

These thoughts found a sympathetic echo in the hearts of influential American liberals associated with *The New Republic* who pursued similar objectives. In 1919 they formed the core of the American delegation to the Paris Peace Conference. Before the war, Zimmern had already met many of them on his visit to the United States. Graham Wallas introduced him to Walter Lippmann who had been Wallas' favourite student during his brief stint at Harvard University. Herbert Croly and Walter Weyl also entered the circle of Zimmern's friends at that time. By the summer of 1915 Croly offered him a permanent job at *The New Republic* should he choose to remain in the United States. Zimmern declined, but promised to write articles and recruit other English writers for the magazine.[95]

Zimmern shared with these Americans the same assumptions about the origins of the war. They thought that the international conflict had been caused by the secretive and exclusive nature of foreign policy-making among the Great Powers. 'What is your own feeling about the possibility of making foreign relations a little more representative, a little more the concern of the whole nation?' Weyl once asked Zimmern.[96] Suggestions of how this situation could be improved were frequently exchanged among these intellectuals. Lippmann complimented Zimmern for his contribution to *War and Democracy*, stating that it is

> the very best book on the war published so far. A sweet tempered and generous book, such as one almost despairs of securing from a nation in the midst of war. I wish I could believe without any further doubt that your crowd represented enlightened England. It would dispense the last doubt I have about the fairness of the essential issues in this war.[97]

As the vanguard of Wilsonian internationalism on both sides of the Atlantic, this group of men aspired to inundate the British political culture with the doctrine of progressivism which had already captured the imagination of the American political and intellectual elites. Zimmern was kept abreast by his contacts at *The New Century* about the political developments in the United States. Like many other British liberals of his time, he saw himself as the harbinger of a new era and was especially eager to introduce his countrymen to Wilson's idealism. What impressed him the most was the high moral tone which accentuated the President's vision of a new world order.

> No ruler has spoken thus since Marcus Aurelius. It is as complete a breach with individualism as with Prussianism. I despair of our pacifists ever learning that the duty of a citizen in a free state is not to weaken the sense of individual obligation to the Commonwealth but to make his State a real moral personality.[98]

Lippmann understood perfectly well what Zimmern meant when he wrote that Lloyd George would be willing to emulate the example of Wilson if exposed to his philosophy.

> He needs to have his arms held up. He needs someone to keep his ideals - real ideals - up to the mark. No one can do that better than the President. He dare not fall behind in the idealists' race. Let the President go on making the running. Let him take all our statesmen's professions at their face value. George will follow partly out of shame, partly out of ambition, partly out of genuine idealism.[99]

Zimmern aimed at influencing domestic policies. He possessed a rare gift of ingratiating himself with diverse political groups in society who sought his advice. Keeping himself unentangled by new occupations which would have limited his mediating role, he was as well respected in government circles as among the working class.

> I want to keep my cosmopolitan standard and a certain sense of detachment, because I feel that is a gift which has been given me, a certain position as a go-between or interpreter, and that I must use it. It is for the same reason that I have undertaken to help the Round Table people, not as entirely one of them, but as a link between them and others whom they might otherwise fail to understand.[100]

At times he advised the political leadership of his country to adopt progressive ideals as the best policy to accommodate the demands of the working-class movement. On another occasion, he lectured the president of the Workers' Educational Association about the necessity to broaden his perspective on the important issues of the day. The workers ought 'to think out a national policy in the way the Round Table has done and tied our members with it, for I recognize that they are incapable, in this generation, of thinking one out for themselves.'[101]

In his philosophical outlook, Zimmern exemplified that group of men which later comprised the membership roster of the Royal Institute of International Affairs. In 1916 he decided that his service to Great Britain would be of greater value if he would spend his time thinking about the terms of a future peace agreement rather than entering the armed forces. Appeasing his conscience, he concluded in a letter to Graham Wallas that his 'Round Table stuff is more useful than private soldiering' and added that 'the chance of helping to make the European settlement a little bit better is more important than anything else just now.'[102] His particular contribution would be in presenting the right ideas - 'the knowledge on which policies are built', whether in the areas of industrial or international relations, to those who hold the reins of power. Writing to Wallas he explained: '... using knowledge in the broad spiritual sense which you and I in our educational thinking have always attached to it. Knowledge unites: policies divide.'[103] Commenting on this attitude of Zimmern, George Martel drew a parallel with the rationale which had been advanced by Curtis and others for founding the Institute of International Affairs:

> This idea of an informed intellectual leadership that would provide the essential knowledge that the public would henceforth require, given their increasing responsibility for the making of foreign policy, was one of the essential foundations upon which the Institute of International Affairs was erected. Not only was this idea one of the keys, but the organisational behaviour of the individuals involved was vital as well.[104]

At the end of 1917 Zimmern and his colleagues at the Department of Political Intelligence (P.I.D.) believed that the Bolshevik Revolution would propel the reform movement to which they belonged to new heights. The overthrow of the Czar was regarded as the beginning of the demise of all autocratic rule. The euphoria which had gripped them at first soon turned to melancholy, as they learned more about the conditions in revolutionary Russia. They emotionally recoiled from the open display of radical despotism which characterised the Soviet leadership style. To them it exhibited all the deplorable features of Prussianism only this time 'upside down'. Since the communist experiment with all its promise and potential had degenerated into a political morass, it lost its attraction for the liberal reformers in Britain. In need of inspiration and guidance, they turned once again their eyes to America. They renewed their contacts to the internationalist and progressive advisors of the President who had filled the ranks of Colonel House's Inquiry. Eustace Percy spearheaded the effort. In May 1918, he warned his colleagues at the P.I.D. that a Republican victory in the presidential elections of 1920 was likely to follow Democratic successes in the voting booths in 1918. If that situation were to materialise, it would be important for Britain to strengthen its ties to America as long as favourable conditions prevailed.[105] He suggested that the British government should solve the lingering commercial problems with the United States by the summer of 1918 and make this 'the basis of the Anglo-American post bellum Entente, which is our central political aim'.[106]

In January 1919 Percy joined the British delegation to the Peace Conference. During his stay in Paris, he shared quarters with Lionel G. Curtis and Ray Stannard Baker (Wilson's biographer) at the Hotel Majestic. Drawing on his previous experience in preparing memoranda on the future Inter-Allied organisation at the P.I.D., he worked side by side with Zimmern, Curtis and others in the League of Nations Section. Wilson's poor showing at the Peace Conference soon put a damper on his exuberance, but he felt an intellectual kinship with the experts in the American delegation. In a letter to Zimmern, he wrote: 'All our American friends share our views very completely if they could only get the President to take sufficient account of actual facts of international relations and prevent him from confining himself to academic principles.'[107]

## 2.6.2    The Commonwealth of Nations

During the Paris Peace Conference, Curtis came to believe that the British Empire would take the lead in the development towards a universal Commonwealth of Nations. This new perspective was the motivating factor to establish the Institute of International Affairs. 'Only one picture comes back to my mind, and that very clearly,' Arnold J. Toynbee recalled when asked in 1958 to describe his impressions of the early days of the Institute,

> an evening meeting at the Majestic, with a pretty large number present, but only one man making himself felt. This was of course Lionel Curtis. He held the floor and dominated the proceedings. Before he had done, the Institute was launched, and he marched out of the room with Headlam-Morley firmly grasped under one arm and Lord Robert [Cecil] under the other. Neither of those two eminent men would have taken the initiative or have been able, if he had taken it, to put the thing through. LC [Lionel Curtis] is the Founder ... My forgetting everything about the launching of the Institute except that one scene, with one figure in it, tells a tale.[108]

The picture we get of Lionel G. Curtis in this account is what we would expect of a man whose growing interest in the study of international affairs at the end of the First World War indicates a fundamental shift in his political philosophy. According to Deborah Lavin, 'he translated his old-fashioned imperialism of Dominion consolidation into a new doctrine of internationalism in which the British Commonwealth of Nations, as the first international organisation, would stand forth as an example of international co-operation and as an influential world power in its own right.'[109]

To be sure, the ultimate goal of the Round Table Group was quite different from the present Commonwealth of Nations, since they wanted to form an imperial federation which would eventually lead to world federation,[110] but they realised that this would only be achieved in the distant future.[111] In the meanwhile they accepted the present imperfect system as an intermediary construction, which would eventually give way to a new world order.[112] In September 1935, in a review of its first twenty-five years, the journal, *The Round Table*, stated:

> Since the war, therefore, though it has never abandoned its view that the only final basis for freedom and enduring peace is the organic union of nations in a commonwealth embracing the whole world or, in the first instance, a lesser part of it, The Round Table has been a consistent supporter ... of the principles upon which the British Empire now rests, as set forth in the Balfour Memorandum of 1926 ... It has held that only by trying the cooperation method to the utmost and realising its limitations in practice would nations within and without the British Empire be brought to face the necessity for organic union.

The principal method chosen by the Group to bring about that 'organic union of nations in a commonwealth embracing the whole world' was to persuade the general public by various means of mass communication, and in particular through the activities of the churches, to accept a world federation 'as the only final basis of freedom and enduring peace'.

Contemplating the implications of federalism on world peace, which can be identified as the core of his political philosophy, Philip Kerr frequently turned to an exposition of the doctrine of the state (usually published in articles of *The Round Table*). He regarded the state, rightly perceived, as 'the noblest of human fabrics'[113], while denigrating its corruption as the worst of perversions.[114] The proper concept of the state was, in his view, based on the ethical teaching of the 'Sermon on the Mount' and the 'Golden Rule'.[115] If the people would follow these Christian precepts, as interpreted by Kerr, they would be animated by a sense of responsibility, based on conscience, for their own actions and for those of their rulers. Such a state must be a democracy - or better, a democratic commonwealth of nations. A particular responsibility, according to Kerr, would rest on the churches in that they would be needed to create the spiritual and cultural conditions for the creation of a world federation:

> To the Christian man loyalty is owned to God, whatever his race, or culture, or language may be, and it is this truth recognized and practised which alone can begin to bring unity and law and peace among the conflicting races and the warring sovereignties which now claim the allegiance of mankind. It is love for and understanding of God which alone can create the conditions in which the federation of man will become a possibility and in which war and the demonic consequences of national sovereignty can be ended.[116]

In contrast to the British Commonwealth, the Prussian state-idea perverted the concept of the state. Its main fault was the veneration of the state as a personified god. If the state is thus deified, the citizens have to follow its dictates blindly. In time, they would be deprived of a sense of individual political responsibility. The cause of the First World War, and generally of all wars, was rooted in such distortions of the doctrine of the state.[117]

Kerr further asserted that it would be incongruent with a sense of responsibility, if an enlightened humankind were arrested in its political development by confining itself to the imperfect set-up of national sovereign states. National frontiers are unnecessary barriers. They prevent the free flow of all the advantages associated with a democratic system. Seen in this way, national sovereignty becomes the primary impediment in the evolution of world order, allowing the powers of darkness (that is, the concept of theocracy) to prevail over the forces of light (that is, the principle of commonwealth).

Just as individuals within a national state are not always inclined to treat others well and must therefore be restrained by law from behaving unsocially,[118] so it must be in the relations of one nation with another. The imposition of an international law would heighten the sense of accountability in the arrangements between different states. The incipient international community would need a judicial system both universally applicable and enforceable. Eventually this would put limits on national sovereignty. Since it is the province of the state to enforce law, there must be some kind of universal state. This political entity of the future, a Commonwealth of Nations, must be based on the principle of federation and permeated by a Christian ethos.[119] On 6 May 1933, in one of his numerous letters to Curtis, Kerr wrote the following:

> It is only Christianity which can create the true Commonwealth, because it is only Christianity which rests its commonwealth on One God, the Father of all, and all men as brethren. True Christianity both extends the Commonwealth to embrace the whole of mankind and, by bringing people into touch with the living God, ensures that so long as they know Him they will manifest that unselfish love which is the only thing which can make the free institutions of a commonwealth - i.e. individual freedom, reign of law, democracy - a living thing and not a shell.[120]

In February 1935 Lord Lothian was invited by Elizabeth Haldane, Secretary of the Burge Trust, to deliver a lecture on international relations. The Burge Memorial Trust was founded in 1926 to commemorate the work for International Friendship of Hubert Murray Burge, formerly Bishop of Oxford and President of the British Council of the World Alliance for Promoting International Friendship through the Churches. The purpose of the annual Burge Memorial Lecture was to promote the cause of international friendship through the churches and to create a better and wider understanding of the international obligations of the Christian people.

On 28 May 1935, almost exactly seven years after the Burge Memorial Lecture was first instituted, Lord Lothian addressed a sympathetic audience at Lincoln's Inn, London. His topic was peace in a future organic world union. It was a remarkable success. Published in pamphlet form, the lecture, 'Pacifism is not Enough, nor Patriotism Either', drew a large readership and became an instant classic of federalist thought.[121]

When Lord Lothian died in Washington in 1940[122], his associate, Sir Edward William Grigg, wrote the obituary for *The Round Table*. Summarising Lothian's fundamental conviction he stated: 'He held that men should strive to build the Kingdom of Heaven here upon this earth, and that the leadership in that task must fall first and foremost upon the English-speaking peoples.' Grigg merely rephrased what Kerr had said before on different occasions. Reflecting on the outcome of the ecumenical World Conference of Life and Work at Oxford (1937), for instance, Kerr stated the following in a letter to the German Pastor Wilhelm Menn[123]: 'I am convinced that when Christianity reaches the point when it is able to bring the Kingdom of Heaven upon earth, it will establish a world federation of some novel kind as the necessary institutional condition by which alone the Kingdom can be maintained in being.'[124]

Lionel Curtis fully agreed with Kerr's sentiments concerning the religious aspects of a 'Commonwealth of Nations'. In *Faith and Works* (1943) he frankly stated that a world commonwealth would be the Kingdom of God on Earth modelled on the Sermon on the Mount, a concept which Curtis borrowed from his reading of Bishop Charles Gore's *The Sermon on the Mount, a Practical Exposition* (1896):

> I, therefore, think of God as a being so creative that He must create other creators, endow them with free-will like his own, and call them to create in partnership with Himself. He has given us a definite task to create what our Lord described as the Kingdom of God upon earth. By that he meant a system of society based on the law of God, which is the duty of men to Himself and each other. Such a system must be a [world] commonwealth, by which I mean the Sermon on the Mount translated into political terms. The British, American, Swiss, Dutch, Scandinavian, and other self-governing nations are political expression of the Sermon on the Mount, though imperfect expressions.[125]

In conversation with Arnold J. Toynbee, Curtis described his role as that of an evangelist crusading for the ideal of world federation, and added that if Christ came back to earth he would find that his precepts were being better practised in the British Commonwealth than anywhere else.[126] In a letter to John Pinder, Charles Kimber, the founder of the Federal Union movement, described, somewhat sarcastically, Curtis' spiritual view of federation:

> Curtis himself saw federation as God's will and as a vehicle for extending the Pax Britannica by way of an Imperial federation to which, I suspect under Lothian's influence, he was prepared to admit lesser breeds if they conformed to Anglo-Saxon good manners. He was tremendously valuable in the early days in giving the movement [Federal Union movement[127]] respectability – or, as he would have said, weight – particularly at Chatham House.[128]

This mythical streak in Curtis' thinking brought him to the conclusion that the British Empire was destined by divine decree to generate a perfect world society, but would die in the process of bringing it into existence: 'Die and ye shall be born again.' In discharging its duty of dispensing liberty, brotherhood, and justice throughout the world the British Empire would disintegrate and thus give birth to a higher form of human co-operation in a world community. The most detailed account of how Curtis envisioned this societal metamorphosis to take place in history was contained in his book, *Civitas Dei* (i.e., the Commonwealth of God).

### 2.6.3    Civitas Dei

Known among his associates as the Prophet,[129] Lionel G. Curtis was the driving force within the Round Table Group in refining the idea of a world commonwealth, pursuing its realisation with the zeal of a new religion.[130] Tireless in advocating a new federal organisation with the British Empire as its focal point, he authored a series of books and articles, culminating in his *Civitas Dei*, which he dedicated to Sir Malcolm Steward, 'one whose life has been devoted to the task of creating the Kingdom of God upon Earth.'[131] In this book, Curtis described what he believed to be 'the first and foremost duty of man'[132], the realisation of what he termed the 'Divine Commonwealth'. Drawing his inspiration from Christ's crucifixion and resurrection, he wrote:

> My thoughts revert to that scene when He that was born at Bethlehem, despised and rejected of men, was scourged and condemned to the death of a slave and a criminal. From that moment of utter despair there sprang the movement which has gone some way to create, and in the ages before us will bring to fulfilment, the Kingdom of God upon earth, the Divine Commonwealth, a human society based on the laws of God, on the one abiding reality, the infinite duty of men to God, of one to another. Of all the lessons brought to my mind in the long task of framing this narrative the deepest is this, that apparent failure, when faced with courage and examined by reason, is the road to superlative triumph. That, I believe, is the true meaning which underlies all that has happened since the dawn which broke upon Easter Day. The spirit of Christ rose from His grave. It moved and yet moves the souls of men to face and accomplish the task which He set them.[133]

Although published in three successive volumes in 1934-1937, *Civitas Dei* was actually a revised and expanded version of a much earlier work of Curtis, *The Commonwealth of Nations* (1916). Combined in one volume in 1938, *Civitas Dei* was circulated under the title *The Commonwealth of God*. The original title was a thinly veiled allusion to Augustine's magnus opus, *De Civitate Dei*. Apparently, Curtis wanted to challenge Augustine's thesis, that the fallen world of this age was fundamentally different from the celestial 'city' of salvation. Repudiating Augustine's theological presuppositions, and intent on reinterpreting the Church Father's spiritual insights, Curtis sought to review the evolution of the commonwealth idea and to show that all of history leads to its fulfilment in the Kingdom of God on earth, which, in his view, was a world state of federalised nations. Moreover, he defined the spiritual essence of the Kingdom as the ethical ideal which Jesus Christ introduced to humankind in the precepts of the two great commandments - to love God and to love one's neighbour as oneself.

Curtis' religious beliefs, convoluted and heterodox as they may have been, nevertheless gripped the imagination of his contemporaries and spurred them on to do their part in expediting the coming of God's kingdom, material and this-worldly, as it was conceived in *Civitas Dei*. 'Curtis's "theology" is quite plainly questionable,' writes Gerald Studdert-Kennedy, 'but on the other hand, it was far more widely shared, and its bearing on his political science, though it has since been neglected, was explicit and obvious at the time.'[134] Of those directly associated with him, only Arnold J. Toynbee discounted the book's thesis in favour of Augustine's. Toynbee's daily reading of Augustine's *Confessions*, and his emotional attachment to it may have been more responsible for this divergence of views than any substantial difference in perspective.[135] Answering Curtis' standard question: 'what is it we are after on this earth?', he responded:

> No doubt the answer is the Civitas Dei; but then one comes to identify this object and here, as you know, I personally, with great affection and respect towards you and your Civitas, put my own treasure in St Augustine - which I fancy may seem to you to be in some inaccessible place beyond the horizon.[136]

Curtis asserted that political wisdom and virtue have been developed throughout history by the creation and operation of free institutions and the practice of self-government. Yet in God's mind, the stage of multiple nation-states governing sovereignly their own affairs was only an intermediate phase in the creation of the ultimate world society. This, according to Curtis, was the enlightened understanding about the divine kingdom which Jesus Christ wanted to communicate to his disciples through a variety of spiritual discourses, and especially through the 'Sermon on the Mount'. Christ's injunction to seek first the Kingdom of God, and his righteousness, supposedly meant that

> the organisation of tribal society into sovereign states, a necessary step to that end, will block its final achievement if the sovereignty of national states is regarded, as it now is, by leaders in church and state, as the last word in human development. We have now reached a stage in the growth of civilisation which cannot go further, and is doomed to go back, until we discover the means of passing from the national to the international state, to the state in the truest and fullest sense of that word ... Human nature has made immeasurable strides since our Lord showed in his own person how divine it can be. But it cannot advance further till men learn to think of the scheme of human relations which he [Christ] conceived as one to be brought from the realm of dreams to the earth in which they live, to be made incarnate in the flesh and blood of a living society.[137]

Yet how could such a 'living society' be brought into existence? Curtis assured any doubtful spirit that, in spite of all opposition, the Commonwealth of God would finally be realised, because 'the supreme Creator had brought into being men made in His own likeness, as partners with Himself in the work of creation, and had left them the task of realising the Kingdom of God upon earth.'[138] Thus the task of designing a political system which would meet God's approval, and bringing about its fulfilment, has been placed into the hands of humankind.[139] Curtis emphasised, however, that a special duty would lie on Christians, as they are aware of God's creative purpose.[140] They would need to mobilise the rest of humankind to join hands with them in building the divine kingdom, which, in keeping with Curtis' interpretation, would be a federal world society.

The first practical step toward the formation of such a society would be the union of a small number of now-independent states into one larger state. The most suitable countries to start with would be those with the same language, similar institutions, and long practice in the art of self-government. Curtis' obvious choice fell on Great Britain, Australia and New Zealand. France, South Africa, and the United States would also qualify as countries suitable for joining the first national commonwealth. The citizens of these countries would quickly develop and demonstrate loyalty to an entity wider than the nation-state as it now is and lead the nations towards the world-commonwealth of the future.[141]

The initial World Commonwealth would have a joint legislature and executive which would impose and collect taxes for federal purposes, operating always upon the individual citizen. Voting and tax-paying for two generations would engender devotion.[142] The federation would find its first common interest in the maintenance of routes between its units, and in time it might be joined by other countries vitally interested in these routes, such as Egypt, India, and Holland.[143] Later would come Belgium and the Scandinavian countries. In this expansion the most difficult step would be the inclusion of the first non-British state. Progress from that point would be both easier and quicker. Thus the British Commonwealth would complete its work as a stage in the long process of political integration which moves toward universal human community in the *Civitas Dei*, the Commonwealth of God.

Although expressing his full support for the League of Nations during its formative stage, even participating in drafting its Charter, Curtis soon changed his opinion after it became clear that there was no hope of peace in a mere league of nations which preserves intact the sovereignty of its states members; which acts only by unanimous decision and even then must depend for action upon forces which remain under control of the states; which has no supreme tribunal with compulsory jurisdiction and no legislature competent to adapt the law to changing conditions; which exercises no authority over the individual citizen and makes no appeal to his loyalty.[144] In *Civitas Dei* he expressed his outright disappointment with the League of Nations due to the diversity of views espoused by its member states. He recommended that the English-speaking nations should withdraw their participation in the League altogether and create their own international organisation. The much-desired admission of the United State and Canada into this organisation would guarantee world peace.

If and when its stability was proved and also its capacity to include other democracies, those even of northern Europe, Canada would, I think, follow suit and by doing so pave the way for its ultimate fusion with the great American Commonwealth. And whenever the people of North America add their strength to an international commonwealth the epoch of world wars in which we are now living will be finally closed.[145]

Again, in his book *World War, its Cause and Cure* (1946) Curtis proposed the union of the United States and Great Britain, as the cornerstone of world federalism.[146]

Curtis perceived the greatest obstacle in realising his internationalist goals in the concept of national sovereignty. 'The change that is needed,' he postulated, 'is first and foremost a change in men's minds. The work of effecting that change is essentially work for the churches; but they cannot begin it till political thinkers have clearly said what the change should be.'[147] Curtis abhorred the emotional attachment, which he perceived in the majority of the people around him, to their own particular country at the exclusion of all the others.[148] To overcome this problem, he put his faith in propaganda, and the chief instrument of that propaganda, he said, must be the Protestant churches. In the closing paragraph of *Civitas Dei* he expressed his confidence that the Christians would discharge their duty, as he saw it, to work towards the realisation of a world commonwealth as the ultimate manifestation of the divine Kingdom.

The great difficulty lies in moving from one stage to the next. It consists no longer in physical obstacles but only in human minds. The difficulty of so changing the minds of men, even in commonwealths most advanced, is hard to exaggerate. It is mountainous in size and as such can only be removed by faith. Because I feel that these mountains can only be moved by faith, I look with hope to repositories of faith, to churches which are based upon faith in the real sense of that word. To leave the language of metaphor, I feel that when once the Protestant churches have learned to regard the creation of a world commonwealth as an all-important aspect of their work in realising the Kingdom of God, an international commonwealth would come into being in a few generations. A bridge would be thrown over the gulf in men's minds which now bars our progress to a higher civilisation. My hopes lies with the churches which are not bound by the chain of their past.[149]

Curtis' trust in the churches' ability to propagate the gospel of world federation was based on his conviction that the public needed to be informed about 'a structure of society based on realities, of a world ordered in accordance with the laws of God', before it would accept a merger of national sovereignties into an international state of some kind.[150] This belief motivated him and Lord Lothian to establish close ties with Church leaders and to play a participatory role in formulating the philosophical and procedural basis of the early ecumenical movement. They exercised an enormous influence on the thinking of Joseph Oldham, the Secretary of the International Missionary Council and organizer of the World Conference on Life and Order in Oxford, 1937:

> Joseph Oldham used the expression "league of churches" because in those days he was profoundly interested in the process whereby the League of Nations had come into being in January 1920. He was in touch with the "Round Table" group, in particular with Lionel Curtis and Philip Kerr, later Lord Lothian, both of whom had taken an active part in the elaboration of the plan for a League of Nations, Curtis as a member of the Peace Delegation at Versailles and Kerr as Lloyd George's private secretary. Both men were also in close touch with General Smuts and Lord Robert Cecil. On 20 September 1952, Oldham wrote to me: "The Round Table group were my great educators in matters of constitutional principle. They clarified my thinking in these matters. I saw clearly that though the Continuation Committee was an organization of church boards it was in principle an entirely new development in church life and that it might lead in the future to new relations between the churches themselves, though I was at the time much too much occupied with IMC [International Missionary Council] post-war problems to look further ahead.[151]

Curtis believed that Church leaders such as Oldham could influence public opinion to such a degree that initiatives would be launched which would ultimately change the geopolitical landscape of the world from some sixty sovereign States to a politically unified human habitat. As future events proved, he would not be disappointed in the ability of the churches to rally the public in support of a 'divine Commonwealth'.


2.7    A spiritual View of the Universe

In a lecture on 'World Order' delivered at Chatham House[152] in spring 1939, Lionel G. Curtis quoted from John Foster Dulles' book, *War, Peace and Change*.[153] He indicated that Dulles had analysed the problem of war and had concluded that national sovereignty was the primary cause of conflicts. That this conclusion was similar to his own views was not coincidental. Avery Dulles, John Foster's son, related the following about his father's close relationship with Curtis: 'Mr. Curtis' thoughts had considerable influence on his own ... He'd have meetings with him and sort of sit at his feet and listen to him as a prophet.'[154] Ever since the publication of *Civitas Dei*, Dulles had advanced its central thesis in his own writings. He was enamoured of the concept that the ethical idea of Christ's teaching, the moral principle of love, was the most dynamic force in history. Moreover, Dulles concurred fully with Curtis' assertion that 'the churches alone can create the necessary public opinion' for the establishment of the commonwealth of God.[155] According to John M. Mulder, 'these ideas apparently influenced Dulles' decision to become active in the church.'[156] The symbiotic relationship between these two extraordinary men and the coalescence of their views concerning the spiritual dimension of international affairs are vitally important in understanding Dulles' active participation in the Federal Council of Churches, especially after the World Conference of Life and Work in Oxford (1937). In the following passage, Mulder makes this point even more obvious:

> It is significant, however, that Dulles was stimulated in the late 1930s by Curtis' ideas of civilization evolving towards the Kingdom of God and the gradual development of an international organization to secure peace. Much of Dulles' writing during the war years and later reflects a similar conception of world order, and while a major influence undoubtedly came from the theologians with whom Dulles was working, the effect of Curtis' somewhat bizarre religious-political philosophy can hardly be ignored.[157]

Contributing an adulatory foreword to the English edition of *War, Peace and Change*, Curtis in turn echoed Dulles' ideas in his Chatham House lecture on 'World Order': 'Each sovereign State tends to look at its own separate and several interests, in disregard of what the results may be to the rest of humanity. For human society there is no government, and so, for [factors affecting] its paramount interests, no control.'[158] The only workable remedy for this intolerable situation would be, 'a world government responsible, not to States, but to all individuals fitted for the trust. That is the goal, however remote, at which we must aim.'[159] In the ensuing discussion, Dr Drummond Shields concurred with Curtis that 'some form of world government was almost certainly the ultimate solution of international difficulties, and a collaboration of democracies was an obvious and natural beginning.' Shields also congratulated the lecturer for his courage and faith in recapitulating the internationalist theme of *Civitas Dei* at a time when nationalism appeared to be sweeping triumphantly across the world.[160] Admiral Drury-Lowe commented on the final chapter of *Civitas Dei* by extracting its pivotal idea. He emphatically stressed Curtis' axiom 'that the great difficulty in moving from one state to another towards the final goal of a World Commonwealth lay in changing the minds of men.' Taking his cue from numerous letters published in the Press, Drury-Lowe opined that such change was already taking place in British society. Many people would begin to recognise the 'great need for moral and spiritual rearmament.'[161] In his final remarks the Admiral stated that only a world-wide spiritual regeneration would suffice to prevent the present order from ending in catastrophe. Only in turning to God would it be possible for humankind to submit itself again to the principles of that higher law which governs the world. Drury-Lowe expressed his hopes that these thoughts would not be brushed aside as merely the product of a visionary mind and added that 'it was not by new weapons nor by new machinery that the world be saved, but by new men.'[162]

Admiral Drury-Lowe's comments were perfectly in harmony with Curtis' own line of reasoning. Earlier in the discussion he had alluded to Professor Toynbee's statement that 'Western Liberalism is merely the political husk of Christianity, without its spiritual kernel'.[163] By doing so he hoped to substantiate his thesis that democracy is not by nature opposed to religion. He objected to the assumption, prevalent among political theoreticians in the nineteenth century, that a democratic system is based on materialistic premises. This erroneous idea supposedly originated at the time of the French Revolution, when leading philosophers confused institutional religion with religion itself, or, as Curtis put it, 'with a spiritual view of the universe'.[164] The reason for such confusion lay apparently in the fact that the established Church was too closely aligned with the *ancien régime*. The revolutionaries were bound to thrust their sword at the hearts of both institutions. Curtis observed, however, that, in his time, a fundamental change had occurred in the popular understanding of democracy as a system built on spiritual principles:

> Marxism, with its by-products Fascism and Naziism, is at last leading the world to realise that the democratic commonwealth is the Sermon on the Mount translated into political terms. The message which President Roosevelt addressed to Congress at the opening of this year (1939) marked an epoch in history; for here was the first executive officer of the greatest commonwealth in the world telling its legislature that the system for which they stand has its roots in religion.[165]

If the Sermon on the Mount had found its political expression in a democratic commonwealth, like the United States of America, then Curtis' appeal to the churches for help in realising the ultimate world commonwealth was, indeed, logical. By 1939 none of the leading members of the Round Table Group would have disputed this assumption, since they had acted upon it with admirable consistency for nearly two decades. Their most valuable contacts within the ecclesiastical establishment in Great Britain were the two principal officers of the International Missionary Council, William Paton and Joseph H. Oldham, who had both studied at Oxford University. They frequently discussed with various members of the Round Table Group, especially with Lionel Curtis, the necessity of establishing a world society.[166] The prototype of such a society would be Curtis' 'Commonwealth of God'.[167] Paton, in particular, was fascinated by the idea of creating a world government or, if deemed impractical under prevailing political conditions, a united Europe as an initial step towards the ultimate goal.[168] Using the International Missionary Council as his platform, he lobbied national governments to accept some form of international organization.[169] In addition to his personal efforts to influence political leaders directly, he authored the book, *World Community* (1938), to disseminate his message more broadly. In it he established the case for a brotherhood of humankind living in a unified world modelled after the Christian community at large.[170]

66

## 2.8    World Community

In the first few pages of *World Community*, Paton asked if it is realistic to believe, as many do, that a brotherhood of humankind is only an empty dream.[171] In looking at the world's situation in the 1930s, the sceptics seemed to have the better part of the argument. In most countries the claims of nationalism and racial superiority carried greater weight for the majority of people than did 'the message of world unity'. Yet, despite the prevalence of these claims, Paton believed they were faulty. They did not take into account the advances of science. He was convinced that the internationalists, not the nationalists, were the true realists, since they had no inclination, as their opposite number seemed to have, to '"put the clock back," "fly in the face of facts," and do other highly unrealistic things.'[172] The technological developments in recent times had apparently validated the arguments of the internationalists. To substantiate his assertion, Paton referred to Lionel Curtis' book, *Civitas Dei*. Far from questioning the thesis that the course of human history would lead inexorably towards the creation of a world commonwealth, he agreed with Curtis that the internationalists would eventually emerge victorious in their dispute with the nationalists. What was needed at this juncture of human development was the support of many historians corroborating the internationalists' claims along the lines which Curtis had drawn in *Civitas Dei*.[173]

Paton believed that the Christian community was the custodian of the principles of world community.[174] The first duty of the Church, as a 'universal society', would be to promote peace by fostering 'a common ethos' among the nations and supporting efforts to unify the world. International law could only then be established as the basis of a 'genuine international order'.[175]

In the name of universal peace, Paton summoned the Church to take a stand against the immoral tendency of the State to play power-politics in foreign affairs. The Christians would be obligated to oppose the idea of the absolute State, in which questions of right and wrong are subject to the dictates of national expediency and aggrandizement. 'Either we believe that there is a morality superior to the State, by which the actions of the State are judged, or we believe that the State is absolute and that what it commands us to do is, because it commands it, right.'[176] Paton did not waver in his conviction that the international Christian community, in its determination to establish 'a better international order', was based upon the principle that morality 'lies beyond the separate wills of States'.[177] However, he disagreed with the view that it had to align itself with every political movement attempting to set up a world organisation. He thought it wrong to place a higher value on the 'relative sphere of political expediency' than on 'the absolute value that attaches to religious duty'.[178] In agreement with the Oxford Report on 'The Universal Church and the World of Nations' (1937), he distanced himself from earlier views among Church officials equating the League of Nations with the Kingdom of God on earth:

In this connection it may fairly be said that while it was right to muster Christian feeling behind the ideal and the fact of the League of Nations, it was wrong for so many to treat the League idea and the League itself as if in them the Kingdom of God had come. "No international order which can be devised by human effort may be equated with the Kingdom of God ... On the other hand the attitude of Christians towards specific proposals in the political sphere should be governed by their obedience to the living God and their understanding of His purpose in Christ."[179]

Paton was disappointed about the inadequacy of political constructs created at Versailles in 1919 to effect peaceful change in international relations.[180] Had Europe been more diligent in seeking political unification after the Great War, it would not have been confronted with the menace of deadly aerial bombardment in 1938.

In another paragraph, Paton admitted that the scornful attacks by German nationalists upon the pronouncements of the World Conference of Life and Work at Oxford (1937) were to a certain degree justified. It was unfortunate, however, that the kernel of truth in these deprecations would also give currency to 'the evils of an unbridled nationalism and racialism'.[181]

They say, in brief, that those who mercilessly lash the excesses of nationalism had nothing to say about the throttling of Germany, the Versailles treaty and its injustices, the taking away of the German colonies and the other measures which German opinion of all shades has regarded as unjust. But when, they say, the national soul reasserts itself in opposition to these injustices, it meets with nothing but misunderstanding and abuse. There is some truth in this, and Christians must take their full share of the blame. There have been voices within the oecumenical Christian movement pleading for a juster view than that of Versailles, but they have not been numerous or strong enough to carry the Churches.[182]

Paton repeatedly asserted that there was still hope of reversing the negative consequences of the Versailles Treaty. He expressed his confidence that the cause of justice would triumph in the end. It would be imperative, however, to supply Christians with accurate facts about the world in which they live. They should be eager to keep themselves informed about foreign affairs. Since the time for peaceful change had arrived, it would be anachronistic to object to the proposal that something should be done to alter the system of sovereign nation-states. For the Church it is never too late to initiate that process of change by supplementing 'the (often) one-sided information available to the public through the ordinary channels, and to remind the public mind of justice, even when it is still relatively safe to be unjust.'[183]

Paton was optimistic that the pervasive influence of Christian teaching and that of internationalists, such as Philip Kerr (Lord Lothian), would eventually lead to the establishment of a world community:

It is scarcely to be doubted that one condition of a stable world order is that there should be some surrender of absolute national sovereignty. Some, like the Marquess of Lothian in his Burge lecture, and others of the Round Table group, definitely envisage the idea of a world-State, and hold that a council of sovereign States [League of Nations] leaves untouched the central problem of unchecked national sovereignty.[184]

Paton further stated that even more moderate proponents of a new world order, such as the ecclesiastics and laymen who had assembled at the Oxford Conference in 1937, would be prepared 'to admit that the claim of each national State to be judge in its own cause is a potent cause of international disorder, and that "the abandonment of that claim, and the abrogation of absolute national sovereignty, is a duty that the Church should urge upon the nations".'[185] Thus he came to the conclusion that, since the churches had widely popularised the idea of the League of Nations, they should now condition 'the minds of their members for this further, and more necessary, though very difficult, advance, and to teach that one absolute condition of a better international world order is that separate nations should be willing to make some surrender of their individual sovereignty.'[186]

In February 1941 Paton published the article, 'The Church and World Order'. He intended to renew the urgent call to the churches to shoulder the task of building an international order after the conclusion of war.[187] Only seven months later this article was followed by the publication of his book, *The Church and the New Order*, which was essentially a lengthy exposition of the same theme.[188] The general thrust of Paton's literary works mirrored Curtis' opinion that the Christian churches should be useful in creating a better understanding among the nations to elevate them to an advanced level of political development. Curtis put it this way: 'The public opinion which is needed to lift the course of human affairs to a higher plane must from its nature be religious in the truest sense of that word. It is for that reason that churches play an indispensable part in such movements.'[189]

Paton's admirable activism was cut short by his untimely death in 1943. The cause he had given his life to would find other, even more determined, advocates. Across the Atlantic John Foster Dulles had already appeared on centre stage in this historic drama as one of the principal proponents of Curtis' Commonwealth of God. His active participation at the World Conference of Life and Work in Oxford (1937) ignited in him a renewed desire to engage in constructive efforts by the Federal Council of Churches to mobilize popular support in the United States for the ideal of a world federation. Eventually he presided over the Council's Commission on a Just and Durable Peace which substantially contributed to the public discussion of postwar peace proposals and laid the foundation for America's participation in the United Nations Organisation.

Notes

[1] George Robert Parkin (1845-1922), the principal of Upper Canada College 1895-1902, was an author and lecturer on imperial federation. In 1902, he became the first secretary of the Rhodes Trust, and he assisted Lord Milner in the next twenty years in setting up the methods by which the Rhodes Scholars would be chosen. His influences remained strong, even thirty years after his death, in the Round Table Group of Canada. His son-in-law, Vincent Massey, and his namesake, George Parkin de T. Glazebrook, were the leaders of the Group in the Dominions.

[2] E.B. Poulton, *John Viriamu Jones and other Oxford Memories* (London: Longmans & Co., 1911) 244-247.

[3] John Ruskin, Kenneth Clark tells us, derived most of his ideas and inspiration 'directly from the source book of all dictatorships, Plato's Republic. He read Plato almost every day.' Kenneth Clark, *Ruskin Today* (New York: Holt, Rinehart & Winston, 1964) 267-268.

[4] John Ruskin, *Lectures in Art*, in *Collected Works*, Vol. 20 (London, 1903) 41.

[5] John Flint, *Cecil Rhodes* (Boston: Little, Brown and Co., 1974) 27; see also C. Newbury, 'Cecil Rhodes and the South African Connection,' in A.F. Madden & D.K. Fieldhouse, eds., *Oxford and the Idea of the Commonwealth* (London: Croom Helm, 1982) 79.

[6] John Ruskin, *A Knight's Faith* (1885), Bibliotheca Pastorum, in *Collected Works*, vol. 31, 505.

[7] J.A. Hobson, *Confessions of an Economic Heretic* (London: George Allen & Unwin, 1938).

[8] Benjamin Jowett (1817-93), the son of a Methodist printer, came to Balliol from St Paul's School as a scholar and remained there all his life. From 1870 to 1893 he was Master of Balliol. See Geoffrey Faber, *Jowett. A Portrait with Background* (Cambridge, Mass.: Harvard University Press,1957).

[9] John MacMillan Brown, *Memoirs* (Christchurch, University of Canterbury, N.Z.: Whitcombe & Tornbs, 1974) 36ff.

[10] William Winwoode Reade, *The Martyrdom of Man* (London: Trübner & Co., [1872] 1874) xxv, 430. The book was still in print in 1968 (Pemberton Publishing Co. republished the 1934 edition).

[11] Charles P. Lucas, *Greater Rome and Greater Britain* (Oxford: Clarendon Press, 1912) 97.

[12] See e.g., Alfred E. Zimmern, *The Greek Commonwealth. Politics and Economics in Fifth-Century Athens* (Oxford: Clarendon Press, 1911).

[13] Richard Jenkyns, *The Victorians and Ancient Greece* (Oxford: Blackwell, 1980) 337.

[14] Sir Alfred E. Zimmern, *The Third British Empire. Being a Course of Lectures delivered at Columbia University* (London: Humphrey Milford, 1926) 34.

[15] Philip Woodruff (pseud. [i.e. Philip Mason]), *The Men Who Ruled India* (London: Jonathan Cape, 1963).

[16] See Deborah Lavin, *From Empire To International Commonwealth*, 125.

[17] See DeWitt Clinton Ellinwood, 'Lord Milner's "Kindergarten", the British Round Table Group, and the Movement for Imperial Reform, 1910-1918,' unpublished Ph.D dissertation, Washington University, 1962, 90.

[18] See Alfred Milner, *The Nation and the Empire. Being a Collection of Speeches*

and Addresses with an Introduction by Lord Milner, G.C.B. (London: Constable and Co., 1913) 499. Toynbee and Milner were co-founders of Toynbee Hall.

[19] See introduction to Arnold Toynbee's *Lectures on the Industrial Revolution* (London: Rivingtons, 1894); and also Edward Crankshaw, *The Forsaken Idea. A Study of Viscount Milner* (London: Longmans, Green and Co., 1952) 21.

[20] Alfred Milner, *Arnold Toynbee. A Reminiscence* (London: Eduard Arnold, [1895] 1901).

[21] *Ibid.*

[22] Milner summarised some of these ideas as follows: 'And for my own part I can imagine no higher ideal which can animate the citizens of my country at the present time than that of a great and continuous national life, shared by us with our kinsmen, who have built up new communities in distant parts of the earth, enabling them and us together to uphold our traditional principles of freedom, order and justice, and to discharge with ever-increasing efficiency our duty as guardians of the more backward races who have come under our sway. That ideal seems to me to embrace all the worthiest aims, whether of narrower or wider scope, which British statesmanship can pursue, and to give to all, who are engaged in any branch of public life, a central meeting-ground and a common inspiration.' Alfred Milner, *The Nation and the Empire*, xlviii.

[23] Arnold Toynbee, *Lectures on the Industrial Revolution in England. Popular Addresses, Notes and other Fragments ... together with a short Memoir by B. Jowett.* [With a prefatory note by Charlotte M. Toynbee] (London: Rivingtons, 1884). The 1905 edition was published by Longmans & Co., London, under the title, *Lectures on the Industrial Revolution of the Eighteenth Century in England together with a Reminiscence by Lord Milner.*

[24] See e.g., Alfred Milner, *The Nation and the Empire*, 195-209.

[25] Leopold Amery became a M.P. for South Birmingham in 1911.

[26] Alfred Milner, *The Nation and the Empire*, 161. On Milner's sympathetic views about socialism, see also *ibid.*, 214, 215.

[27] See John Marlowe, *Milner. Apostle of Empire. A Life of Alfred George the Right Honourable Viscount Milner of St James's and Cape Town, KG, GCB, GCMG, (1854-1925)* (London: Hamish Hamilton, 1976) 178, 179; and also Walter Nimocks, *Milner's Young Men. The 'Kindergarten' in Edwardian Imperial Affairs* (London: Hodder and Stoughton, [1968] 1970) 145.

[28] See Edward Crankshaw, *The Forsaken Idea. A Study of Viscount Milner*, 156; Milner's lectures were posthumously published in six articles in *The National Review*, XCVI (January-June, 1931) 36-53, 185-203, 336-356, 477-499, 641-655, 758-776. Leo Maxse, editor of *The National Review*, was the brother of Lord Milner's widow.

[29] See also Milner's introduction in his book, *The Nation and the Empire*, xi-xlviii; and Walter Nimocks, *Milner's Young Men*, 11.

[30] Edmund Garrett, 'Milner and Rhodes,' in Charles S. Goldman, ed., *The Empire and the Century. A Series of Essays on Imperial Problems and Possibilities by various Writers. With an Introduction by C.S. Goldman ... and a Poem by Rudyard Kipling entitled 'The Heritage'* (London: John Murry, 1905) 481.

[31] See letter to George R. Parkin, dated December 15, 1893; as cited in John Evelyn Wrench, *Alfred Lord Milner. The Man of No Illusions 1854-1925* (London: Eyre & Spottiswoode, 1958) 146-147; the original letter is deposited in the *Private Papers of Sir George Parkin*, Public Archives of Canada, Ottawa. Milner again

expressed his antipathy for existing political institutions in his letter to Parkin, dated June 30, 1896, in *Private Papers of Sir George Parkin*. See also Alfred Milner, *The Nation and the Empire*, 90.

[32] Letter, Milner to Congdon, 23 November 1904, in Cecil Headlam, ed., *The Milner Papers. South Africa, 1899-1905*, Vol. 2 (London: Cassell & Co., 1931-1933) 506. The first volume covers the years 1897-1899.

[33] A.M. Gollin, *Proconsul in Politics. A Study of Lord Milner in Opposition and in Power 1854-1905* (London: Anthony Blond, 1964) 166-167. See Walter Nimocks, *Milner's Young Men*, 204; Nimocks refers to a letter from Oliver to Milner, December 26, 1914, in *Milner Papers*, Oxford University; and also A.M. Gollin, *Proconsul in Politics*, 247. The fact that Frederick S. Oliver was a member of the Round Table Group is attested by John E. Wrench, in *Alfred Lord Milner*, 294.

[34] See Vladimir Halpérin, *Lord Milner and the Empire. The Evolution of British Imperialism.* [With a foreword by The Rt. Hon. L.S. Amery, P.C., C.H.] (London: Odhams Press, 1952) 158.

[35] Lord Hankey, the Secretary of the War Cabinet (1916), and of the Imperial War Cabinet (1917), described Milner's activities as Minister without Portfolio thus: 'My recollection is that Milner was wonderful in tackling a great variety of jobs where mere co-ordination was necessary involving agriculture, food, shipping, coal and fuel, shipbuilding, steel and other metals, railways and railway material, ports and manpower.' As cited in John E. Wrench, *Alfred Lord Milner*, 335.

[36] See John E. Wrench, *Alfred Lord Milner*, 331.

[37] Lionel G. Curtis gives credit for the introduction of the label, 'Milner's Kindergarten', to Sir William Marriott who used the nickname derisively in an attempt to create trouble for Milner in Johannesburg. Marriott's use of the term is not dated; see Lionel G. Curtis, *With Milner In South Africa* (Oxford: Basil Blackwell, 1951) 344-345; on Marriott, see *Dictionary of National Biography*, Second Supplement, Vol. II, 571-572. More commonly, though not as authoritatively, the origin of the term is traced to its use by the Cape Colony statesman John X. Merriman, in the conflict over the suspension of the Cape Colony constitution. In a speech in the Cape Parliament on September 11, 1902, Merriman asked whether Milner intended to set up 'a sort of kindergarten of young Balliol men - (laughter) - to govern this great country?' As cited in Sir James Tennant Molteno, *Further South African Recollections* (London: Methuen & Co., 1926) 27.

[38] See DeWitt Clinton Ellinwood, Jr., 'Lord Milner's "Kindergarten", the British Round Table Group, and the Movement for Imperial Reform, 1910-1918,' 63.

[39] Milner's Kindergarten has been aptly described by Leopold Amery: '... the most characteristic feature of Milner's organization, the element on which he relied for his personal staff, for the work of the high commissioner's office, of the Inter-Colonial Council, ... as well as for much of the work of the colonial administrations themselves, was his 'Kindergarten', the young Oxford men whom he collected or who collected themselves round him. His belief in youth, energy and adaptability combined with first-class brains was abundantly justified by the result. The 'Kindergarten' often made mistakes. Their ideas about money were sometimes overgenerous. Their manner occasionally too cocksure. But by sheer enthusiasm, ability, devotion to duty, and passionate loyalty to their chief, they achieved a gigantic task.' Leopold S. Amery, *My Political Life*, 3 vols. (London: Hutchinson, 1953) Vol. I, 177. Although reflecting Amery's characteristic admiration for himself and his friends, this is an excellent

statement of the spirit and position of the Kindergarten.

[40] See Walter Nimocks, *Milner's Young Men*, 35-36.

[41] Robinson adopted the family name of Dawson in 1917, in accord with a family inheritance. John Evelyn Wrench, *Geoffrey Dawson and Our Time* (London: Hutchinson, 1955) 146. In order to avoid confusion, he will henceforth be referred to as Dawson, by which name he is best known.

[42] See Walter Nimocks, *Milner's Young Men*, 28, 53, 145.

[43] See *ibid.*, 41.

[44] See [Lord Brand], 'Philip Kerr. Some Personal Memories,' *The Round Table* (June, 1960), no. 199, 235.

[45] The following list gives the members or close associates of the Kindergarten. All of them had studied at Oxford University, a good number of them were fellows at All Souls College: Patrick Duncan (later Sir Patrick); Philip Kerr (later Lord Lothian); Robert Henry Brand (later Lord Brand); Lionel Curtis; Geoffrey Dawson (until 1917 Robinson); John Buchan (later Lord Tweedsmuir); Dougal Orne Malcolm (later Sir Dougal); William Lionel Hichens; Richard Feetham; John Dove; Basil Williams; Lord Basil Blackwood; Hugh A. Wyndham; George V. Fiddes (later Sir George); John Hanbury-Williams (later Sir John); Main S.O. Walrond; Fabian Ware (later Sir Fabian); William Flanvelle Monypenny; see DeWitt Clinton Ellinwood, 'Lord Milner's "Kindergarten", the British Round Table Group, and the Movement for Imperial Reform, 1910-1918,' chap. III: 'Milner Forms a "Kindergarten",' 55-92.

[46] See R. Stokes, *Political Ideas of Imperialism* (Oxford: Oxford University Press, 1960) *passim*.

[47] Lionel G. Curtis, 'A Criterion,' *Journal of the British Institute of International Affairs*, I (1922); as cited in Deborah Lavin, *From Empire To International Commonwealth*, 260.

[48] Lord Milner to Geoffrey Robinson, September 14, 1907; *Geoffrey Dawson Papers*.

[49] See Stephen Gwynn, ed., *The Anvil of War: Letters between F.S. Oliver and His Brother 1914-1918* (London: Macmillan & Co., 1936) 16.

[50] See Frederick Scott Oliver, *Alexander Hamilton: An Essay on American Union* (New York: G.P. Putnam's Sons Pub., 1921) 502. The first English edition seems to have been published in 1906.

[51] Basil Williams, ed., *The Selborne Memorandum: A Review of the Mutual Relations of the British South African Colonies in 1907* (Oxford: Oxford University Press, 1925) xvii.

[52] See letters, Alfred Milner to Geoffrey Robinson, August 21 and September 21, 1906, *Dawson Papers*.

[53] *Ibid.*, September 21, 1906. Quoted by Milner from Curtis' initial letter.

[54] Basil Williams, ed., *The Selborne Memorandum*, xvi.

[55] Letter, Alfred Milner to Geoffrey Robinson, August 21, 1906.

[56] See Basil Williams, ed., *The Selborne Memorandum*, xvi-xxi.

[57] Letter, Geoffrey Robinson to Alfred Milner, January 7, 1907, *Milner Papers*, Box SA I.

[58] Letter, Alfred Milner to Geoffrey Robinson, April 17, 1908, *Dawson Papers*.

[59] Letter, Geoffrey Robinson to Alfred Milner, February 3, 1907, *Milner Papers*, Box SA III.

[60] [Lionel Curtis], *The Government of South Africa*, 2 vols. (n.p.: Central News

Agency, Ltd., 1908).

[61] J.R.M. Butler, *Lord Lothian (Philip Kerr) 1882-1940* (London: Macmillan,1960) 28.

[62] *Ibid.*

[63] See Closer Union Societies, *Proceedings at the Annul Meeting of the Association of Closer Union Societies at Johannesburg, March 3, 4, & 5, 1909* (Johannesburg: Argus Co., Ltd., 1909).

[64] Letter, Alfred Milner to Geoffrey Robinson, September 14, 1987, *Dawson Papers.*

[65] Letter, Lionel G. Curtis to Alfred Milner, October 31, 1908, *Milner Papers*, Box SA IV.

[66] Walter Nimocks, 'Lord Milner's "Kindergarten" and the Origins of the Round Table Movement,' *South Atlantic Quarterly*, LXIII (Autumn, 1964), 517. The interview with Lord Brand was conducted on May 3, 1960.

[67] Letter, Lionel G. Curtis to Richard Jebb, December 6, 1908, *Jebb Papers.*

[68] Letter, Lionel G. Curtis to Leo Amery, March 29, 1909, *Leopold S. Amery Papers.*

[69] Letter, Lionel G. Curtis to Lord Selborne, 18 October 1907, MS Selborne 71; as cited in Deborah Lavin, 'Lionel Curtis and the Idea of Commonwealth,' in Frederick Madden & D.K. Fieldhouse, eds., *Oxford and the Ideal of Commonwealth* (London: Croom Helm, 1982) 99.

[70] *Ibid.*

[71] *Ibid.*

[72] *Ibid.*

[73] The others were Richard Feetham, F.S. Oliver, Lord Lovat, G.L. Craik, Lionel Hichens and L.S. Amery.

[74] As cited in David Watt, 'The Foundation of the Round Table. Idealism, Confusion, Construction,' *The Round Table* 60 (November 1970), London, 426.

[75] *Ibid.*

[76] See e.g., John Marlowe, *Milner. Apostle of Empire*, chapter 10 (The Round Table), 205-213; Walter Nimocks, *Milner's Young Men*, chapters 9 (Lord Milner's part in founding the round table movement) and 11 (The *Round Table*); A.M. Gollin, *Proconsul in Politics. A Study of Lord Milner in Opposition and in Power 1854-1905* (London: Anthony Blond, 1964) chapter VII ('Damn the Consequences' and The Round Table); Walter Nimocks, 'Lord Milner's "Kindergarten" and the Origins of the Round Table Movement,' *South Atlantic Quarterly*, LXIII (Autumn, 1964) 507-520; James Eayrs, 'The Round Table Movement in Canada, 1909-1920,' *Canadian Historical Review*, XXXVIII (March, 1957) 1-20; Carroll Quigley, 'The Round Table Groups in Canada, 1908-38,' *Canadian Historical Review*, XLIII (Sept., 1962) 204-224; John Conway, 'The Round Table. A Study in Liberal Imperialism,' unpublished Ph.D dissertation, Harvard University, 1951; DeWitt Clinton Ellinwood, Jr., 'Lord Milner's "Kindergarten", the British Round Table Group, and the Movement for Imperial Reform, 1910-1918,' unpublished Ph.D dissertation, Washington University, 1962.

[77] Deborah Lavin, *From Empire To International Commonwealth*, 108; see also Deborah Lavin, 'Lionel Curtis and the Idea of Commonwealth,' in Frederick Madden & D.K. Fieldhouse, eds., *Oxford and the Ideal of Commonwealth*, 100.

[78] See John Marlowe, *Milner. Apostle of Empire*, 212.

[79] See John Marlowe, *Milner. Apostle of Empire*, 212; see also Walter Nimocks, *Milner's Young Men*, chapter 11: 'The Round Table,' 179-196; and DeWitt Clinton Ellinwood, 'Lord Milner's "Kindergarten", the British Round Table Group, and the Movement for Imperial Reform, 1910-1918,' chap. VI: 'The Wider Stage: Beginnings of the Round Table Movement, 170-212; chap. VII: 'To Save the Empire: The Cooperative Study of the Empire-Commonwealth, 1910-1916,' 213-267; chap. VIII: 'Stating the Problem of Empire; The Public Side, 1910-1914,' 268-319; chap. IX: 'The War Years: An Ambiguous Fulfilment,' 320-35.

[80] See Alan C. Johnson, *Viscount Halifax. A Biography* (London: Robert Hale, 1941) 57.

[81] Deborah Lavin, 'Lionel Curtis and the Founding of Chatham House,' 62.

[82] See John Marlowe, *Milner. Apostle of Empire*, 178 (Marlowe refers to the *Milner Papers*, Box 97, Bodleian Library, Oxford University, for details).

[83] Lionel G. Curtis, *Dyarchy* (Oxford: Oxford University Press, 1920) 74.

[84] It was the policy of *The Round Table* not to reveal the identity of its authors. It seems likely, however, that the statement quoted above was made by Philip Kerr; see John Marlowe, *Milner. Apostle of Empire*, 210, 211.

[85] The first issued of *The Round Table* was published in November 1910. The editor stated that the purpose of this journal was 'to present a regular account of what is going on throughout the King's dominions, written with first-hand knowledge and entirely free from the bias of local political issues and to provide a means by which the common problems which confront the Empire as a whole can be discussed with knowledge and without bias ... The *Round Table* does not aim at propounding new theories or giving voice to ingenious speculations ... [but] ... the founders ... have an uneasy sense that ... the methods of yesterday will not serve in the competition of to-morrow ... It is an anomaly that there should be no means of marshalling the whole strength of the Empire effectively behind its will, when its mind is made up ... If there is a common problem ... there should be some other means than the circulation of formal official despatches, or a meeting of Premiers only once in four years, whereby it can be publicly discussed and a decision quickly reached.' See Walter Nimocks, *Milner's Young Men,* 188-190.

[86] The following list gives the editors of *The Round Table* from 1910 to 1946: From: December, 1910 Philip Kerr; June 1, 1913 Philip Kerr and Edward Grigg jointly; January 1, 1917 R. Coupland, acting Editor; June 1, 1919 Geoffrey Dawson, acting Editor, assisted by John Dove, November 22, 1920; John Dove (during the Editor's illness in 1929 and 1930, the number for December, 1929, was edited jointly by Mr. Kerr and Mr. Horsfall, those for March and June, 1930, by Mr. Horsfall, and that for September, 1930, by Mr. Curtis and Mr. Hodson. From this time on Mr. Hodson was assistant editor, but was mainly engaged in travelling abroad on behalf of the review); April, 1934 H.V. Hodson, acting Editor; July, 1935 H.V. Hodson; July, 1938 - January, 1939 V.T. Harlow, deputy Editor (Mr. Hodson in Australia); October, 1939 - June, 1941 R. Coupland, acting Editor; for June number, 1941 Henry Brooke, acting Editor; September number, 1941 Henry Brooke, acting Editor; September number, 1942 Geoffrey Dawson, acting Editor; January, 1945 Dermot Morrah, acting Editor; January, 1946 Dermot Morrah, Editor; see DeWitt Clinton Ellinwood, 'Lord Milner's "Kindergarten", the British Round Table Group, and the Movement for Imperial Reform, 1910-1918,' 378.

[87] For biographical data on these men see the following: Robert Henry Brand:

*Who's Who, 1958*, 343-344; Geoffrey Dawson (Robinson): John Evelyn Wrench, *Geoffrey Dawson and Our Time* (London: Hutchinson, 1955); *The History of the Times*, Vols. III, IV; 'Geoffrey Dawson,' *The Round Table*, XXXV (1945) 99-102; *The Times*, November 8, 1944, 7; John Dove: Robert Henry Brand, ed., *The Letters of John Dove*; 'John Dove,' *The Round Table*, XXIV (1934) 463-68; *Dictionary of National Biography, 1931-1940*, 237; *The Times*, April 19, 1934, 9; William Lionel Hichens: 'Lionel Hichens,' *The Round Table*, XXXI (1941) 5-16; *Dictionary of National Biography, 1931-1940*, 426-427 (written by Edward Grigg); *The Times*, October 17, 1940, 7; Edward Grigg: 'Edward Lord Altrincham,' *The Round Table*, XLVI (1956), 110-112; *Who's Who, 1955*, 5051; *The Times*, December 12, 1955, 13.

[88] The obituary of Lord Milner in *The Round Table*, June 1925, XV, 427-430.

[89] In the sketch of Milner in the *Dictionary of National Biography*, written by Basil Williams of the Kindergarten, we read: 'He was always ready to discuss national questions on a non-party basis, joining with former members of his South African "Kindergarten" in their "moot", from which originated the political review, *The Round Table*, and in a more heterogeneous society, the "Coefficients", where he discussed social and imperial problems with such curiously assorted members as L. S. Amery, H. G. Wells, (Lord) Haldane, Sir Edward Grey, (Sir) Michael Sadler, Bernard Shaw, J. L. Garvin, William Pember Reeves, and W.A.S. Hewins.'

[90] See A.M. Gollin, *Proconsul in Politics*, 166.

[91] The Round Table Group's view of history is elaborated in all of Curtis' books.

[92] See Philip Kerr, *The Round Table*, August 1911, I, 422-423.

[93] Sir Alfred E. Zimmern, *The Greek Commonwealth. Politics and Economics in Fifth Century Athens* (Oxford: Clarendon Press, 1911).

[94] Letter, Arnold J. Toynbee to Paget Toynbee, 20 April 1915, *Toynbee Papers*, box 67.

[95] Letter, Herbert Croly to Alfred E. Zimmern, 8 July 1915, *Zimmern Papers*, box 14, ff.198-199.

[96] Letter, Walter Weyl to Alfred E. Zimmern, 5 May 1915, *ibid.*, f.175.

[97] Letter, Walter Lippmann to Alfred E. Zimmern, 7 June 1915, *ibid.*, ff.180-181.

[98] Letter, Alfred E. Zimmern to Walter Lippmann, 24 April 1917, *Zimmern Papers*, box 15, ff.60b-60c.

[99] *Ibid.*

[100] Letter, Alfred E. Zimmern to Mrs. Albert Mansbridge, 29 August 1915, *Mansbridge Papers*, BL, Mss. 65257; as cited in Gordon Martel, 'From Round Table to New Europe. Some intellectual Origins of the Institute of International Affairs,' in Andrea Bosco and Cornelia Navari, eds., *Chatham House and British Foreign Policy 1919-1945*, 29.

[101] Letter, Alfred E. Zimmern to Albert Mansbridge, 25 August 1915, *ibid.*, 30.

[102] Letter, Alfred E. Zimmern to Graham Wallas, 14 April 1916, *Wallas Papers*, 1/46,f.37; as cited in Gordon Martel, 'From Round Table to New Europe. Some intellectual Origins of the Institute of International Affairs,' in Andrea Bosco and Cornelia Navari, eds., *Chatham House and British Foreign Policy 1919-1945*, 30.

[103] *Ibid.*

[104] *Ibid.*, 30.

[105] See Memorandum by Eustace Percy, 'The U.S.: Party Politics and the November Elections,' Confidential, 23 May 1918, Public Record Office, FO371/4360; as referred to by Gordon Martel, 'From Round Table to New Europe. Some intellectual

Origins of the Institute of International Affairs,' 32.

[106] See Minute by Percy on 'War Trade Organisation in the U.S.,' Confidential, 6 August 1918, Public Record Office, FO371/4360; as referred to by Gordon Martel, 'From Round Table to New Europe. Some intellectual Origins of the Institute of International Affairs,' 32.

[107] Letter, Eustace Percy to Alfred E. Zimmern, 16 January 1919, *Zimmern Papers*, box 16, f.36.

[108] 'Early Days of Chatham House,' 10, Chatham House Archive (CHA), 2/1/2A; as cited in Deborah Lavin, *From Empire To International Commonwealth*, 166.

[109] Deborah Lavin, 'Lionel Curtis and the Founding of Chatham House,' 61.

[110] See Deborah Lavin, 'Lionel Curtis and the Idea of Commonwealth,' in Frederick Madden & D.K. Fieldhouse, eds., *Oxford and the Ideal of Commonwealth*, 97-121; Richard Mayne, John Pinder, John C. de V. Roberts, eds., *Federal Union: The Pioneers. A History of Federal Union* (London: Macmillan, 1990) 8; and also Michael Burgess, 'Empire, Ireland and Europe: A Century of British Federal Ideas,' in Michael Burgess, ed., *Federalism and Federation in Western Europe* (London: Croom Helm, 1986) 137-138.

[111] See speech delivered by Alfred Milner in Johannesburg on March 31, 1905, in Alfred Milner, *The Nation and the Empire*, 90-91.

[112] In a favourable review of Ramsay Muir's book, *The Expansion of Europe. The Culmination of Modern History* (London: Constable & Co., [1922] 1939), the editor of *International Affairs*, the journal of the Royal Institute of International Affairs, wrote as follows: 'The book records the failure of the League of Nations, and sketches the outline of a new world order by which European civilization may yet be saved. It is to be a federation of States which will consent to their sovereignty being limited in three definite respects. First, they must abandon the right to be judges in their own cause and to make war at their own pleasure. Second, they must pursue a common policy of opening the channels of trade. And third, they must accept a common regulation of the conditions under which subject people, whether civilized or backward, are to be governed.' RIIA, *International Affairs* [1939], vol. XVIII, no. 3 (London: Chatham House) 849-850.

[113] See e.g., Lord Lothian, 'The Demonic Influence of National Sovereignty', *The Universal Church and the World of Nations*, in Joseph H. Oldham, ed., *Church, Community, and State*, 7 Vol. (London: George Allen & Unwin, 1938) 6.

[114] See *ibid.*, 16.

[115] See John Pinder & Andrea Bosco, ed., *Pacifism is not enough. Collected Lectures and Speeches of Lord Lothian (Philip Kerr)* (London: Lothian Foundation Press, 1990) 65.

[116] Lord Lothian, 'The Demonic Influence of National Sovereignty,' *The Universal Church and the World of Nations*, 20.

[117] See *ibid.*, 11-13.

[118] See *ibid.*, 8.

[119] See *ibid.*, 18.

[120] Letter, Lionel G. Curtis to Philip Kerr, 6 May 1933; as cited in J.R.M. Butler, *Lord Lothian (Philip Kerr) 1882-1940* (London: Macmillan, 1960) 100-101.

[121] Lord Lothian, *Pacifism is not Enough - nor Patriotism either* (Oxford: The Clarendon Press, [1935] 1941).

[122] See H. Montgomery Hyde, *The Quiet Canadian. The Secret Service Story of*

*Sir William Stephenson* (London: Hamish Hamilton, 1962) 47, 48.

[123] Pastor Wilhelm Menn had also contributed a preparatory paper to the Oxford Conference, entitled 'The Church of Christ and the International Order', but was prevented by Hitler from taking part in the Conference personally.

[124] Letter, Philip Kerr to Pfarrer Wilhelm Menn, 27 July 1937; as cited in J.R.M. Butler, *Lord Lothian (Philip Kerr) 1882-1940*, 100.

[125] Lionel G. Curtis, *Faith and Works* (London: Oxford University Press, 1943) 12.

[126] See Arnold J. Toynbee, *Acquaintances* (London: Oxford University Press, 1967) 146.

[127] The Federal Union Movement will be discussed in chapter 5.

[128] Letter, Sir Charles Kimber to John Pinder, 29 February 1980; as cited in Richard Mayne & et al., eds., *Federal Union: The Pioneers. A History of Federal Union* (London: Macmillan, 1990) 10, 11.

[129] See Arnold J. Toynbee, *Acquaintances*, 130, 131; and also DeWitt Clinton Ellinwood, 'Lord Milner's "Kindergarten", the British Round Table Group, and the Movement for Imperial Reform, 1910-1918, 215, 216.

[130] It is interesting to note that Lionel G. Curtis was born in an Anglican rectory; the religious influence is evident in many of his writings. Two other members of the Round Table Group had similar Christian backgrounds. Richard Feetham was also born in an Anglican rectory, while John Buchan came from a family of ministers in the Free Church of Scotland. Buchan's writings, such as *Pilgrim's Way. An Essay in Recollection* (Cambridge, Mass.: Houghton Mifflin, 1940), are replete with biblical phraseology.

[131] Lionel G. Curtis, *Civitas Dei* (London: George Allen & Unwin, [1934-1937] 1950). *Civitas Dei* was the most complete expression of the philosophy of the Round Table Group as a whole.

[132] See Lionel G. Curtis, *Civitas Dei*, 742.

[133] *Ibid.*, 654. Deborah Lavin indicates that the intellectual origin of Curtis' axiom was not Christ's teaching, but rather the philosophy of T. H. Green: 'Curtis defined freedom not as absence of constraint but as a social relation, and he transformed Green's proposition that "among ourselves there is at least a potential duty of every man to every man" into an absolute of his own, constantly reiterated: "the infinite duty of each to all". If the self-governing Commonwealth was to be based on the mutual duty of all its citizens, then citizenship must be extended to all.' Deborah Lavin, 'Lionel Curtis and the Idea of Commonwealth,' in Frederick Madden & D.K. Fieldhouse, eds., *Oxford and the Ideal of Commonwealth*, 102.

[134] *Curtis MSS*, 24 May 1938, Bodleian Library, Box 12, f.143, as cited in Gerald Studdert-Kennedy, 'Christianity, Statecraft and Chatham House: Lionel Curtis and World Order,' *Diplomacy & Statecraft*, Vol.6, No.2 (July 1995), 476.

[135] See C.T. McIntire, 'Toynbee's Philosophy of History in his Christian Period,' in C.T. McIntire and Marvin Perry (eds.), *Toynbee: Reappraisals* (Toronto: University of Toronto, 1989).

[136] Gerald Studdert-Kennedy, 'Christianity, Statecraft and Chatham House: Lionel Curtis and World Order,' 476.

[137] Lionel G. Curtis, *Civitas Dei*, 655. Curtis stated that, in speaking of the Kingdom of God on earth, Jesus Christ was really expounding the concept of the perfectibility of human nature, first conceived by Greek philosophers, in seeking to

fulfill the social duty to God and mankind. Curtis also believed that the principle of a universal society which Christ supposedly taught to his followers had already been put in practice on a small scale in Greece many centuries ago (*ibid.*, 699-700).

[138] *Ibid.*, 676.

[139] See *ibid.*, 740, 743.

[140] See *ibid.*, 741-742.

[141] See *ibid.*, 733-734.

[142] See *ibid.*, 732.

[143] See *ibid.*, 733.

[144] See *ibid.*, 728-729.

[145] *Ibid.*, 944.

[146] Lionel G. Curtis, *World War, its Causes and Cure: The Problem considered in view of the Release of Atomic Energy* (New York: Putnam, 1946) 161.

[147] Lionel G. Curtis, *Civitas Dei*, 730. Two pages later Curtis stated: 'This brings us back to the point that the real difficulty in creating an international commonwealth exists, not in the facts of nature, but only in the state of men's minds' (*ibid.*, 732).

[148] See *ibid.*, 714-715.

[149] *Ibid.*, 744-745.

[150] *Ibid.*, 730.

[151] W.A. Visser 't Hooft, *The Genesis and Formation of the World Council of Churches* (Geneva: World Council of Churches, 1982) 11.

[152] The headquarters of the Royal Institute of International Affairs at 10 St. James Square, London.

[153] Lionel G. Curtis, 'World Order,' *International Affairs*, May-June, 1939, Vol. XVIII., No. 3 (London: Royal Institute of International Affairs) 6: 'The position is better stated, than I can state it by Mr. Foster Dulles on page 102 of his book *War, Peace and Change.* "The world," he writes, "is thus in imagination peopled with some sixty super-beings." These imagined beings are endowed with primitive and conflicting desires. There as yet exists no authority to provide, as between such desires, other solvents than that of might. The "ethical" solution also fails to operate because group authorities are not deemed to be subject thereto, or to have any duty to each other. The personified States are not endowed with the spirit of sacrifice and renunciation. The "ethical" principle operates, to be sure, upon the individual group members, and creates a willingness on their part to sacrifice for others. But the "others" tend more and more to become the personified States to the exclusion of more universal causes.'

[154] Avery Dulles, *Oral History Collection*, 1966, 24-25.

[155] Lionel Curtis, *Civitas Dei*, xliii. Curtis stated further 'When political thinkers provided the necessary guidance, the churches can then begin to change public opinion and so enable the statesmen to act.'

[156] John M. Mulder, 'The Moral World of John Foster Dulles', 164.

[157] *Ibid.*

[158] Lionel G. Curtis, 'World Order', 6. In the following Curtis stated his opinion as to the reason why the League of Nations, although designed to usher in a new world order, was inadequate to function as a world government; see *ibid.*, 7-8.

[159] *Ibid.*, 8.

[160] *Ibid.*, 16.

[161] *Ibid.*

[162] *Ibid.*

[163] Lionel G. Curtis, 'World Order,' 11.

[164] *Ibid.*

[165] *Ibid.*

[166] Joseph H. Oldham requested that, after his death, his personal correspondence should be deposited at Rhodes House Library in Oxford.

[167] The expression 'the Commonwealth of God' was also used by ecumenical leaders of the Federal Council of Churches; see e.g., Samuel Z. Batten, *The New World Order*, 22 (Batten is quoting from Ward & Edwards' book, *Christianizing Community Life*): 'The Commonwealth of God as the ideal social order has come only as far and as fast as men have consciously joined with the purpose of Jesus. Constantly betrayed he is never defeated ... He voices both the ideal of man and the eternal purpose. He joins together in his personality the will of God and the desires of men. He makes the divine human and the human divine. The future belongs to those who work with him. They share his immortality of purpose and power. To create the Christian Commonwealth by Christianizing community life -- this is to bring the new Heaven and the new Earth.'

[168] See Eleanor M. Jackson, *Red Tape and the Gospel. A Study of the Significance of the Ecumenical Missionary Struggle of William Paton (1886-1943)* (Birmingham: Phlogiston Publishing, 1980) 269.

[169] See Darril Hudson, *The Ecumenical Movement in World Affairs*, 76-77.

[170] William Paton, *World Community* (London: Student Christian Movement Press, 1938) 13-14.

[171] *Ibid,* 16.

[172] *Ibid.*

[173] See *ibid.* Paton referred to the Preface to vols. II and III in Lionel G. Curtis, *Civitas Dei.*

[174] See *ibid.*, 57.

[175] *Ibid.*, 151-152.

[176] *Ibid.*, 153.

[177] *Ibid.*

[178] *Ibid.*, 153-154.

[179] *Ibid.*, 154. Paton quoted from the Oxford Report (1937), Joseph H. Oldham, ed., *Church, Community and State*, Vol. 8: *The Churches Survey Their Task* (London: George Allen & Unwin, 1938) 171.

[180] *Ibid.*

[181] See *ibid.*, 155.

[182] *Ibid.*

[183] *Ibid.*, 156.

[184] William Paton, *World Community*, 156; his emphasis.

[185] *Ibid.*, 156-157. Paton referred to the Oxford Report (1937), in Joseph H. Oldham, ed., *Church, Community and State*, vol. 8: *The Churches Survey Their Task*, 173.

[186] *Ibid.*, 157.

[187] William Paton, 'The Church and World Order' (including a review of Bishop Bell's book *Christianity and World Order*), *The Student Movement* vol. XL (12 February 1941) 63

[188] William Paton, *The Church and the New Order*, S.C.M. Press Religious Book Club edition No. 23, London, 1941. The book was first published in September of 1941.

[189] Lionel G. Curtis, *Civitas Dei*, 723.

# 3

# THE PROBLEM OF NATIONAL
# SOVEREIGNTY

In 1936, Henry P. Van Dusen told Dr Joseph H. Oldham, the Secretary of the Commission of Research of the Universal Christian Council, that John Foster Dulles, who had by then become a widely renowned exponent of international law, was well qualified to write a preparatory paper for the World Conference of Life and Work at Oxford (1937). He also informed Oldham about Dulles' active interest in the affairs of the Presbyterian Church[1] and the Federal Council of Churches.

Van Dusen's close friendship with Dulles dated back to the liberal-fundamentalist controversy in the Presbyterian Church. In 1923 the fundamentalist faction in the Presbyterian General Assembly of New York sought to prevent the ordination of Van Dusen, accusing him of holding liberal-modernist views. Dulles was asked to prepare a brief in defence of Van Dusen. Although the General Assembly, controlled by conservatives, rejected the appeal, it was subsequently accepted by the New York City Presbytery. Van Dusen was allowed to embark on a highly successful clerical career and become one of the most outstanding proponents of the ecumenical movement. Through the years Dulles and Van Dusen served together on different commissions of the Federal Council of Churches. They also met frequently at Union Theological Seminary, where Dulles was a trustee and Van Dusen a professor. In November 1945, Van Dusen succeeded Henry Sloane Coffin[2], as president of the seminary, largely upon Dulles' recommendations.[3] The most significant point of contact between these two men, however, was their common membership in the Council on Foreign Relations.

Predictably, Van Dusen's high opinion of Dulles left its intended impression on Oldham[4], who, on his visit to the United States in 1936, was eager to meet the American lawyer. Subsequently, Dulles attended a number of meetings of the American committee of the Universal Christian Council which was responsible for preparatory planning of the Oxford Conference. Soon it became clear that Dr Oldham's ability in organising a popular movement among the churches would be ideally complemented by Dulles' keen sense of political realism on questions regarding international relations. Both realised that they needed each other in mobilising the churches against manifestations of extreme nationalism. Dr Oldham saw in John Foster Dulles qualities of character and intellect which would be of immeasurable value to his work of organising the World Conference of Life and Work in Oxford, 1937. Yet not even he could imagine the progress which would be accomplished in formulating the Church's position on world order and peace as a result of Dulles' presence at Oxford. Unknown to both men at the time, the meeting which ensued marked the beginning of a remarkable collaboration in the ecumenical movement. They aspired to capture the imagination of the Christian public with a grand ideal, transcending narrow-minded national self-interest, the ideal of a unified world society living in peace and justice. To educate the churches, and through them the society at large, about international co-operation was seen by both men as the primary antidote of war. It was regarded as essential in preventing a repetition of the fiasco which had followed America's refusal to join the League of Nations in 1920.

Dulles heartily agreed to write a paper on his favourite topic of peaceful change in preparation of the Oxford Conference. A few months later he sent Oldham his article entitled 'The Problem of Peace in a Dynamic World', which was circulated among a select number of Christian scholars and Church leaders for critical assessment[5] and subsequently published in volume seven of the Oxford series on *Church, Community, and State*.[6] The same article also appeared in the Christian magazine *Religion in Life* in America in spring 1937.[7]

### 3.1    Unification of the World

In 'The Problem of Peace in a Dynamic World', Dulles outlined the basic concepts of peaceful change and attacked what he regarded to be an unhealthy and obsolete concept of national sovereignty.[8] He cautioned against becoming too quickly disheartened at the slow progress of eliminating war. Advances in overcoming the main obstacles to peace, created by pride and selfishness, did not keep pace with enlightened expectations. Human egotism could only be offset, he asserted, by superseding it with 'some sentiment more dominant and gripping and which would contain in it the elements of universality as against particularity.'[9] No other organisation would be as uniquely qualified to accomplish this task as the Church because 'in the eyes of God, all men are equal and their welfare is of equal moment ... It is only through an approach of such universality that there is any promise of a solution.'[10] In this statement as in several others, Dulles idealised the Christian Church as an exemplary community which had demonstrated the ability to transcend the limitations of the nation state, echoing the belief of his father, a liberal Presbyterian minister, that the Church should always project its transnational character to the world.[11] In so doing, it would contribute to the swell of pacific sentiments which had already begun to influence government policy since the end of World War I. The devastations of that conflict prompted politicians to propose a 'new world system' in which war would be outlawed.[12] Until then, 'the sovereignty-war system' would continue to dominate the political landscape of the world. Since international law was only a collection of legal codes regulating the declaration and prosecution of war and the rights and duties of neutrals, Dulles felt keenly its inadequacy to prevent recurring outbursts of war. Even peace conferences, such as those held at The Hague in 1899 and 1907, did not surpass the limitations of a system which recognised the right of sovereign nations to settle their disputes by violent means. Their primary purpose was to balance the accounts of previous conflicts by awarding the victorious parties strategic advantages in the case of another territorial dispute. Prompted by the development of new weaponry, the Hague Conferences also introduced better guidelines in waging war so that its savagery and destruction could be kept to a minimum. Thus, they unwittingly strengthened the war system by making its prosecution more bearable.[13]

In discussing at great length different theories about the origins of war, Dulles developed the thesis that perpetual peace would not be attainable unless the war system itself would be eliminated. In conclusion, he stated: 'Where then does the solution lie? The grandiose solution lies in the abolition of the entire concept of national sovereignty and the unification of the world into a single nation. All boundary barriers are thus automatically levelled.'[14] This solution, however, would be too radical in its application. Dulles realised that the notion of simultaneously uniting all nations under one government would be unacceptable to a world accustomed to the set-up of different nation-states. Yet there was an alternative approach of bringing peace to an agonizing humanity:

> Our requirement is not that there be no boundaries but that safety valves be cut through the barriers of boundaries so that human energy will diffuse itself peacefully and not be suppressed and compressed within a rigid envelope until a bursting pressure is attained.[15]

Dulles pointed to the early history of the United States as a useful guide to determine the extent of the apertures needed to assure a peaceful diffusion of friction between neighbouring nations. Despite the fact that America had, in his time, largely abandoned its original federal design, Dulles thought that it was still instructive to contemplate the conditions which existed at the time the Union was formed. The former colonial states exercised the same sovereign rights as any other nation and consequently kept a jealous eye on each other. At times their dealings with one another deteriorated almost to the point of open hostility. 'Yet through the adoption of a multilateral treaty known as the Constitution, they have found an essential basis for peace in the renunciation by each of the right to interfere with the interstate movement of people, goods, and ideas.'[16] The decisive moment in bringing the states under the rule of a federal government occurred when the decision was reached to invest in Congress the power to issue a single currency. Each state abrogated the right to mint its own money, but retained the authority to determine its social, educational, and religious policies.

> In some [states] the common law prevails, in others the civil law. Each has its own courts and its own system of taxes -- having only recently given the Federal Government the power also to impose income taxes. Each has its own armed force for the preservation of internal order. Legal, social, labour, and material conditions have, in fact, varied greatly as between the states.[17]

Since the state boundaries were no longer formidable barriers, they did not 'arouse any effort on the part of one state to extend its own barriers at the expense of another.' Money could easily be transferred between citizens of different states for capital investment or loans. Interstate commerce and the exchange of ideas were greatly facilitated, because U.S. citizens could now travel unhindered to any part of the nation. A surplus of energy, which accumulated in densely populated states, could easily be channelled to other areas of the country. To alter the state boundary lines themselves by armed force lost its significance as a means to improve one's economic standing.[18] In the last paragraph of his article, Dulles finally stated that he looked to Church leaders in particular to guide the world into a peaceful future:

> It is these nations [the Western democracies] which can still exercise a leadership in world affairs. It is they who above all should want a warless world, for neither democracy nor religion can thrive under the menace of war. The objective is thus one which should logically command their full support. But, unhappily, pure reason does not suffice to assure action. Reason can chart the course. It can point out what are the obstacles, the human weaknesses, that interpose. But to overcome these obstacles is the task of spiritual leadership.[19]

In writing this paper Dulles wanted to diminish that 'great affection' of the people for the division of nations 'by artificial lines into compartments'. He noted that the 'system of dividing the surface of the earth among some sixty nations and allowing each to do as it pleases has become an outmoded feature in international affairs.'[20] The same theme occurred repeatedly in Dulles' public address and writings.[21]

Dulles must have been aware of the revolutionary content of his message to the churches,[22] especially since he kept in close contact with individuals, such as Arnold J. Toynbee, who were conscious of the radical nature of their internationalistic creed. In an address at the Fourth Annual Conference of the Institute for the Scientific Study of International Relations, Copenhagen, June, 1931, Toynbee stated, for example:

> We are at present working discreetly but with all our might to wrest this mysterious force called sovereignty out of the clutches of the local national states of our world. And all the time we are denying with our lips what we are doing with our hands, because to impugn the sovereignty of the local national states of the world is still a heresy for which a statesman or a publicist can be, perhaps not quite burned at the stakes, but certainly ostracized and discredited.

It was a daring feat in the mid 1930s to recommend the abolition of independent nation-states which, of course, would include the United States. One might expect that Dulles would have caused a public outcry among patriotic Americans by the sheer audacity and magnitude of his proposition, or, at least, be regarded as controversial. In general, however, his articles were received favourably.[23] A world society, after all, was the perennial dream of humankind throughout the centuries. To suggest, however, that Dulles was an unrealistic dreamer or theorising philosopher would be to underrate his genius. He was a man of clear vision and intellectual resourcefulness. His penetrating insight into the true nature of world politics made him a prophet, visualising and articulating the great and immanent vision of an international community. At a later occasion, in 1942, meeting with the British Foreign Minister Anthony Eden, Dulles was still gripped by the same idea which he pursued with unrelenting passion until the end of his life. Eden, while entertaining his guest, 'allowed Foster to expatiate at length on his ideas for world government and European federation.'[24]

By using the ecumenical movement as the preferred vehicle to express his opinions, Dulles chose, as his primary target group, the Christian public in the English-speaking world. His goal was to motivate the churches to become actively involved in building a global society. He wanted to reverse the political trends which in his view were leading towards international anarchy and disorder.[25] The first step in restoring a sense of sanity to the realm of foreign relations was to lead the nations to 'an intellectual and emotional conviction that the existing system is so bad that it must be changed, even though that means, for some, forgoing advantages that they have the power to grasp.'[26] Addressing the graduating class at Princeton Theological Seminary on May 16, 1944, Dulles admitted, however, that a change of perspective regarding the disastrous 'power system' of national sovereignty is only gained on the stony road of 'hard and cruel experience'.[27] He hoped that the two world wars had taught the nations to settle their disputes by appealing to principle - the organising of a world community - rather than by brute force. A rational approach to the solution of conflicts between nations would be needed in the future. Dulles cautioned, however, that the danger of reverting to the familiar state of power politics during the phase of general confusion at the end of war is always present. He warned that 'if this happens after this war, we will again fail to have the state of mind which must precede any genuine progress toward world order. To prevent that psychological relapse must be the concern of those, like yourselves, who aspire to moral leadership.'[28] Thus he challenged a new generation of pastors to guide their future congregations into the unfamiliar terrain of a new world order as the only sure hope of peace. That it would be a difficult assignment to complete was made clear to these seminarians in Dulles' concluding remarks:

> To achieve world order is a long, hard task. It will only have begun when the fighting stops. It is not a task for those who are weary or of faint hearts. It calls for men who are clear of vision, strong of faith, and competent in deed. Fortunately, there is a goodly number of those men among our leaders and among the rank and file of our people. How much they can achieve, and how quickly, depends on whether their ranks are steadily augmented. We need many more who possess and will use the qualities Christ taught. To assure that is your task.[29]

Advocating the need for a unified world with unrelenting fervour in Church circles from the late 1930s to the mid 1940s he elevated the issue of a world federation to the status of a religious concern of first importance. At the end of the Second World War he would explicitly state: 'To create the moral foundation for world order was ... the foremost task of the churches.'[30] Based on that 'moral foundation' a social structure would emanate which would be characterised by peace, justice, and equality.


3.2     The Social Structure of a World Society

Difficult as it may be for us to understand today, however, Dulles predicted that the social structure of a just world society would be modelled on the prototypes of totalitarian countries like Soviet Russia and Nazi Germany. In the same article that featured his proposition to abolish the independent nation-state, written in preparation of the ecumenical conference in Oxford 1937, he discussed the benefits of Communism and Fascism, and the ideal social policy to be adopted in the future world state:

> How are we to overcome the obstacles created by pride and selfishness? ... We can get rid of them only by replacing them by some sentiment more dominant and gripping and which will contain in it the elements of universality as against particularity. This is no visionary dream. Before us today we have the spectacle of Communism and Fascism changing almost overnight the characteristics of entire peoples. Millions of individuals have been made into different and, on the whole, finer people. Elemental virtues are again treated as matters of concern. Immoralities and dishonestness,

personal prides and prejudices are replaced by courage, self-sacrifice and discipline. There is a conscious subordination of self to the end that some great objective may be furthered.[31]

John Foster Dulles believed that Communism and Fascism were inspiring spectacles from which the American Christians should learn a lesson in successful social engineering. In *War, Peace, and Change* (1939), which was by far his most significant literary accomplishment, Dulles elaborated this thesis in further detail, eliciting the following comments by Albert N. Keim:

> Dulles saw fascism and communism as outstanding contemporary examples of the skilful combining of the ethical and political solutions. There was, he believed, an "inherent interconnection" between the ethical and the political solution in any viable polity.[32]

During the Second World War Dulles became more cautious in his public references to the Nazi movement, but for most of the 1930s he openly defended the political model of Fascism. In a speech at Princeton in March 1936, he suggested that what was happening in Germany and Italy was all part of the inevitable struggle between the new 'dynamic' nations and 'static' nations like England and France, and Americans must adjust themselves to the changes that were coming. He added that, although 'distasteful', the Nazi revolution in Germany represented a change that it would be better to accept rather than go to war to stop, and that if everyone yielded gracefully, then Hitler, National Socialism, and its excesses would prove to be a passing phase. On the eve of World War II Dulles still entertained these sentiments. Ron Chernow, in *The Warburgs. A Family Saga*, states:

> Jimmy [James Paul Warburg] always thought Dulles a pompous stuffed shirt, a view amply confirmed when Dulles intoned, "Only hysteria entertains the idea that Germany, Italy or Japan contemplate war upon us." Not without a touch of admiration, Dulles described the Axis powers as the "dynamic have-not nations" whose legitimate demands must be met.[33]

To come to a better understanding about Dulles' sympathetic attitude towards European totalitarianism in the 1930s, one needs to examine his transcontinental business connections during that period of time.

### 3.2.1   The Nazi Controversy at Sullivan & Cromwell

After Hitler had come to power in Germany, some wealthy German Jews, distinguished clients of Sullivan & Cromwell, turned to John Foster Dulles for help against Nazi oppression. Eleanor Dulles, who cohabitated at the time with David Blondheim, an American Jew, frequently spoke her mind about the intolerable situation of Jews in Germany.[34] Once John Foster rebuked his sister for her 'impertinent' comments about the significance of the growing anti-Semitic sentiments in Nazi Germany, which she had observed first-hand while on a visit in Berlin. In response he told her that he had seen them himself but thought them the temporary by-products of a much more important and fundamentally positive change in the power structure of Europe.[35]

Leonard Mosley writes that many of Dulles' friends on Wall Street, as well as Allen, Eleanor, and some of his partners at Sullivan & Cromwell, were perplexed about his complacency over what was happening in Germany. John J. McCloy[36], a fellow lawyer, expressed puzzlement over Dulles' ambivalent attitude to the Nazis.[37]

The answer to this apparent ambiguity in Dulles' behaviour might have been, as Mosley suggests, his realisation that the allied powers had committed a gross inequity against Germany at Versailles in 1919 by imposing on its people an unrealistic burden of reparation payments. He contended that this injustice 'must be paid for', and that Adolf Hitler was one of the 'bills' the allies would have to accept and meet.[38]

Allen, who had placed himself at the head of the anti-Hitler faction at Sullivan & Cromwell, was adamant in his opinion to sever all official connections to Nazi Germany. Invited by Fritz Thyssen, the German steel tycoon, he had attended a meeting at the Nazi headquarters in Berlin and was deeply offended by 'a lecture on the blindness of Americans to the evils of Jewish international finance.'[39] John Foster admitted later that this non-cooperative attitude of his brother had 'extremely hurt him'.[40] Eventually, after some heated discussions, the other partners threatened to resign from Sullivan & Cromwell and set up a rival firm. Even then, John Foster would not yield the field to them. 'At a stormy meeting of the partners', writes Mosley, 'Foster vehemently defended his policy of leaving Germany well enough alone, and stressed the financial loss the firm would suffer if it abandoned its German clients.'[41] There was much truth in the latter statement, because Sullivan & Cromwell, as James S. Martin, the Chairman of the Economic Warfare Section of the Department of Justice, pointed out in a postwar investigation[42], managed in co-operation with the German law firm of Albert & Westrick[43] much of the legal procedures in the matter of reparation and foreign loan negotiations for the Schroder[44] and J. Morgan banking interests in Germany.[45] To overcome the impasse, an emotionally distressed John Foster Dulles finally gave in to the demands of his law partners.[46] In 1935, Sullivan & Cromwell closed its office at the Hotel Esplanade in Berlin.[47] Refuting frequent charges of pro-Naziism in later days, Allen would state that this decision was reached unanimously in protest against Hitler's totalitarianism. 'You couldn't really do an honest piece of law in Germany after the Hitlerian laws began to be passed and the Hitlerian discipline clamped down on the country. And I remember very well the reason for the closing. There was no particular incident, except that we didn't feel you could practice law there.'[48] Considering the circumstances, it is understandable that Allen did not tell the whole story, which was undoubtedly known to him.

The fact that John Foster concurred reluctantly with the majority decision at Sullivan & Cromwell to discontinue the firm's legal representation in Berlin did not prevent him from pursuing single-handedly numerous business interests in Nazi Germany. At least once per year from 1934 to 1939, with the sole exception of 1938, he travelled to Berlin in an official capacity.[49] On one of these business trips, in early 1936, he discussed financial matters with the Minister of Economics and Reichsbank president, Hjalmar Schacht.[50] Schacht, an old friend of Dulles, would soon distinguish himself as Hitler's financial genius. On the same occasion, Dulles consulted with Dr Heinrich F. Albert, a member of the law partnership Albert & Westrick, Sullivan & Cromwell's principal liaison in Germany since the early 1920s. Albert's impeccable Nazi credentials[51] and his long-standing connections with the German intelligence establishment[52] opened up lucrative business opportunities for Sullivan & Cromwell with a number of large German enterprises, such as the Hansa Steamship Company.[53]

In the autumn of 1944, at the height of the presidential election campaign in the United States, Senator Claude Pepper (D, FL), alleged that J. Henry Schroder Banking Corporation (Schrobanco) had financed Hitler's rise to power through its intermediary, Baron Kurt von Schröder.[54] These accusations were actually directed towards the bank's legal advisor, John Foster Dulles, who was widely expected to become Secretary of State of a new Republican administration.[55] Senator Joseph F. Guffey of Pennsylvania hurled similar charges against Dulles in a congressional speech at the same time.[56] Understandably, Schrobanco denied the allegations and described Senator Pepper's insinuations as 'unqualifiedly false', while ignoring those of Senator Guffey.[57]

The journalists, Drew Pearson and Walter Winchell, joined in the fray and accused Dulles of having assisted 'the banking circles [J. Henry Schroder Banking Corporation] that rescued Adolf Hitler from the financial depths and set up his Nazi party as a going concern.' They claimed that Dulles, in his legal capacity at Sullivan & Cromwell, had maintained professional ties with Baron Kurt von Schröder. Moreover, Pearson suggested that Dulles had displayed an unusual affection for other fascist dictators and their political allies, such as General Franco of Spain and Count René de Chambrun, the son-in-law of Laval, and had advised the 'Swedish SKF'.[58] In 1946 and 1947 Dulles' alleged connections to the Nazis were again impugned in articles of *The Protestant*[59] and the *Social Questions Bulletin*[60]. They repeated most of the Pearson charges. In addition, a whole series of attacks upon Dulles were published in *In Fact*, edited by George Seldes.[61] In early 1947, Raymond Walsh informed the American public on his national radio program that Dulles had rendered legal services to the German chemical concern I.G. Farben during the war.[62] In the same year, Congressman Adolph J. Sabath of Illinois raised the question of Dulles' earlier links to Hitler's armament industry in a congressional speech.[63] A few months later Harold L. Ickes, Roosevelt's former Secretary of the Interior, took up the same issue and branded Dulles a fascist sympathizer.[64]

91

Although Ickes retracted some of his accusations again in 'Looking Forward Backwards', an article published in *The New Republic* (November 21, 1949), he did not change his negative assessment of Dulles as a politician of questionable convictions.[65] In 1949, while running for a Senate seat in New York, Dulles was again confronted with allegations of having espoused Fascism throughout the 1930s. At the height of the campaign he was even accused of anti-Semitism. Although Dulles did not defend himself personally against any of these charges, members of the Federal Council's Commission on a Just and Durable Peace and political supporters repeatedly spoke out in his defence.[66] There is sufficient evidence to demonstrate, however, that Dulles stood in direct contact with individuals close to the banking and chemical industry of Nazi Germany.[67] Ronald W. Pruessen, a sympathetic biographer of Dulles, finds it impossible to absolve him from charges that he had harboured fascist sentiments throughout the 1930s:

> If, as Dulles and his supporters always later maintained, he felt considerable repugnance toward the Hitler regime and guided his firm to a decision that it was impossible to do legal business in Nazi Germany, his qualms were hardly categorical in execution. As one historian has suggested, a far more accurate gauge of the sentiments of American businessmen toward Germany during the 1930s is a measurement of their actions rather than their words: this is certainly applicable to John Foster Dulles.[68]

Even the letter sent to the editor of *The Christian Century*, signed by Bennett, Niebuhr, Nixon, and Oxnam, which attributed pure motives to Dulles' collaboration with Nazi-controlled companies, stated that '[a]ny corporation lawyer of like position will find that policies of certain of his clients are open to social criticism.'[69]

3.2.2    The Schroder Connection

In the late 1920s John Foster Dulles, who had by then become a senior partner at Sullivan & Cromwell, was appointed chief legal advisor of the Schroder investment bank (Schrobanco). Sullivan & Cromwell and Schrobanco were both located in the same building, owned by the Bank of New York, at the corner of Wall Street and William Street.[70] Allen W. Dulles, John Foster's brother and a partner at Sullivan & Cromwell, became a director of the Schroder bank in New York and was retained as its legal counsel from 1938-1942. He was also an old friend of Frank C. Tiarks, a partner in the Schroeder Bank in London since 1902.[71]

In 1936 the Rockefellers selected Schrobanco to forge a link between the financial establishment of America and Nazi Germany. For that purpose they formed a new investment bank, Schroder, Rockefeller & Company, Inc. (Schrorock) at 48 Wall Street, which would handle the underwriting and general securities business of J. Henry Schroder Banking Corporation and the Rockefeller interests.[72] Avery Rockefeller, son of Percy Rockefeller[73], who had previously worked behind the scenes at Schrobanco, became the director and vice president of the new bank. Carlton Fuller, another banker at Schroders, was appointed president.[74] John and Allen Dulles were chosen as the new company's lawyers.[75]

In 1938, Frank C. Tiarks (1874-1952), Managing Director of J. Henry Schroder & Co. in London and a director of the Bank of England in 1912-1946[76], acted as Hitler's financial representative in Great Britain.[77] After the First World War, Tiarks had worked closely with the German banking establishment. At the request of Lord Milner, who occupied an important post at the War Office at the time, he had agreed to serve as financial adviser to the British Army of Occupation in Germany, with the title Civil Commissioner. Roberts notes that this was 'a role for which he [Tiarks] was uniquely qualified by virtue of his membership of the Court of the Bank of England and his strong business and personal ties to Germany.'[78] For instance, Tiarks became particularly involved in the business affairs of three private banks in Cologne, notably J.H. Stein, the family firm of Baron Bruno's wife, Deichmann & Co., and Sal. Oppenheim & Cie.

The interests of Schroders in Germany were managed predominantly by the merchant firm, Schröder Gebrüder, in Hamburg, and its affiliated bank in Cologne, the J.H. Stein & Co[79], in which SS-Oberführer Baron Kurt von Schröder was a partner.[80] Kurt von Schröder was also Hitler's representative to the Bank for International Settlements[81] and a director of International Telephone & Telegraph (I.T.T.) subsidiaries in Germany.

3.2.3    The I.T.T. Network

In 1941 Sosthenes Behn, the president of I.T.T., who was known for his admiration of Hitler,[82] tried to acquire General Aniline & Film Corporation, the American subsidiary of the German I.G. Farben cartel.[83] The Treasury Department, however, placed this company under the control of the Alien Property Custodian[84] before the business transaction could be carried out.[85] Leo T. Crowley, the director of the Alien Property Custodian agency, was advised by John Foster Dulles, his principal legal counsel, to appoint Ernest K. Halbach, a former I.G. Farben official, as chairman of General Aniline & Film,[86] and Victor Emanuel, as a director of the board. These appointments were certainly not accidental.[87] Victor Emanuel, a director of Standard Gas & Electric, had for many years enjoyed a close business relationship with Schrobanco.[88] Subsequently, Crowley, Halbach, and Emanuel allowed this subsidiary of the German I.G. Farben cartel, which was a gigantic conglomerate of chemical firms in its own right, to remain intact throughout the duration of the war, supporting Hitler's war effort by delivering strategic war chemicals to Nazi associates in South America.[89]

On November 19, 1945 Baron Kurt von Schröder revealed under oath that Behn, prevented from buying into the I.G. Farben cartel, invested 250,000,000 Reichmarks through I.T.T.'s subsidiary Lorenz A.G. in Focke-Wulf A.G., an aircraft manufacturing firm producing fighter planes used against the Allies.[90] According to Schröder's testimony, I.T.T. 'substantially increased' the initial investment sometime later. While the United States was fighting against the Axis Powers during the Second World War, the American entrepreneur Sosthenes Behn was making huge profits from Hitler's armament industry,[91] without which it would have been impossible for the German army to embark on its far-flung operations.[92] It should be noted, however, that Behn was also a substantial supplier of communications and electronic equipment to the Allied armies.[93] Anthony Sampson portrays accurately this grotesque situation:

> The wartime annual ITT reports were full of patriotic references, and pictures of the American flag flying over ITT's plants. Behn was building up a stronger base in America, and in September 1942 he announced a great new ITT plant in New Jersey. ITT laboratories in America, helped by a contingent of refugee French engineers from Paris, achieved some valuable inventions, including the High Frequency Direction Finder, nicknamed Huff-Duff, which was used to detect German submarines attacking the Allied convoys in the Atlantic. Thus while ITT Focke-Wulf planes were bombing Allied ships, and ITT lines were passing information to German submarines, ITT direction finders were saving other [Allied] ships from torpedoes.[94]

In line with his general business philosophy Sosthenes Behn also invested I.T.T. capital in the Swedish Enskilda Bank, which financed the gigantic ball-bearing cartel generally known as SKF (A.B. Svenska Kullagerfabriken).[95]


3.2.4    A.B. Svenska Kullagerfabriken

Hugo von Rosen, the cousin of Field Marshal Hermann Göring, and William L. Batt, vice-chairman of the United States War Production Board, were directors of SKF in America throughout the war.[96] SKF was another international armament production company which, in the words of Higham, 'was concerned only to make profits, trade on both sides of the fence in wartime, and act as a front for German interests.'[97] Recognising the strategic significance of ball-bearings to the prosecution of war, Hugo von Rosen, accompanied by a group of board members, visited the SKF plants in Germany and Italy, to assure the most proficient co-operation with the company's principal customer, the High Command of the Axis Powers. While in Germany Hugo von Rosen also initiated precautionary measures in case the British blockade would make it difficult for these plants to honour their contracts with Nazi affiliates in Latin America. He promised his managers that, if such a situation were to develop, SKF in Philadelphia would immediately step in and deliver the products. This promise held true even after Roosevelt had declared war on Japan and its allies.[98] In late December 1941 it became expedient to place the different SKF subsidiaries in the United States under American ownership in order to prevent the Treasury Department from confiscating them. For this delicate task, the SKF directors enlisted the assistance of John Foster Dulles, who effectively protected the U.S. holdings of the international ball-bearing conglomerate by establishing a voting trust with himself and William L. Batt as trustees.[99]

Despite these and other efforts to keep the Axis armament industry intact, it became obvious, in 1943, that the Allies would eventually defeat their enemies. Perceiving the historical significance of this development, Dulles became increasingly involved in the postwar planning of the U.S. State Department. He knew that the Allies were themselves interested in unifying the world under their auspices. According to Emery Reves' book, *The Anatomy of Peace* (1946), an American-dominated new world order would rise phoenix-like from the ashes of the most devastating war in human history. Reves postulated that 'human society can be saved only by universalism', a belief also shared by Dulles. However, Reves' subsequent assertion took that idea a step further. He stated that 'unless the Christian churches return to this central doctrine of their religion and make it the central doctrine of their practice, they will vanish before the irresistible power of a new religion of universalism, which is bound to arise from the ruin and suffering caused by the impending collapse of the era of nationalism.'[100] Dulles probably disagreed with that statement. In the mid-1940s Dulles could look back on many years of dedicated service to the Federal Council of Churches, especially in formulating the Council's position on social and international issues. His participation at the Oxford Conference of Life and Work in 1937 was certainly one of the most memorable events in his life. It was consistent with earlier attempts in the 1920s to promote the concept of new world order through his participation in different commissions of the Federal Council.

3.3     In the Service of the Churches

During the 1920s Dulles attended the Park Avenue Presbyterian Church in New York, serving as a voting elder on the church's session. On Armistice Sunday Roswell P. Barnes delivered a sermon at the church which commented favourably on Woodrow Wilson's progressive idealism. After the sermon Dulles, visibly impressed by what he had heard, invited Barnes to his home to discuss the subject further. The conversation which followed clarified Dulles' thinking about the utility of the churches in international affairs. 'It was one of the earliest indications,' writes John M. Mulder, 'that Dulles was beginning to appreciate the role which the churches might play in foreign affairs.'[101]

In 1921 Robert E. Speer, the president of the Federal Council of Churches, persuaded Dulles to become a member of the Commission on International

Justice and Goodwill.[102] The Council entrusted to this commission the responsibility of formulating the Christian position on global issues. Attracted by its Wilsonian and internationalist ethos, Dulles agreed to complete one term of service.[103] In 1923 he left the commission, only to join the National Conference of the Christian Way of Life. The most distinguished service which he rendered to the Presbyterian Church was his masterful defence of the liberal faction within the Presbyterian denomination during the controversy-filled years of 1924 to 1926. Henry Sloane Coffin, the president of Union Theological Seminary, was among those who praised him for his successful fight against the traditionalists within the ranks of the Presbyterian Church. Following the favourable vote of the Synod of New York in 1926 concerning the ordination of pastoral candidates of liberal convictions, Dr Coffin wrote in a letter that the decision of the Judicial Committee was a great triumph for Dulles. Addressing Dulles directly, he stated: 'The decision [of the synod] practically embodied your entire brief. I cannot thank you enough nor tell you how sincerely I admire the masterly way you prepared that brief.'[104] Tertius van Dyke, the pastor of the Park Avenue Presbyterian Church, in commenting on Dulles' activities to affect changes of traditional church policies, said that he 'made a genuine contribution to the living history of the Presbyterian Church'.[105]

In 1923, the Presbyterian General Assembly appointed him to the membership of the American delegation which was to be sent to the Universal Christian Conference on Life and Work in Stockholm, 1925 (although Dulles actually never went to Stockholm).[106] A few days later he was invited as an official delegate to the Presbyterian General Assembly. The following year, the Presbytery of New York commissioned him to the General Assembly in Grand Rapids, Michigan. Throughout the early 1920s he also served on the Church Extension Committee of the Presbyterian Church and its Committee to Study 'War'.[107]

John D. Rockefeller, Jr., in 1931, invited him to serve on the Inquiry Commission of the Foreign Mission Board of the American Baptist Church. This commission would spend half a year in India, Japan, and China to gather information on the situation of foreign missions. Dulles, however, declined to take part in this enterprise, giving as a reason the inability to travel overseas for any extended length of time. His responsibility as senior partner of Sullivan & Cromwell, arguably New York's most prestigious law firm, was demanding his full attention and could not be left unattended for six months. This might have been an excuse. Sometime later he was quite able to leave his post at the law firm for long periods of time.[108] At that stage in his life Dulles had, however, significantly lessened his involvement within the churches. His zeal of earlier days had been dampened over the seemingly fruitless effort to mobilise the Christian public to work for a new world order. After years of frustrating attempts to establish a truly international order, and faced with the inevitable demise of the League of Nations caused by its impotence to deal with conflicting nationalistic aspirations, he saw his own need of inspiration and direction in finding a new approach to achieve world government. In 1937 Dulles, therefore, decided to travel to Europe to preside over the International Study Conference[109] held in Paris under the auspices of the League of Nations.[110]

3.4     The International Studies Conference, Paris 1937

Despite its French location the International Study Conference was organised by the British Royal Institute of International Affairs (RIIA).[111] Thus it was not surprising that Dulles, as a founding member of the Institute of International Affairs (as it was then called), initially cherished great hopes about the outcome of this conference in terms of promoting international co-operation. Convened under the motto of 'Peaceful Change', a group of politicians, lawyers, and university professors[112] discussed the subject of how grievances in Europe, specifically those of Germany and Italy, might be resolved without resort to an armed conflict. The deliberations, however, grew distasteful, as it became clear that the opinions expressed by most participants were emotionally charged denunciations of National Socialism and Fascism, lacking the rudimentary qualities of constructive criticism. Dulles, who had been an admirer of the Nazi movement ever since he attended that momentous meeting on 27 January 1932, in Düsseldorf, when Hitler first sought the support of industrialists[113], became impatient with his disputants, describing their remarks as irrelevant to the purpose of the discussions. In the presence of his son Avery, he expressed his dissatisfaction with the results of the study conference. Avery Dulles later recalled his father's disposition as follows: 'He [John F. Dulles] felt the people attending were not able to rise above their nationalistic self-interest and prejudices.'[114] John F. Dulles summarised the problem of his colleagues, as he perceived it, in an article entitled 'The Churches and World Order': 'I saw the impossibility of bringing the delegates present even to discuss the agreed topic of "peaceful change" lest it might be inferred that their own nations admitted the possibility of change to its [sic] disadvantage.'[115] In retrospect Dulles described his disillusionment with the outcome of the Paris Conference as something he had not expected. He had falsely placed his confidence in the excellent credentials of its participants.

> [At the Paris Conference] the students and men experienced in public affairs drawn from substantially the same nations as were represented at Oxford and selected to represent the best contribution which each country could make to an unofficial, dispassionate, and scholarly study of the chosen problem ... would have been [unable] ... to agree [had an agreed report been attempted] either as to the nature and scope of the problem itself or the proper approach to its solution.[116]

In fact, says Toulouse, 'as he reflected upon it sometime later, he viewed it as a complete waste of time.'[117]

Soon, however, his frustrations gave way to a feeling of renewed vitality in pursuing the cause of world federation. He entered into the realm of highly principled and open-minded Church leaders and would emerge as a totally changed person. Dulles' indifference towards a personal cultivation of his faith did not detract from his overall service to the churches, because of his strong belief in the brotherhood of humankind and his ambition to serve the cause of international peace.[118] His commitment to the social and material progress of humankind reflected exactly the tenets of the Federal Council's 'Social Creed of the Churches' of 1908 and its many subsequent pronouncement on the conditions of a just and egalitarian world society.[119] The purpose of the Oxford Conference of Life and Work to infuse the Christian churches with a renewed sense of determination to change social conditions and work for international co-operation squared perfectly with Dulles' aspirations.

### 3.5     The World Conference of Life and Work, Oxford 1937

In an article published in *Religion in Life* in 1938, Dulles revealed his motive for accepting the invitation to come to Oxford which Dr Oldham had extended to him personally two years earlier: 'It seemed to me that I might there find the answer to certain questions which perplexed me.'[120] Dulles' search for answers at the Oxford Conference focussed on one primary concern. He wanted to find out what influence the Church would be able to exercise in dealing with the problem of nationalism.[121]

Disillusioned by the unexpected failure of the Paris conference, Dulles and his wife Janet left France and crossed the Channel *en route* to Oxford. Toulouse, commenting on the significance of this journey, writes:

> While the trip across the Channel from the continent of Europe to the British Isles is a short one, that distance hardly signifies the momentous change in the way Dulles framed solutions to international problems after making the trip.[122]

Regardless of any expectation he might have had, his presence at Oxford in the midst of 450 delegates representing 125 different Christian denominations, helped him to appreciate the strategic importance of the World Conference of Life and Work and the social and international aspirations of its leaders.

### 3.5.1     Church, Community, and State

At the convocation of the Conference on Church, Community, and State, in Oxford, 1937, the Christian community could look back on a thirty-year history of bringing the ecumenical vision of international co-operation to life. This history began at the turn of the century, when a few clergymen had taken the initiative to mobilise the Christian public in promoting world peace. Recognising the need to organise their efforts more systematically, these early activists summoned like-minded Christians to the Second Hague Peace Conference in 1907. (Incidentally, as secretary of the Chinese delegation, John F. Dulles participated at the Second Hague Conference, accompanying his grandfather, John Watson Foster.)[123] The theoretical basis of calling for an intensified struggle to uphold peace in a world of increasing political tension and polarisation was freely discussed at the plenary sessions of the conference. The delegates decided, however, against formulating a theology of peace. As pragmatists they were more concerned about practical steps to ensure peace than to formulate a theological statement for the prevention of war. They justified their activism in the political arena by arguing that a spontaneous and decisive response to the social challenges of the day was imperative to the well-being of churches in particular and of Western civilisation in general. Not feeling the need to base their concepts of peace on a biblical foundation, they were at liberty to consider general principles derived from philosophical, social and economic thought.

The early ecumenical leaders placed human suffering next in importance to the question of war. The International Missionary Council, under the leadership of Joseph H. Oldham and William Paton, committed itself to alleviate, wherever possible, the appalling conditions of social oppression which were seen as the primary cause of suffering. Its social program reached a considerable following in the 1920s, but it fell short of establishing a general acceptance among the Missionary Council's more conservative constituency. It was flawed in the eyes of many, because of its failure to take theological questions into consideration.

The World Alliance was founded in 1914 to promote international friendship, especially between English and German Christians. Its leadership seized upon conflicts between nations to exercise public pressure on international organisations and statesmen to solve the disagreements peacefully. During the First World War its moralistic pronouncements did not elicit any immediate response by statesmen on either side of the conflict. The Alliance ultimately became irrelevant to both its dwindling base of supporters and its intended target group, the heads of state of the warring nations.

In the early 1920s Nathan Söderblom, the Archbishop of Uppsala, initiated the Life and Work movement which was to become a dynamic force within the ecumenical movement. He believed that there could be no real co-operation among the churches unless they resolutely faced concrete problems permeating the social order in Western societies, such as unemployment, racism, social inequality, and war. Söderblom was particularly interested in studying the regulating mechanism of capital and labour. He also paid close attention to the relationship between Church and State. By his massive influence and eloquence, the Archbishop convinced ecclesiastics and Christian laymen of many countries to address these social and political issues personally as well as corporatively. Consequently, in 1925, the first of the great ecumenical assemblies in the twentieth century was held in Stockholm. The Universal Christian Conference on Life and Work was attended by 528 delegates of 31 churches from 38 nations who gathered for the service of worship in Stockholm Cathedral, on August 14. The delegates had responded to a 'Letter of Invitation' declaring that 'the world's greatest need is the Christian way of life not merely in personal and social behaviour but in public opinion and its outcome in public action, a goal involving the responsibility of putting our hearts and our hands into a united effort that God's will may be done on earth as it is in heaven'. 'To this end', the message went on,

> ... we will consider such concrete questions as that of industry and property, in relation to the Kingdom of God; what the Church should teach and do to help to create right relations between the different and at times warring classes and groups in the community; how to promote friendship between the nations and thus lay the only sure foundation upon which permanent international peace can be built.[124]

Immediately following the opening service, the delegates were received at the Palace by the King of Sweden who assured them that the aim of the Conference was no less important than that of the Council of Nicea. The purpose of Nicea had been to define the nature of Christ and therefore the essential content of the Christian religion. Due to Söderblom's influence, however, the Life and Work conference was concerned exclusively with social and economic problems, not with doctrinal questions. The ecumenical gathering was sponsored by the Federal Council of the Churches of Christ in America, the World Alliance for Promoting International Friendship through the Churches, and the British Conference on Christian Politics and Citizenship.

The Life and Work movement lost its momentum in subsequent years, failing to define its specific role in the arena of international affairs. In the face of world-wide economic depression, the rise of totalitarian dictatorships, and the menacing threat of a second world war the ecumenical movement remained on the side-lines as a social force, and played no part in shaping historic events. If it was to return to the centre of public awareness, it would have to demonstrate that in most social issues of the day the relationship between Church and State was of fundamental importance.[125]

In 1934 at the Universal Christian Council for Life and Work in Fanø, Denmark, the assembled Church leaders decided to convene a world conference on 'Church, Community and State' at Oxford in a few years time.[126] Gripped by the urgency of the situation, Joseph H. Oldham, the Secretary of the International Missionary Council, resigned his position in order to organise the conference. Unlike the Stockholm Conference of 1925, Oxford, 1937, was not content with broad generalisations about the social and international significance of the Gospel. It was specific and realistic in dealing with the complexities of the political and economic scene. Its participants were anxious to communicate a strong sense of unity in spite of the widening gap between the different nations to which they belonged. They hoped to become a redeeming influence of peace in a fragmented world as members of the same faith community.

The Oxford Conference prepared the ideological ground of what Reinhold Niebuhr later described as an impressive system of Christian pragmatism. This was largely due to Oldham's extraordinary efficiency in revitalising the social influence of the churches in the midst of an increasingly secularised society. 'In the interrelation of these social realities', Oldham's 'Letter of Explanation to the Churches' declared, 'is focussed the great and critical debate between the Christian faith and the secular tendencies of our time. In this struggle the very existence of the Christian Church is at stake.'[127] To examine the scope and explore the implications of that 'great and critical debate', a series of symposia was organised on different aspects of the central theme: 'Church, Community, and State'. Conscious of its historic mission, the ecumenical movement seized the opportunity to define what it perceived to be humankind's intended destiny.

Of all the ecumenical gatherings, the Life and Work Conference at Oxford was one of the most determinative in formulating the social ethic of an incipient new world order. During the three years preceding the conference, papers on different subjects relative to the main theme were circulated for comment among a wide range of experts before being re-edited by the original contributors for publication.[128] Joseph H. Oldham, the Chairman of Life and Work's Research Department, in collecting the material, availed himself of the services of a young, but already well-known, Dutch theologian, Willem A. Visser 't Hooft.[129] Later, these preparatory studies were published in seven volumes, entitled 'The Church and Its Function in Society'; 'The Christian Understanding of Man'; 'The Kingdom of God and History'; 'Christian Faith and the Common Life'; 'Christ and Community'; 'Church, Community and State in Relation to Education'; and 'The Universal Church and the World of Nations'.[130] Important contributions to these volumes were made by a number of highly accomplished theologians, including Kenneth S. Latourette, William Temple, Reinhold Niebuhr, and Paul Tillich.

Since the Oxford Conference was addressing concrete problems of secular society, it became imperative to bring into the discussions a considerable number of experts in public affairs. The Section on Church and State, for example, was presided over by Max Huber, former President of the World Court at The Hague and later of the International Red Cross; Francis B. Sayre, Assistant Secretary of State, and Alanson B. Houghton, a former United States Ambassador to Great Britain, were among the American members of the same group. Distinguished experts on international law filled the ranks of equally accomplished academicians in the section meetings, including G.M. Gathorne-Hardy, Walter Van Kirk[131] and Charles P. Taft. The most renowned authority in the field of Political Science, Professor Ernest Barker of Cambridge, participated in the discussions on Church and Community chaired by Sir Walter Moberly, Chairman of England's University Grants Committee. Intellectuals of the standing of R. H. Tawney[132], John P.R. Maud, André Philip, Sir Josiah Stamp, and Sir Alfred E. Zimmern were present to advise the theologians on matters of history and science.

The Oxford Conference also marked the recognition of the Federal Council of Churches of Christ in America (FCC) as the dominant force within the ecumenical movement leading its constituent churches towards the creation of the World Council of Churches.[133] The president of the FCC, Albert W. Beaven, participated in the proceedings of the conference. In one of the section meetings he led the discussion on the problems of the economic order. Samuel McCrea Cavert, who was to succeed Beaven as president of the Council, accompanied Henry A. Atkinson[134], Walter M. Horton and others, to the meetings on the Universal Church and the World of Nations. William Adams Brown of Union Theological Seminary[135] was one of the presiding officers. John C. Bennett, soon to become a professor of the same school, was secretary of the section on 'The Church and the Economic Order'.[136] John A. Mackay, the president of Princeton Theological Seminary, was chairman of the section on 'The Universal Church and the World of Nations', and Henry Sloane Coffin, Mackay's counterpart at Union Theological Seminary, presided over the section on 'The Church and Education'. John R. Mott was appointed chairman of the Business Committee.

Attending the conference as a representative appointed by the Universal Christian Council, John Foster Dulles participated in the deliberations of section meetings, listened to challenging speeches at the plenary sessions, and deepened his personal ties with many assembled clergymen and Christian laymen. They offered him the opportunity to examine at close range the potential of the churches to form a worldwide alliance in pursuing a better international order. The respect for Dulles' integrity extended to him by the ecclesiastical community was only surpassed by his admiration of the loving atmosphere exhibited by the Christian assembly at Oxford. He was profoundly impressed by the practical outworking of unity - 'irrespective of national or racial differences'[137] - among the representatives of numerous Christian traditions that he could observe all around him. The Christian virtue of brotherly love permeating this conference stood in sharp contrast to the 'distrustful atmosphere of national competition' that had prevailed at Paris only a short while before, overshadowing the proceedings and prohibiting any agreeable discussion on international order.[138] In an address to the graduating class of Princeton Theological Seminary on May 16, 1944, Dulles described the congenial environment he had found at the Oxford Conference:

[T]he 1937 Oxford Conference on Church and State ... was made up of men and women who, like those who gathered at Pentecost, came 'from every nation under heaven.' There was but one bond of unity - that was faith in God as revealed by Jesus Christ. As at Pentecost, that bond of unity enabled us to understand each other. We discussed matters which, before, I had seen always give rise to violent dispute. We found intelligent, practical agreement as to how such matters should be dealt with. We did not find any formulas of quick and easy solution. But we did find that the toughest problems could be tackled in ways which, instead of creating discord, drew men together in fellowship.[139]

In exchange for his keen interest in the proceedings of the conference he was offered a platform to voice his ideas of what he perceived to be the foremost duty of the Christian Church.[140] At the Oxford Conference Dulles was put in charge of a committee to draft the report on 'The Universal Church and the World of Nations'.[141] Reciprocating the trust extended to him by the ecumenical leaders, he regarded it as a great privilege to formulate the Church's position on world order in co-operation with a team of renowned scholars of international affairs. During the session meetings and while drafting the report, he felt a close intellectual affinity with Arnold J. Toynbee, the Director of Studies of the Royal Institute of International Affairs.[142] At least four other members of the RIIA were present at the Oxford Conference, namely Philip Kerr (Lord Lothian), Sir Alfred E. Zimmern, G.M. Gathorne-Hardy, and Lord Robert Cecil.[143]

### 3.5.2    The Universal Church and the World of Nations

'At a time when the hearts of men fail them for fear,' the Oxford report on 'The Universal Church and the World of Nations' notes solemnly, 'the Conference calls upon the members of the Churches to remain steadfast in their faith in God and in Jesus Christ, the Saviour of all mankind.'[144] This summons is followed by a description of the critical situation confronting the world in the summer of 1937.[145] Yet, despite the seemingly hopeless state of international affairs, the authors find a reason to be optimistic: 'We need not despair; the world belongs to God; to believe in His power and love is not to escape from reality but to stand upon the rock of the only certainty that is offered to men.'[146] Counting on this unshakeable reality, the authors state confidently, 'a special ground of faith and courage amid the perplexities of our age is that the Christian Church is becoming truly oecumenical.'[147]

#### 3.5.2.1   True Ecumenicity

The report continues to define the nature and purpose of the ecumenical movement, in being the first indication that the Church has begun to act on the 'God-given vision of the Church Universal', a new realisation of the fundamental truth that the 'Church is one'.[148] The authors pay special tribute to the missionary movement of the nineteenth century, which, by being obedient to the Great Commission, has made 'the bounds of the Christian community co-extensive with the habitable globe'. In spite of this positive accomplishment, they also recognise that there is still a great measure of disunity among the different Christian denominations and regret the lack of true fellowship, especially with the Church of Rome, which was not represented at the conference.

In turning their attention to the international sphere in which the Church tries to work out its true ecumenicity, the authors point out that the Church brings a unique insight into the task of achieving a better world order, the reality of a world brotherhood: 'To those who are struggling to realize human brotherhood in a world where disruptive nationalism and aggressive imperialism make such brotherhood seem unreal, the Church offers not an ideal but a fact, man united not by his aspiration but by the love of God.'[149]

The ecumenical leaders at Oxford tried to define the international character and communal nature of the Church, as a supranational brotherhood, which transcends racial and cultural distinctions. It is telling that they advanced a sociological, rather than a biblical, concept of the Church, and thus revealed their primary intention of pursuing a socio-political, rather than a spiritual, agenda in addressing the needs of the world.[150]

3.5.2.2  World-wide Brotherhood

In 1938, the implications of this ecumenical program were spelled out explicitly by William Paton in his book *World Community*. He argued that, by creating a world-wide brotherhood, the Christian churches had succeeded in establishing a degree of unity among themselves which was unprecedented in human history. The reality of a unified Church would not only provide a model for secular designs of an international brotherhood, it would also be a strong stimulus to unite the nations under one government. Paton believed that the foundations of a world community had thus already been laid by the ecumenical movement. He emphasised, however, that the Christian concept of brotherhood would still be fundamentally different from its secular equivalent. By necessity, a world community would need to start, 'from the nation as a given fact'.[151] It would then proceed in federating different national units with one another to form a greater supranational entity which would eventually comprise the whole world. In contrast, the Church would not begin 'with an aspiration after brotherhood on the part of separate elements or units; it offers at the very start of all inquiry the given fact of unity in Christ. It says not "Become brethren," but rather "Sirs, ye *are* brethren."'[152]

The Oxford Report continues to assert that no international order devised by human effort may be equated with the Kingdom of God. Its authors recognise, however, that 'a true conception of international order requires a recognition of the fact that the State, whether it admits it or not, is not autonomous, but is under the ultimate governance of God.'[153] The international order, therefore, constitutes an essential part of the divine kingdom. Christians are challenged to act according to the standards of this kingdom when confronted with specific proposals in the political sphere. They should be governed by their obedience to the living God and their understanding of His purpose in Christ.[154] The Church's 'vision of world brotherhood,' writes Keim, 'provided precisely that unifying principle which the world lacked. The church, properly mobilized, with her loyalties centered on universal and transcendent principles, could become a powerful antidote to the rampaging nationalism threatening mankind.'[155]

Considering that Sir Alfred E. Zimmern, the Montague Burton Professor of International Relations at Oxford University, was a contributor of a preparatory paper to the Oxford Conference, entitled 'The Ethical Presuppositions of a World Order'[156], and co-authored this particular section of the Oxford Report with John Foster Dulles[157], it is highly significant to take a brief look at certain passages in his book *Spiritual Values and World Affairs* (1939).[158] There he explained his reservations against equating any man-made world order with the Kingdom of God.

### 3.5.2.3  Spiritual Values and World Affairs

In the preface of *Spiritual Values and World Affairs*, Zimmern stated that this volume contains the substance of a series of university lectures delivered between 24 January and 4 March 1939. In the opening chapter he explained further that these lectures were intended primarily for students in the Faculty of Theology at Oxford University, though they were attended by others also. In referring to the broadly phrased book title, he noted that it was not his desire to limit himself to a specific religious communion or form of religious experience. In general, however, he would base his discussion on Christian lines and relate it to the Christian Gospel.[159]

From the first page of the book to the last Zimmern reviews and analyses different concepts of world order, propagated by men like Woodrow Wilson and Henri Bergson. His purpose was to show the value of informing public opinion on issues of world order along the lines suggested by Elihu Root, the founder of the Council on Foreign Relations:

> Fifteen years ago, one of the wisest political thinkers of our generation, Mr. Elihu Root, reflecting on the demand for "popular diplomacy", summed up this whole issue in a few sentences: "When foreign affairs were ruled by autocracies or oligarchies", he wrote, "the danger of war was in sinister purpose. When foreign affairs are ruled by democracies the danger of war will be in mistaken beliefs. The world will be the gainer by the change, for, while there is no human way to prevent a king from having a bad heart, there is a human way to prevent a people from having an erroneous opinion. That way is to furnish the whole people, as a part of their ordinary education, with

correct information about their relations to other peoples.[160]

In the first chapter, the author noted that over the last twenty years the Church had become increasingly more interested in international affairs. This interest had found expression in a number of ways such as public statements of representative Church bodies and high ecclesiastics.[161] Sermons on international issues also heightened the general awareness of world affairs in churches across the country. Zimmern saw the combined effect of these activities as 'a factor of considerable - sometimes perhaps, decisive - importance in the national life of this country [Great Britain], not to speak of the overseas Dominions and the United States.'[162] It certainly indicated the enormous effort within the Church to create an international mind-set among its parishioners.

Without wishing to dampen the enthusiasm of the ecumenical movement for international institutions, Zimmern criticised its leaders for equating the imperfect system of man-made organisations with the Kingdom of God. He recalled one incident in the early days of November 1918 when one of his friends at the Foreign Office[163] gave him a copy of a personal letter to the Archbishop of Canterbury. According to this letter, his friend had been much disturbed by a resolution of the Lambeth Conference which suggested that the projected League of Nations was the beginning of a new world order. In their enthusiasm the Church leaders apparently believed that the incipient world organisation would be a first instalment of the Kingdom of God on earth.[164] Zimmern's friend expressed his grave concern about the well-publicised campaign to encourage Christians to place their hopes in an institution which, in his view, was only a piece of political machinery. He also warned the Archbishop that, in a fallen world, there would always be the possibility of failing to meet inflated expectations. This danger was especially present in attempting to bring peace and prosperity to a war-stricken world by means of an association of nations. Failure could engender wide-spread disillusionment in the mechanisms of international co-operation, and Christians might turn to fanatical brands of utopianism and lose credibility in the public eye.

In retrospect, Zimmern could only bemoan the fact that the course of events had largely justified his friend's apprehensions:

Is not this exactly what has happened? Did not many Christians in the twenties fall into the temptation of seeking a sign from Heaven and of believing that they had found it in Geneva? And have we not witnessed in the thirties - not in this country alone - the stampede of a disappointed generation to other forms of this-worldly idealism, which a Lambeth Conference would be the first to discountenance?[165]

Sensing his duty to restore the Church's tarnished reputation, he reminded the ecclesiastical authorities to regain a proper perspective 'in all such manifestations of sympathy and in all efforts to guide public opinion in regard

106

to the League of Nations policy.'[166] It should always be the Christian's first concern to keep in sight those overriding considerations which are purely spiritual in nature. This did not mean, Zimmern intimated, that he wanted to dissuade the ecumenical leaders from showing their enthusiasm for the League of Nations. On the contrary, he applauded their decision to identify themselves with the political aspirations of a large group of internationally minded fellow countrymen. His criticism was directed, rather, against their erroneous reading of the League's relative importance in the international arena of the day. The Christian leaders missed the point that an association of nations, formed on a voluntary basis in pursuance of a common defence policy, was not and could never be identical with a functional world government. The League, at its best, was only a 'short-distance issue' since its jurisdiction did not extend into the private sphere of individual citizens.[167] Thus Zimmern encouraged the Church to develop a long-term perspective in regard to the establishment of a new world order. He warned its leaders not to succumb to the temptation of circumventing 'the more difficult tasks, the long-distance tasks', in their efforts to create a genuine world community.[168]

Intimately involved with the proceedings of the League of Nations, Zimmern had observed first-hand the inability of a mere alliance of sovereign nation-states to sustain his enthusiasm about its future prospects.[169] Expressing his own disillusionment in the practical outworking of a collective security system, which had been designed to embrace the whole world but failed to secure the participation of the United States[170], he did not want to lose the Church as an ally in mobilising a grassroots movement for a better world order in the future. He feared that the ecumenical movement would forfeit its broad public support if it continued to place all its eggs in the basket of a dysfunctional system of global governance. Consequently, he counselled restraint in equating the League of Nations with the Kingdom of God on earth:

> And finally, should not the Churches, whilst manifesting their sympathy for the League of Nations, have warned Christians in season and out of season against the delusion that the League could in any way be associated with the conception of the Kingdom of God? I would be almost ashamed to emphasize this had I not so constantly heard and read utterances and statements to the contrary - suggestions that the League was in some way part of a Messianic scheme, a milestone on the road to an ultimate World Commonwealth.[171]

In giving this advice to Church leaders, Zimmern did not object to the concept of a world commonwealth as a political device to prevent war and its devastating consequences. As a matter of fact, he had for long been one of its most ardent advocates as an original member of the Round Table Group. His point was simply that it belonged in the domain of political science, not of religion. In referring to the Gospel teaching about the Kingdom, which made a clear distinction between matters pertaining to the religious and the political sphere, he mildly rebuked the Church for its reluctance to recognise and act upon that fact.[172] He asserted that the primary task of analysing the current situation in world affairs must remain the prerogative of a group of 'dispassionate, conscientious, fair-minded scientific students of international affairs'.[173] The Church should look to them - the members of the Royal Institute of International Affairs (RIIA) - for guidance in questions of political significance. Belonging, as he did, to the cadre of the RIIA, Zimmern placed his full confidence in this group of two thousand five hundred political scientists to lead the way into a new dispensation of world history.[174] Having thus set his priorities, he did not see a strict dichotomy between the duty rendered to Caesar and that to God, and objected to the notion that the values of science and of the spirit are merely juxtaposed, with no inner connection between them.[175] Granting to the Church the right to exert its moral influence on political and social issues, including international affairs, he still doubted whether the ecumenical movement would be able, 'to frame judgements, to educate opinion, and to construct policies in regard to these issues'[176], without drawing on the expertise of the Royal Institute of International Affairs.

In spite of concerted efforts by civil and religious organisations, the establishment of a world government, which had seemed so promising in 1919, remained still a distant possibility in the late 1930s. What prevented speedy progress towards its fulfilment was, in Zimmern's view, the tardiness of a large section of society 'to submit itself to any intelligent discipline in these matters.'[177] He meant that many Englishmen had not yet embraced the progressive idea of abrogating their own national sovereignty in favour of a world government. Consequently, he believed that 'a generation or more of education in international relations would be required before even the more politically mature peoples will be ready to cooperate in transforming the ideas and principles of the [League of Nations] Covenant into practical working policies.'[178]

### 3.5.2.4   Demonic Evil of National Sovereignty

Although written two years earlier, the Oxford Report had already described the inherent difficulties of creating an international order. The authors recognised that the greatest obstacle in establishing a world federation is found in the present political arrangement in which nations are allowed to act sovereignly within their own borders. Different solutions were offered of how the system of sovereign nation-states can be exchanged by a world order system. Naturally, the authors appealed to the churches to facilitate this change of systems:

> Various means have been suggested on the political plane for dealing with this problem. The simplest and most radical is to abolish the system of power-relations by subordinating the concept of independent sovereignty

through the establishment of a federal system. Another solution, attempted in the League of Nations, is to create an organization providing for constant and regular cooperation between States, thus promoting common habits and standards which may in time form the basis of a common law. So far as the present evil is political the heart of it is to be found in the claim of each national State to be judge in its own cause. The abandonment of that claim, at least to that extent, is a duty that the Church should urge upon the nations.[179]

This passage in the Oxford report reflects Philip Kerr's argumentation in the preparatory paper which he had submitted previously to the Conference organisers. At some length Kerr, a devoted Christian Scientist, who had grown up in a strict Roman Catholic family, exhorted the churches to counteract (according to the title of his essay), 'the demonic influence of national sovereignty.' Christianity, by the illumination of God's Spirit, would precondition humanity to reject the selfish adherence to nationalism and embrace a democratic world order:

For the manifestation of the Spirit among men will lessen the egotism of nationalism, will weaken the hold of despotic political creeds and pagan philosophies, and will substitute brotherly love and trust for envy, hatred, greed, and suspicion in international relations, both political and economic. It will mean a transformed human nature in which men and nations will not only feel their unity but will be able to trust one another because they act on the same just and honourable and unselfish standards. When this Christian transformation of man through love and understanding of the One True God has gone far enough, the nature and purposes of mankind will be so changed that it will be natural, easy, indeed inevitable, to bring into being institutions which will deal with international problems from the standpoint of the well-being of humanity as a whole, and whereby the legislative, executive, and judicial functions of the world federation will be exercised under some kind of democratic control, and in accordance with moral and spiritual law, and without any of the despotic, repressive, illiberal features which would necessarily characterize a world state to-day. For the Spirit of the Lord will inform its policy and its acts, and 'where the Spirit of the Lord is there is liberty.'[180]

Throughout the length of his paper Kerr railed against national sovereignty in graphic language and castigated it as the sole cause of war. He believed that demonic consequences would flow from it. In particular, he mentioned 'economic nationalism'[181], as one of these nefarious effects which in turn produced 'vast unemployment and capital losses through the cessation of international trade, the dislocation of the world balance between supply and demand, and the overthrow of democracy by dictatorship in country after country.'[182] Moreover, national sovereignty was also the relentless adversary of the League of Nations. Apparently, in a perverse twist of fate, the purpose of the League had been inverted to its very opposite. Instead of uniting the world peacefully, it forced the nations 'to come back to competitive armaments and alliances and to the military time-table.' Kerr deplored the League's impotence to heal the gangrene of national sovereignty.

> A League of sovereign states therefore tends to become a system not for the revision of treaties in the interests of justice, but to become an alliance system of those who are interested in the status quo. The essential weakness of the League is disclosed in the fact that the allegiance of the citizen is owed to his own state and not to the League, and that when the views of the two conflict it is the decisions of his own state that he must obey.[183]

Despite this pathetic state of affairs, the League of Nations was still exemplary in two specific areas: (1) it represented humankind's first recognition of its need to submit to the reign of law under a world government; and (2) it opened up new diplomatic channels for the peaceful resolution of international disputes.[184] Kerr realised, however, that certain preconditions would need to be met before the League could make good on all its promises. The most important of these were the requirement of universal membership and the nations' willingness to subordinate their own interests to the League's arbitration. Unfortunately the record of history showed that in these essential points the League of Nations was conceptually flawed and limited in its effectiveness by forces outside its control.

> But because it [the League] is based upon the complete national sovereignty of its members it begins to be paralysed as soon as one or more powerful states resign membership or repudiate their obligations under the Covenant, for contract is utterly different from common sovereignty. No league of sovereign states can establish peace in the political sense of that word ... Because its members are sovereign the League can exercise neither legislative, executive, judicial, nor taxing power.[185]

Kerr observed that the League functioned well as long as the political and economic *status quo* was preserved. Eventually, however, it succumbed to the undermining influence of national sovereignty, and thus became seriously impaired to counter the evil manifestations of economic nationalism. The only means at its disposal to alter the *status quo* was an appeal to 'the voluntary consent of those most immediately concerned'. Yet regrettably some nations, bent on pursuing a war policy, were not prepared to listen.[186] As a result,

> '[c]ollective security' has almost vanished because economic sanctions are of little value unless universally applied, and military sanctions and even effective economic sanctions against a powerful sovereign state involve a risk of war which members are not prepared to assume unless their own vital interests are involved.[187]

Kerr suggested that the only solution which he believed would be able to combat 'the demonic evils' inherent in a nation-state system was 'the creation of a common sovereignty representing all men and nations by the pooling of that part of state sovereignty which deals with supernational matters, in a world federation.'[188] As would be expected from a leading member of the Round Table Group, Kerr defined 'world federation' as 'a state which, in its own sphere, will command the allegiance of mankind, will be able to legislate for, judge, and tax everybody, and which will be responsible to everybody while leaving the national state freedom to deal with affairs in the national sphere.'[189] In propounding a federal solution Kerr followed closely the blueprint of Curtis' *Civitas Dei*. Looking at the situation objectively, he rightly recognised, as Curtis had done before him, that a world federation could not be established arbitrarily overnight. Smaller groups of nations sympathetic to the federal idea would need to unite at first and then expand their territory gradually by accretion of other states.[190] The final product would be a political unit embracing the whole world. 'When such a body comes into being,' Kerr asserted, 'then and then only will war end and the perversions and destructions inherent in the competition of national sovereignties be ended on earth.'[191]

In the final section of his paper, Kerr outlined the specific role of the churches in facilitating the 'federation of nations into a single world commonwealth'.[192] In discussing some practical aspects, he cautioned his audience to avoid two extremes. They should not seek to establish a world federation which would be either too strong politically or too weak. If it were too strong, tyranny would take over and stifle freedom of thought and initiative. The free exercise of religion would be the first victim of such a repressive system. Yet, if it were too weak, the cultural, religious, and linguistic differences among the nations would soon work havoc on the federal system and tear it apart. A mediating position could only be achieved if Christianity would provide humankind with a common loyalty, not to a political entity, but to God. Kerr was convinced that this truth, if appreciated and followed, would bring 'unity and law and peace among the conflicting races and the warring sovereignties which now claim the allegiance of mankind.'[193] Consequently, '[i]t is love for and understanding of God which alone can create the conditions in which the federation of man will become a possibility and in which war and the demonic consequences of national sovereignty can be ended.'[194] This was the supreme challenge set before the churches. They were summoned to prevail not only against the encroaching 'paganism and secularism of our age', but also to triumph over the 'political and economic division of which the national state is the most ruthless and powerful.'[195] Thus, in conclusion, Kerr encouraged the Christian churches to build the Kingdom of God on earth.

> The ecumenical Church of Christ will not do this by becoming absorbed in the political and economic programmes and ideals of the time. Neither will it do so by standing apart from the public questions of the age. Christianity produces as acute transformations and controversies in the body politic in

which it is lived, as it does in the individual who begins to practise it. The Church will accomplish its mission by being faithful to the unchanging spiritual law of God rather than to the experiences of men, and by being the expression of that active and practical love and wisdom of God towards men which, once it is reflected in society, will inevitably produce the Kingdom of God among the nations of the earth.[196]

Since the Oxford report on the 'Universal Church and the World of Nations' singled out the concept of national sovereignty as the main problem in international relations, the assembled church delegates must have discovered in Kerr's remarks a definite congruence of thought and unity of purpose. In following his line of reasoning, they expressed their appreciation for his concise presentation of a rational framework and an outline of practical steps to achieve a better world order. He had reminded them that their principal task in realising this program of true ecumenicity was to advocate a common ethos ('the unchanging spiritual law of God') among the nations as the basis of international law:

All law, international as well as national, must be based on a common ethos - that is, a common foundation of moral convictions. To the creation of such a common foundation in moral conviction the Church as a supra-national society with a profound sense of the historical realities, and of the worth of human personality, has a great contribution to make.[197]

The call to create a 'common foundation of moral convictions' must have struck a familiar chord in the hearts of many Church leaders, since it was to this end that they had directed their efforts for decades. They faithfully discharged their duty of enlightening the nations with the principles of a new social ethic which they derived from a liberal interpretation of the gospels.[198] Believing in the righteousness of their cause, they saw themselves rendering an indispensable service to humankind in eliciting its presumed sense of oneness, as brothers and sisters, under the Fatherhood of God.

In *The Church and the New Order*, William Paton referred to a private memorandum of Arnold J. Toynbee, in which the latter described the preaching of 'the Gospel of God as the Lord of the nations' as the only way to produce an international ethos among the peoples of the world:

There is no other way of creating an international ethos than the preaching of the Gospel of God as the Lord of the nations, and as the Father of the men, women and children out of whose mutual relations the mirages called nations are conjured up. It is only through a sense of the common Fatherhood of God that we can hope to awaken a sense of the brotherhood of Man. Thus there can be no international ethos without a religious basis.[199]

Paton admitted that Toynbee's reference to the Gospel of God had a broader meaning than generally understood by Christians. It did not necessarily

112

exclude the ethical teachings of other religions. Toynbee was hopeful that the barriers of race, nationality, and language might be overcome, at least potentially, by applying the spiritual principles of different faith traditions.[200] Although sympathetic to Toynbee's pantheistic view, Paton still believed that Christianity is the religion most likely to succeed in uniting the nations. He was convinced that 'in so far ... as the Church realizes its own nature and mission, and is in fact that which its Lord desires it to be, it cannot but increase in the world the amount of basal trust and commitment of human beings to one another across the boundaries of nations.'[201] Thus he concluded that the Christian Church, by displaying its ecumenical unity and moral conviction, can make a significant contribution in developing an international ethos as the foundation of law in a new world order.[202]

The delegates at the Oxford Conference argued along the same lines. They recognized, according to John A. Mackay, one of the committee chairmen, two basic approaches to the solution of international problems. The first was to proceed from the multiplicity of nations with their own interests towards co-operation and international peace. The second was to move from a central or unifying principle – Jesus Christ and the moral law – toward the resolution of international conflicts.[203] Most of the delegates, notably William Paton, opted for the second solution. Samuel M. Cavert recalled that this was mainly due to the influence of Dulles who thought that the Oxford Conference presented 'great possibilities for creating an international ethos [through the Church] which would be essential as any foundation for any lasting international political structure.'[204] The first responsibility of the Church would thus be to inform the general public about international affairs. Referring explicitly to the Oxford report, Darril Hudson states:

> Recognising that the attitudes of peoples in western societies supported much injustice, it was urged that the national churches should furnish more reliable news than that available through controlled news agencies. The churches should also educate their constituencies, young and old alike, in those areas making for peace, such as understanding current world problems. On the basis of such information, Christians could urge informed opinions on political leaders favouring peaceful change and avoiding war. The Church should urge the abrogation of the claim of absolute sovereignty in order to create a system, such as the League of Nations, for achieving a better international order.[205]

Yet as long as human beings were living under the constant threat of extreme nationalism, economic exploitation, and war, the churches would need to unite their forces to transform the present sovereignty system into a world order system wherever possible: 'It therefore particularly devolves upon Christians to devote themselves to securing by voluntary action of their nations such changes in the international order as are from time to time required to avoid injustice and to promote equality of opportunity for individuals throughout the world.'[206] It is important to note that the authors defined 'peaceful change' as a 'voluntary action of nations' to abrogate their own sovereignty to an international authority.[207] They believed that the international order would inevitably change, peacefully or forcefully, but preferred the first alternative, 'voluntary action', as the means of achieving that change.[208]

In the next section of the report the authors delineate different attempts of how an international order must be organised. Mention is made of the League of Nations, which is valued as the most notable among the many organisations interested in the achievement of international order.[209] Christians are urged to have a clear understanding of the League's status and character. Although the League did not fulfill all the expectations originally placed into its peace-making mechanisms, the authors proudly assert that 'no alternative conception or method of comparable range has come to light in the intervening period, and the need for an agency of international co-operation is as great as ever, if not greater.'[210] Yet it is also recognised that this first assembly of nations did not create a genuine world community, because the attitude and practice of power-politics based on the sovereignty system remained an unchanged fact after 1920.

The League, the report on 'the Universal Church and the World of Nations' concludes, is therefore only 'a means to certain ends'.[211] A great price – the abrogation of national sovereignty – has still to be paid in order to create 'the conditions of effective international action'.[212] Despite a resurgence of nationalism in Europe in their own time, the authors looked optimistically into the future: 'In proportion as these ends [creation of a world government] are desirable so will their attainment make a large demand on those qualities of energy, good faith, and readiness to pay the price.'[213]

The report contains some additional sections on 'The Permanent Court of International Justice', 'Treaties' and 'The Church as Peace-maker'. These are followed by two separate discussions on 'The Church and War' and 'The Church's Witness', which are divided up into further subsections. Darril Hudson summarises the content of these passages as follows:

> The Church must witness to a better international order. It must not permit racial barriers to exist. Religious freedom should be sought and upheld; Christians should not, however, attempt to have special civil status in other nations. The churches must educate public opinion on international affairs. They must warn of the dangers of uncontrolled rearmament and insist on the possibility of its limitation.[214]

The report finally ends on a positive note. The Christian leaders resolved to work toward the creation of an international order by setting up their own ecumenical organisation:

> We commend with thankfulness the efforts of those movements which are working for the cause of international understanding through the Churches.

We rejoice in the decision taken by the Conference to recommend the creation of a World Council of Churches, and we urge that the study of the problems dealt with in this report should be included in its aims.[215]

The Church delegates expressed their general satisfaction with the report, as being identical with the high ideals of the ecumenical movement that they had formulated provisionally at the Stockholm Conference in 1925 and now in greater detail and binding force at Oxford. The selection of Willem A. Visser 't Hooft, as the first General Secretary of the World Council of Churches, at its founding conference in Amsterdam, 1948, gave further impetus to the influence of this internationalist declaration, since Visser 't Hooft shared with John A. Mackay the chairmanship of the section meeting on 'The Universal Church and the World of Nations', at Oxford, and was one of the two officers primarily responsible for approving the content of this particular report.

3.5.3    A Life-changing Experience

The impact of the Oxford Conference upon Dulles' life has been recounted many times.[216] Dulles himself has described it repeatedly in published articles and speeches[217] calling it 'one international event that ... stands out above all the others.'[218] More than a decade later, he vividly recalled his experience at Oxford to the Presbyterian church in Watertown where he had been christened as an infant. He told his listeners that it was 'then [at Oxford] I began to understand the profound significance of the spiritual values that my mother and father had taught.'[219] Dulles' sister Margaret remembered 'the tremendous impression' which the Oxford Conference had etched in her brother's mind. He had left America in Spring 1937 with 'the kind of hopelessness of the difficulties of the economic world', she said, and had been emotionally refreshed by Church leaders who were 'full of idealism as well as practicality'.[220]

3.5.3.1   The Influence of a Christian Upbringing

Commenting on Dulles' change of attitude in 1937 Toulouse traces its origin back to the influence of his Christian parents: 'Oxford obviously brought Dulles to a renewed appreciation of his past, and this caused him to re-evaluate his perspective in international affairs.'[221] Nurtured in the religious atmosphere of a small Presbyterian manse, his childhood upbringing had certainly left its imprint on his mind.[222] After Oxford, noted the theologian Bennett, Dulles 'went back to his heritage to a certain extent, and there was a certain continuity.'[223] From an early age he had read the Bible regularly, even committing large portions of the Scriptures, like the Gospel of John, to memory. Allen, his younger brother, once remarked that John Foster knew the whole Bible by heart.[224] If this was not quite true, Dulles was certainly well versed in biblical teaching. He developed a habit of always carrying a small New Testament with him.[225] As Secretary of State, he once boasted that nobody in the Department of State knew as much about the Bible as he did.[226] In disputes he always quoted a Bible verse in defence of his position. Allen came to dislike this annoying habit of his brother, because he could never reply in kind and expose the casuistic reasoning behind Foster's use of Scripture. John Foster's son, Avery, revealed later that his father 'was somewhat selective in his reading of the New Testament, but he did read it frequently and he got themes from it which he felt harmonized with his own philosophy of life.'[227] As an example of how his father personalised the meaning of biblical passages to integrate with his own particular outlook on life, Avery Dulles added the following remarks:

> He [John F. Dulles] took things from the Sermon on the Mount like "Seek first the Kingdom of God", and interpreted the texts in a pragmatic way, saying that if you are devoted to the moral law you will succeed, your efforts will be crowned with temporal success ... he felt it necessary to have a moral vision and faith, and be convinced that what you are doing and saying is objectively right, and not just a matter of expediency.[228]

Whatever the nature of his faith in the protective surroundings of his parents' home, the real test of its authenticity came when he embarked on his career of a Wall Street corporate lawyer.

### 3.5.3.2 The Cold Business World of Wall Street

After establishing himself as a successful lawyer, Dulles became much more independent in his thinking about the meaning and relevance of Christianity. In his mind he began to recast the biblical concepts inculcated since early childhood, into an abstract system of moral principles devoid of any real continuity with its spiritual roots. This nonchalant attitude towards the theological aspects of the Christian faith was probably the product of the rough intellectual climate permeating the business community of New York City.[229] 'Its [financial] transactions', writes Hoopes,

> are marked by a pervasive coldness; the dealing is hard, tough, impersonal and not infrequently ruthless; the stakes are high and the play is for keeps. Having been thrust into this arena to be tested for survival, Dulles proved in the event to be a shrewd and powerful gladiator, and, not surprisingly, took on along the way a number of characteristics essential not for survival alone but for conspicuous success.[230]

The ambivalent business ethic on Wall Street, with its primary objective of accumulating wealth by whatever means, must have exercised a strong influence on Dulles. The pragmatic approach of speculators, industrialists, and bankers in gaining financial fortunes and political power became a conspicuous factor in the young lawyer's personal, professional, and public life. Considering his religious upbringing, Dulles might well have followed the dictates of his higher conscience in the moral ambiguities which confronted him frequently, rejecting a course of pure expediency. Yet Hoopes seems to believe that Dulles was hardly ever burdened with excessive scruples in his dealings on Wall Street. Certainly at times, his ambition to achieve high social status[231] and financial success prevailed over idealistic notions of moral rectitude:

> If his background indicated there would be at least an initial collision between the values of Watertown and the values of Wall Street, it seems to have been cushioned by the influences of Grandfather Foster, Princeton, law school and European travel. If Dulles understood that the hard calculations of advantage which dominate the American business ethic are of doubtful compatibility with the teachings of Christ, he found he could readily live with the discrepancy, meanwhile pursuing a pragmatic course for the benefit of his client, his firm and himself.[232]

The cold reality of the business world on Wall Street revealed, to some degree, Dulles' readiness to replace the biblical basis of his Christian heritage by a more utilitarian code of ethics. That he could so easily exchange the dogmas of Christianity for a simplified notion of a subjective 'Moral Law' was partly due to his father who had introduced him at a tender age to the writings of German philosophers. His sister, Eleanor, later wrote that philosophers like 'Berkeley, Schopenhauer, Nietzsche, Hegel, and Bergson grew familiar early.'[233] While a college student at Princeton University, Dulles pursued the study of philosophy with singular devotion. His senior thesis on 'The Theory of Judgment', written on nineteen double-spaced pages, was deemed of such high quality that it earned him the Chancellor Green Mental Science Fellowship. This fellowship entitled him to enrol for one year at the Sorbonne in Paris to study under the renowned French philosopher and Nobel Prize winner, Henri Bergson.[234]

An extended intellectual history of Dulles, if attempted here, would have to include a detailed study of Bergson's concept of 'peaceful change', a concept which was to become the most dominant theme in almost all of Dulles' speeches, and a phrase which he used innumerable times in his writings.[235] His most famous address, given at the founding conference of the World Council of Churches in Amsterdam, 1948[236], was a masterful exposition of Bergson's idea of change, a view of reality in which everything is in a constant state of flux. 'The core of Dulles' view of international affairs,' writes Albert N. Keim, 'was an evolutionary Bergsonianism.'

For Bergson, evolutionary flux was the essential reality. Fuelling that constant flux was an endemic tension between dynamic and static forces. War, for Bergson, was a consequence of the failure of the dynamic and static forces in world affairs to maintain a flexible equilibrium. Dulles had quite clearly taken his distinguished teacher's ideas and made them his own.[237]

Dulles had also written a study paper entitled 'The Christian Citizen in a Changing World' for that conference.[238] Yet it has to be said that he interpreted Bergson's concept of peaceful change in his own unique way, and thus contributed to the ideological basis of the ecumenical movement its most revolutionary element.[239] Already in 1924 he had presented a program for peaceful change to the Presbyterian General Assembly. In his address to the Church assembly he declared that, if this program did not proceed from a peculiarly Christian premise, it should be considered all the better.[240]

For most of his adult life, Dulles felt more at home in the company of financiers, politicians, economists, and intellectuals than among ecclesiastics. Despite his activism on behalf of the FCC, he maintained an ambivalence over his personal views about the Christian faith. He never associated with exponents of traditional Christianity, but rather opposed them, mostly in legal and doctrinal matters, with all the intellectual ability and professional expertise at his disposal.

### 3.5.3.3   Faith in the Brotherhood of Humankind

Evaluating Dulles' Christian commitment, Mark G. Toulouse noted that 'Dulles was not a pious individual. Nor did he, at this time [1926], make any meaningful contribution to the church in a theological sense.'[241] During his college years and his early professional life he rarely referred to Christianity, religion, or morality in personal letters or other writings. In 1918 in a note addressed to his mother he expressed doubts about the Christian faith, questioning whether or not he really had any religion.[242] The decision to become a lawyer instead of a Presbyterian minister, as was expected of him, nearly broke his mother's heart.[243] But it would not motivate him to change his mind. Thomas E. Dewey[244], who did not meet Dulles until 1937, later commented, 'I think he spent some years as an atheist.'[245] During the course of his intimate relationship with Dulles, Dewey had many opportunities to probe the deeper recesses of his associate's complex personality.[246] Although Dulles would never allow himself to be seen as an atheist in public, in private the matter might have been different. Therefore Dewey's assumption that Dulles spent some years as an atheist carries considerable weight in that it comes from someone who knew him well.[247] After the spiritually stimulating experience at the Oxford Conference[248], he described himself as a Christian layman with 'somewhat diluted beliefs'.[249] Even the fact that Dulles was active in church circles, prior to 1937, especially in the early 1920s, does not necessarily mean that he was a devout Christian in any orthodox sense. Perusing some of his numerous sermons, the evidence of Dulles' religious expressions suggests rather that his understanding of the basic tenets of Christianity was superficial.[250] Toulouse does not hesitate to emphasise Dulles' disinterest in 'reading any serious theological works', quoting a statement of Dulles' son Avery to that effect: 'He [John Foster] did not enter into questions of a sheerly dogmatic nature.'[251] In a Senate hearing, Milton Mayer called Dulles 'a worldly man ... who wants to be a Christian without performing the Christian mission.'[252] Yet considering Dulles' life as a whole it might be better to classify him as a 'so-called Christian humanist'[253] rather than an outright atheist. The theologian John Coleman Bennett thought Dulles had evolved his own form of 'secularized Calvinism'.[254] This variety of Christian humanism resembled closely his father's doctrine of 'social utility'.[255] Platig asserts that it was clearly Dulles' 'utilitarian ethic which brought about his acceptance of Christianity and not vice versa.'[256] 'The theological baggage he [Dulles] brought with him from Watertown,' writes Townsend Hoopes[257], 'was a good deal lighter than has been supposed.'[258] In concrete terms, this meant that Dulles' spiritual orientation was never set on close adherence to doctrinal propositions.[259] Hoopes further states:

> Even after his "rediscovery" of religion in 1937 [at the Oxford Conference], his theology consisted almost solely of a generalized faith in a "universal moral law", which he failed to define, yet assumed every man could grasp and should obey; that, plus a belief that the church has a role to play in the political process, and a conviction in the supreme worth of the individual.[260]

Dulles' faith was more an idealised commitment to the betterment of humankind in this world than a conscious acceptance of a transcendental reality. His religious orientation was neither exclusively Christian nor was he interested in missionary ventures to 'Christianize' the world. He never seemed to believe in the necessity to pay homage to a higher being, his devotion being directed rather to the 'universal brotherhood of man'.[261] Yet he always couched his humanistic creed, as expounded in numerous public speeches, in Christian terminology.

In 'World Brotherhood through the State', an address delivered under the auspices of The Brotherhood of St. Andrew, at the Convention Hall, Philadelphia, on September 8, 1946, Dulles reminded the assembled masonic brethren of their duty, 'to advance the general welfare of mankind'.[262] A dedication to create the brotherhood of nations would lie at the heart of this task. The Covenant of the League of Nations and the Kellogg-Briand Pact had not failed to deliver their promised blessings of peace. The fault lay, rather, in the wrong attitude of the principal victors at Versailles, who wished to dominate the vanquished nations. This attitude prevented the Peace Treaty (and those international treaties that followed) from warding off 'the evil spirits who brought the peace to a quick and ignominious end'.[263] Christ had never promised to bring a static peace to this world, nor had he described peace as a condition of tranquility. Instead, he spoke of the sword as symbolic of his coming, pointing to the revolutionary aspects of the gospel. God's children would be obliged to fight constantly against the imperfections of world order. They would direct their efforts to bring about that dynamic peace of which Christ had actually spoken, a peace 'that does not stifle but encourages efforts to promote human welfare.'[264] Toward that end, the Christians would need to lead the peoples of this world.

As an outstanding example of what had been accomplished already, Dulles mentioned that the non-Roman churches of fifteen countries had founded the Commission of the Churches on International Affairs only one month before (August 1946) at a conference in Cambridge, England.[265] In unanimous agreement with the other Church delegates, Dulles, as chairman, had decreed that the purpose of the Commission would be 'to discuss the part which the churches might take in world affairs'.[266] In a subsequent statement it was announced that 'the judgment and guidance of the Christian conscience upon international problems must be clearer and more decisive than hitherto'.[267] Building upon the earlier work in the United States of the Commission on a Just and Durable Peace[268], the Commission of the Churches on International Affairs would promote the brotherhood of humankind, based on moral law, on a world-wide scale:

> It can be expected that that Commission will recognize that peace requires the co-operation of men of all nations, races, and creeds and that the principles upon which world order depends are those which men of good will throughout the ages have accepted as part of the moral law. A great body of Christian churches, representing many denominations and many races, is committed, as never before, to subject the conduct of nations to moral law.[269]

In 1944 Dulles had already reminded Christian audiences in numerous speeches that they do not 'alone possess the qualities of mind and soul upon which [the] solution depends.'[270] Although 'Christians believe that the moral law has been most perfectly revealed by Jesus Christ,' it had to be recognised that 'the moral, or *natural*, law is revealed through other religions, and can be comprehended by all men, so that it is a force far more universal than any particular religion.'[271] In the 1950s he still defined his belief as the application of principles derived from 'the natural and moral law which have wider acceptance than Christianity'.[272] At that time he became an active member of World Brotherhood, along with many other famous politicians, academicians and financiers.[273] In an address at the 'Festival of Faith' of the San Francisco Council of Churches, on June 19, 1955, Dulles defined the moral law as a pantheistic concept undergirding each religion, which imbues the United Nations with the moral force of its principles.[274]

In short, Dulles did not believe in the orthodox tenets of Christianity, but rather in a selective and subjective interpretation of Christ's moral teaching. It

120

was an abstract faith in the expediency of the generally recognisable 'Moral Law', as defined by Dulles himself, governing the affairs of the universe as an impersonal force.

Dulles experienced at Oxford what some of his biographers later described as an intellectual 'conversion'.[275] This meant that he left the conference with the impression that the Christian churches could serve as a powerful social force in the process of eliminating the trappings of nationalism and the barriers of the 'sovereignty system'. The churches represented, in his view, the most effective instrument in educating public opinion about the advantages of a new world order.[276] In the *Oxford Report* he remarked that 'many voices in all nations are lifted in these days in favour of a more just international order and the removal of inequalities of opportunity.'[277] The reappraisal of the usefulness of the ecumenical movement in establishing the Commonwealth of God, i.e., a world federation, would never lose its influence on his mind and emotions. Oxford taught him that it would indeed be possible to transform the spiritual values of the Christian community into practical contributions to the cause of international organisation.[278] The essential value which Dulles gained as the result of his participation at the Oxford Conference was, therefore, more a renewed appreciation of the churches' capacity in influencing foreign affairs than any spiritually invigorating effects it might have had on his personal faith.[279]

Dulles' discovery of the Church as a powerful agent of change at Oxford Conference was continuously reinforced by the extraordinary expansion of the Christian movement in the United States and abroad. Church attendance remained on a consistent upward trend from the mid 1930s to the late 1940s. By 1947, Church leaders ranked higher in public esteem than government officials and businessmen.[280] Dulles was enthused about the growing influence of the churches in general society. By taking advantage of this influence and directing it into the right channels he would be able to fulfill the dream of creating a universal brotherhood of humankind, an ideal which he shared with many ecumenical leaders.[281] In perfect unison the assembly at Oxford defined the nature and purpose of the Universal Church, as follows:

> The thought and action of the Church are international in so far as the Church must operate in a world in which the historical Christian bodies share with the rest of mankind the division into national and racial groups. They are oecumenical in so far as they attempt to realize the Una Sancta, the fellowship of Christians who acknowledge the one Lord. This fact of the oecumenical character of the Church carries with it the important consequence that the Church brings to the task of achieving a better international order an insight that is not to be derived from ordinary political sources. To those who are struggling to realize human brotherhood in a world where disruptive nationalism and aggressive imperialism make such brotherhood seem unreal, the Church offers not an ideal but a fact, man united not by his aspiration but by the love of God.[282]

This was in keeping with the ecumenical vision which had been formulated almost two decades earlier by Samuel Z. Batten of the FCC in his book, *The New World Order* (1919):

> If there is to be a new world it must come first of all through a new spirit in the nations. There must be created an international mind and conscience; we must learn to think of humanity as one family and to have a world patriotism; they must keep their minds free from jealousy and selfishness, and must base their policy and practice upon true and Christian principles; they must be as quick to resent injustice by a nation as by an individual. Humanity must become an ideal in order that it may become an actuality. World patriotism must be a faith, a chivalry, before it can be an organization. International peace must become an aspiration, a religion, before it will become a reality.[283]

Dulles' radical change of perspective concerning the potential of the ecumenical movement in reaching a world-wide audience with the message of unity, ecclesiastical as well as secular, following the Oxford Conference was really more a renewed dedication to the socio-political program of the FCC in direct continuation of his earlier participation in the Council's activities.

### 3.5.4    The Churches Survey Their Task

The Oxford Conference established itself as a celebrated landmark in Christian social thinking. For nearly a quarter of a century the published material of the conference was constantly referred to as the authoritative statement in Protestant social ethics. W. A. Visser 't Hooft was later to note that the study volumes, especially on the Oxford theme, served to stimulate thinking in theological faculties, in forums and among lay groups. The Professor of Church History in the University of Chicago, J. H. Nichols, believed that 'the authority of the Oxford Reports was unprecedented, at least in Protestant social ethics, and their competence enabled them to rank with the best of secular thought, a phenomenon scarcely seen since the seventeenth century.'[284]

In three areas the influence of the Conference on the ecumenical movement can clearly be observed: (1) Oxford initiated a new concern for the church in its corporate life. To a large degree, the church reacted to the resurgence of totalitarianism in Europe. The confrontation with what was happening in the political arena emphasised the importance of the church as a world-wide community of believers rooted in a historical continuity, not dependent on any contemporary culture and not limited to nation, race or class, but having its own distinctive ethical code derived from the Scriptures. (2) The conference signalled a transition to what might be termed 'the new social gospel'. At Oxford the Church recognised that its one-sided appeals to follow Christ's example of love were not enough in a world in which the stubborn facts of man's selfishness and its manifestations in the power structures of society were visible everywhere. (3) Oxford stimulated a serious consideration of the social sciences by theologians.

After the conference the division between the social and the theological aspects of the Christian faith were much less emphasised. In time the churches began to disregard the dogmatic side of their belief, deemed to be incompatible with the ethos of the ecumenical movement, in favour of the Gospel's social ethics. Due to the decisive influence of the FCC at Oxford, the tenets of the Social Gospel, as embodied in the Social Creed of 1932, became almost universally accepted in defining the true mission of the Church. In short, the Federal Council's goal was to build the Kingdom of God on earth. To understand more fully what the Church leaders set out to do, we need to examine some of the social policies which had been promulgated by the FCC since its inception in December 1908.

Notes

[1] Dulles was an elder in the Park Avenue Presbyterian Church. He frequently shared the pulpit there with his pastor, Tertius Van Dyke.

[2] Henry Sloane Coffin was president of Union Theological Seminary from 1926 to 1945.

[3] See Leonard Mosley, *Dulles. A Biography of Eleanor, Allen, and John Foster Dulles and their Family Network* (London: Hodder and Stoughton, 1978) 190.

[4] According to Samuel McCrea Cavert's recollection of these events expressed in an interview with Mark G. Toulouse, Van Dusen told Dr Oldham referring to John F. Dulles: 'Here was a man they ought not to miss.' Mark G. Toulouse, *The Transformation of John Foster Dulles. From Prophet of Realism to Priest of Nationalism* (Macon, GA: Mercer University Press, 1985) 51.

[5] In a promotional brochure, advertising the book series of the Oxford Conference, the publishers stated: 'This series of six volumes, specially prepared for the World Conference at Oxford last July, is in active preparation and should be on sale in the late autumn. Leading scholars and churchmen of all nations have collaborated in preparing them. No finer group of religious thinkers has ever before been brought together. All the material has been circulated amongst the writers themselves before taking final shape and they have had the further criticism of a wider circle of their colleagues throughout the Christian world. It may justly be claimed for the books that they are the beginning of a process which may lead to a clarification of the issues confronting men. especially Christians, in the modern world. *These books are of the utmost value to all earnest churchmen* (George Allen & Unwin Ltd, 40 Museum Street, London, W.C.1; italics in the original).

[6] John F. Dulles, 'The Problem of Peace in a Dynamic World,' in Joseph H. Oldham, ed., *Church, Community and State*, Vol. 7: *The Universal Church and the World of Nations* (London: George Allen & Unwin, 1938) 143-168

[7] John F. Dulles, 'The Problem of Peace in a Dynamic World,' *Religion in Life*, Vol.6, No.2, Spring, 1937.

[8] See John Foster Dulles, 'The Problem of Peace in a Dynamic World,' in Joseph H. Oldham, ed., *The Churches Survey Their Task*, 154; see also John Foster Dulles,

'The Problem of Peace in a Dynamic World,' *Religion in Life*, 197.

[9] See John F. Dulles, 'The Problem of Peace in a Dynamic World,' in Joseph H. Oldham, ed., *Church, Community and State*, 167.

[10] As cited in Mark G. Toulouse, 'Working Towards Meaningful Peace: John Foster Dulles and the F.C.C., 1937-1945,' *Journal of Presbyterian History* 61:4 (Winter 1983) 395.

[11] See *ibid.*

[12] See John F. Dulles, 'The Problem of Peace in a Dynamic World,' in Joseph H. Oldham, ed., *Church, Community and State*, 145.

[13] *Ibid.*

[14] *Ibid.*, 154.

[15] *Ibid.*, 155.

[16] *Ibid.*

[17] *Ibid.*, 155, 156.

[18] *Ibid.*, 156.

[19] *Ibid.*, 168.

[20] John F. Dulles, 'The Problem of Peace in a Dynamic World,' in Joseph H. Oldham, ed., *The Churches Survey Their Task*, 167, 168.

[21] See, e.g., John F. Dulles, 'Peaceful Change within the Society of Nations' (1936), *JFD Papers*; 'The Problem of Peace in a Dynamic World' (1937), *Religion in Life*; John F. Dulles, 'The American Churches and the International Situation,' December 1940; 'Christianity in this Hour' (April 21, 1941), *JFD Papers*; John F. Dulles, 'Address at Union Theological Seminary,' (May 19, 1941), *JFD Papers*; John F. Dulles, 'Peace without Platitudes,' *Fortunes*, XXV (January 1942); John F. Dulles, 'Towards World Order' (March 5, 1942), in Francis J. McConnell, et al., *A Basis for the Peace To Come* (New York: Abingdon-Cokesbury Press, 1942); John F. Dulles, 'The Churches and World Order,' Address delivered to the graduating class of Princeton Theological Seminary on May 16, 1944, published in *Theology Today*, October, 1944, in Henry P. Van Dusen, ed., *The Spiritual Legacy of John Foster Dulles.*

[22] O. Frederick Nolde, Associate Secretary General of the World Council of Churches, admitted in an interview in 1965 that he believed Dulles had pursued radical policies during his time as chairman of the Commission on a Just and Durable Peace: 'There was a very considerable meeting of minds in the arena of world affairs because what Dulles was after at that time was revolutionary.' As cited in Richard D. Challener and John M. Fenton, 'Recent Past Come Alive in Dulles "Oral History,"' University: A Princeton Quarterly (Spring 1967), 6.

[23] See Richard D. Challener and John M. Fenton, 'Recent Past Come Alive in Dulles "Oral History,"' University: A Princeton Quarterly (Spring 1967), 6.

[24] See Leonard Mosley, *Dulles*, 120.

[25] Dulles referred occasionally to the world system prevailing in the late 1930s and early 1940s as the sovereignty-war system; see e.g., John F. Dulles, 'The Problem of Peace in a Dynamic World,' in Joseph H. Oldham, ed., *The Churches Survey Their Task*, 153.

[26] John F. Dulles, 'The Churches and World Order,' in Henry P. Van Dusen, ed., *The Spiritual Legacy of John Foster Dulles*, 29.

[27] *Ibid.*

[28] *Ibid.*, 29, 30.

[29] *Ibid.*, 30.

[30] A statement of John F. Dulles, as cited in 'Manual of Laymen's Missionary Movement' (April 4, 1945) 1, *JFD Papers*.

[31] John F. Dulles, 'The Problem of Peace in a Dynamic World,' in Joseph H. Oldham, ed., *Church, Community and State*, 167-168. See also John Foster Dulles, 'The Problem of Peace in a Dynamic World,' *Religion in Life*, 206, 207.

[32] Albert N. Keim, *John Foster Dulles and the Federal Council of Churches, 1937-1949*, unpublished Ph.D thesis, The Ohio State University, 1971, 21, 22.

[33] Ron Chernow, *The Warburgs. A Family Saga* (London: Random House, 1993) 491. See also James Paul Warburg, *The Long Road Home. An Autobiography of a Maverick* (Garden City, N.Y.: Doubleday & Co., 1964) 179, 180.

[34] Leonard Mosley, *Dulles*, 89.

[35] *Ibid.*, 89, 90.

[36] John J. McCloy became U.S. High Commissioner in Germany after World War II. From 1953 to 1970 McCloy was the chairman of the board of the Council on Foreign Relations and simultaneously one of its directors (until 1972).

[37] Leonard Mosley, *Dulles*, 90; see also Townsend Hoopes, *The Devil and John Foster Dulles*, 47: 'John J. McCloy, who was later United States High Commissioner in Occupied Germany, said with reference to the prewar period that "I was always puzzled to see just where Foster Dulles stood ... with the Nazi business and what his feeling was about the oncoming menace from Germany. I rather gathered the impression that he was not particularly concerned about it."'

[38] Leonard Mosley, *Dulles*, 90.

[39] *Ibid.*, 88.

[40] *Ibid.*, 91.

[41] *Ibid.*; see also Townsend Hoopes, *The Devil and John Foster Dulles*, 47

[42] James Steward Martin, in his official role at the State Department, was investigating the structure of Nazi industry. He observed that American and British businessmen tried to occupy key positions in this postwar investigation to divert and even prevent investigation of Nazi industrialists. To cover their own tracks and complicity in the machinations of the Third Reich, they asserted that these German industrialists were innocent of the crimes committed by the Nazis. Martin is sceptical about this thesis and presents evidence that would suggest a conscious attempt to conceal the collaboration of Nazi industrialists with American and British businessmen.

[43] See James S. Martin, *All Honorable Men* (Boston: Little, Brown, Co., 1950) 53. The cooperation between Sullivan & Cromwell and Albert & Westrick continued unabated during the years of Nazi rule in Germany. See also *ibid.*, 52, 209.

[44] The spelling of the name 'Schroder' appears in its three variant forms throughout this chapter. If the name refers to the American or English branches of the Schroder investment banks, it is usually written in its anglicized form (without the o-Umlaut [ö]). If it refers to the German branch, it is written with the o-Umlaut (ö) or its alternative spelling 'oe'. This rule is, however, not consistently followed in some quotations.

[45] See Richard Roberts, *Schroders. Merchants & Bankers* (London: Macmillan, 1992) 192: 'Sullivan and Cromwell had close ties with Germany, where the firm handled bond issues and related matters for several provincial governments and private corporations. It maintained an office in Berlin, and the business from German clients was lucrative.' Richard Roberts informs us that 'the return of Germany to the gold

standard following the success of the Dawes Loan of October 1924 was the cue for an even greater involvement in German finance by J. Henry Schröder & Co. Commercial opportunity was certainly a powerful incentive, but Baron Bruno was also motivated by a strong desire to assist with the economic reconstruction of Germany. Short-term finance by acceptance credits and advances to German clients averaged £ 5.2 million per annum in 1924-28, almost double the annual average of 1920-23 ... The clients were much the same as in the early 1920s, predominantly Hamburg merchant firms, Schröder Gebrüder heading the list, and manufacturers and banks elsewhere in Germany ... There was a significant increase in the number of industrial and utility companies making use of Schröders' facilities on a larger scale in 1929-30, notably Allgemeine Electrizitäts Gesellschaft (AEG) ... In these years Schröder's acceptances and advances for German clients averaged £ 6.2 million per annum, more than ever before and almost half of the firm's total.'

[46] See Townsend Hoopes, *The Devil and John Foster Dulles*, 47.

[47] The present writer was unable to find out if Sullivan & Cromwell closed its Hamburg office. Even if we assume that this office was also closed, Sullivan & Cromwell still continued to operate through the German law firm Albert & Westrick, as it had done since the early 1920s.

[48] Transcripts of interviews with Allen W. Dulles and Eustace Seligman, *The Oral History Collection*. Eustace Seligman, a partner at Sullivan & Cromwell, stated that 'we closed that office in Berlin when it became apparent that Mr. Hitler was going to take over the government. We got out somewhat in advance .... Mr. Dulles [John Foster] was very active in that.' It should be noted, however, that the Berlin office of Sullivan & Cromwell was closed in 1935, two years after Hitler had assumed power in Germany, not 'somewhat in advance' of the events transpiring in January 1933. Far from being 'very active in that', John Foster vehemently opposed that decision. See also *Christian Century*, LXI:43 (October 25, 1944) 1224-1225.

[49] See Dulles' passport and correspondence, *JFD Papers*.

[50] Dulles' business correspondence with Nazi clients gives a partial picture of the on-going legal activities of Sullivan & Cromwell after the cessation of official representation in Berlin; see e.g., letters, Hjalmar Schacht to John F. Dulles, September 27, 1935; John F. Dulles to George S. Brown, January 29, 1936; John F. Dulles to Hjalmar Schacht, June 15, 1937. These and other letters are contained in the *JFD Papers*.

[51] See H. Montgomery Hyde, *The Quiet Canadian. The Secret Service Story of Sir William Stephenson* (London: Hamish Hamilton, 1962) 70, 71; and also Charles Higham, *Trading with the Enemy. An Exposé of The Nazi-American Money Plot 1933-1949* (London: Robert Hale, 1983) 95, 142, 155.

[52] See James S. Martin, *All Honorable Men*, 52-53.

[53] See letters, John F. Dulles to Heinrich F. Albert, December 27, 1935; June 15, 1939, *JFD Papers*.

[54] See e.g., 'Pepper Links Dulles to Nazis, Sees Peace Threatened, Warns Nation Against Witch-Hunt,' *In Fact*, XV (August 18, 1947) 1-3.

[55] See Richard Roberts, *Schroders*, 296.

[56] Speech of Senator Joseph F. Guffey of Pennsylvania on floor of the Senate in United States Congress, *Congressional Record*, 78th Congress, 2nd Session (Washington, D.C.: Government Printing Office, 1944) XC, Part 6, 8058-8061; see also letter, JFD to Luman J. Shafer, September 16, 1944, *JFD Papers*; and *Christian*

*Century*, LXI:43 (October 25, 1944) 1224-1225.

[57] See Richard Roberts, *Schroders*, 296. Roberts quoted from a statement issued to the press by Gerald F. Beal on 12 October 1944; see SA Schrobanco papers. Gerald F. Beal, an executive director of Schrobanco, was also a member of the Council on Foreign Relations.

[58] See *Capital Times* (Madison, Wisconsin: September 26, 1944), 20; *ibid.* (September 28, 1944), 28; and *ibid.* (September 29, 1944), 24; and also Ronald W. Pruessen, *John Foster Dulles*, 123. It is a matter of record that Dulles had represented the Bank of Spain in a case against the Federal Reserve Bank of New York. *Ibid.*, 122-123; Pruessen refers to the following sources: John Foster Dulles, Inzer B. Wyatt, Richard G. Pettingill, Memorandum on Behalf of Plaintiff, Banco de Espana Sigmund Solomon, L71/239, etc., June 2, 1938, United States District Court for the Southern District of New York; letter, JFD to Henry L. Stimson, January 26, 1939, *JFD Papers*.

[59] See Kenneth Leslie, 'John Cardinal Dulles?,' *The Protestant*, VII (August-September, 1946) 6-8; Kenneth Leslie, 'Cable to Dulles,' *ibid.*, 5-6. *The Protestant* was not associated with any Christian group, but was a private enterprise.

[60] The *Social Questions Bulletin* was an unofficial organ of the Methodist Federation for Social Action. Source for this statement is private correspondence in the files of the Commission of a Just and Durable Peace; as referred to by Jessie June Burroway, 'Christian Witness Concerning World Order. The Federal Council of Churches and Postwar Planning 1941-1947,' unpublished Ph.D thesis, University of Wisconsin, 1953, 27.

[61] See 'Hitler's Backers, U.S. Bankers, and Mr. Dewey's Mr. Dulles,' *In Fact*, X (October 30, 1944) 1-2; 'Pro-Nazi Ties of Marshall's Adviser,' *ibid.*, XVI (December 8, 1947) 3-4; 'Schroeder Scandal,' *ibid.*, XVII (March 22, 1948) 3; 'The Suppressed Dulles Story,' *ibid.*, XX (October 24, 1949) 3-4. For some other charges of pro-Nazism against Dulles see the following: 'On Mr. Dulles and What To Do About Him,' *Soviet Russia Today*, XV (July, 1946) 6-7; 'Vishinsky Wasn't First,' *New Masses*, LXV (October 14, 1947), 3-5; Howard Watson Ambruster, *Treason's Peace. German Dyes and American Dupes*, The Beechhurst Press, New York, 1947.

[62] See transcript of J. Raymond Walsh broadcast, February 26, 1947, *JFD Papers*.

[63] See speech by representative Adolph J. Sabath of Illinois on floor of the House, United States Congress, *Congressional Record*, 80th Congress, 1st Session, 1947, XCIII, Part 4 (Washington, D.C.: Government Printing Office) 4607.

[64] See letter, JFD to George C. Marshall, March 10, 1948.

[65] See Harold L. Ickes, 'Looking Forward Backwards,' *The New Republic*, CXXI (November 21, 1949), 16, *JFD Papers*. For another example of a partial retraction see 'In Justice to Mr. Dulles,' *New Republic*, CXI (November 20, 1944), 647.

[66] See speech of Senator Arthur H. Vanderberg of Michigan on floor of Senate in U.S. Congress, *Congressional Record*, 78th Congress, 2nd Session, 1944, XC, Part 6 (Washington, D.C.: Government Printing Office, 1944) 8061; Luman J. Shafer, 'The Christian in Politics,' *Post War World*, Vol. I (October 16, 1944) 2; 'John Foster Dulles,' *The Christian Century*, LXI (October 25, 1944) 1224-1225; John C. Bennett, Reinhold Niebuhr, Justin Wroe Nixon, and G. Bromley Oxnam, 'Concerning Mr. Dulles,' *ibid.*, 1231.

[67] See e.g., Ronald W. Pruessen, *John Foster Dulles*, 132: 'Dulles's cartel activities, on the other hand, make the righteousness of his later denials of German associations grate somewhat harshly. His two definite attachments with the

International Nickel Company and Solvay & Cie. spanned the years when these clients were developing and maintaining cartel relationships with, among others, Germany's I. G. Farben. As legal counsel, director, and executive committee member for both companies throughout the 1930s, it is clear that Dulles was actively and specifically engaged in arranging those cartel relationships. See also Gabriel Kolko, 'American Business and Germany, 1930-1941,' *The Western Political Quarterly,* XV (December 1962) 713-728.

[68] *Ibid.,* 132. Several pages earlier in his biography of Dulles, Pruessen had already asserted that 'there is good reason not to leave the question of Dulles's associations with Nazi Germany too hastily. A thorough study of his legal work suggests that there are some major activities which may be of key importance in this regard. To telescope somewhat, something of the spirit if not the letter of the critiques of Dulles and his business associates proves to be correct after all.' *Ibid.,* 126.

[69] John C. Bennett, Reinhold Niebuhr, Justin Wroe Nixon, and G. Bromley Oxnam, 'Concerning Mr. Dulles,' *ibid.,* 1231.

[70] See Richard Roberts, *Schroders,* 225.

[71] Richard Roberts lists the partners of Sullivan & Cromwell who became also directors of Schrobanco: 'There was also a succession of partners of Sullivan & Cromwell, Schrobanco's legal counsel: Allen Dulles, the brother of John Foster Dulles, 1938-42; De Lano Andrews, 1943-55; and Norris Darrell, 1955-63.' Richard Roberts, *Schroders,* 280, 281. See also James S. Martin, *All Honorable Men,* 51-52.

[72] See Richard Roberts, *Schroders,* 290.

[73] Percy Rockefeller, born 1878, was the son of William D. Rockefeller (brother of John D. Rockefeller) and inherited part of the Standard Oil fortune. Percy was a director of Guaranty Trust from 1915-1930.

[74] See *New York Times,* November 24, 1929; and also Richard Roberts, *Schroders,* 290.

[75] See Charles Higham, *Trading with the Enemy,* 22.

[76] See Richard Roberts, *Schroders,* 123; see *ibid.,* 177.

[77] See James & Suzanne Pool, *Who Financed Hitler. The Secret Funding of Hitler's Rise to Power 1919-1933* (New York: The Dial Press, 1978) 311, 312; see also *ibid.,* 462-464, and the research material collection in '*Christian Century* editorial' file, *JFD Papers.*

[78] Richard Roberts, *Schroders,* 260.

[79] The J.H. Stein Bank in Cologne was to become one of the main conduits of funds provided for by international financiers to support the National Socialist movement in general and Himmler's SS in particular. This explains why U.S. Army Colonel Bogdan was anxious to divert the attention of post-war U.S. Army investigations away from the J.H. Stein Bank that held the secrets of the associations of American subsidiaries with Nazi authorities while World War II was in progress. James Steward Martin recounts how during the planning meetings of the Finance Division of the Control Commission he was assigned to work with Captain Norbert A. Bogdan, who, in his civil profession, was vice president of the J. Henry Schroder Banking Corporation of New York. Martin relates that 'Captain Bogdan had argued vigorously against investigation of the Stein Bank on the grounds that it was "small potatoes".' James S. Martin, *All Honorable Men,* 52, 54-56.

[80] As listed by the Kilgore Committee, Schröder's political acquisitions in the early 1940s were as follows: SS Senior Group Leader; Iron Cross of First and Second

Class; Swedish Consul General; International Chamber of Commerce - Member of administrative committee; Council of Reich Post Office - Member of advisory board; German Industrial and Commerce Assembly - Presiding member; Reich Board of Economic Affairs - Member; Deutsche Reichsbahn - President of administrative board; Trade Group for Wholesale and Foreign Trade - Manager; Akademie für Deutsches Recht (Academy of German Law) - Member; City of Cologne - Councillor; University of Cologne - Member of board of trustees; Kaiser Wilhelm Foundation - Senator; Advisory Council of German-Albanians; Goods Clearing Bureau - Member; Working Committee of Reich Group for Industry and Commerce - Deputy chairman. Schröder's banking connections were equally impressive and his business connections (not listed here) would take up two pages: Bank for International Settlements - Member of the directorate; J.H. Stein & Co. Cologne - Partner (Banque Worms was French correspondent); Deutsche Reichsbank, Berlin - Advisor to board of directors; Wirtschaftsgruppe Private Bankgewerbe - Leader; Deutsche Verkehrs-Kredit-Bank, A.G., Berlin (controlled by Deutsche Reichsbank) - Chairman of board of directors; Deutsche Überseeische Bank (controlled by Deutsche Bank, Berlin) - Director. Source: United States Congress, Senate Hearings before a Subcommittee of the Committee on Military Affairs, *Elimination of German Resources for War*. Report pursuant to S. Res. 107 and 146, July 2, 1945, Part 7, 78th Congress and 79th Congress (Washington, D.C.: Government Printing Office, 1945); see also *New York Times*, April 28, 1929.

[81] See Charles Higham, *Trading with the Enemy*, 1-2.

[82] See Anthony Sampson, *The Sovereign State. The Secret History of ITT* (London: Hodder and Stoughton, 1973) 27, 44.

[83] See Charles Higham, *Trading with the Enemy*, 36; and also Anthony Sampson, *The Sovereign State*, 31.

[84] See James S. Martin, *All Honorable Men*, 67-68.

[85] See H. Montgomery Hyde, *The Quiet Canadian*, 123-126; and also FCC Inter-Office Memorandum, February 27, 1943.

[86] Not only John Foster Dulles, but also his brother Allen, were involved in protecting GAF from being identified as a subsidiary of I.G. Farben, thus assuring its continuous collaboration with the Nazi armament industry. See Charles Higham, *Trading with the Enemy*, 216.

[87] See Charles Higham, *Trading with the Enemy*, 138-141.

[88] Roberts describes the close relationship between the different Schroder Investment banks and Standard Gas & Electric; see Richard Roberts, *Schroders*, 290-291.

[89] See Charles Higham, *Trading with the Enemy*, 99.

[90] The original statement of Schröder is contained in *The Trial of the Major War Criminals before the International Military Tribunal* (German ed.), Volume XXXVI, Nuremberg, 1947-1949, 532. During World War II International Telephone and Telegraph was making cash payments to *Reichsführer-SS* Heinrich Himmler. These payments enabled I.T.T. to protect its investment in Focke-Wulf; see United States Congress, Senate Hearings before a subcommittee of the Committee on Military Affairs, *Scientific and Technical Mobilization*, 78th Congress, 1st session, S. 702, Part 16 (Washington, D.C.: Government Printing Office, 1944) 939. See also Anthony Sampson, *The Sovereign State*, 28.

[91] See Anthony Sampson, *The Sovereign State*, 32-33.

[92] See Charles Higham, *Trading with the Enemy*, 99.

[93] Behn did not only supply communications and electronic equipment to Roosevelt's army, but also, by means of his British company, Standard Telephones and Cables, to Churchill's forces; see Anthony Sampson, *The Sovereign State*, 32.

[94] See *ibid.*, 39. Higham notes the disturbing fact that all these diverse activities of I.T.T. were not only well-known to the State Department, but also seemingly encouraged; see Charles Higham, *Trading with the Enemy*, 99-100.

[95] See Charles Higham, *Trading with the Enemy*, 116-117: 'With its 185 sales organizations throughout the world, SKF ... represented virtually every industrial combine in Sweden and every member of the board was part of the companies that controlled the entire Swedish economy. Founded in 1907, SKF, with its subsidiaries, was the largest manufacturer of bearings on earth. It controlled 80 percent of bearings in Europe alone. It also controlled iron ore mines, steel and blast furnaces, foundries and factories and plants in the United States, Great Britain, France, and Germany. The largest share of its production until late in World War II was allocated to Germany; 60 percent of the worldwide production of SKF was dedicated to the Germans ... And ball bearings were among the most powerful weapons of The Fraternity's sophisticated form of wartime neutrality. Their inventor and the power behind their production and distribution as SKF chairman was Sven Wingquist, a dashing playboy friend of Göring and the Duke and Duchess of Windsor. He was a prominent partner in Jacob Wallenberg's Stockholm Enskilda, the largest private bank in Sweden - a correspondent bank of Hitler's Reichsbank.'

[96] See *ibid.*, 116, 118-119.

[97] *Ibid.*, 116, 117: 'Tiny ball bearings were essential to the Nazis: The Luftwaffe could not fly without them, the tanks and armored cars could not roll in their missions of death. ITT's Focke-Wulfs, Ford's autos and trucks for the enemy, would have been powerless without them. Focke-Wulfs used at least four thousand bearings per plane: roughly equivalent to those used by the Flying Fortresses. Guns, bombsights, electrical generators and engines, ventilating systems, U-boats, railroads, mining machinery, ITT's communications devices - these existed on ball bearings.'

[98] See *ibid.*, 122: 'As war went on, it became necessary to cloak SKF shipments to South America in case members of the FBI should discover what was going on. As a cover, von Rosen set up a subsidiary that took a leaf out of the Standard Oil book. Registered in Panama, it was protected by Panamanian laws from American seizure. Ball bearings travelled from American ports on Panamanian registered vessels. Over 600,000 ball bearings a year travelled in this manner to Nazi customers in South America including Siemens, Diesel, Asea, and Separator, as well as Axel Wenner-Gren's Electrolux and Behn's ITT ... When Germany began to run short of ball bearings in 1943, despite the vast shipments from Sweden and its own local production, more were needed from South America. So von Rosen arranged for reshipment from Rio and Buenos Aires via Sweden. The British, utterly dependent on SKF for their own ball bearings, appeased the dubious corporation by issuing special Navicerts allowing vessels to pass unsearched through the blockade to Sweden. Even the Russians concurred - they, too, needed SKF.'

[99] See *ibid.*, 118, 120-121.

[100] Emery Reves, *The Anatomy of Peace* (London: George Allen & Unwin, 1946) 75.

[101] John M. Mulder, 'The Moral World of John Foster Dulles,' 161. Mulder refers to Roswell P. Barnes' sermon, 'Working for Peace as a Churchman,' June 14, 1959,

Dulles Memorial Library, Interchurch Center, New York City.

[102] See letters, Robert E. Speer to JFD, 28 June 1921; JFD to Robert E. Speer, n.d., *JFD Papers*, Box 4; see also letter, Sidney L. Gulick to JFD, 30 November, 1925, *JFD Papers*, Box 7.

[103] See letters, Tertius Van Dyke to JFD, 6 March 1922, *JFD Papers*; Samuel McCrea Cavert to John F. Dulles, 29 December 1922, *JFD Papers*.

[104] Letter, Henry Sloane Coffin to JFD, 15 October 1926, *JFD Papers*, Box 7. Henry Sloane Coffin was Professor of Practical Theology at Union Theological Seminary from 1904 to 1926. He was President of the Seminary from 1926 to 1945. As a member of the American delegation attending the Oxford Conference in 1937, he presided over the section meetings on 'Church, Community, and State in Relation to Education'; see Joseph H. Oldham, ed., *The Churches Survey Their Task. The Report of the Conference at Oxford, July 1937, on Church, Community, and State*, 302.

[105] Letter, Tertius Van Dyke to JFD, 25 January 1926, *JFD Papers*, Box 7.

[106] In 1925 the Federal Council had participated in the Stockholm conference. One hundred and fifty delegates from the United States attended and declared for the same social gospel, which had helped to bring about the formation of the Federal Council in 1908. This position met with great opposition from the German delegates, because of its social and not spiritual emphasis.

[107] See letters, E.C. Carter to JFD, 12 December 1923; JFD to E.C. Carter, 14 December 1923, *JFD Papers*, Box 5; Henry Atkinson, General Secretary of the Presbyterian Assembly, to JFD, 29 May 1923, *JFD Papers*, Box 5; Henry Atkinson to Theodore R. Savage, 8 January 1933, *JFD Papers*, Box 110.

[108] Memorandum, JFD to William Nelson Cromwell, 16 June 1931, *JFD Papers*, Box 9; letter, William Nelson Cromwell to JFD, 23 October 1931, *JFD Papers*, Box 7.

[109] See International Institute of Intellectual Cooperation, *Peaceful Change, Procedures, Population, Raw Materials, Colonies*, Proceedings of the Tenth International Studies Conference, Paris, June 28th-July 3rd, 1937, Paris, 1938, 620.

[110] It was the biennial meeting of the Institute of Intellectual Cooperation. Through the League of Nations, the Royal Institute of International Affairs was able to extend its intellectual influence into countries outside the Commonwealth. This was done, for example, through the Intellectual Cooperation Organization of the League of Nations. This Organisation consisted of two chief parts: (1) the International Committee on Intellectual Cooperation, an advisory body; and (2) The International Institute of Intellectual Cooperation, an executive organ of the Committee, with headquarters in Paris. The International Committee had about twenty members from various countries. Gilbert Murray was its chief founder and was chairman from 1928 to its disbandment in 1945. The International Institute was established by the French government and handed over to the League of Nations (1926). Its director was always a Frenchman, but its deputy director and guiding spirit was Sir Alfred Zimmern from 1926 to 1930. It also had a board of directors of six persons. Gilbert Murray was one of these from 1926.

[111] See Stephen King-Hall, *Chatham House*, 71-72.

[112] See *ibid.*, 72-73.

[113] See Greg Poulgrain, 'Dean Rusk. A Reflection,' *Australia & World Affairs* 26, Spring 1995, 28. In fact, in 1937, while travelling in Europe, John F. Dulles would have liked to meet Hitler again or, at least, listen to his mesmerizing speeches. Avery Dulles described his father's fascination with 'the successful demagogue' in precise

terms: 'He was very interested in the techniques of capturing the interests of the electorate ... He saw in Hitler the example of a person who could capture the enthusiasm of the people ...' Leonard Mosley, *Dulles*, 96. Dulles' biographer, Mosley, added the following words to these comments: 'But at the last moment he [Dulles] decided against it [a trip to Germany in 1937], perhaps feeling that the possibilities for embarrassment outweighed the opportunities for demagogic instruction.' *Ibid.*

[114] *Ibid.*, 97.

[115] John F. Dulles, 'The Churches and World Order', in Henry P. Van Dusen, ed., *The Spiritual Legacy of John Foster Dulles*, 25.

[116] John F. Dulles, 'As Seen By a Layman,' in Henry P. Van Dusen, ed., *The Spiritual Legacy of John Foster Dulles*, 40.

[117] Mark G. Toulouse, *The Transformation of John Foster Dulles*, 50.

[118] See John F. Dulles, 'The Church's Role in Developing the Basis of a Just and Enduring Peace,' in *When Hostilities Cease*, Addresses and Findings of the Exploratory Conference on the Bases of a Just and Enduring Peace, Chicago Temple, May 27-30, 1941, Commission on World Peace of the Methodist Church, Chicago, 1941, 15-17.

[119] See John Foster Dulles, 'As Seen By a Layman,' *Religion in Life*, VII (Winter, 1938) 36; in Henry P. Van Dusen, ed., *The Spiritual Legacy of John Foster Dulles*, 13.

[120] *Ibid.*

[121] See Mark G. Toulouse, *The Transformation of John Foster Dulles*, 51.

[122] *Ibid.*

[123] See Mark G. Toulouse, *The Transformation of John Foster Dulles*, 33.

[124] G.K.A. Bell, ed., *The Stockholm Conference of 1925. Official Report of the Universal Christian Conference on Life and Work held in Stockholm, 19-30 August 1925* (London, 1926) 18.

[125] See Samuel McCrea Cavert, *On the Road to Christian Unity* (New York: Harper & Brothers, 1961) 29.

[126] See *Minutes of the Meeting of the Universal Christian Council for Life & Work*, Fanø, Denmark, 1934, 47ff.

[127] See also Joseph H. Oldham, ed., *Church, Community and State*, Vol. 7: *The Universal Church and the World of Nations*, vii.

[128] See *ibid.*, viii-ix.

[129] Visser 't Hooft also collaborated with Oldham in writing a foundational study on the Oxford theme, *The Church and its Function in Society*, published before the conference, and subsequently included as the first volume of *Church, Community, and State*, 8 Vols. (London: George Allen & Unwin, 1938). In the United States this series was published under the title, *The Oxford Conference*, 7 Vols. (Chicago: Willett, Clark & Co., 1937). Since this edition has gone out of print, a new edition, edited with an interpretive introduction by Harold L. Lunger, was published under the title, *Foundations of Ecumenical Social Thought. The Oxford Conference Report* (Philadelphia: Fortress Press, 1966).

[130] Joseph H. Oldham, ed., *Church, Community, and State*, 8 Vols. (London: George Allen & Unwin, 1938).

[131] Walter W. Van Kirk (1891-1956), Methodist minister, was secretary of the Federal Council's Department of International Justice and Goodwill, 1925-1950, and director of the Commission on a Just and Durable Peace throughout its existence. In this Commission he worked under the chairmanship of John F. Dulles. From 1950 until 1956 he was the executive of the National Council of Churches for International

Affairs. Van Kirk was also a member of the Council on Foreign Relations and, like Dulles, a delegate at the United Nations Founding Conference in San Francisco, 1945.

[132] R.H. Tawney was a founding member of the Institute of International Affairs at the Hotel Majestic in Paris. In his book, *Equality*, he discussed the concept of world federation at great length. See R.H. Tawney, *Equality* (London: Allen & Unwin, [1931] 1938).

[133] See letters, William Adams Brown to JFD, 8 January 1926, *JFD Papers*, Box 7; Tertius Van Dyke to JFD, 7 October 1935, *JFD Papers*, Box 14.

[134] Henry A. Atkinson was one of six associate secretaries of the Commission on the Church and Social Service of FCC, and one of five members of its Secretarial Council. Serving as secretary of the FCC's Commission on International Justice and Good Will, Atkinson was also a member of the Committee of Direction of its Commission on Councils of Churches and a secretary of the Committee on Interchange of Preachers and Speakers Between the Churches of America, Great Britain and France.

[135] William Adams Brown was elected one of the Conference's co-chairmen. Samuel McCrea Cavert stated that Brown played a prominent role in the Life and Work movement culminating in the founding of the World Council of Churches. See Samuel McCrea Cavert, *The American Churches in the Ecumenical Movement 1900-1968* (New York: Association Press, 1968) 163.

[136] See Robert C. Mackie & Charles C. West, ed., *The Sufficiency of God. Essays on the Ecumenical Hope in Honor of W. A. Visser 't Hooft* (Philadelphia: Westminster Press, 1965) 124.

[137] John F. Dulles, 'Faith of our Fathers', in Henry P. Van Dusen, ed., *The Spiritual Legacy of John Foster Dulles*, 6. In 'The Church's Contribution Toward a Warless World', Dulles wrote that at Oxford he had met men of 'conflicting nationalities' who, while sharing a Christian perspective, found that 'the difficulties between their nations ... quickly fell into the category of those matters which are calmly discussed and peacefully settled.' John F. Dulles, 'The Church's Contribution Toward a Warless World', *Religion in Life*, IX (Winter, 1940) 39.

[138] John F. Dulles, 'Faith of our Fathers,' in Henry P. Van Dusen, ed., *The Spiritual Legacy of John Foster Dulles*, 6.

[139] John F. Dulles, 'The Churches and World Order,' *Theology Today* (October, 1944), in Henry P. Van Dusen, ed., *The Spiritual Legacy of John Foster Dulles*, 25.

[140] See Ronald W. Pruessen, *John Foster Dulles*, 187: 'For a passing moment, he [Dulles] seems to have felt that church leaders and intellectuals active in the international ecumenical movement might be valuable allies in pushing for the world reforms he was then advocating. The meetings at Oxford proved very exciting, as men like Reinhold Niebuhr, R.H. Tawney, Paul Tillich and T.S. Eliot listened attentively to his ideas.'

[141] See Edward Duff, *The Social Thought of the World Council of Churches* (London: Longmans, Green, and Co., 1956) 261; Samuel M. Cavert, *Oral History Collection*, 1965; and Ronald W. Pruessen, *John Foster Dulles*, 187. Pruessen states that 'the end product [of the report] read like a polished version of his [Dulles'] 1935 *Atlantic* article.' *Ibid.*, 188; the title of the article was 'The Road to Peace,' *Atlantic Monthly*, CLVI (October, 1935) 492-499; see Joseph H. Oldham, ed., *The Churches Survey Their Task*, 167-187; see also Universal Christian Council, *The Message and Decisions of Oxford on Church, Community and State*, New York, 1937, 3-7, 31-53,

76-88.

[142] See Albert N. Keim, 'John Foster Dulles and the Federal Council of Churches of Christ, 1937-1949,' 15.

[143] In *The Church and the New Order*, William Paton referred specifically to the opening line of an address of Robert Cecil, which had made a strong impression on him: 'I shall never forget Viscount Cecil beginning a speech at the Oxford Conference of 1937 with the remark that the most important task of the Churches in seeking to further international order and goodwill was to preach the Gospel.' William Paton, *The Church and the New Order* (London: SCM Press, 1941) 152. For information about Robert Cecil's contribution at the Conference, see W. A. Visser 't Hooft, *Memoirs* (Geneva: WCC Publication, 1973) 72.

[144] Joseph H. Oldham, ed., *The Churches Survey Their Task. The Report of the Conference at Oxford, July 1937, on Church, Community, and State*, 167.

[145] See *ibid.*

[146] *Ibid.*, 167-168.

[147] *Ibid.*

[148] *Ibid.*, 168.

[149] *Ibid.*, 169.

[150] See Albert N. Keim, 'John Foster Dulles and the Federal Council of Churches of Christ, 1937-1949,' 11-12: 'The new ecumenicity was based on a new view of the church. '"Let the church be the Church," was the rallying cry at Oxford. In essence this was a call for a new "churchly" sociology and politics. The Christian community ought to exhibit the quality of life which it espoused for society as a whole.'

[151] William Paton, *World Community*, 55. Paton stood in succession of former ecclesiastics, such as W.H.P. Faunce, who had already much earlier propagated the ideal of a brotherhood of humankind in the context of a new world order. In *Christian Principles Essential to a New World Order* (1919), Faunce stated: '"Thou shalt love thy neighbor" has deep philosophy behind it, for if you can truly love your neighbor, you can love anybody else in the world. But does not this respect mean simply the old doctrine of the brotherhood of man? Yes, and no. No, if by brotherhood is meant a warm and generous feeling which may vanish tomorrow when neutralized by a more primitive and powerful instinct. Yes, if we mean the clear understanding of a permanent fact. Brotherhood is not sentiment, it is intellectual understanding. Love is not in the last analysis emotion; it is perception -- perception of the values under the surface of another personality or behind the strange costume and speech of another people. We cannot like all men, but we can and must love them -- that is, perceive and appreciate their value and hold it as a precious possession. To place underneath the world-order the steady perception that all nations are members one of another is the first step in Christianizing the relation of states.' W.H.P. Faunce, *Christian Principles Essential to a New World Order* (New York: Association Press, 1919) 10.

[152] *Ibid.*

[153] Joseph H. Oldham, ed., *The Churches Survey Their Task*, 171.

[154] See *ibid.*

[155] Albert N. Keim, 'John Foster Dulles and the Protestant World Order Movement on the Eve of World War II,' *Journal of Church and State*, 3 (1978) 75; see also John Foster Dulles, 'As Seen by a Layman,' *Religion in Life* 7 (Winder 1938), 36-44.

[156] See Joseph H. Oldham, *Church, Community, and State*, Vol. 7: *The Universal*

*Church and the World of Nations*, 27-56.

[157] See Darril Hudson, *The Ecumenical Movement in World Affairs* (London: Weidenfeld & Nicolson, 1969) 159. Zimmern's relationship with one of the leading officers of the ecumenical movement has intermittently come to light. In the context of describing his impressions of the Oxford Conference, Marc Boegner, the president of the French Protestant Federation and co-founder of the World Council of Churches, wrote: 'Requests for this meeting had come from various quarters, and a number of eminent men were anxious to attend: John Foster Dulles; the Oxford professor Sir Alfred Zimmern, with whom I had long maintained a relationship of mutual trust and friendship ...' Marc Boegner, *The Long Road to Unity* (London: Collins, 1970) 130.

[158] Sir Alfred E. Zimmern, *Spiritual Values and World Affairs* (Oxford: Clarendon Press) 1939.

[159] See *ibid.*, 5.

[160] *Ibid.*, 48-49; see also 69-70.

[161] *Ibid.*, 1.

[162] *Ibid.*

[163] Zimmern did not identify his friend by name.

[164] See *ibid.*, 6.

[165] *Ibid.*

[166] *Ibid.*, 67.

[167] *Ibid.*, 69.

[168] *Ibid.*

[169] See *ibid.*, 41: 'Undoubtedly, the fact that the League of Nations had to be established within the traditional framework of the so-called Family of Nations - nations strong and weak, responsible and irresponsible, politically mature and politically immature, all brought in together seemingly on equal terms - was an important factor in its enfeeblement, one might even say, its corruption. It also accounts for the inherent weakness of what is called International Law - that is, the rules which are supposed to regulate the conduct towards one another of these unequal members of the so-called Family of States.'

[170] See *ibid.*, 104-105.

[171] *Ibid.*, 69.

[172] See *ibid.*, 70.

[173] *Ibid.*, 75. It is not surprising that Andrew R. Osborn, in *Christianity in Peril. The New World Order and the Churches* (1941), argued along the same lines as Zimmern did, even to the point of summarising in a lengthy passage the thesis of *Spiritual Values and World Affairs*: 'The nature of these difficulties has been indicated by Sir Alfred Zimmern, professor of International Relations in the University of Oxford, in the opening chapter of his book on *Spiritual Values and World Affairs*. He points out that in the last twenty years the churches in England have occupied themselves with international relations. He holds that this interest involves a corresponding responsibility on the part of church leaders and individual ministers to have accurate knowledge and to consider the probable effect of their proposals; otherwise their utterances will lack discrimination and wisdom. The author indicates clearly that the danger is a real one, that in the name of Christianity utterances may be made which will do harm instead of good. He points out that the field of international affairs is one "where ignorance and inexperience are peculiarly dangerous, and where amateurs, even gifted amateurs, can do untold harm," and adds: "It is open to doubt

whether the direct influence of the Churches on British foreign policy in the last twenty years has done more good than harm." As an instance of what he means he refers to a manifesto published in the *Manchester Guardian* of 21 January 1932. The signatories included sixteen bishops of the Church of England and a number of prominent Free Church ministers ...' Andrew Rhodes Osborn, *Christianity in Peril. The New World Order and the Churches* (New York: Oxford University Press, 1942) 137ff.

[174] See Sir Alfred E. Zimmern, *Spiritual Values and World Affairs*, 75-76.

[175] See *ibid.*, 75.

[176] *Ibid.*, 76.

[177] *Ibid.*

[178] *Ibid.*, 70.

[179] Joseph H. Oldham, ed., *The Churches Survey Their Task. The Report of the Conference at Oxford, July 1937, on Church, Community, and State*, 172-173.

[180] Philip Kerr (Lord Lothian), 'The Demonic Influence of National Sovereignty', in Joseph H. Oldham, *Church, Community, and State*, Vol. 7: *The Universal Church and the World of Nations* (London: George Allen & Unwin, 1938) 20.

[181] *Ibid.*, 3.

[182] *Ibid.*, 16.

[183] *Ibid.*, 18.

[184] *Ibid.*, 17.

[185] *Ibid.*, 17.

[186] *Ibid.*, 18.

[187] *Ibid.*

[188] *Ibid.*

[189] *Ibid.*

[190] *Ibid.*, 19.

[191] *Ibid.*, 18.

[192] *Ibid.*, 19.

[193] *Ibid.*, 19.

[194] *Ibid.*

[195] *Ibid.*, 23.

[196] *Ibid.*

[197] Joseph H. Oldham, ed., *The Churches Survey Their Task. The Report of the Conference at Oxford, July 1937, on Church, Community, and State*, 173-174.

[198] See chapter 4.

[199] William Paton, *The Church and the New Order*, 160 (emphasis in the original).

[200] *Ibid.*: 'He [Toynbee] goes on to point out ... that genuinely religious elements in Islam, Hinduism, Buddhism, and other religions offer hope of reaching an *ethos* overcoming the barriers of race, nationality and language.' In the last volume of his monumental *The Study of History* Toynbee confessed his pantheistic creed as follows: 'In claiming to possess a monopoly of the Divine Light, a church seems to me to be guilty of hybris. In denying that other religions may be God's chosen and sufficient channels for revealing Himself to some human souls, it seems to me to be guilty of blasphemy. If it is inadmissible to call oneself a Christian without holding these tenets, then I am not entitled to call myself a Christian; ... [that] "the heart of so great a mystery can never be reached by following one road only" - is an article in my creed which neither my head nor my heart will allow me to abandon.' Arnold J. Toynbee, *The Study of History*, Vol. VII (Oxford: Oxford University Press, 1947) 428.

201 *Ibid.*, 161-162.

202 *Ibid.*, 170.

203 John A. Mackay, *Oral History Collection*, 1965, 5-6.

204 Samuel M. Cavert, *Oral History Collection*, 1965, 5.

205 Darril Hudson, *The Ecumenical Movement in World Affairs*, 158.

206 Joseph H. Oldham, ed., *The Churches Survey Their Task. The Report of the Conference at Oxford, July 1937, on Church, Community, and State*, 174.

207 *Ibid.*

208 *Ibid.*

209 See *ibid.*, 175.

210 *Ibid.*, 176.

211 *Ibid.*, 177.

212 *Ibid.*

213 *Ibid.*

214 Darril Hudson, *The Ecumenical Movement in World Affairs*, 159.

215 Joseph H. Oldham, ed., *The Churches Survey Their Task. The Report of the Conference at Oxford, July 1937, on Church, Community, and State*, 187.

216 See e.g., Federal Council of Churches, *Federal Council Bulletin 24*, no. 1 (January 1941), New York, 6. Van Dusen said, for example, 'it was a milestone in Mr. Dulles' own intellectual development that any biographer ought to take serious account of.' Henry P. Van Dusen, *Oral History Collection*, 1965, 2-3.

217 Dulles' mentioned the influence of the conference upon him in each of the following published speeches: 'As Seen by a Layman'; 'The Churches' Contribution'; 'The Churches and World Order'; and 'Faith of Our Fathers.' Most of them are reprinted in Henry Van Dusen, ed., *The Spiritual Legacy of John Foster Dulles.*

218 John F. Dulles, 'The Churches and World Order,' *Theology Today* (October, 1944), 341-348; reprinted in Henry P. Van Dusen, ed., *The Spiritual Legacy of John Foster Dulles*, 23.

219 John F. Dulles, 'Faith of Our Fathers,' in Henry Van Dusen, ed., *The Spiritual Legacy of John Foster Dulles*, 7.

220 Margaret Dulles Edwards, *Oral History Collection*, 1965, 2.

221 Mark G. Toulouse, *The Transformation of John Foster Dulles*, 35. Allen Macy Dulles, John Foster's father, was a Presbyterian minister, whose theological convictions are described by Toulouse as follows: 'Foster's father, the Reverend Allen Macy Dulles, was a liberal Protestant minister, one who was greatly influenced by the theological trends of the day. The last two decades of the nineteenth century saw the development of the Social Gospel movement, which claimed a leadership that desired to awaken the social consciousness of the churches. Major figures included Washington Gladden (1836-1918), Francis Greenwood Peabody (1847-1936), Walter Rauschenbusch (1861-1918), and Josiah Strong (1847-1916). Strong's *Our Country: Its Possible Future and Present Crisis* was published in 1885. As probably the most influential book of the nineteenth-century Social Gospel genre, Strong's book represents Protestant liberalism's confidence in applied science and guided evolution. Further, Strong's ideas closely parallelled the political Progressivism developing at the same time. On the social side, the older Dulles was deeply influenced by the works of Strong and Rauschenbusch. On the theological side, as his own book *The True Church* (F.H. Revell, New York, 1907) bears witness, he was heavily indebted to the work of Ritschl, Harnack, and McGiffert.' Mark G. Toulouse, *The Transformation of John*

*Foster Dulles*, 4-5. In 1904, Reverend Dulles left his Presbyterian parsonage in Watertown to accept an appointment as the professor of Theism and Apologetics at Auburn Theological Seminary.

[222] Recounting his childhood experiences, Dulles, on a visit to Watertown, in 1952, remembered that his 'family had a rigorous schedule of worship. On thinking back, it seems to me that we averaged over 10 services a week. It is not surprising that that made an impression. It was an impression that was not always enjoyable at the time, but the older I have grown and the wider has been my experience, the more I have appreciated that early religious upbringing and have seen how relevant it is to the far-flung and changing scenes of life.' John F. Dulles, 'Address before the Watertown Chamber of Commerce,' 30 April 1952, *JFD Papers*, Box 307; see also John F. Dulles, 'Faith of Our Fathers,' Address at the First Presbyterian Church, Watertown, New York, Sunday, August 28, 1949, in Henry P. Van Dusen, ed., *The Spiritual Legacy of John Foster Dulles*, 5.

[223] John C. Bennett, interview with Mark G. Toulouse, as cited in Mark G. Toulouse, *The Transformation of John Foster Dulles*, 22.

[224] See Leonard Mosley, *Dulles*, 24.

[225] See John Robinson Beal, *John Foster Dulles*, 28; Mark G. Toulouse, *The Transformation of John Foster Dulles*, 6-7.

[226] Louis L. Gerson, *John Foster Dulles* (New York: Cooper Square Publishers, Inc., 1967) xi.

[227] Leonard Mosley, *Dulles*, 98.

[228] *Ibid.*

[229] See Townsend Hoopes, *The Devil and John Foster Dulles*, 34.

[230] *Ibid.*, 34-35.

[231] Hoopes describes this tendency in Dulles' social and professional life to establish himself early in his career as a successful lawyer and to become part of New York's high society; see *Ibid.*, 37. Besides his senior partnership at Sullivan & Cromwell, which employed 20 partners and 80 lawyers, John F. Dulles held directorships in fifteen companies at various times, including the Bank of New York, the American Bank Note Company, the American Agricultural Chemical Company, the North American Company, the Edison Company of Detroit, the International Nickel Company of Canada, and the British firm of Babcock and Wilcox; see Richard Goold-Adams, *The Time of Power. A Reappraisal of John Foster Dulles* (London: Weidenfeld and Nicolson, 1962) 41.

[232] Townsend Hoopes, *The Devil and John Foster Dulles*, 35. Hoopes states further that 'in the dozens of speeches he [Dulles] later made to church groups, in the many articles he wrote, and in his moralistic pronouncements as Secretary of State, there was rarely any reference to sin, no admission that ethical decisions are fraught with moral ambiguity, and no evidence of an understanding that the dimension of self-interest, self-preservation and self-righteousness is implicit in every exercise of power. But what he lacked in theology, he more than made up for in self-certitude; and as the years passed, and particularly following his categorical commitment to anti-Communism and his coming to power as Secretary of State, this quality seemed to transform itself into an awesome moral self-righteousness. The judgments continued to be those of Dulles, but he conveyed the sense of acting as the agent of a higher power, as if, someone said, he had "a pipeline to God". He left Jamison Parker, a young aide of his latter years at the State Department, with the strong impression that "to cross him

was to cross the deity.'" *Ibid.*

[233] Eleanor Lansing Dulles, *John Foster Dulles. The Last Year* (New York: Harcourt, Brace and World) 161.

[234] Michael A. Guhin states: 'Dulles took some interest in the international law courses at the Sorbonne, but found more interest in Henri Bergson's lectures in philosophy. Perhaps Bergson's concept of "creative evolution" - especially the idea that the intellect is merely one factor in biological adaptation serving a pragmatic function in the struggle for life - played a role in the strengthening of the young Princetonian's naturalistic leanings.' Michael A. Guhin, *John Foster Dulles*, 23.

[235] See Mark G. Toulouse, *The Transformation of John Foster Dulles*, 124; quoting from John F. Dulles, 'Peaceful Change,' *International Conciliation*, no. 369 (April 1941) 493.

[236] See the World Council of Churches, *Man's Disorder and God's Design*, Vol. V: *The First Assembly of the World Council of Churches* (New York: Harper and Brothers, 1949) 36-39. Dulles actually delivered two addresses, the first made to the plenary session and the second immediately following the speech of Professor Josef L. Hromadka of Prague. Both speeches marked 'a high point of interest' for the Assembly.

[237] Albert N. Keim, 'John Foster Dulles and the Federal Council of Churches of Christ, 1937-1949,' 18-19. See also Mark G. Toulouse, *The Transformation of John Foster Dulles*, 124. In a footnote Toulouse states that 'one can find the basis for much of what Dulles wrote concerning change in Henri Bergson, *Creative Evolution*, trans. Arthur Michel (New York: Henry Holt and Company, 1911).' Bergson's teaching must be seen as one of the most substantial and lasting influences on Dulles' mind helping him to form a distinct philosophy of life.

[238] John F. Dulles, 'The Christian Citizen in a Changing World,' in The World Council of Churches, *Man's Disorder and God's Design*, Vol. IV: *The Church and the International Disorder* (New York: Harper and Brothers, 1948) 73-114.

[239] See John R. Beal, *John Foster Dulles*, 51.

[240] John F. Dulles, 'Criticisms of Mr. Hatch's Report on War,' 1924, 6, *JFD Papers*.

[241] Mark G. Toulouse, *The Transformation of John Foster Dulles*, 25.

[242] See letter, 'Mother' to 'Foster', December, 1918, *JFD Papers*.

[243] Henry P. Van Dusen remembered that a minister once suggested to Dulles: 'Foster, your mother must have been terribly disappointed when you didn't become a minister.' 'Nearly broke her heart,' was his reply. See Henry P. Van Dusen, *Oral History Collection*, 1965, 13.

[244] Thomas E. Dewey was an influential member of the Council on Foreign Relations for many years. As the presidential candidate of the Republican Party he was the unsuccessful opponent of Franklin D. Roosevelt and Harry S. Truman at the elections of 1944 and 1948, respectively.

[245] Thomas E. Dewey, *Oral History Collection*, 1965, 10; as cited in Townsend Hoopes, *The Devil and John Foster Dulles*, 35.

[246] For details of the relationship between Thomas E. Dewey and John F. Dulles, see the following articles: John Chamberlain, 'John Foster Dulles. A Wilsonian at Versailles, This Famous Lawyer May Be Dewey's Secretary of State,' *Life* XVII (21 August 1944) 96; Forrest Davis, *The Saturday Evening Post*, CCXVII (September 9, 1944) 25 and *ibid.*, (September 16, 1944) 20; James B. Reston, 'John Foster Dulles and

His Foreign Policy,' *Life*, XXV (October 4, 1948) 131-132; Alden Hatch, 'The Men Around Dewey,' *Harper's Magazine*, CXCVII (October, 1948) 42-43. It should be noted, however, that all of these accounts differ on the actual origins of the relationship, but they agree on its intimacy from about 1937 on.

[247] Toulouse contests Dewey's allegation that Dulles was an atheist for some years: 'Some of the speculation that he [Dulles] had nothing to do with religious activities until around 1937 is based upon Thomas Dewey's statement in 1965 that, so far as he knew, Dulles spent many of these years as an atheist. The evidence just does not support Dewey's assumption, however.' Mark G. Toulouse, *The Transformation of John Foster Dulles*, 9.

[248] Henry P. Van Dusen believed that during the 1920s Dulles was an 'inactive' Presbyterian layman and that the Oxford Conference in 1937 not only stimulated Dulles' interest in working in the church but also represented a recovery of his faith. See Henry P. Van Dusen, *Oral History Collection*, 1965, 3-4.

[249] John F. Dulles, 'As Seen by a Layman,' *Religion in Life* VII (Winter, 1938) 36; in Henry P. Van Dusen, ed., *The Spiritual Legacy of John Foster Dulles*, 13. See also Mark G. Toulouse, *The Transformation of John Foster Dulles*, 9.

[250] See especially the sermons published in Henry P. Van Dusen, ed., *The Spiritual Legacy of John Foster Dulles*, which presumably contain his most spiritual addresses. Instead, they are replete with political statements devoid of spiritual content which is distinctly Christian in origin.

[251] Mark G. Toulouse, *The Transformation of John Foster Dulles*, 8, quoting Avery Dulles, interview, conducted by Philip A. Crowl, 1966.

[252] See statement by Milton Mayer in U.S. Congress, Senate Hearings before the Committee on Foreign Relations, *North Atlantic Treaty*, 81st Congress, 1st Session (Washington, D.C.: Government Printing Office, 1949) 825.

[253] The present author follows E. Raymond Platig's use of the word 'humanist', as a name for that type of self-realisationist ethical thinker whose ethic is naturalistic in origin. Platig refers to Lucius Gavin's article, 'Major Ethical Viewpoints', in *Encyclopedia of Morals*, Vergilius Ferm, ed. (New York: Philosophical Library, 1956) 317-318, to point out that the term 'Christian humanist' is, in the view of orthodox Christianity, self-contradictory and necessitates the modifier 'so-called'. Platig continues: 'The more generous orthodox Christians might, therefore, describe Dulles as a so-called Christian humanist and the less generous might accuse him of being a humanist masquerading behind convenient Christian categories. The fact that Dulles' earlier ethical thought was naturalistic rather than theological would add some weight to this charge. On the other hand, those who claim to be both idealistic perfectionists and Christians would find little reason to deny the Christian label to Mr. Dulles' position. Such Christians, however, would probably agree that there is nothing uniquely Christian about their idealistic perfectionism, but rather that they share the essentials of their ethical position with pure humanists. In a sense, Dulles makes this same point when he finds evidence of the moral law in all great religions (and even outside of any religious framework) ...' E. Raymond Platig, 'John Foster Dulles. A Study of His Political and Moral Thought Prior to 1953 with Special Emphasis on International Relations,' dissertation, University of Chicago, 1957, 161.

[254] John Coleman Bennett, *Oral History Collection*, 1965, 23; see also Townsend Hoopes, *The Devil and John Foster Dulles*, 35.

[255] See Townsend Hoopes, *The Devil and John Foster Dulles*, 35.

[256] E. Raymond Platig, 'John Foster Dulles,' 131.

[257] It might be of interest to note that Townsend Hoopes, a fellow-member with Dulles in the Council on Foreign Relations for many years, does not even once refer to the Council in his 562-page book.

[258] Townsend Hoopes, *The Devil and John Foster Dulles*, 35.

[259] Eleanor Lansing Dulles stated in an interview with Mark G. Toulouse that her oldest brother was mostly motivated in his life by a faith in 'the force of good', not by any set of Christian doctrines: 'I have never known how much Foster went along with the doctrines of the church - the Apostles Creed, that kind of thing. I've never known. It's hard to know ... But there was something about the atmosphere of religion in the family that carried over to us in varying degrees - and to Foster, I think more than the rest of us probably - that there was this force for good, and if it's a force for good, and if you want to be good, you associate yourself with it - and that's going to influence your life. Whatever the formula he adopted, it meant a good deal to him. And I just don't know the terms of this formula. I don't remember that we ever discussed it among ourselves after we were adults.' Mark G. Toulouse, *The Transformation of John Foster Dulles*, 8, 9.

[260] Townsend Hoopes, *The Devil and John Foster Dulles*, 35.

[261] *Ibid.*, 34.

[262] John F. Dulles, 'World Brotherhood Through the State,' in Henry P. Van Dusen, ed., *The Spiritual Legacy of John Foster Dulles*, 114; originally published in *Vital Speeches of the Day*, Vol. XII (October 1, 1946) 744ff. In this address Dulles repeatedly equated 'Christ's Gospel' with 'human welfare'. At another occasion he wrote that 'free societies ... best reflect the Christian concept of the nature of man and his relationship to God and to fellow man. They best assure progressive peaceful change to what may, from time to time, seem the greatest good of the greatest number.' John F. Dulles, 'The Task of World Peace,' *The Commercial and Financial Chronicle*, CLXVI (August 21, 1947) 749.

[263] John F. Dulles, 'World Brotherhood Through the State,' in Henry P. Van Dusen, ed., *The Spiritual Legacy of John Foster Dulles*, 116.

[264] *Ibid.*

[265] The conference was held under the auspices of the World Council of Churches (in the process of formation) and the International Missionary Council; see Federal Council of Churches, *Biennial Report* (1946), New York, 61; *New York Times*, August 4-8, 1946, *passim*; and Norman Goodall, *The Ecumenical Movement* (London: Oxford University Press, 1961) 94. See Commission of the Churches on International Affairs, *Annual Reports*, London; deposited at the British Library; shelfmark: P.P.1014 [13 volumes]. The membership list is printed in each volume, except the first.

[266] John F. Dulles, 'World Brotherhood Through the State,' in Henry P. Van Dusen, ed., *The Spiritual Legacy of John Foster Dulles*, 120. The *New York Times* of February 25, 1946, reported the purpose of the Commission: 'To stimulate the churches of all nations to a more vigorous expression of the demand of the Christian conscience in relation to the political policies of governments.' On July 30, 1946, the same newspaper quoted John Foster Dulles as follows: 'We are aiming at a top organization [Commission of the Churches on International Affairs], international in character, to coordinate the thinking and action of Protestant denominations through their national organization. We will attempt to make it do for religion what labor does through the World Federation of Trade Unions.'

[267] *Ibid.*

[268] See Federal Council of Churches, 'Progress Report by New Commission on World Affairs,' *Federal Council Bulletin* 30, no. 1 (January, 1947), New York, 16.

[269] John F. Dulles, 'World Brotherhood Through the State,' in Henry P. Van Dusen, ed., *The Spiritual Legacy of John Foster Dulles*, 120.

[270] John F. Dulles, 'Draft Article', April 29, 1942, 5, *JFD Papers*.

[271] John F. Dulles, 'Can Freedom Win', Address delivered at St. Lawrence University on June 8, 1952, 7, *JFD Papers*. In 1947, Dulles stated that 'the moral law, happily, is a universal law. It is reflected by many great religions. Even without religion there is general agreement on "right" and "wrong" in their crude and obvious aspects ... But Christians believe that, through Christ, the moral law has been revealed with unique clarity.' John F. Dulles, 'The Task of World Peace', *The Commercial and Financial Chronicle*, CLXVI (August 21, 1947) 751; see also John F. Dulles, 'Moral Leadership', *Vital Speeches of the Day*, XIV (September 15, 1948) 708; John F. Dulles, 'U.S. Solicits Opinions of American Republics on Japanese Settlement', *The Department of State Bulletin*, XXIV (April 16, 1951) 617; John F. Dulles, 'A Policy of Boldness', *Life* XXXII (May 19, 1952) 154.

[272] John F. Dulles, Speech upon receiving the Peace Medal of St. Francis, February 20, 1952, 1, *JFD Papers*. See also John F. Dulles, *War and Peace*, 187.

[273] In June 1950 at the suggestion of Paul Hoffman the National Conference of Christians and Jews founded World Brotherhood at UNESCO House in Paris, France. The officers of World Brotherhood were Konrad Adenauer (German Chancellor), William Benton (U.S. Senator; Assistant Secretary of State, Trustee and Vice President of University of Chicago*)*, Arthur H. Compton (General Chairman of World Brotherhood; Nobel Prize in Physics [1927]; Co-chairman of National Conference of Christians and Jews; professor at Washington University), Paul Henri Spaak (NATO Secretary General), Paul G. Hoffman, Herbert H. Lehman (U.S. Senator), John J. McCloy (Chairman of Chase Manhattan Bank), and Adlai Stevenson (U.S. United Nations Ambassador). Other members and supporters of World Brotherhood included: President Eisenhower; John Foster Dulles; Allen W. Dulles (CIA director); Henry R. Luce (owner of *Time* magazine and *Life*); President John F. Kennedy; and Supreme Court Justice Earl Warren.

[274] See John F. Dulles, 'The Moral Foundation of the United Nations,' in Henry P. Van Dusen, ed., *The Spiritual Legacy of John Foster Dulles*, 131: 'The success of the United Nations have been largely due to those throughout the world who believe that there is a God, a divine Creator of us all; that he has prescribed moral principles which undergird this world with an ultimate authority equal to that of physical law; that this moral law is one which every man can know if only he opens his heart to what God has revealed; that these moral principles enjoin not merely love and respect of the Creator but also love and respect for fellow man, because each individual embodies some element of the Divine; and that moral principles should also govern the conduct of nations ... Thus, as we gather here as representatives of many faiths held throughout the world, we can find much ground for satisfaction. It has been demonstrated that the religious people of the world can generate the motive power required to vitalize a world organization by providing it with principles which are guiding not merely in theory but in fact.'

[275] E. Raymond Platig asserts 'that what we called Dulles' religious conversion was intellectual in nature.' It was a natural outgrowth of Dulles' previous commitment

to a utilitarian ethic. He changed his former belief about the role of the Christian faith in a modern society, because, after Oxford, he came to realise that 'Christianity was socially useful for purposes of universal human welfare.' E. Raymond Platig, 'John Foster Dulles,' 130, 131. This meant that Dulles saw the main purpose of Christianity in bringing happiness and prosperity to the human race; see John F. Dulles, *War, Peace and Change*, 118.

[276] See John F. Dulles, 'The Faith of Our Fathers,' in Henry P. Van Dusen, ed., *The Spiritual Legacy of John Foster Dulles*, 7: 'From then on [Oxford Conference] I began to work closely with religious groups - Protestant, Catholic, and Jewish - for I had come to believe that, of all groups, they could make the greatest contribution to world order. Most of all I worked with the Commission on a Just and Durable Peace of the Federal Council of the Churches of Christ in America.'

[277] Joseph H. Oldham, ed., *The Churches Survey Their Task. The Report of the Conference at Oxford, July 1937, on Church, Community, and State*, 175.

[278] See E. Raymond Platig, 'John Foster Dulles,' 322.

[279] This assessment concurs with that of John M. Mulder, in 'The Moral Wold of John Foster Dulles: A Presbyterian Layman and International Affairs, *Journal of Presbyterian History*, 49:2 (Summer, 1971), 161, fn. 16.

[280] See Will Herberg, *Protestant-Catholic-Jew. An Essay in American Religious Sociology* (New York: Doubleday & Co., 1955) 59, 63-64; and also Samuel McCrea Cavert, *The American Churches in the Ecumenical Movement 1900-1968*, 189, 190. Cavert refers to successive editions of *The Yearbook of American Churches*, edited by Benson Y. Landis, National Council of Churches, New York, especially the editions of 1952, 254-265, and 1955, 296.

[281] See Albert N. Keim, 'John Foster Dulles and the Federal Council of Churches of Christ, 1937-1949,' 13, 14: 'The [Oxford] conference was decisive in Dulles' evolution as a churchmen. He came away convinced that the church was peculiarly qualified to promote solutions to the outstanding world order problems besetting mankind. The church's common faith and common hope, coupled with its universal character, made it potentially at least, a unique vehicle to challenge the petty particularities of nation and culture. Its vision of world brotherhood provided precisely that unifying principle which the world lacked. The church, properly mobilized, with its loyalty centered on universal and transcendent principles, could become a powerful antidote to the rampaging nationalism threatening mankind.' See also John F. Dulles, 'As Seen by a Layman,' *Religion in Life*, 9.

[282] Joseph H. Oldham, ed., *The Churches Survey Their Task. The Report of the Conference at Oxford, July 1937, on Church, Community, and State*, chapter V: 'The Universal Church and the World of Nations,' Section II, 'The Oecumenical Church,' 169.

[283] Samuel Z. Batten, *New World Order* (New York: American Baptist Publishing Society, 1919) 116. On page 118 Batten wrote the following: 'In our time humanity is facing the question of an organization of the nations in a society of states. It is becoming clear that humanity is one, that the nations are the interrelated and interdependent members of one body, and that each nation is under obligation to take thought for the things of others, and to look not alone on the things of self but also on the things of others. It is necessary therefore for the nations that believe in world humanity and international justice to express their common life in some form of international organization. There is no such thing as absolute liberty for the individual;

he is a part of society, and must be willing to accept his place in the social order and consent to have his interests measured by the welfare of all. There is no more justice for the claim of absolute sovereignty on the part of a nation than on the part of an individual. "Absolute sovereignty," says a suggestive writer, "means absolute anarchy." The one nation must therefore think of itself as a part of humanity and learn to live with others in terms of justice and peace; it must realize that nothing can be really good for itself which is evil to the rest; it must come to perceive that whatever policy blesses all blesses each.'

[284] James H. Nichols, *Democracy and the Churches* (Philadelphia: The Westminster Press, 1951) 235; see also Ruth Rouse & Stephen Charles Neill, eds., *A History of the Ecumenical Movement 1517-1948* (London: SPCK, 1967) 591.

# 4

# THE PROMISE OF A NEW SOCIAL ORDER

In the early 1930s the Federal Council of Churches (FCC) became much more articulate in expressing its aspirations to revive the ecumenical spirit among the different denominations in America. Despite the Council's official policy to co-operate with its constituent churches primarily on the basis of a common purpose, the general emphasis of interdenominational collaboration was increasingly placed on establishing an organic union of participating churches. This development of closer union had always been tacitly pursued by the leadership of the FCC and was part of the vision of its more progressive members. Initially, most of the progress of ecumenical interaction was accomplished by the leaders of the Council, as they carried on their co-operative work among missionary and educational agencies. Yet functional solidarity in the work of the denominations before 1930 was still limited to isolated joint ventures. Contrary to the expectations of most ecumenical sceptics, however, the interest in organic unity among various denominations was rekindled during the 1930s. This was a surprising turn of events, as it had appeared that the co-operative idea had exhausted itself before 1932 by the sheer impracticality of its design and purpose.


4.1     The New Enthusiasm for Organic Unity

A series of favourable circumstances precipitated a new eagerness among the churches to seek organic unity. The first of these was the declining importance of doctrinal distinctiveness among denominations. Liberal theology, gradually permeating the American ecclesiastical scene, reduced interest in sectarian peculiarities and cleared the way for improved interdenominational relations. Doctrinal indifference became such a general phenomenon that it brought about organic mergers of churches on an increasing scale. Several important church unions took place in the 1930s. This happened first among churches of similar doctrinal and ecclesiastical backgrounds and then among churches of very different backgrounds. The Congregational churches and a group of Christian churches decided in 1931 to form the Congregational Christian denomination. In 1934 the Evangelical Synod and the Reformed Church in the United States joined hands in establishing the Evangelical and Reformed Church.[1] The most memorable church unification occurred in 1939, when the Methodist Episcopal Church united with the Methodist Episcopal Church South and the Methodist Protestant Church to form the Methodist Church. At that time this was the largest single church merger in American church history.[2]

After 1932 the FCC was less reticent about publicly encouraging such mergers than it had been before 1930. The ecumenical movement in America began to assume an aggressive posture in encouraging and guiding the trend for church union. In the process of extending its influence the Council embarked on a triumphalist journey, shaping the ecclesiastical landscape in America and around the world according to its own ecumenical design. It was to leave indelible imprints on the pages of modern church history. The FCC had finally come to maturity.

As a clear sign of future intentions, the leadership of the Council took a bold stand for the cause of ecumenism at the Indianapolis quadrennial in 1932. In his plenary speech the president of the Council, Bishop Francis J. McConnell[3], delineated the strategy of organic union among the American churches: 'If we keep going steadily in this direction [toward a larger Christian unity], we shall eventually discover that we have union and do not have to create it. All that will be necessary will be to ratify something that has come into being without artificial promotion.'[4] Sending out the directive to his ecclesiastical constituency, McConnell set out to conquer his country for the ecumenical ideal. This strategy was to become increasingly popular in succeeding interdenominational meetings.

The concept of achieving a union of churches as a by-product of the existence and activities of the Council was not an original contribution of McConnell. It had been inherent in the program of the ecumenical movement from its beginning. Samuel McCrea Cavert, for example, bore witness to the Council's penetrating and ongoing influence on both its constituent churches and other Protestant denominations, as he stated:

> Thoughtful observers increasingly agree that the Federal Council has abundantly demonstrated its indispensability to the effectiveness of Protestantism, providing a necessary centre of collective activity and a united leadership in the most crucial, moral and spiritual problems confronting the nation and the world.[5]

And then he added this insight: 'While itself not an agency for organic union, the Federal Council of Churches is constantly creating the conditions out of which union can naturally come.'[6]

The February issue of the *Christian Herald* (1933) declared that the FCC was the greatest collective achievement of North American Protestantism. It seemed to imply that organic unity could only become a reality as the concomitant of a growing unity of action. If such purposeful action failed to materialise, however, the work of organised Christianity could be profoundly hindered in many fields.[7]

On the occasion of the Council's twenty-fifth anniversary (1933) the editor of the *Christian Century* mentioned succinctly what he perceived as the causes for the irrefutable demise of the denominational missionary enterprise; 'the five times too many churches, the too many ministers and theological seminaries, and the too many missionary societies.' These facts, he claimed, presented enough evidence to convince everybody that the churches were being forced into 'all sorts of irrelevant and unspiritual stunts and vices in order to keep going.' In his concluding remarks he postulated: 'Surely the Federal Council will face this condition, surely it will not meet and sojourn again without making a constructive proposal for a united administration of Christian mission – not by a board, as proposed by the *Laymen's Report*, but by a united church.'[8]

The Christian Century surmised that the efforts of the Council, as a unifying agency, would have been more successful had it not been for the pathetic diversification and self-determination of the constituent churches. The realisation that the Council was merely the creation of some twenty eight denominations (as of 1933), and could not independently surpass the limitations of denominationalism was a sobering thought to the ecumenical enthusiasts of the religious journal.

The *Christian Century* assumed the self-appointed task of challenging the FCC to become more determined in seeking Christian unity. In 1935 it published two articles, one by E. Stanley Jones and the other by Finis Idleman, insisting on a comprehensive restructuring of Protestantism.[9] Idleman called on the Council to create a department of Christianity, claiming that in 1935 the situation of the churches would require such assertive action.

E. Stanley Jones fervently pleaded for the confederation of several denominations as the Church of Christ in America, which would consist of various branches such as the Baptist, Methodist, Presbyterian, and Episcopal.[10] He discarded the suggestion, falsely attributed to him, that he wanted to see the various denominations become a monolithic entity. He insisted that his plan was calling for a federal union, not a federation.[11] What he envisioned was a union of all Protestant churches based on the model of the U.S. Constitution of 1787. The various branches would come together on the simple doctrinal basis found in Matthew 16:16-19. He defended his proposal on the grounds of the urgent necessity to unite, in view of the task confronting the church.[12]

This plan was far more sweeping in its intent than any previous proposal made by a representative of the FCC. Jones was certainly aware that his plan would elicit adverse reactions from denominational sources. In the midst of mounting opposition to his radical idea, Jones tried to calm the fears of his disputants by asserting that his plan would not require anyone to give up what was fundamentally good in any branch, but each would give its good to the best.[13]

Yet Jones was less than candid in his statements. The whole plan rested upon an indifference to the development of Christian theology from the Council of Nicea onwards, and it actually called upon the creedal churches, the Presbyterian and the Lutheran, for example, to surrender the heritage of the Reformation. Loyalty to biblical theology was to bow to loyalty to unity for the sake of unity. Yet, despite these drastic implications, Jones was not prepared to retract his proposal. He adamantly defended the principle of federal union.

In 1937 the executive committee of the FCC created the Commission on Christian Unity, stating that such an operation was the natural outcome of the national preaching mission.[14] It was more a docile response to the pleas of the *Christian Century* and E. Stanley Jones and to the call of the Asbury biennial of December 5, 1936. The *Christian Century* greeted the arrival of the Commission with an optimistic, but still moderate, enthusiasm.[15]

The Commission on Christian Unity was actually organised and began to function in September 1937. By March 1938 it was able to give its first report on what had been accomplished in promoting unity among the churches.[16] In this report to the Council the Commission analysed the various proposals for church union that had been brought forward and found them sadly lacking in substance and realism.[17] It was particularly critical of E. Stanley Jones's plan because it retained in the united church the denominational structure in the form of branches. The committee agreed that this approach, which allowed the several churches to retain their own doctrinal positions, forms of worship, and methods of government, was not compatible with the kind of unity discussed at the Edinburgh Conference on Faith and Order (1937). The report denied that there was a basic disagreement between those who insisted on the definite authority of the Scriptures for ordering the creeds and worship of the church, and those who insisted on the individual experience of divine grace as the definitive norm in these matters. The committee of the Commission came to the conclusion that 'we have not reached the time in the United States when any plan for union is satisfactory.'[18]

The matter of unity and union came up again in 1939 when the Commission on Christian Unity presented another report to the executive committee as a response to a request from the 1938 General Assembly of the Presbyterian Church, USA, asking for advice on the E. Stanley Jones plan for church union and a recommendation for 'fuller unity in Christian service'.

In answer to this request the executive committee gave the recommendation that, in view of the heartening progress being made in the reorganisation of the World Council of Churches (in the process of formation), and in view of the recent unification of certain denominations and the prospective mergers of others, any comprehensive effort for American church unity should be postponed until such issues as 'the nature of the church' were settled. The executive committee also decreed that the unity contemplated under the plan formulated by Stanley Jones could be realised through an increasing co-operation with the FCC.[19]

In 1941 the FCC went on record as agreeing with the request of the General Assembly of the Presbyterian Church, USA, of May 1938 for greater unity of planning and activity in the area of home missions.[20] Besides the emphasis of the FCC in promoting Christian unity, another equally important domestic event was the restructuring of the Federal Council.


4.2    The Restructuring of the Federal Council

In preparation for the Council's expanded responsibilities in an age of social chaos, many influential ecclesiastics insisted on a thorough overhaul of its organisation, to enable it to meet the new challenges of the day. This reorganisation of the structure of the Council was the task of the 1932 quadrennial, which met at Indianapolis in December, just one month after Roosevelt's election victory over the incumbent Herbert Hoover. It proved to be the most consequential meeting of the Council after the Philadelphia conference of 1908, and would remain so until the founding conference of the National Council of Churches in 1950. The process of reorganisation was carefully pursued over a period of four years. At the Rochester quadrennial of 1928 a special committee was commissioned to study the function and structure of the FCC and present its findings in 1932.[21] Sweeping changes were introduced as a result of this committee's recommendations. The Council added five new areas of ministry to those which were already part of its work.[22] The new areas were: (1) evangelising the churches; (2) cultivating the devotional life of church members; (3) putting a stronger emphasis on Christian education as the basis of a healthy social consciousness; (4) offering its service to the churches to fight the social injustice of the day and, most importantly of all, (5) eliminating war as an instrument of national policy by establishing a new world order.[23] This committee also recommended that it would be advantageous to the Council if its popular image were perceived as that of representative and not a hierarchical body. It should be noted, however, that in spite of the insistence of this committee that the FCC should give the appearance of being a representative body and not a hierarchical one, revision of its organisation resulted in more centralisation, and also placed greater authority into the hands of the larger denominations, which were decidedly the most liberal members of the Council. The conservative voice was reduced to a whisper as a result of this reorganisation.

Furthermore, it was suggested that the Council should fulfill two distinct functions in the area of public relations: (1) witnessing on moral issues on which there was sufficient common agreement to make a pronouncement possible, and (2) studying and discussing the issues on which there was insufficient common accord, and publishing the results of such discussions.[24]

The special committee also urged the Council to adopt the earlier report of the executive committee on restructuring. The report was immediately adopted. According to its stipulations, three members from each of the constituent denominations would henceforth be members of the Council, and each denomination would also be entitled to one additional member for every one hundred thousand members. The interval between the Council's general meetings was shortened from four to two years. It was felt that the Administrative Committee had outlived its usefulness. Appropriate action was taken to terminate its function. The executive committee was reconstituted to be composed of two delegates from each denomination and one additional delegate for each church possessing fifty thousand members over the first five hundred thousand.

In 1932 the Federal Council's Commission on Goodwill Between Christians and Jews, which was founded in 1922, became an independent organisation. This kind of organisational change, however, occurred only a few times in the history of the Council. In 1935 a committee was created to nominate and supervise the chaplains in the federal penitentiaries; in 1937 Seward Hiltner was named as its chairman and charged with obtaining for these positions men who had training not only in theology but in psychology and sociology as well. That year, 1937, the Committee on Religion and Mental Health was created.

In 1940 the Council itself was reorganised, the first real change since the reorganisation of 1932. At the Atlantic City biennial it was decided that each denomination could also appoint laymen, but the total number of laymen could not exceed one third of the total number of delegates. There was also a provision that the churches could name up to twelve additional delegates, but they were to be designated as representatives of state and local councils of churches. This last innovation was part of a concrete program designed to strengthen the FCC at the grassroots level and give it wider popular appeal and support.

Of greater importance during this decade was the development of the Council's public image and denominational support. Although it began the era with the loss of the Presbyterian Church, U.S.A., from its membership, which marked the most important defection in the Council's history from 1908 to 1950, its record was still one of growth in membership. The increase in denominational membership would have been more impressive if the mergers between constituent Council members, previously referred to, had not occurred.

Although the Church of God withdrew from membership in 1933 because of the arrangements favoured by the FCC in regard to the establishment of new congregations, this was the last defection during the decade. In 1933 the recently formed United Church of Canada became an affiliate member. Five years later, in 1938, the Syrian Orthodox Church joined, the first non-Protestant church to do so, thus changing the original nature and purpose of the

Council. In 1940 the Protestant Episcopal Church entered into full membership, and the same year overtures were made by the Presbyterian Church, U.S.A. to rejoin the Council. In 1940 there were twenty constituent members of the Council representing a total membership of about twenty million people.

The restructuring of the FCC went hand in hand with a revision of the Social Creed of 1908. The Church leaders were convinced that this Creed had lost its function as an appropriate expression of the Council's social and economic philosophy. It no longer served its original purpose of confronting the economic and social problems in American society at large.


4.3     The Social Creed of 1932

The most significant event of the Indianapolis quadrennial was the endorsement of the Social Creed of 1932. This was the result of a series of earlier efforts of the FCC to prepare the ground for such a development. In 1919 Samuel Z. Batten, an American Baptist pastor and leader of the FCC, had already proclaimed the inception of a new social order as the manifestation of God's kingdom on earth. He stated:

> Upon the men of this time is breaking the light of a new social order. The outstanding fact of today is the rediscovery of the kingdom of God. To the world this comes almost as a new revelation from heaven. For eighteen hundred years men have believed in this kingdom and have prayed for its coming; but now at last conception of its meaning becomes larger and more true. We are coming to see that the kingdom of God in Christ's conception never means anything less than a righteous human society on earth. Christ has come, not to condemn the world, but to save the world. He has come to reveal a kingdom in heaven and to realize a kingdom on earth. He has come not alone to save people out of the world and fill them for a far-away heaven; but to make a heaven here. He has come not to patch up human society and make the world a little less intolerable for men; but to make all things new and to create a new social order.[25]

In the early 1930s, the reality of a righteous human society on earth was still a long way off from what Batten had envisioned. Several articles in the *Federal Council Bulletin* during 1932, therefore, began to discuss the need to revise the outdated Social Creed of 1908. Toyohiko Kagawa, a Japanese churchman, asserted in the January issue that the propagation of the Christian gospel must include the total reconstruction of society. The Church should aspire to nothing less than the constitution of Christian collectivism. 'It is evident,' he wrote, 'that we must Christianise industry and get rid of the acquisitive motive in economic life. It seems to me that we cannot solve our problems on the basis of individualism.'[26] His idea was to replace the supposedly defunct capitalist system with a number of Christian co-operatives

151

modelled after the pattern of the medieval guild system. The FCC was enthused about Kagawa's proposal and incorporated it (in a modified form) in its revised version of the Social Creed.

The Social Creed of 1932 adopted at Indianapolis declared that the churches should stand for: 1. Practical application of the Christian principle of social well-being to the acquisition and use of wealth, subordinating speculation and the profit motive to the creative and co-operative spirit. 2. Social planning and control of the credit and monetary systems and the economic processes for the common good. 3. The right of all to the opportunity for self-maintenance; a wider and fairer distribution of wealth; a living wage, as a minimum, and above this a just and fair share for the worker in the products of industry and agriculture. 4. Safeguarding of all workers, urban and rural, against harmful conditions of labour and occupational injury and disease. 5. Social insurance against sickness, accident, want in old age and unemployment. 6. Reduction of hours of labour as the general productivity of industry increases; release from employment at least one day in seven, with a shorter working week in prospect. 7. Such special regulations of the conditions of work of women as shall safeguard their welfare and that of the family and the community. 8. The right of employees and employers alike to organise for collective bargaining and social action; protection of both in the exercise of this right; the obligation of both to work for the public good; encouragement of co-operatives and other organisations among farmers and other groups. 9. Abolition of child labour; adequate provision for the protection, education, spiritual nurture and wholesome recreation of every child. 10. Protection of the family by the single standard of purity; educational preparation for marriage, home-making and parenthood. 11. Economic justice for the farmer in legislation, financing, transportation and the price of farm products as compared with the cost of machinery and other commodities. 12. Extension of the cultural opportunities and social services now enjoyed by urban populations to the farm family. 13. Protection of the individual and society from the social, economic and moral waste of any traffic in intoxicants and habit-forming drugs. 14. Application of the Christian principle of redemption in the treatment of offenders, reform of penal and correctional methods and institutions, and of criminal court procedure. 15. Justice and equal rights for all, mutual goodwill and co-operation among racial, economic and religious groups. 16. Repudiation of war, drastic reduction of armaments, participation of international agencies for the peaceable settlement of all controversies; the building of a co-operative world order. 17. Recognition and maintenance of the rights and responsibilities of free speech, free assembly, and free press; the encouragement of free communication of mind with mind as essential to the discovery of truth.[27] The creed closed with an appeal for a new social order in a new age of faith.[28]

The Social Creed of 1932 saw, in the union of Churches, the outward expression of a collectivist Protestantism. Many followers in the social-gospel movement called fervently for the realisation of the kingdom of God. They were convinced that a unified front of Protestant Churches would be necessary, even essential, to build this kingdom, as defined by Walter Rauschenbusch and his successors.

The course which the Council chose in pursuing its social agenda was outlined later that year in another article, 'The Spiritual Challenge of the Economic Crisis.'[29] The article conceded that the church's responsibility did not include the task to define an industrial policy or structure for a new economic order, even though this is what it set out to do. The author, a certain Reverend William Boddy of the First Presbyterian Church of Chicago, declared: 'It seems too that there is a new imperative lacing the Cross, not as a dogma of theology, not as the source ... of vesper hymns, but as a way of life ... In short, the church in this day must teach that Jesus had undertaken nothing less than changing man over the whole range of his life, from an acquisitive to a contributive being.'[30]

The Commission on the Church and Social Service spearheaded the campaign for a Christian collectivism among the American public by preparing a message which was delivered on Labour Day 1932. This message directly advocated a redistribution of wealth in the United States and also among the nations of the world. It asserted that only by the intelligent regulation and management of finance, credit, and industry could the kingdom of God be advanced for the common good. It pleaded for the extension of minimum-wage laws, and the payment of the highest wages possible in order to achieve the redistribution of wealth and to realise the kingdom of God.[31]

It became clear that the thinking of a large segment of the leadership of the Council was dominated by political and economic idealism. The proliferation of theological liberalism was equally prominent among the same group of clerics.

There can be no doubt that the social affirmations of 1932 were, on the surface, more open in their demand for a collectivist society in America than the original creed of 1908. A detailed study of the original document reveals, however, that it foreshadowed most of the statements of 1932. The original differed from its revised form in that it did not intend to subordinate the profit motive to a new co-operative spirit and it did not openly call for the collective control of the economic processes, credit and finance for the common good. Yet the idea of collectivism had certainly formed the basis of the Social Creed of 1908.

The new Social Creed mirrored in many aspects the proposals of the New Deal which, in turn, served as a platform on which the Council would erect its many projects designed to meet the social and economic crisis of the 1930s. The statement of 1932 enabled the FCC to welcome Roosevelt's radical policies with open arms, because the economic conditions of 1932 were much more favourable for expressing the idealism inherent in the earlier version.[32] The *Journal of Religious Education* and the *Christian Endeavour World Commonweal* (Roman Catholic) opined that the Social Creed of 1932 made great progress towards the application of Christian principles to the solution of the pressing problems of the day, and urged all Catholics to give it sympathetic approval.[33] The editor of the *Christian Herald* also gave enthusiastic endorsement to the new draft of the Social Creed. A similar endorsement came from *The Christian Century* which embraced the new creed with excitement and declared that the FCC had made the bold choice and the right one.[34] In short, the new creed was greeted with an astonishing openness and ready acceptance, except for some scattered criticism from the more conservative Presbyterian and Lutheran journals.

Equipped with a new and more precise statement of its objectives, the Council was well prepared to contend for social justice at home and abroad. Focusing on the ideal of a Christian collectivism, the growing number of Walter Rauschenbusch's disciples tried to eliminate pathological social behaviour such as greed and injustice. They pursued with singular devotion the objective of fulfilling their postmillennial vision of the Kingdom of God on earth.


4.4     The Kingdom of God on Earth

After 1932 the social gospel was propagated with renewed vigour. It received much greater emphasis, as an expression of the Federal Council's philosophy, than at any time previously. Yet it remains unclear why the social gospel was so popular among the leadership of the Council in the early 1930s. The general Christian public had no great enthusiasm for the social dictum of Walter Rauschenbusch. It was more concerned about the propagation of the gospel in its historic evangelical context.

One cause of the resurgence of the social gospel was unquestionably the impact of the depression on the morale of the people. The Council was reacting to the adverse conditions of the economic depression plaguing the nation. But this does not sufficiently explain why the Council perceived it as its foremost task in evangelism from 1934 on. Other reasons undoubtedly contributed to this new emphasis on proclaiming the social gospel. A new commitment to the concept of the kingdom of God on earth needed to be generated among the people at large and from the constituencies of the member churches, a commitment that had been notably absent for some time. Unless the Council succeeded in mobilising a grassroots movement of socially conscious Christians it would never realise the goals set out in the Social Creed. Thus the new emphasis on propagating the principles of the Social Creed was again designed to attain the kingdom of God on earth rather than to reach lost souls with the Gospel of the Lord Jesus Christ.

During the 1930s the *Federal Council Bulletin* urged its audience to propagate the social gospel. It exhorted its readers to reject any notion that there was a basic conflict between the preaching of the gospel as such and the need to make known the Social Creed of the FCC. The Federal Council knew that unless it could secure a deep dedication to the ethical principles of the

Gospel, and a deep commitment to the Jesus who was presented as the living embodiment of these ethical ideals, there would be no motivating power for Christians to struggle for the realisation of the kingdom of God in the national life. Without adhering to basic Scriptural concepts, therefore, the Council's social appeals were couched in biblical terminology. Although mentioning the sin problem frequently, it was usually in the context of sins against society rather than sin against God. Regeneration was masterfully redefined as a new social awareness. The substitutionary atonement of Christ upon the cross was deemed insignificant and was rarely if ever mentioned. The Reformation dictum, that humankind can find peace with God only by being justified by faith, was simply ignored as without relevance. The residue of evangelical concepts which could be found in their gospel messages were mostly based on Arminian theology. Some Council members favoured a semi-Pelagian or Pelagian approach in evangelism.

In 1935 Samuel McCrea Cavert defined the role of the FCC in propagating the social gospel:

> The first and basic task of the Church is to help men gain and hold a sense of the spiritual meaning of life ... If the Church fails here it fails everywhere and becomes a broken cistern from which thirsty men can draw no water. The second great task of the Church is to hold before men the Christian ideal of life and to train them for Christian living. The idea that by some external magic we can secure a Christian society without training the individual Christian motives is a subtle illusion. We cannot permanently solve a single problem without changing the human heart.[35]

McCrea Cavert recognises clearly that the hearts of men must undergo a basic transformation before the society, in which they live, can be changed. The 'spiritual meaning of life' mentioned above refers to a transcendental quality of life which rises above the mundane and purely material interests of daily existence. Yet the author did not attribute any significance to the work of the Holy Spirit in regeneration, conversion, and sanctification.

Against this background of a socially motivated gospel ministry, the FCC entered upon its self-conferred task with a new determination under the direction of Dr William Hiram Foulkes, who succeeded Dr Charles Goodell as secretary for evangelism early in 1933, and then under William S. Abernathy, who took office in January 1935.

In 1934 the Council began to use a new, more aggressive, strategy to evangelise the American public, as it became increasingly clear that the previous approach was failing to reach many segments of society. Accordingly, in 1935, a national preaching mission was announced for the autumn of that year. The membership of the preaching mission was drawn almost exclusively from Northern church circles and, of these, largely from the Northern Baptist Convention and Northern Methodist churches. Some of the most famous preachers in the country offered their services in propagating the social gospel: Albert Beaven, former President of the FCC and president of the Rochester-Colgate Divinity School; Lynn Harold Hough, Dean of Drew Seminary; Bishop Ivan Lee Holt of St. Louis; Paul Scherer; George A. Buttrick; and E. Stanley Jones. Most of them shared a common theological outlook. They were the recognised paragons of liberal theology. Despite the predominance of these preachers, some evangelicals were also named as participants of the mission. They included the Methodist Bishop Arthur Moore of Atlanta and Pastor George W. Truitt of the First Baptist Church of Dallas.

The national preaching mission was well underway in 1936. The Council reported that missions had been held in twenty-eight cities and that the total attendance for the meetings was about twenty million with some twenty-three thousand ministers participating. Although the FCC was well pleased with these statistics, the preaching mission was continued in 1937 with an even greater number of ministers participating. In 1940 the Council organised a new series of national evangelistic events with the inauguration of the National Christian Missions program. The first was held in Kansas City, Missouri, in September 1940 and the last in Los Angeles in March 1941; each mission lasted one week. The missions were held in twenty cities and over two hundred speakers took part. E. Stanley Jones participated in all twenty-two missions. Murial Lester of London and Adolf Keller of Geneva also played prominent roles.

In 1938 the FCC concentrated its preaching missions on university campuses. This evangelistic campaign was not officially part of the national preaching mission, but another facet of the nationwide crusade to propagate the social gospel. It was certainly one of the more successful propaganda enterprises established under the tutelage of the FCC. Missions were held in sixteen colleges and universities with sixty-six preachers involved. E. Stanley Jones and T.Z. Koo were the featured speakers at many of the schools. They skilfully presented the social gospel and liberal Christianity in an attractive form to their student audiences. Some one hundred and thirteen thousand students attended these meetings, which were held at such schools as Ohio State University, and the universities of Illinois, Pennsylvania, North Carolina, and Wisconsin.

In 1939 the growing crisis in Europe and the outbreak of war in September of that year brought a shift of interest among the students, and the university missions were gradually phased out. Yet even in 1939 preaching missions were conducted on twenty college and university campuses. In spite of this unified and well financed attempt to make liberal theology appealing to large numbers of students, it is not clear that these efforts left any lasting impressions on their minds. Many of them discovered that liberal theology, despite its pacifist philosophy, could not sufficiently answer the pressing question of how to avert war in a modern world. The idealism of liberal theologians was useless in dealing with the crisis of armed conflict confronting Europe and America.

Unable to assess the true impact of the preaching missions, and elated by the positive, but mostly superficial, reception of the social gospel, the Council regarded the national campaign an overall success. At least it accomplished its purpose of calling the Christian public to arms, to defend a western civilisation on the verge of overthrow by irreligion. The Council once more stressed the reasonableness of the Christian faith in a personal God, its appropriate provisions for the deepest needs and aspirations of human life, and its redemptive, creative powers in organising and shaping a bewildered society after the standards and ideals of the kingdom of God.[36]

If there be any remaining doubt as to the purpose of the mission E. Stanley Jones should set it at rest. We believe that we see the goal and we believe that men can get hold of that power to move on to that goal. That goal is the Kingdom of God on earth. The Kingdom of God is a new order standing at the door of the lower order. The higher order, founded on love, justice, goodwill, brotherhood and redemption, stands confronting this lower order founded on selfishness, exploitation, unbrotherliness, with its resultant clash and conclusions ... it [the higher order] will finally replace this lower order, for it is God's order. We shall present Christ as the open door to that era. We shall unfold the possibilities of that era both within the individual and the collective will.[37]

In 1940 the Council launched a new project, the annual Worldwide Communion Sunday. The first was held on October 6, 1940. In this it followed the example of the General Assembly of the Presbyterian Church, USA, which had earlier initiated a similar event.

To reach the broad masses in the big cities with the social gospel, the Council began to expand its radio broadcasting program, using the facilities of several networks. Already in 1939 the Council claimed that it had at least one Christian message on the radio every day of the year. In that year Oscar Blackwelder, Ralph Sockman, Paul Scherer, Daniel Poling, Harry Emerson Fosdick, Frederick K. Stamm, Harold Paul Sloan, John Sutherland Bonnell, Jesse Bader (secretary for propagation for the FCC), Norman Vincent Peale, and Joseph Sizoo, were preaching over the air waves on behalf of the Council. In general, these programs were based on liberal theology, though a few moderate evangelicals were included to give the programs a wider hearing among those who were conservative and preferred the evangelical message. The content of the messages was usually on a high cultural level, appealing to the more educated classes of the country.

4.5    Progressive Social Experimentation

The social climate in the 1930s presented new challenges to the FCC. The world at home and abroad had drastically changed and taken on a different appearance from that which it had throughout most of the 1920s. The economic disturbances which had come in the wake of the New York stock market crash in 1929 allowed the Council to broaden and accelerate its various activities on the home front, steering them on a more progressive course. The

Great Depression prepared all sections of American society for a wide acceptance of social legislation in the hope that it would alleviate the prevailing misery and hopelessness among the general population. The Council's leadership realised the inherent potential of this unusual opportunity to experiment with radical ideas. Against the backdrop of economic depression the world at large seemed full of opportunities to condition the social consciousness of most people to seek a just world society. The Council's long-cherished expectations regarding a just redistribution of wealth seemed to be approaching the point of realisation. The leadership of the Council believed that the cause of economic equality was advancing, and would automatically generate a peaceful society. But the rising tide of totalitarianism in Europe and Asia would rudely shatter these illusions. The world fell increasingly under the spell of ruthless dictators.

The executive committee of the Council was horrified at the advances of National Socialism and Fascism on the European Continent. In sharp contrast, it welcomed and heartily supported the appearance of Roosevelt's New Deal.


4.6     The Federal Council and the New Deal

As the New Deal program was made public in the period of March to June 1933, the FCC approved unreservedly the measures taken by Roosevelt. During the first two years of the Democratic administration, from 1933 to 1935, the enthusiasm of the Council's leadership for the New Deal grew until it knew no bounds. In this speech to the Dayton biennial in December 1934, President Albert Beaven challenged the churches to participate in the radical changes being effected in the political, industrial, and economic life of the nation. With a keen sense of urgency he insisted that the church should never be content with the *status quo*.[38]

In his statement Beaven declared war against the Republican party, the opponents of the New Deal, but most of all against the social structure of the old order. His idealism was driving him to radical conclusions about the demise of the social order of capitalist America. He separated, for example, the right to own property from human rights.[39] Questionable as this separation is, both in its logical and theological presuppositions, American liberalism has embraced it as the primary principle of its social and economic policy for over a century. It has exercised an irresistible attraction to all varieties of liberal thought.

A qualified endorsement of the New Deal, as it existed in 1933, was announced at the Council's September 1933 meeting. The executive committee issued a statement that interpreted the National Recovery Administration in the light of the Social Creed of 1932:

> We do not suggest that the national recovery program embodies the full social idea of Christianity, or that the success of the program would leave no

desirable social goals unattained. The Christian conscience can be satisfied with nothing less than the complete substitution of motives of mutual helpfulness and goodwill for the motive of private gain, and the removal of the handicaps which our economic order now inflicts upon large numbers, particularly on certain occupational and racial groups. But we would call the attention of the members of our churches to the fact that the recovery program aims a vigorous blow at some of the more grievous types of exploitation and injustice.[40]

In the following section the report expressed its unabated admiration for the Roosevelt program for taking severe measures against child labour and for confirming the right of the working class to organise, as it was then guaranteed in the National Industrial Recovery Act of 1933. The statement was also highly appreciative of the codes provided for by this act because they insisted on forming new ways of ethical functioning by the diverse classes in the economic order. The executive committee conceded that, 'whatever its inevitable weaknesses, the National Industrial Recovery program implies the practicability of a more co-operative economic order, socially controlled for the common good and a willingness to relinquish special privileges and power.'[41] That it called for a large degree of experimentation in the economic and political life of the nation and that 'it is not to be supposed that a flawless program could be developed quickly in a time of great stress and anxiety,'[42] was a foregone conclusion. Although the churches would not feel called upon to approve every aspect, particularly the technical details of the many measures that had been implemented, the committee did recommend to the members of its constituent churches that they co-operate in the attainment of the ideals toward which the national recovery program was directed and the endorsement of its main social and spiritual implications for the congregational life.[43] To publicise this statement, the FCC convened a special meeting in Washington early in December 1933 to face the emergency then confronting the churches and the nation and to take whatever action it could. The outcome of this special conference was to result in a far-reaching change in the relationship of the secular state to the ecclesiastical authorities. The FCC initiated an amalgamation process which in time blurred the distinction between its new social order and the New Deal. It became apparent that the differences which still existed between the social order envisioned by the Council and Roosevelt's new world order was one of degree not of substance. The Social Creed of 1932 was more demanding in its stipulations than the New Deal legislation was willing or able to be. Although acceptable in many respects, Roosevelt's social policy was not bringing in the Kingdom of God quickly enough for the Council's liberal theologians. Still basically leading toward collectivism, the New Deal was not accomplishing the degree of social and political collectivism that would bring about the realisation of that kingdom. The Council's representatives offered a clear challenge to reluctant politicians who did not see the vision as clearly as they would have wished.

To an increasing number it seems clear that both Christianity and social science point toward a more collective economy in which the strong shall bear the burdens of the weak and in which the weak shall be made strong. What is needed is a loyalty to Christian ideals and good will that is strong enough to break through a hampering social structure even though we are unable to see the distant scene.[44]

The most dramatic moment at the special meeting in Washington was reached as both President Roosevelt and Henry Wallace, Secretary of Agriculture[45], addressed the assembled clergymen and established the grounds of a close working relationship between state and church from the vantage point of the political authority. The outward pretence of upholding the constitutional provision of a clear separation between the religious and secular realms of society was conscientiously maintained, but in reality it was brushed aside in favour of a close co-operation to usher in a new age, as it was hoped, of material prosperity and social harmony. In speaking of the prosperity that he envisioned for the nation, Roosevelt said:

It can be a prosperity built on spiritual and social values rather than on special privileges and special power. Toward this new definition of prosperity the churches and the governments, while wholly separate in their functioning, can work hand in hand. Government can ask the churches to stress in their teaching the ideas of social justice, while at the same time government guarantees to the churches ... the right to worship God in their own way. The churches, while they remain wholly free from the suggestion of interference in government, can at the same time teach millions of followers that they have the right to demand of the government of their own choosing the maintenance and furtherance of a more abundant life.[46]

A close analysis of this address shows that Roosevelt saw in the churches a force of social change in American society. The Social Creed of 1932 had led the Council into a situation in which it would do the will and bidding of the state. The Council had come a long way from its early stance that it would never become the auxiliary of a political party and would never actively endorse or support a particular economic or political program.

The speech of Henry Wallace was even more revealing than Roosevelt's. Wallace explicitly challenged the Protestant churches to initiate a sweeping change that would bring it into closer harmony with the New Deal:

I am wondering if the religion we shall need during the next hundred years will not have much more in common with the Christianity of the second and third centuries or possibly even with that of the Middle Ages than with the Protestants of the past one hundred years. The strong personal initiative conferred by the Protestants' religion must in some way be merged into a powerful religious attitude concerning the entire social structure ... I am not talking about welfare drives and other forms of charity which good men among the Protestants, Jews and Catholics alike support so loyally. The thing

I am talking about goes far deeper. It is an attitude that will not flow from external compulsion but that will spring from the hearts of the people because of an overwhelming realisation of a community of purpose. Perhaps the times will have to become even more difficult than they have been during the past two years before the hearts of our people will be willing to join together in a modern adaptation of the theocracy of old.[47]

In this address to the FCC Wallace insisted on a radical reformation of Christianity itself. Only a willingness on the part of the churches substantially to alter its dogma and practice would suffice to meet the needs of the day. The old virtue of helping those who had suffered hardships must give place to a new conception of a community of purpose. The basis for such a change is disclosed in the closing paragraph of his address:

This spiritual cooperation to which I refer depends for its strength on a revival of deep religious feeling on the part of the individual in terms of the intellectual concept that the world is in very truth one world, that human nature is such that all men can look on each other as brothers, that the potentialities of nature and science are so far-reaching as to remove many of the ancient limitations. This concept which now seems cloudy and vague to practical people must be more than the religious experience of the literary mystic. It must grow side by side with a new social discipline. Never has there been such a glorious chance to develop this feeling, this discipline as in this country today.[48]

According to Wallace, the new religious feeling must come from the realisation that the world is one – an emphasis which would presumably lead to a principled detachment from the competing propositional claims of truth made by the religions that actually inhabit that 'one world'. It would be the outgrowth of the new sociological knowledge made available by science, not the belief in a sovereign God. Wallace placed his emphasis more on the creation of a new humanism than the imposition of a new theocracy.

It is both interesting and revealing that the leadership of the FCC would see a kinship between the philosophy of Franklin Roosevelt and Henry Wallace and its own concept of the kingdom of God on earth. The insistence that the social aims of the New Deal did not fully meet the requirement of this secularised concept of the kingdom of God is nothing more than an acknowledgment that the humanistic theology of the Council was more progressive in its implications than the philosophy of the New Deal architects, who faced the political realities of the hour and of what could and could not be pushed through Congress.

Nevertheless, the editor of the *Bulletin* was enthusiastic about this address. He stated that Wallace was a man of vision who aptly visualized a better social order and devoted his energies to securing a co-operative instead of a competitive economic organisation. As his address showed, the editor alleged, Wallace had been influenced both by the Old Testament prophets and by the life and teaching of Jesus.[49] Henry A. Wallace was certainly a very religious person. His beliefs, however, were not rooted in historic Christianity. Wallace became notable for his mystical outlook on life.[50]


4.7     The Cause of World Peace

After the Council had greeted the general program of the New Deal of 1933 and 1934 with much acclaim, an unexpected change occurred. A curious disinterest in Roosevelt's domestic policy became evident both in the issues of the *Federal Council Bulletin* and in the annual reports. Besides some isolated references to various features of the legislation, the New Deal as such received hardly any attention after 1934, a fact which appears strange and on the surface difficult to comprehend. Yet there is a reason which may account for the apparent indifference. The New Deal was a daily reality in American life. It had such close affinity to the principles of the Social Creed of 1932 that the Council was quite satisfied with its collectivist program and heartily applauded its success, not as a direct participant, but more as a spectator. Roosevelt was a shining troubadour on the political scene who had mastered with unusual brilliance the science of social engineering. His New Deal legislation seemed secure beyond the reach of conservative attacks.

After 1935 the Council commented only occasionally on the domestic program of the New Deal. By then the pressing problem of world peace seemed to become a much greater concern to the Council. The rise of totalitarianism in Germany and Italy threatened, as it seemed, to evolve into another world war. It was feared that the disturbance of world peace could have negative side effects on the domestic program of the New Deal. Every effort needed to be made to reverse the trend towards international anarchy and aggression. That the Council became less interested in the problems of labour and industry had no serious repercussions. More important issues were the order of the day.

The menacing reality of Hitler's totalitarian regime and the threat of another world war confronted the FCC with the greatest crisis in its entire history. It became painfully aware that little could be done to alleviate the brutality of the Nazi persecution of Christians and different minority groups or to avoid the conflict in Europe. In this situation the leadership of the Council decided to embark on a time-honoured course of action. Marshalling all the influence and strength at its disposal, the Council took up the banner of pacifism to prevent the United States from again becoming involved in a European conflict. Determined to launch another great peace campaign, the FCC would once more be at the centre of the pacifist movement. The attack of the Japanese on America's Pacific fleet at Pearl Harbor (December 7, 1941) ended this campaign abruptly. But for the time being the leaders of the Council turned their attention exclusively to the problems of peace and war. Being assured that their social program at home was well administered by the governing Democratic Party, they were at liberty to plan their pacific strategy and ready to carry it out.

At the beginning of its peace initiative the Council made use of a public inquiry into the machinations of the American arms industry and investment banks in relation to Woodrow Wilson's decision (despite his non-interventionist election platform of 1916) to enter into World War I. It was generally assumed that the J. P. Morgan bank, standing at the apex of Wall Street's financial élite, greatly influenced and aided the war-mongering elements in American politics and mass media to safeguard its loans to the allied forces. The assumption that financial capitalism offered a willing hand to bring about untold misery and destruction to millions of people was not only widespread in secular liberal circles, but also very attractive to the Council's liberals. They quickly used this situation to further their own agenda for economic and industrial change at home by denigrating major segments of the industrial complex.

For this reason the executive committee of the FCC supported the public campaign for an official investigation of the arms industry. In March 1934 a sensational article appeared in *Fortune* under the title 'Arms and the Men'. In its pages a shocking story was told of shady deals and devious methods of great munitions manufacturers of Europe in their efforts to bring about wars that would make them immeasurably wealthy.[51] The whole story was reprinted in the *Congressional Record* on the initiative of Senator Nye. He wanted to impress on susceptible members of Congress the importance of calling for an official investigations. One month later, on April 12, seemingly moved by the tale of the *Fortune* story the Senate approved a resolution to inquire into the machinations of armament manufacturers and dealers. With the acquiescence of Senator Pittman, chairman of the Senate Committee on Foreign Relations, Vice-President Garner charged Senator Nye with the responsibility of conducting the investigations. A special Congressional committee was authorised to determine the extent of influence exercised by the 'merchants of death' on the shaping of a favourable popular opinion for America's involvement in World War I. Senator Nye's primary intention was to reveal to the American public the machinations of Wall Street in dragging the United States into a European war for no other reason than to safeguard their loans to the Allies and so to increase their profits. If his suspicions were to be confirmed by the hearings as he confidently assumed and the evidence widely dispersed across the nation, it would produce a fundamental upsurge of isolationist sentiments everywhere. He sincerely hoped it would drown 'the drums of war that beat a cadence of death for the poor and a rhythm of riches for the wealthy.'[52] While the American public in general was highly appreciative of the Senator's assignment, the State Department was less enthused about it. Secretary Hull was deeply distressed about the unexpected appointment of a Republican senator to such an important position by a Democratic majority in Congress:

Had I dreamed that an isolationist Republican would be appointed I promptly would have opposed it ... The appointment of Nye was a fatal mistake because the committee proved that the United States had been drawn into the First World War by American bankers and munitions makers.[53]

The Committee began its hearings on September 4, 1934. The FCC reinforced its earlier action by sending a statement of unreserved support for the Nye investigation. Albert Beaven, the Council's acting president, wrote the declaration in the name of the executive committee. Without doubt it represents the strongest expression of Beaven's sentiments on this matter; perhaps it was the most passionate pacifist statement the Council had ever issued.

As president of the Federal Council and at the request of the Council's Executive Committee I am writing to urge you and your associates to let nothing prevent the continuance of our inquiry until all the pertinent facts relevant to the manufacture and sale of war materials by American firms are made a matter of official record. Moreover, we protest against the suggestion that these hearings, if continued, be continued under the cloak of secrecy. The public is entitled to the facts irrespective of the effect which the publication of these facts may have upon individuals or groups of individuals in our own or other countries. The Christian thinking people of the nation are thoroughly aroused over this situation. A wave of moral indignation is sweeping through the churches against what appears to be a conscienceless and unscrupulous attitude taken by the armament and munition makers who are willing, apparently, to jeopardize the peace of the world for the sake of private gain .... The churches are determined to do all within their power to rid the world of war. They do not believe that this can be attained until the private traffic in arms and munitions is placed under strict national and international control.[54]

For obvious reasons this statement is of great significance in analysing the Council's public policy. In the first place, it is clear that the Nye investigation was to be used to disparage American capitalism by casting a slur on one part of the industry. It was to become the Council's favoured strategy to extend governmental control of industry by campaigning against the arms manufacturers and exporters. Several years later the Democratic administration would use the coming of war for the same purposes. Secondly, it is equally apparent that the FCC had already decided upon the guilt of the munition makers without waiting for a final verdict. The task which was left to the Nye committee was to confirm what the Council had already concluded. The Council was hardly assuming an objective posture about the issue. In the actual event the conclusion of the Council was well founded, as it became gradually clear that many of the charges levelled against 'the merchants of death' proved correct[55], although not all the findings indicated a direct complicity of the armament industry in precipitating war. The American historian Charles C.

Tansill proved, writes David L. Hoggan, 'as early as 1938 that the Nye Congressional Committee was wrong in its original assumption that the "merchants of death (Morgan, Rockefeller, etc.)" ordered President Wilson to enter the European war when he did. There is now general agreement that the ultimate decision on war or peace remained with Wilson.'[56] Still, the Nye hearings brought to light a sordid story of great magnitude. Tansill summarised the findings as follows:

> There were some colourful chapters dealing with the malign activities of highly paid lobbyists who used their influence to secure lucrative contracts. Some of the testimony pointed to the fact that manufacturers of munitions ardently believed in a "one world" of business. There were intimate ties that bound these "merchants of death" into an international trust. Within this business circle many trade secrets freely circulated, patents were exchanged, and the volume of trade was diverted into certain favored channels. It was also brought out that some American army and naval officers had been of great service to armament firms, and that the Army and Navy departments, in order to speed a "preparedness program", had given definite encouragement to the same corporations. This encouragement went so far as to permit manufacturers to copy designs of equipment that had been tested and perfected in government laboratories. Products made from these plans were freely sold to foreign governments.[57]

The greatest embarrassment to the American government was brought about by the publication of secret files kept under seal in the Department of State. In the assumption that this material would not be passed on to newspaper reporters, Secretary Hull made them available to the Nye Committee. Although the Committee took every conceivable precaution, some of the most compromising information seeped out to the public. The documents supposedly evidenced that the Chinese Government had diverted a large wheat loan into the open coffers of armament dealers. It was insinuated that King George V had put pressure on Poland to buy its arms from British firms.[58] The publication of the secret correspondence between the House of Morgan and the British Government during the years 1914-1917 implicated one of the most important American investment banks with a serious breach of the Neutrality legislation, while the United States government quietly accommodated, if not encouraged, these infractions of its publicly stated policy. The British Ambassador protested in unmistakable terms about Hull's connivance, albeit unwillingly, in revealing to the American public the close co-operation between Wall Street firms and the British Government. Of such explosive revelations the common person in the street should have been kept ignorant, the Ambassador maintained, as the American people were prone to misinterpret the real intentions of Wall Street and thus place an unjustified odium on the British Foreign Office for eliciting its assistance in a time of unprecedented crisis.

In spite of these damaging revelations the House of Morgan was not subpoenaed. This would have raised further embarrassing questions concerning the genuineness of Wilson's commitment to strict neutrality before April 2, 1917. Secretary Hull made a serious effort to enlist the support of President Roosevelt to keep the Nye Committee 'within reasonable limits'.[59] But the President was not inclined to offer any assistance in concealing the blood-stained record of the House of Morgan.[60] He did not prevent the nation from venting its anger against greedy and unscrupulous Wall Street industrialists, speculators, and bankers. 'Thanks to this lack of Presidential pressure,' concluded Tansill,

> the Nye Committee unearthed a vast amount of data of great value to historians. These documents clearly showed the economic forces that helped to prepare the hostile climate of opinion against Germany that eventually led to American intervention in 1917. An important part of this evidence revealed the rich financial harvest gathered by some business firms as a result of the conflict.[61]

Once again,' writes Chernow, 'the timid Jack Morgan was transmogrified into a venal, snarling monster. As *Time* magazine said, "Before the Committee for settlement was a scandalous question: should J. P. Morgan be hated as a war-monger second only to Kaiser Wilhelm?"'[62]

Thirdly, the FCC applied tremendous political pressure on a congressional investigating committee instituted by the American government. This action could not be interpreted simply as a campaign of moral indignation on the part of the churches. From the very beginning it displayed the conspicuous marks of political activism, based upon a political agenda. It was certainly a far cry from the earlier position assumed by the Council, namely that it would not stoop down into the trenches of political agitation.

The Council tried to assist the Nye committee[63] by issuing a pacifist statement called 'To Christians of All Lands'. It was a clarion call for international peace emphasising the Council's invitation to the churches worldwide to join in a crusade not only against war itself, but against all preparations that could lead to conflict.[64] Conceding that the international situation was fraught with danger, as a consequence of nationalism and a pathological war psychology, the statement pointed out that American Christians could not stand as the accuser of any single nation, for they were just as guilty as Christians in other countries. In that solemn hour it was the duty of the churches of Christ to stand firm and steadfast.

> Many Christian bodies in the United States have said that our churches should never again be used in preparation for war but should be used in the promotion of peace. They have said that the church should not sanction war or bless it. They have said that war is a denial of the gospel they profess. In any dilemma between loyalty to country or to Christ, they have said that they would follow Christ ... We invite the people of the churches of the world to join us in proclaiming anew our citizenship in a kingdom that is without

geographical or racial division. By virtue of a common loyalty to the Lord, Christians everywhere have a kinship with one another. Their loyalties, accordingly, are first to God and after that to the nation of which they are a part ... We believe that the churches of Christ around the world should with all possible dispatch say to their respective governments that they cannot and will not give their moral support to war as a method of settling international difficulties, nor will they become a party to the mad race in armaments now in progress in so many parts of the world ... We believe that the hour has come when all Christians should unite in urging the nations to make renewed effort to resolve existing international differences on a peaceful basis. We cannot and will not believe that the people of the world desire that a relatively small number of persons shall precipitate an international crisis that would seem to make inevitable a resort to military violence.[65]

The Council was not satisfied with merely pleading for the cause of peace. It also launched a public crusade by demanding that the American government should impose severe economic sanctions on any aggressor nation. The Council strongly insisted on the nationalisation of the munition industry in order to ensure its strict control by the state department. It also demanded that the naval construction provided for under the Vinson Bill be stopped at once and all offensive weapons be destroyed. The most sweeping proposal taken before the American government was that it should dismantle its air force and use its planes exclusively for peaceful purposes.[66] This radical position of unilateral disarmament and strict governmental control of the armament industry exposed the Council's most basic problem. It had little or no understanding of the causes of war. To invite an aggressor to embark on a course of conquest a nation only needed to weaken its military defense unilaterally.

In December 1934, the FCC organised the National Conference on the Churches and World Peace, which convened in Dayton, Ohio. The tone of this conference is evident from the resolutions passed and the affirmations adopted: 'Resort to military violence for the settlement of international, interracial, economics, or class disputes is sin.'[67] And further:

We are convinced that in order to avoid a calamitous race of armaments with Japan, the United States should be prepared to make substantial concessions by agreeing to abolish naval vessels and other weapons of aggression so as to make impossible a war across the Pacific.[68]

On the basis of these resolutions and affirmations, the Council followed the recommendations of its own Department of Good Will and International Justice to approve of the neutrality proposals then before Congress. Probably it was mere coincidence that the Neutrality Act of 1935, in its final form, included substantially all of these demands. The similarity between the act and the position of the Council cannot necessarily be credited to the latter's influence, except insofar as the Council was itself reflecting the general isolationist mood of the country prior to Pearl Harbor.[69]

At the biennial meeting held at Asbury Park, New Jersey, in December 1936 the Council announced a nine-point program as a guideline for the diplomatic and military policies of the Roosevelt administration. Seeking to implement its position on world peace, it asked the government to fulfill its Good Neighbour Policy for the western world, to extend the provisions of the Neutrality Act of 1935, to enter the World Court, to exercise moderation in its military policies, to work for the national and international control of the arms traffic, to extend the reciprocal trade agreements provided for by an act of 1934, to make it clear that the American armed forces could not and would not be used for protecting overseas material interests, and to improve relations with Japan.[70] These programs and resolutions, particularly the nine-point program of 1936, constituted the peace platform of the Council until September 1939.

The Neutrality Act of 1937, the apex of such legislation in the years before the actual outbreak of hostilities in Europe, fulfilled even more of the demands advanced by the FCC. It is difficult to assess the direct contribution of the FCC to its passage, for in 1937, as in 1935, isolationist feelings were a powerful factor in congressional thinking. The Act omitted, for example, the provisions sought by the Council on the national and international control of arms traffic.

The leaders of the FCC refused to admit that their support of the Neutrality legislation could actually be counterproductive to a genuine peace policy. Still extolling with boundless optimism the ability of the social gospel to maintain peace in a chaotic world of would-be conquerors, the Council had not yet appreciated that pacifism would simply play into the hands of ambitious and power-seeking politicians. The ecclesiastical leadership falsely believed that a strong neutral policy towards belligerent nations, including an embargo on arms, credits, and loans, would be sufficient to prevent war, if coupled with a policy to advance internationalism.[71] In reality, the Neutrality Acts were applied in a rather different fashion.

Although President Roosevelt occasionally professed great sympathy for the Council and its works, he most certainly did not endorse certain features of the acts of 1935 and 1937, both of which restricted his presidential authority in foreign affairs.[72] He had no scruples to circumvent the provisions of the Neutrality Acts, if such action was called for to accomplish personal objectives. Although temporarily prevented by strong isolationist opposition led by Senator William E. Borah of Idaho, he tried to persuade Congress in July 1939 to repeal the embargo provision of the Neutrality Acts. He felt that the unfairness of these laws should be redressed by allowing him to choose which party of potential belligerents he favoured to support in the future. Convening a special session of Congress at the outbreak of war Roosevelt called again for a revision of the neutrality laws to grant the Allied Powers exclusive rights to obtain munitions in the United States.[73] In November 1939 the embargo on war supplies was lifted. Roosevelt's intention became obvious

168

in a conversation with Philip Kerr (Lord Lothian), the British Ambassador, on June 16, 1940, as Britain staggered toward the abyss of military defeat by Hitler:

President Roosevelt then told the Ambassador [Philip Kerr] that ... the United States would certainly allow British ships to use American facilities for reforming and supply, and that, while they might not have formally declared war on Germany because of constitutional difficulties, they would in effect be a belligerent "assisting the Empire in every way and enforcing the blockade on Germany". This tremendous decision to back the seemingly hopeless cause of Britain with all the material and moral encouragement he could supply was entirely Roosevelt's own; it was taken against the advice of the majority of the White House official circle, and at a time when his position in the country in an election year was far from secure. He immediately followed it up by giving his Cabinet a new bi-partisan look, having anticipated over the past six months that the development of "a real crisis" in the shape of a German victory in Europe would justify him in largely dispensing with what he called "strictly old-fashioned party government".[74]

The Federal Council's naivete in believing that Roosevelt's public attestations to keep America out of the war were sincere cannot be faulted. The President was too clever to divulge his real intentions to those who would have opposed him had they known. He did not want to alienate the principal proponents of the American peace movement prematurely, realizing, as Charles A. Beard[75] noted, that their internationalist agenda played into his hands.

Subsidized and powerful private agencies engaged nominally in propaganda for "peace" are among the chief promoters of presidential omnipotence in foreign affairs. They look to the President rather than Congress for assistance in advancing their ideas of America's obligation to join other "peace-loving" nations in ordering and reordering the world. Moreover, as these agencies in turn subsidize professors and "students of international relations" by the hundreds, they thereby help to exalt presidential "leadership" and, correspondingly, degrade the Senate or the House of Representatives or both with regard to their responsibilities in foreign affairs. Consequently, American education from the universities down to the grade schools is permeated with, if not dominated by, the theory of presidential supremacy in foreign affairs. Coupled with flagrant neglect of instruction in constitutional government, this propaganda in universities, colleges, and schools has deeply implanted in the minds of rising generations the doctrine that the power of the President over international relations is, for all practical purposes, illimitable. The theory of limitless power in the Executive to conduct foreign affairs and initiate war at will, unhampered by popular objections and legislative control, is of course old in the history of empires and despotisms. It was long accepted and practised by despotic monarchies. It was held and applied by Hitler and Mussolini. It is now the theory, as well as the practice, of totalitarian governments everywhere. But such governments have never been under the delusion that limitless power can be exercised over foreign affairs and war, while domestic affairs and domestic economy are left free and the authority of government over them is constitutionally limited.[76]

Although the Council was mostly unaware of the implication of its peace initiative, there were many people in the country who recognised what was involved in the brand of pacifism it was promoting. As a result, a new wave of vigorous criticism arose against the Council. There was a growing conviction of many that the Council was hardly interested in preserving the national independence and economic prosperity of the American people. In this critical situation, it became increasingly clear to the ecumenical leadership that it needed the endorsement of a public figure with a conservative reputation to abate some of the criticism of its detractors. They approached John Foster Dulles, knowing quite well that his public image as a conservative was merely a facade. 'I don't think,' noted Henry P. Van Dusen, 'that we felt, in the context in which we saw him, that Dulles was conservative at all. I would say he was a moderate liberal ... Among his closest legal colleagues, he was regarded as, if not a radical, a liberal.'[77] But exactly for that reason the Church leadership thought Dulles would be the ideal choice. They were elated when he accepted the chairmanship of the Federal Council's 'Commission to Study the Bases of a Just and Durable Peace' in 1941. Two years later, they appointed him to the Executive Committee of the Council. Dulles served in this capacity until his resignation in 1950.

As Van Dusen rightly observed, Dulles was never a conservative in the true sense of the word. Despite his successful attempt in portraying himself as a genuine Republican, at a time when the Grand Old Party was still largely viewed as conservative, Dulles was a full-blooded liberal. In the late 1940s and throughout the 1950s he became particularly known for his bi-partisanship. Michael A. Guhin describes the early stages of Dulles' developing political philosophy thus:

> The combination of Dulles' moderate political liberalism and internationalism prevented any identification with the non-internationally minded, more conservative segment of American society. He never did belong to the die-hard group of the Grand Old Party and, at times, his internationalist complexion caused him either to shift party alliances or to disagree openly with the more conservative element.[78]

Prior to becoming Secretary of State, he never denied his ideological adherence to Wilsonian progressivism, least of all in his published works, but was always careful to express his radical ideas in pious words. In the spring of 1938, for example, the left-liberal magazine *The Nation* invited him 'as one of a small group of articulate liberals in foreign policy' to write a 300-word statement about the problems in Europe. In his short essay Dulles touched on the issue of isolationism versus interventionism. 'The sum of the whole matter is this,' he wrote, 'that our civilization cannot survive materially unless it be redeemed spiritually ... Here is the final challenge to our churches.'[79]

Dulles wanted to encourage the churches to bring society to the point at which it would voluntarily embrace internationalism. He did not mean that they should implore the people to seek personal reconciliation with God.


4.8     The Geneva Conference

In the summer of 1939 it became increasingly obvious that the outbreak of war was unavoidable. The FCC was desperately looking for an effective resolution of the diplomatic imbroglio which held the European capitals in its grip. Most Church leaders believed, as did many pacifists during the interwar years, that economic conditions were the primary cause of war.

In January 1938 the Belgian economist, Dr. Paul Van Zeeland, had proposed a plan to call for a world economic conference. He was convinced that war could be prevented if government officials would meet face to face to discuss economic issues such as monetary reform, trade, colonies, and economic assistance. To Van Zeeland's great disappointment, Great Britain and France rejected the idea. The international situation was deteriorating so rapidly at the time that an economic conference was seen as ineffective to reverse the downward trend.

In the wake of the Munich Agreement, the idea of a world conference was brought up again, this time in the United States. Albert W. Palmer, the president of Chicago Theological Seminary, supported Van Zeeland's proposal and urged the churches in *The Christian Century* to arouse world opinion in support of an economic conference. In his passionate appeal Palmer called Munich a triumph of pacifism. Since the churches constituted the peace movement's most active element, Palmer challenged them to use this opportunity to broaden their sphere of influence and preserve their credibility. 'Let the American churches, through the Federal Council, invite the churches of the world unitedly to urge upon their governments the calling of such a conference.'[80] In case the governments would not co-operate, Palmer suggested the churches should organise their own conference.

The FCC endorsed Palmer's idea at once. Two weeks later Edgar Dewitt Jones, the president of the FCC, and twenty other Church leaders met with Roosevelt to seek his support for an economic conference. The President received them courteously. After the meeting the Church delegation left with the impression that he would act in accordance with their petition, only to discover later, as many other delegations before them, that Roosevelt was not at all inclined to do so.[81] In December 1938, Palmer expressed his disappointment in another article in *The Christian Century*, summoning the churches to hold their own conference. In conclusion he wrote that they would need to be the conscience of the world.[82]

In January 1939, the FCC drafted a proposal for a conference and submitted it to the Provisional Committee of the World Council of Churches in Paris. In the meantime the international situation had eroded again so drastically that the European members of the committee rejected it. They had lost faith in an economic solution.[83] Nevertheless, they agreed to organise a small conference of economic experts to give them an official platform to exchange ideas and present their findings to the churches. This compromise was acceptable to the Americans, as long as the most competent and well-respected experts would be invited. It was hoped that the governments would pay attention to their recommendations.[84]

In July of that year, the Provisional Committee of the World Council of Churches convened the International Conference of Lay Experts and Ecumenical Leaders in Geneva. A twelve-member delegation of the FCC, including John Foster Dulles, was sent to the conference. George A. Buttrick, the president of the FCC, issued the following instructions to the departing delegates. 'I assume,' he wrote, 'that all of you have read Mr. Dulles' book *War, Peace and Change*, which is, more than any other book, the basic document for your discussions.'

In his memoirs, W. A. Visser 't Hooft stated that the Provisional Committee intended to assemble a group of fifteen laymen 'with thorough knowledge of international affairs' and fifteen theologians and church leaders.[85] In the end, they secured the participation of thirty-six participants, including Max Huber (Switzerland), Alfred E. Zimmern (Great Britain), Charles Rist (France), and F. M. van Asbeck (Netherlands). Visser 't Hooft also mentioned that two reputable Germans, O. H. von der Gablentz and Wilhelm Menn, were present at the conference.[86] During the five days of meetings two primary questions were considered for discussion and study. What could be done by churches and individual Christians (1) to arrest the drift towards war and (2) to move closer to the establishment of an international order?[87]

The serenity of the garden at the Hotel Beau Sejour, where the delegates met, stood in sharp contrast to the tense atmosphere which surrounded the discussions. 'War psychology enveloped us like a fog of poison gas,' Palmer deplored later.[88] In one of the debates Dulles defended the position of allowing Hitler a free hand in redressing the injustices inflicted on Germany by the Versailles Peace Treaty, and added that he would be prepared to concede to the Nazis the right to pursue their own course in international affairs without interference from other nations. Sir Alfred E. Zimmern disagreed vehemently with this viewpoint. He felt that, in dealing with Nazi Germany, the western democracies had been far too lenient. In tolerating Hitler's lust for conquest, they had contributed to the volatile situation in Europe. This clash of opinions was, according to Visser 't Hooft, one of several 'difficult moments' which occurred at the conference.[89]

Another bone of contention between the European delegates and Dulles

172

was the latter's insistence on creating an international organisation. Dulles' insisted on including the statement that 'power of any kind, political or economic, must be co-extensive with responsibility' in Section I of the Conference report, which defined the presuppositions of the delegates. Despite his formidable powers of persuasion the American lawyer could not convince the Europeans entirely of its implied meaning. Becoming one of the most strongly held credos of Dulles in the 1940s, this statement expressed his belief that, on matters affecting the interrelationship of nations, such as monetary policy, trade, and immigration, an international authority, based on a federal construct, should be created to monitor policies and mediate disputes.[90] In a letter to Lionel G. Curtis describing his impressions of the Church conference in Geneva, Dulles was particularly disenchanted with the Europeans' 'complete lack of comprehension of the real significance of the federal system' as a possible ultimate solution for international disorder.[91]

In the days following his return to the United States, and as a direct result of his participation at the Geneva conference, Dulles was more than ever convinced that some kind of supranational agency must be established. Interestingly enough, his rationale for creating such an organisation was not to prevent war (the argument he usually employed), but to accelerate the process of change in setting up a new world order.[92] Expressing his ideas to Quincy Wright, Dulles suggested to begin with publicising the concept of a 'consultative' agency, weaker than the League, open-ended, and geared to deal with specific functional or technical problems such as trade, law or finance. He thought that it would be impossible at the present evolutionary stage of international affairs to confer on any international organisation the power to impose military or economic sanctions, nor should it perform policy assignments which would infringe on the sovereignty of nation-state. The primary consideration should be to preclude any potential reaction against internationalism. At a later stage, however, these functional activities could be integrated into the statutes of international law and form the basis of institutional arrangements which might eventually approximate some kind of world polity. Dulles would always insist that 'world government cannot be created; it must grow in response to need.'[93]

## 4.9 Hawks and Doves

At the outset of the war in Europe John Foster Dulles became entangled in the increasingly rancorous controversy which raged between interventionist and noninterventionist clergymen in the United States. In a nationally broadcasted radio message on 8 September 1939, a few days after Britain and France had declared war on Germany, George A. Buttrick, the president of the FCC, asked his audience to support a policy of neutrality:

> We must be neutral from high and sacrificial motives - not for physical

safety, not in an attempt to maintain an impossible isolation from world problems, assuredly not for commercial gain, but rather because we know that war is futile and because we are eager through reconciliation to build a kindlier world.[94]

Immediately following the broadcast, the FCC issued a statement entitled 'The American Churches and the European War,' which castigated war as 'an evil thing contrary to the mind of Christ'. The United States government was again urged strongly to stay out of war. Essentially in agreement with the FCC the National Peace Conference sent a similar message to the President a few days later.[95] By the end of September 1939 *The Christian Century* claimed euphorically that most American churches were opposed to war. The editor Charles Clayton Morrison still feared, however, that the churches may succumb to the mounting forces of a virulent interventionism, as they had done in 1917.[96] To counteract militarist influences, he decided to publish a serialized version of Ray Abrams' *Preachers Present Arms*, which denounced Protestant jingoism during the First World War. On October 18, 1939 the executive committee of the FCC commended President Roosevelt in a letter for his efforts to keep the country out of the conflict and implored him to co-operate to the best of his abilities with other nations in restoring peace. Roosevelt was asked to consider an internationalist solution to the problem of war: 'We urge the development of some form of world order,' the letter concluded, 'in which certain aspects of the sovereignty of the individual state would be limited in the interests of the world community.'[97]

Soon, however, dark clouds rose on the horizon which cast an ominous shadow over the pacifist cause of the churches. Reinhold Niebuhr showed first signs of uneasiness about noninterventionism in his Gifford Lectures in Scotland at the end of 1939. Deeply concerned about the threat to democracy caused by the American refusal to help Britain and France in its struggles against the Nazis, he authored a series of articles, which he called 'Leaves from the Notebook of a War-Bound American.' He passionately denounced the evil of totalitarianism which seemed unstoppable on its march to conquer the world. On the eve of his return to the United States in early 1940, Niebuhr began to call for America's entry into the war.[98]

Standing at the helm of the interventionist faction within the FCC which was steadily gaining in popularity among Church leaders, Niebuhr issued a public statement, entitled 'The American Churches and the International Situation.' Urging the churches to refrain from war hysteria, Niebuhr contended that to remain neutral about the European conflict would not be in America's best interest, since it was more than a battle between competing power blocks. There was a fundamental moral difference between the Axis powers' lust for conquest and the Finns' heroic defence of their country against the Russian aggressor. America's war objective should be to preserve freedom which would suffer a fatal blow everywhere in the case of an Axis victory.[99] At that time Niebuhr was not yet convinced that a new world order would arise out of the ashes of the old, once hostilities had ceased. The statement was endorsed by thirty-two prominent Church leaders. Dulles was one of the signatories. Shortly after the statement was made public, John Foster freely admitted to Quincy Wright that he had reluctantly appended his name to the document. On the question of war guilt his views deviated substantially from those expressed in the statement. He believed that the Allies were just as responsible as the Axis Powers for causing the outbreak of hostilities. The western democracies had failed to diffuse a volatile situation in the years leading up to the war in that they had prevented peaceful change from taking place in international affairs. Dulles contended, furthermore, that the moral issue was hardly as one-sided as the statement made it out to be. In his view the European conflict showed the classical signs of a clash between competing imperialisms.[100]

Dulles was never easily intimidated or swayed to change his position if he was certain of its expediency in achieving his goals. Sometimes, however, he shifted the emphasis of his argumentation from one aspect to another to make a more convincing case for his position. While he had emphasised in late 1939 that the western democracies were equally to blame for causing the war, because they did not allow the so-called 'have not' powers to meet their legitimate needs, he began to stress the futility of force in solving international conflicts in the early 1940s. Refuting some claims of Granville Clark's peace proposal, he contended that the author placed too much credence on the effectiveness of force. 'I do not think peace is maintained primarily by force, but rather by the creation of sound economic conditions, so that men of violence are kept in the minority instead of becoming the leaders of great mass revolts.'[101] Three days later in conversation with a friend he stated essentially the same opinion: 'I have always felt that the measure of force necessary to maintain peace was the measure of the unsoundness of the social order.'[102]

In April 1940 Dulles rejected outright the argument that the United States should assist Britain and France with everything short of war. His rationale was that a nation should refrain from putting its prestige on the line if it did not possess adequate means to protect it. He was certain that the American people would resist the decision to send its armies to Europe merely to preserve the western democracies. A victory of Nazi Germany would be deplorable, to be sure, but it would not match the negative effects of war itself which the United States would suffer. 'The greatest menace ... is war itself, and the means necessary to win a modern war.'[103] Dulles surprisingly argued in his letter to Thomas Debevoise that it may not be so tragic to let Britain and France fall to the Germans, if they were not strong enough to maintain their own political independence. The United States could win the war for them, but this would be only a temporary solution at best to guarantee their survival.[104]

In early May 1940, the Nazi victories in Scandinavia threatened a defeat of the Allies. The interventionist faction within the FCC, led by Reinhold Niebuhr and Henry P. Van Dusen, became increasingly concerned and issued another statement urging the American government to sustain the British and the French in their struggle. Still cautious in demanding a declaration of war against Germany, they called for moral and material support. Nearly all of those who had signed the January statement appended their signatures again with the notable exception of John Foster Dulles. He steadfastly refused to sign, even after Van Dusen implored him in a telegram to change his mind. A personal petition from Henry Sloane Coffin and an earnest message from William Adams Brown were greeted with the same negative response.[105]

If the interventionist clergymen chafed over John Foster's seeming betrayal, the pacific noninterventionists were delighted. A day after Dulles' refusal to sign the statement had become known, Walter W. Van Kirk[106], secretary of the FCC's Department of International Justice and Goodwill and a co-member of the Council on Foreign Relations, sent him a letter. 'I can't tell you how grateful I am for your view,' wrote Van Kirk. 'I had expected that in a period of international stress there would be a tendency on the part of some of our preachers to stand where most of them had stood in 1917-1918. I had not supposed, however, that the drift would set in so quickly.'[107] This letter was followed by other communications from clergymen commending Dulles in similar terms for his principled stance. Those who applauded his decision, however, were soon disappointed, when Dulles also refused to endorse the noninterventionist manifesto. In late May, George A. Buttrick, Harry Emerson Fosdick, and Ralph Sockman had published a refutation of the Niebuhr-Van Dusen declaration which they wanted him to sign.[108] Although sympathising with the noninterventionists during the early phase of the war, Dulles was careful to keep himself out of the controversy because he felt that neither group represented his own position adequately. He adopted a quasi-isolationist position while remaining an internationalist at heart. In his speech at the National Council of the Y.M.C.A. in Detroit, on October 28, 1939, he stated: 'I dislike isolation, but I prefer it to identification with a senseless repetition of the cyclical struggle between the dynamic and static forces of the world ... The fundamental fact is that the national system of wholly independent sovereign states is completing its cycle of usefulness.'[109] Thus he saw 'neither in the underlying causes of the war, nor its long range objectives, any reason for the United States becoming a participant in the war.' 'Were we now to act,' he maintained, 'it would be to reaffirm an international order which by its very nature is self-destructive and a breeder of violent revolts.'[110]

The champion of isolationism, Charles A. Lindbergh, came out in public to demand a *modus vivendi* with Hitler, and Dulles supported him. In a personal letter he commended the famous aviator for his isolationist stance:

> I am very glad you spoke as you did. I do not agree with everything that you said, but I do agree with the result, and I feel that there is grave danger that, under the influence of emotion, we will decide upon a national policy which is quite the reverse of what we had more or less agreed upon when we were thinking clearly.[111]

176

In a gesture of gratitude, Dulles offered his legal services to Lindbergh during the incorporation of the America First Committee (AFC).[112] It is rather doubtful, however, that Dulles ever concurred unreservedly with the isolationist position of the AFC. In fact, he was annoyed by critics who associated him publicly with Lindbergh's organisation. One of the reasons he gave for refusing to become an AFC member sheds some light on at least one aspect which caused him to seek a mediating position between the interventionists and isolationists.

> I am making my first interest in these matters my work with the Federal Council of Churches, where I have just become Chairman of an important committee they are setting up to study international relations. My ability to achieve the long range objectives I have in mind and my influence with the group would be hurt if I were publicly identified with one or another of the groups actively involved in the current phases of the problem.[113]

Thus, his temporary involvement in the isolationist movement must be seen simply as a matter of expediency, supporting the AFC as long as the consequences of its activities coincided with his own goals of preserving American neutrality prior to Pearl Harbor. He was too much of an internationalist to throw in his lot with a group of conservative nationalists who were almost completely at variance with him ideologically. Ronald W. Pruessen rightly observes that the epithet 'Isolationist' is a label that simply fails to stick.[114] Dulles intimated at times that, under certain circumstances, he would discard isolationist sentiments:

> I am not an "isolationist", indeed I have generally been called an "internationalist" ... I would not oppose affirmative action if our policy were based upon a genuine understanding of the causes of the present crisis and was intelligently designed to achieve a world order whereby recurrent crises might hereafter be avoided.[115]

Commenting on the interventionist controversy in the United States a quarter century earlier, he frankly admitted that he had supported Wilson's war effort: 'I was willing and eager to see the United States go into the World War under the leadership of Wilson. I felt that he had perceived and might correct the inherent defects in our present world system.'[116] In a letter to William E. Borah, who chaired a Senate committee, investigating infringements of the neutrality legislation, Dulles explained why he had refused to testify in favour of the isolationist movement:

> My general feeling is that if the world is bound into a cycle of recurrent violence, then I should like to see the United States avoid involvement. I fear this is the situation in Europe today. However, I am "isolationist" only in this sense and believe that if any program could be evolved which would break the cycle and give some promise of re-establishing a real era of peace rather

than mere armistice, then we should play our part [in entering the war].[117]

Arguing that isolationism is untenable in an interdependent world, Dulles told Arthur Sulzberger, publisher of the *New York Times*, that he rejected the 'old-time nationalistic slogans like "America First" or "Defend America".' No country could stay in isolation for long and prosper.[118] Dulles thus confounded some of his critics, such as James P. Warburg and Wendell Willkie, who attacked him openly for his alleged isolationist sentiments. Unable to silence his political detractors completely, he was repeatedly accused after the war of having weakened the United States' resolve to defeat the Axis powers. Ronald W. Pruessen writes that 'some [critics of Dulles] went on to lambast him for urging a cowardly and irresponsible path on his fellow citizens.'[119]

After the German invasion of France the dispute between the noninterventionists and interventionists within the executive committee of the FCC started to become public knowledge. To abate the embarrassment over its internal division the Church leadership decided to publish a revised declaration working doggedly on a new formula throughout June 1940. In the meantime the executives of Christian agencies in Geneva had formed an International Consultative Group and called on the United States to shoulder its responsibility for freedom in the world. The Group claimed that the possibility of an Allied victory had become remote and Christians everywhere should contemplate the serious consequences of a Nazi Europe.[120] Abhorred by the thought of a German victory, the executive committee of the FCC urged the United States to save basic human values by entering the war. Admittedly this solution would not be a cure-all, only the lesser of two evils. The churches were exhorted to honour the rights of both pacifists and soldiers, to care for war victims regardless of nationality and political ideology, and, above all, to preserve the bonds of ecumenical fellowship across national boundaries. The scale had tipped noticeably in favour of the interventionists in the higher echelons of the FCC. In a letter to William W. Van Kirk Dulles deplored the defeat of the pacifist faction within the Church leadership. He was especially incensed about the portrayal of the Axis Powers as evil personified in contrast to that of the Allies as the righteous defenders of a moral cause. The churches had to bear part of the blame for that misrepresentation.

> I am struck by the fact that history shows that in every so-called "Christian" country, in time of war or international stress, the church has uniformly become the hand-maiden of national politics. The church leaders then see the moral issue as identical with the national issue and call upon church members as a matter of religious duty to support its own national leaders as being "right." ... I greatly hoped that in the present crisis the Christians church in this country could avoid concentrating upon the admitted evils elsewhere, slurring over the admitted evils at home and thereby becoming, in my judgment, hypocritical and unChristian.[121]

In his response Van Kirk agreed with Dulles, but admitted regretfully that the noninterventionist faction within the FCC had become a minority. 'It is increasingly clear that my views are not the views of a large number of the members of the executive committee.'[122] Instead of giving in to the opinion of the dominant interventionist faction, the pacifistic clergymen continued the fight for their position. By October 1940 the two sides had run into serious disagreements with one another and had reached a deadlock. It was feared that the public image of the FCC would suffer lasting damage. To restore a modicum of unity, at least on the surface, an informal meeting was convened at Dulles' home. Spokesmen of both points of view were in attendance. The noninterventionist faction was represented by Henry Atkinson, Harry Emerson Fosdick, William W. Van Kirk, and Roswell P. Barnes. Their counterparts were Henry Sloane Coffin, William Adams Brown, and Samuel McCrea Cavert. Some men were also present who preferred to take a neutral posture. They were A. L. Warnshuis, H. A. Hatch, J.A. Franklin, and A. K. Chalmers. Meanwhile, Van Dusen and Niebuhr on the interventionist side and Palmer, Buttrick, and Morrison on the other chose to remain absent.[123]

Dulles was asked by those present to draft a statement which would emphasise the essential unity of the churches despite divisive issues which remained unresolved. On 18 October 1940 Dulles passed the statement on to the entire executive committee of the FCC. Subsequently, he wrote a position paper based on the comments he received from the Church leadership and called it 'The American Churches and the International Situation'. The main premise of the paper was that Christians should rise above the hatreds of war in order to preserve the bonds of a world-wide fellowship of churches. Furthermore, they should show to the world the type of repentance and humility which distinguished their belief in the spiritual supremacy of God rather than the state.[124] On December 10-13, 1940 at the biennial meeting of the FCC in Atlantic City the Department of International Justice and Goodwill presented the paper to the six hundred delegates in attendance who endorsed it officially on behalf of the FCC.[125] Many of the delegates lauded it 'as one of the most significant pronouncements of recent years.'[126]

As it turned out, the Dulles paper was far less interventionist than the earlier one published in June. *The Christian Century*, long since the voice of the noninterventionists, praised it as a 'remarkable' essay which 'will stand for a long time as conclusive evidence that as of December 1940, the churches of this nation still retained their sanity, and what is more, their Christian faith in God as reconciling love.'[127] Apparently, Dulles chipped in his lot discreetly with the noninterventionists. As could be expected, the interventionists were rather displeased. In February 1941, they published the first issue of *Christianity and Crisis* under the editorship of Reinhold Niebuhr to voice their opinions. The publication cost of the journal was defrayed by a group of prominent clergymen belonging to the interventionist faction.

In March, 1941, Bishop Henry Hobson launched his interventionist Fight for Freedom Committee. Its sponsors listed several executives of the FCC who were colleagues of Dulles. Earlier, Albert W. Palmer had formed the Ministers No War Committee and initiated a Churchmen's Campaign for Peace through Mediation. The purpose of the program was to recruit pastors for the noninterventionist cause.

Eventually, in March 1941, when Roosevelt signed the Lend-Lease Act, the pretended neutrality of America was deliberately set aside in support of the Allies. The hawks and doves within the FCC adjusted their arguments accordingly. The interventionists prepared a statement of the FCC pressing the United States for an early declaration of war. The noninterventionists, reconciling themselves to the thought of America's inevitable entry into the conflict, turned their attention to formulating specific war objectives, calling them 'peace aims'.

Dulles, by now chairman of the FCC Commission on a Just and Durable Peace, began immediately to articulate the conceptual framework of a peace settlement which meshed perfectly with his expertise in broad policy questions. A noticeable change had taken place at the North American Ecumenical Conference in Toronto, to which Dulles had been invited. The hawks and doves still clashed on occasion, but they managed to calm their tempers and reach broad agreements whenever the discussion shifted to peace aims.[128] 'The ecumenical churchmen at Toronto,' writes Albert N. Keim, 'while differing sharply on the matter of involvement in the war, were amazingly united in their vision of what constituted a desirable international order. They were, at the risk of overgeneralization, basically Wilsonian internationalists, and that pleased Dulles.'[129] John Foster was relieved to see that the wounds of the interventionist controversy were finally healing. William W. Van Kirk also recognized the beneficial influence of the Commission on a Just and Durable Peace in uniting the Church leadership to pursue a common goal. In a memorandum to Samuel M. Cavert, his superior at the FCC, he stated that 'the persons whom I have named broadly represent varying views. Given a fair amount of statesmanship, it should be possible for us, through a Commission of this kind, to prevent an unfortunate division within our ranks in times like these.'[130]

Henry P. Van Dusen, one of the leaders of the interventionist camp, noted in 1942, after the successful conclusion of the National Study Conference at Delaware, Ohio, that the representatives of American Protestantism, who until three months ago had been bitterly divided, found a consensus on important proposals for a postwar world. He believed that reconciling the hawks and doves with each other and putting them to work on long range peace issues was one of the best contributions of the Commission on a Just and Durable Peace. Dulles deserved much of the credit for this result. He devised an organisational structure which allowed the different groups to come together and deliberate on a mutually agreeable subject, i.e., the building of the Kingdom of God on earth.[131]

[1] Ruth Rouse & Stephen Charles Neill, eds., *A History of the Ecumenical Movement, 1517-1948*, Vol. 1, World Council of Churches, Geneva, (1954) 1986, 498.

[2] *Ibid.*, 497.

[3] McConnell retired from his presidential office of the Federal Council soon afterwards.

[4] Federal Council of Churches, *Quadrennial Report* (1932), New York, 19.

[5] Federal Council of Churches, *Federal Council Bulletin* 16, no. 10 (November-December 1933), New York, 4.

[6] *Christian Century*, November 29, 1933, 1496. On the other hand, the *Christian Century* sounded a very critical note about the Indianapolis quadrennial and its 'timid' stand on denominationalism: 'Our denominationalist system is spiritually bankrupt. The foundations on which the denominations have been accustomed to justify their existence have been steadily subsiding for many years ... Our sects are all operating on the momentum from the past, rather than on power generated in the living present' (*ibid.*, 1496).

[7] See also Federal Council of Churches, *Quadrennial Report* (1932), New York, 12.

[8] *Ibid.*

[9] This article was published in *Christian Century*, October 9, 1935, 1278-79.

[10] See Federal Council of Churches, *Federal Council Bulletin* 20, no. 4 (April 1937), New York, 3-5.

[11] See Samuel McCrea Cavert, *The American Churches in the Ecumenical Movement 1900-1968*, Association Press, New York, 1968, 159, 160: 'One of the interests of the Commission was in exploring some form of unity among denominations that would pass beyond voluntary cooperation. During the National Preaching Mission Stanley Jones had begun to suggest this, and his farewell message before returning to India was entitled "The Next Great Step-Unite." The type of union which he advocated was midway between a federation, in which cooperating denominations retain full sovereignty, and a merger in which the denominations disappear. In the federal union which he urged, each denomination would become a "branch" of a united church, delegating certain functions and powers to the central body and retaining all authority not thus delegated. This would be legal union, Dr. Jones argued, even if the denominations maintained their own doctrinal standards, ministries, and forms of worship. He was confident that once such a union had been definitely initiated the denominational differences would be gradually overcome. After several years of his one-man crusade Dr. Jones felt he had sufficient popular support to warrant organizing it, and launched "The Association for a United Church." For more than a decade it kept up a promotional effort but the plan never reached the point of being seriously considered by any denomination. Out of much ferment of discussion there emerged a growing conviction that, whatever might be a more remote goal, the one forward movement that was practicable in the near future was the combining of all the existing instruments of cooperation into one inclusive interdenominational structure. It was felt that such a reorganization would have the double value of securing a more efficient operation in all fields of common responsibility and also of presenting to the nation a more adequate picture of the essential oneness of the churches.'

[12] See Federal Council of Churches, *Federal Council Bulletin* 20, no. 4 (April 1937), New York, 4: 'But I do not see how the Christian Church can do the things I have suggested unless we get together. Our denominationalism simply cannot do the task. A divided church in a divided world has little authority. The next great step within Christendom is for the church to unite. I suggest that we drop our denominational label as separate churches and have one church, the Church of Christ in America and under this central unity we have branches, the Baptist Church ... We would be brought together in the General Assembly of the Church of Christ in America.' See also E. Stanley Jones, *The Next Great Step*, The Association for a United Church, Boston, n.d.

[13] *Ibid.*, 5.

[14] *Ibid.* 20, no. 5 (May 1937), New York, 6.

[15] See *Christian Century*, April 21, 1937, 513.

[16] See Federal Council of Churches, *Federal Council Bulletin* 21, no. 3 (March 1938), New York, 9-10 for the complete text.

[17] This report was published in Federal Council of Churches, *Biennial Report* (1938), New York, 21-24.

[18] *Ibid.*, 23.

[19] Federal Council of Churches, *Federal Council Bulletin* 22, no. 9 (September 1939), New York, 7-8. A conference had been held in Utrecht in May 1938 to draft a constitution for the World Council. The Federal Council sent Kenneth Scott Latourette, Lewis S. Mudge, F. H. Knubel, James DeWolf Perry, J. Ross Stevenson, William Adams Brown, Samuel McCrea Cavert, Henry Smith Leiper, and Dean Luther Weigle as delegates. By September 1938 the proposed constitution had received favourable action by the General Assemblies of the Presbyterian Church, USA and the Presbyterian Church, U.S., the General Council of the Congregational Christian Church, the General Synod of the Evangelical Church, the General Synod of the Reformed Church in America, and the Northern Baptist Convention. By the end of the year five other denominations had taken similar action.

[20] A beginning of co-operation in this area had been made in 1935 with the signing of the National Comity Agreement by six of the larger denominations, but it applied only to towns with less than 1,500 population.

[21] This report in published in Federal Council of Churches, *Annual Report* (1932), New York, 29-56.

[22] *Ibid.*, 28.

[23] *Ibid.*, 30. This committee also discussed the question of the proper relationship that should exist between the Council and those promoting church union. Admitting that there was a great division of opinion on this matter, the committee simply declared that the function of the Council was to help the denominations express the unity that they already possessed.

[24] *Ibid.*, 30.

[25] Samuel Zane Batten, *The New World Order*, 4-5.

[26] Federal Council of Churches, *Federal Council Bulletin* 15, no. 1 (January 1932), New York, 6.

[27] *Ibid.* 16, no. 1 (January 1933), New York, 9.

[28] See *ibid.*: 'We may legitimately expect that the collective mind of the nation will be equal to the intellectual and administrative tasks involved, especially under the stress of critical social conditions, if the moral qualities required are in sufficient power. What our people lack is neither material resources nor technical skills -- these

we have in abundance -- but a dedication to the common good, a courage and an unselfishness greater than are now manifest in American life. The tasks are beyond us and their accomplishment will be indefinitely delayed or frustrated, unless there be a nationwide spiritual awakening which has social gains. Our supreme social need is spiritual awakening. In our extremity arising out of harrowing social conditions throughout the world, we therefore turn anew to Christ; for the faith of great endeavour, for an overwhelming disclosure of God in the life of humanity, for the dedication of innumerable individuals to the creation of a more Christian social order, and for the assurance that what needs to be done, with God's help can be done.'

[29] Federal Council of Churches, *Federal Council Bulletin* 15, no. 9 (September 1932), New York, 12.

[30] *Ibid.*

[31] *Ibid.*, 23-24.

[32] The Indianapolis quadrennial also gave a much fuller and more radical statement of its position in its 6,000-word exposition, 'The Social Order and the Good Life' which served as the basis for the creed of 1932.

[33] *Commonweal,* December 28, 1932.

[34] For a thorough commentary on this creed, see the *Christian Century*, January 4, 1933, 6-8.

[35] Federal Council of Churches, *Federal Council Bulletin* 18, no.10 (November-December 1935), New York, 5.

[36] *Ibid.*, 7. The Council had tried to begin a Youth for Christ preaching mission in 1933 but it was unsuccessful; see also Federal Council of Churches, *Federal Council Bulletin* 20 (June 1937), New York, 8.

[37] *Ibid.*, 19, no. 8 (October 1936), New York, 5.

[38] Beaven asserted: 'It is not possible for the church to say in a voice commanding enough so that the world can hear, in the name of the Lord, that any proposal of society or government which asks for the backing of Christian people, but which would protect property at the expense of people, would protect the privileged at the expense of the underprivileged, would seek material profit rather than the enrichment of life, would rely upon force rather than justice, would manipulate and control the gifts of God in nature for the interests of the few as against the many, would breed the fears that destroy rather than the confidence that releases and strengthens, would exploit humanity rather than enlarge the life which humanity lives -- cannot be consistent with the purposes of God and the teachings of Jesus and cannot have our support.' Federal Council of Churches, *Annual Report* (1934), New York, 26-27.

[39] The *Christian Century* (November 23, 1933, 1945) adroitly pointed out that the Council should come to the aid of President Roosevelt's formulation of a sharp ethical antithesis between property rights and human rights.

[40] Federal Council of Churches, *Federal Council Bulletin* 16, no. 10 (October 1933), New York, 6.

[41] *Ibid.*

[42] *Ibid.*

[43] *Ibid.* In *The Third American Revolution* (New York, 1933) Benson Y. Landis, assistant secretary of the Department of Research of the Federal Council, wrote that the New Deal was trying to carry out a large part of the program of the churches that had been set forth in the Social Creed of 1932. He praised the Roosevelt 'revolution' as a robust young collectivism waging a battle against the old rugged individualism.

[44] Federal Council of Churches, *Federal Council Bulletin* 18, no.4 (April 1935), New York, 5.

[45] Henry Agard Wallace, Secretary of Agriculture (1933-40), vice-president (1941-45), Secretary of Commerce (1945), presidential candidate of the ultra-leftist Progressive Party (1948).

[46] Federal Council of Churches, *Federal Council Bulletin* 17, no. 1 (January 1934), New York, 7-8.

[47] *Ibid.*, no. 2 (February 1934), New York, 6.

[48] Federal Council of Churches, *Federal Council Bulletin* 17, no. 1 (January 1934), New York, 7.

[49] *Ibid.*

[50] See Dwight Macdonald, Henry Wallace. The Man and the Myth (New York: Garland Publ., Inc., 1979) 116-127: 'Formal religion, however, is not the important part of Wallace's abundant other-worldly life. He delighted especially in esoteric knowledge, strange creeds in which the scientific and the supernatural are blended. His faith ... seems to be an amalgam of Buddhism, Judaism, Zoroastrianism, Mohammedanism, and Eddyism'. To which might be added: theosophy, spiritualism, numerology, and astrology. 'Wallace dabbles in astrology and can draw a horoscope. He is quite familiar with the theory that the future can be predicted from certain markings on the Great Pyramid' (118); and Norman D. Markowitz, The Rise and Fall of the People's Century. Henry A. Wallace and American Liberalism, 1941-1948 (New York: The Free Press, 1976) 333-342.

[51] See especially *Fortune* IX, (March 1934), 52-57, 113-126.

[52] Charles Callan Tansill, *Back Door to War. The Roosevelt Foreign Policy 1933-1941* (Chicago: Henry Regnery Co., 1952) 211.

[53] Cordell Hull, *The Memoirs of Cordell Hull*, Vol. I, 398.

[54] See Federal Council of Churches, *Annual Report* (1934) 142-43. See also Dr. Beaven's letter to Senator Nye: 'The Federal Council of Churches is deeply interested in the thorough prosecution of the investigation of the munitions industry which has been going forward under the direction of the Senate committee of which you are Chairman ... As President of the Federal Council and at the urgent request of the Council's Executive Committee, I am writing to urge you and your associates to let nothing prevent the continuance of your inquiry until all of the pertinent facts relevant to the manufacture and sale of war materials by American firms are made a matter of official record.' 'Federal Council Supports Munitions Inquiry,' *Federal Council Bulletin* 17, no. 11 (November-December, 1934), New York, 21.

[55] See H. C. Engelbrecht & F. C. Hanighen, *Merchants of Death* (New York: Dodd, Mead, and Co., 1934). Alarmed at similar trends of accelerated American rearmament in the early 1930s, the authors described the historical developments set in motion immediately before and during the First World War, which precipitated the outbreak of war and America's final entry in April 1917. Corroborating their arguments with substantial evidence, they placed the blame solely on profit seeking and power hungry investment bankers and armament industrialists. They write: 'Fifteen years have elapsed since the "war to end all wars." Yet the arms industry has moved forward with growing momentum as if the pacific resolutions of the various peoples and governments had never existed. All these technical improvements and the industry bear an uncomfortable resemblance to the situation during the epoch preceding 1914. Is this present situation necessarily a preparation for another world struggle and what, if any,

are the solutions to these problems?'

[56] David L. Hoggan, *The Myth of the 'New History'. Techniques & Tactics of the Mythologists of American History* (Torrance: Noontide Press, [1965] 1985) 14.

[57] Charles Callan Tansill, *Back Door to War*, 212, 213; Tansill refers to the following sources: *Hearings Before the Special Senate Committee on the Investigation of the Munitions Industry,* 73[th] Congress, 2nd session (Washington, D.C.: US Government Printing Office) pts. 1-17; William T. Stone, 'The Munitions Industry,' *Foreign Policy Association Reports*, No. 20, 1935; and H. C. Engelbrecht, *One Hell of a Business*, New York, 1934.

[58] Cordell Hull, *The Memoirs of Cordell Hull,* 380.

[59] See *ibid.*, 400-402.

[60] See Richard Lewinsohn, *The Profits of War through the Ages* (New York: E.P. Dutton) 103-104, 222-224: 'The 500 million dollar loan contracted in autumn 1915 brought to the group of bankers, at whose head Morgan was, a net profit of 9 million dollars ... Again, in 1917, the French government paid to Morgan's and other banks a commission of 1,500,000 dollars, and a further million in 1918. Besides the issue of loans there was another source of profit: The purchase and sale of American stock which the Allies surrendered so that they could buy munitions in the States. It is estimated that in the course of the war some 2000 million dollars passed in this way through Morgan's hands. Even if the commission was very small, transactions of such dimensions would give him an influence on the stock market which would carry very real advantages ... His hatred against war did not prevent him, citizen of a neutral country, from furnishing belligerent powers with 4,400,000 rifles for a matter of $194,000,000 ... The profit were such as to compensate to some degree his hatred of warfare. According to his own account, he received, as agent of the English and French governments, a commission of 1% on orders totalling $3,000,000,000. That is, he received some $30,000,000 ... Besides these two chief principals, Morgan, however, also acted for Russia (for whom he did business amounting to $412,000,000) and for Italy and Canada (figures for his business with the last two not having been published) ... J.P. Morgan, and some of his partners in the bank, were at the time shareholders in companies that were ... concerns which made substantial profits from the orders he placed with them ... It is really astonishing that a central buying organization should have been confided to one who was buyer and seller at the same time.'

[61] Charles C. Tansill, *Back Door to War*, 213, 214. In *The Profits of War*, Richard Lewinsohn makes the following statement: 'The Kennecott Company, one of the Guggenheim group, made a profit in 1917 amounting to 70 % of the capital invested ... The corresponding profits of the Utha Copper Company ... were 200 % ... But even this was surpassed by the Calumet and Hecla Copper Mining Company who won the palm with 800 % in 1917' (Richard Lewinsohn, *The Profits of War*, 153-154). See also *Report of the Federal Trade Commission on War-Time Profits and Costs of the Steel Industry*, June 25, 1924, 29.

[62] Ron Chernow, *The House of Morgan* (New York: Simon & Schuster, 1990) 400; see also *Time* magazine, January 20, 1936.

[63] Against the background of the Council's unreserved support of Roosevelt's New Deal legislation and his interventionist foreign policy, it was certainly a clear indication of the Council's willingness to forgo principles in favour of expediency that it rallied behind the staunchly conservative and isolationist Republican Senator Gerald P. Nye of North Dakota. But it also shows how deeply entrenched the pacifist

convictions of the Council had been at that particular period of time. Even the Council's repudiation of pacifism after Pearl Harbor and its full endorsement of Roosevelt's war effort cannot negate this fact.

[64] See Federal Council of Churches, *Federal Council Bulletin* 17, no. 5 (May 1934), New York, 6-7.

[65] See *ibid.*, 6.

[66] See Federal Council of Churches, *Federal Council Bulletin* 17, no. 6 (June 1934), New York, 7.

[67] Federal Council of Churches, *Federal Council Bulletin* 18, no.1 (January 1935), New York, 4.

[68] *Ibid.*, 11.

[69] A clear distinction should be made between Christian pacifism and isolationism. There were many secular isolationists who had no connections to the Federal Council and the passage of this and subsequent neutrality acts was probably more due to their influence than to that of the Council.

[70] See Federal Council of Churches, *Federal Council Bulletin* 20, no.1 (January 1937), New York, 7.

[71] See Federal Council of Churches, *Annual Report* (1935), New York, 39.

[72] For Franklin Roosevelt's role in the struggle for the passage of neutrality legislation, see Charles A. Beard, *President Roosevelt and The Coming of War, 1941* (New Haven: Yale University Press, 1948).

[73] See e.g., Thomas A. Bailey & Paul B. Ryan, *Hitler vs. Roosevelt. The Undeclared Naval War* (London: Collier Macmillan Publishers, 1979); Charles C. Tansill, *Back Door to War* (Chicago, IL: Regnery, 1952); Charles A. Beard, *President Roosevelt and The Coming of War, 1941* (New Haven: Yale University Press, 1948).

[74] H. Montgomery Hyde, *The Quiet Canadian. The Secret Service Story of Sir William Stephenson* (London: Hamish Hamilton, 1962) 32, 33.

[75] Charles A. Beard was the president of the American Political Science Association and of the American Historical Association. In 1948 he was awarded the Gold Medal of the National Institute of Arts and Letters for the best historical work of the preceding decade. Incidentally, Beard was a founder of Ruskin College, Oxford.

[76] Charles Austin Beard, *President Roosevelt and The Coming of War, 1941*, 590.

[77] Henry P. Van Dusen, *Oral History Collection*, 1965, 41, 43.

[78] Michael A. Guhin, *John Foster Dulles*, 19, referring to a letter of Dulles addressed to Ambassador John W. Davis, *JFD Papers* (July 14, 1920). Guhin further remarks: 'Although John W. Davis, Democratic candidate for the presidency in 1924, was a friend of Dulles, familiarity was not the only if even the main, reason why the latter supported Davis in 1920 and 1924. In short, Ambassador Davis was internationally minded and Dulles was strongly advocating, among other things, United States membership in the League of Nations and no "return to normalcy." When Davis failed to receive the Democratic nomination in 1920, Dulles was "considerably disappointed" with both candidates and awaited developments to decide whether to be a Republican or Democrat ... In 1924 Dulles wholeheartedly supported Davis and supplied him with a list of issues on which he thought the Republicans were particularly vulnerable to criticism. Dulles supported the Harding-Hughes plan for adherence to the Permanent Court of International Justice, while claiming President Coolidge, in spite of announced support, was actually indifferent to the proposal' (*ibid.*).

[79] John F. Dulles, draft manuscript prepared for *The Nation* (March 1938), Box 138, *JFD Papers*; as cited in Albert N. Keim, 'John Foster Dulles and the Protestant World Order Movement on the Eve of World War II,' *Journal of Church and State*, 3 (1978) 76.

[80] Albert W. Palmer, 'Call a World Economic Conference!' *The Christian Century* (9 November 1938), 1368-1369.

[81] Charles Clayton Morrison, 'Editorial,' *The Christian Century* (30 November 1938), 1453.

[82] Albert W. Palmer, 'What Should the Churches Do Now?' *The Christian Century* (21 December 1938), 1575.

[83] See Samuel McCrea Cavert, 'Moving toward the World Council,' *The Christian Century* (22 February 1939), 242-244.

[84] Charles Clayton Morrison, 'Editorial - Toward a World Convergence,' *The Christian Century* (8 March 1939), 312.

[85] See Willem A. Visser 't Hooft, *Memoirs* (Geneva: WCC Publication, 1973) 110.

[86] See *ibid.*; and also Conference Memoranda, 1939, *JFD Papers*, Box 138. The Americans were Henry A. Atkinson, John F. Dulles, Charles Fenwick, James H. Franklin, Georgia Harkness, Ivan Lee Holt, G. Ashton Oldham, Albert W. Palmer, John R. Mott, Henry Smith Leiper, Roswell P. Barnes, Mrs. Graham Spry. All but the last person were to serve on the Commission on a Just and Durable Peace later (see ch. 5).

[87] See W. A. Visser 't Hooft, *Memoir*, 110.

[88] Albert W. Palmer, 'A Christian Fourteen Points,' *The Christian Century* (13 September 1939), 1102.

[89] W. A. Visser 't Hooft, *Memoirs*, 111.

[90] See Albert Keim, 'John Foster Dulles and the Federal Council of Churches, 1937-1949,' 33.

[91] See letter, JFD to Lionel G. Curtis, July 19, 1939, *JFD Papers*, Box 138, as cited in Albert N. Keim, 'John Foster Dulles and the Protestant World Order Movement on the Eve of World War II,' *Journal of Church and State*, 3 (1978) 78.

[92] See Albert Keim, 'John Foster Dulles and the Federal Council of Churches, 1937-1949,' 36.

[93] Letter, JFD to Quincy Wright, December 19, 1939, *JFD Papers,* Box 138; as cited in Albert N. Keim, 'John Foster Dulles and the Protestant World Order Movement on the Eve of World War II,' *Journal of Church and State*, 3 (1978) 79.

[94] Charles Clayton Morrison, 'Editorial - Peace and Neutrality Sought by American Churches,' *The Christian Century*, 20 September 1939, 1124.

[95] Charles Clayton Morrison, 'Editorial - Peace and Neutrality Sought by American Churches,' 1125.

[96] 'Correspondence,' *The Christian Century*, 27 September 1939, 1172.

[97] Charles Clayton Morrison, 'Editorial - The Federal Council's Message,' *The Christian Century*, 18 October 1939, 1262-63.

[98] Reinhold Niebuhr, 'Leaves from the Notebook of a War-Bound American,' *The Christian Century*, 25 October 1939, 1298-99; 15 November 1939, 1405-6; 6 December 1939, 1502-3; 27 December 1939, 1607-8.

[99] Special Correspondence, 'Emphasize War Responsibility,' *The Christian Century*, 31 January 1940, 152.

[100] Letter, JFD to Quincy Wright, 24 January 1940, Box 8, *JFD Papers*.

[101] Letter, JFD to Granville Clark, 4 March 1940, Box 138, *JFD Papers*.

[102] Letter, JFD to Helen Miller, 7 March 1940, Box 138, *JFD Papers*.

[103] Letter, JFD to Thomas Debevoise, 30 April 1940, Box 138, *JFD Papers*.

[104] See *ibid.*

[105] Letters, Box 7, *JFD Papers*.

[106] A graduate of Ohio Wesleyan University and of Boston University School of Theology, Dr. Van Kirk held several Methodist pastorates in Massachusetts before joining the staff of the Federal Council in 1925. Serving first as Associate Secretary of the Commission on International Justice and Goodwill, he became the Secretary of the Commission in 1934. Eventually, he became the Secretary of the corresponding department of the National Council of Churches. Dr. van Kirk was also a Director of the National Peace Conference, a clearinghouse for many other peace organisation in the United States, and a Committee member of Dulles' Commission on a Just and Durable Peace.

[107] Letter, Walter W. Van Kirk to John Foster Dulles, 11 May 1940, Box 7, *JFD Papers*.

[108] See letter, William Adams Brown to John Foster Dulles, 24 May 1940, Box 7, *JFD Papers*.

[109] John F. Dulles, 'America's Role in World Affairs', address to Detroit YMCA, October 28, 1939, *JFD Papers*.

[110] *Ibid.*

[111] Letter, JFD to Charles A. Lindbergh, November 1939, *JFD Papers*.

[112] See Ronald W. Pruessen, *John Foster Dulles*, 183.

[113] Letter, JFD to America First Committee, 4 December 1940, Box 131, *JFD Papers*.

[114] Ronald W. Pruessen, *John Foster Dulles*, 183.

[115] Dulles address, March 22, 1939, *JFD Papers*.

[116] *Ibid.*

[117] Letter, JFD to William E. Borah, April 3, 1939, *JFD Papers*.

[118] Letter, John F. Dulles to Arthur Sulzberger, 21 May 1941, Box 7, *JFD Papers*.

[119] Ronald W. Pruessen, *John Foster Dulles*, 183.

[120] See *New York Times*, 9 June 1940, 1:20.

[121] Letter, JFD to William W. Van Kirk, 13 June 1940, Box 19, *JFD Papers*.

[122] Letter, William Van Kirk to John Foster Dulles, 28 June 1940, Box 7, *JFD Papers*.

[123] Federal Council of Churches memoranda, October 1940, Box 207, National Council of Churches Archives, New York, New York, as cited in Albert N. Keim, 'John Foster Dulles and the Protestant World Order Movement on the Eve of World War II,' *Journal of Church and State*, 3 (1978), 85.

[124] See *Federal Council Bulletin* 24, no. 1 (January 1941); *Biennial Report* (1940); and 'Policy During the War Urged on Churches,' *New York Times*, 11 December 1940, 21.

[125] 'The Churches and the International Situation,' Federal Council of Churches manuscript, December 1940, Box 207, National Council of Churches Archives, New York, New York; as cited in Albert N. Keim, 'John Foster Dulles and the Protestant World Order Movement on the Eve of World War II,' 85.

[126] *Federal Council Bulletin* 24, no. 1 (January 1941), 2.

[127] Harold E. Fey, 'News of the Christian World - Outline Policy for Crisis,' *The Christian Century*, 25 December 1940, 1623.

[128] 'The World Church: News and Notes - Toronto Ecumenical Conference,' *Christianity and Crisis* (30 June 1941), 8.

[129] Albert N. Keim, 'John Foster Dulles and the Protestant World Order Movement on the Eve of World War II,' 87.

[130] Memorandum, Walter W. Van Kirk to Samuel M. Cavert, 9 April 1940, Box 197, National Council of Churches Archives, New York, New York; as cited in Albert N. Keim, 'John Foster Dulles and the Protestant World Order Movement on the Eve of World War II,' 87.

[131] See Henry P. Van Dusen, 'The Churches Speak,' *Christianity and Crisis* (6 April 1942), 1.

# 5

# THE PROSPECT OF A JUST AND DURABLE PEACE

5.1     The Commission on a Just and Durable Peace

In February, 1940, John Foster Dulles gave a keynote speech on 'The Churches and the International Situation' at the National Study Conference of the FCC in Philadelphia. His Christian ideals prompted him to revitalise the ideal of an international organisation capable of preventing armed conflict between individual nations. He argued that the war which had broken out in Europe a few months earlier was a result of international irresponsibility on the part of sovereign nations and called on the churches to assist in applying a 'Wilsonian' solution to that problem. This would entail, among other things, the internationalisation of colonial areas, the creation of an international court to settle disputes, and the acceptance of the idea of collective security. Before this could be done, however, two obstacles would need to be removed: (1) the elevation of the personified state to the status of a quasi-deity and (2) the exaggerated sense of moral superiority held by the contending nation-states. Dulles believed that the churches would be able to overcome both obstacles by reasserting the supremacy of God and thereby effectively diluting the pervasive statism of the times. Dulles concluded his speech by making an emotional appeal to the churches to become involved in creating the conditions which would secure universal peace.

> We must ... work and plan on the assumption that we will have another opportunity to create a new world order. But if so, two things seem certain: One is that this second opportunity, if it is to be vouchsafed us, will be our last, and the other is that there can be no new world order without the active participation of the United States, which alone combines the resources, intellectual capacity, and prestige to lead the war – in a world which

otherwise is distraught and largely ruined.[1]

Henry Sloane Coffin and Henry P. Van Dusen issued at once a public statement, apparently in response to Dulles' challenge, in which they expressed their hope that the defeat of the Axis powers would bring the age of nationalism to an ignominious end and usher in a new era of internationalism.[2] Dulles was impressed by the global perspective of the Federal Council's leading officers. Subsequently, he accepted the offer to become chairman of the Commission on the American Churches and the Peace and War Problems.[3] From the beginning, the Commission was beset by jurisdictional disputes. Despite energetic attempts to salvage the situation, Dulles did not succeed in getting the Commission off the ground.[4] At an informal dinner in October, 1940, the leadership of the Federal Council discussed alternative ways to disseminate Protestant thinking about the design of a postwar world. An agreement was reached to dismantle the troubled agency and to put in its place a new study commission. The ecumenical leadership decided to present the proposal at the Federal Council's Biennial meeting scheduled for December, 1940. In a statement drawn up by Dulles, the churches were urged to establish a commission designed to 'clarify the mind of our churches regarding the moral, political and economic foundations of an enduring peace.' The other tasks the Commission was supposed to fulfil were as follows: First, to prepare the people of our churches and of our nation for assuming their appropriate responsibility for the establishment of such a peace; second, to maintain contacts with the Study Department of the World Council of Churches (now in process of formation); third, to consider the feasibility of assembling representative gatherings of Christian leaders, lay and clerical, if and as this may serve to mobilize a sentiment of Christian peoples to bring about a peace which will reflect Christian principles.[5] The delegates at the conference expressed their approval and endorsed a motion to establish 'The Commission to Study the Bases of a Just and Durable Peace.'[6] To forestall any problems, the Commission would be answerable directly to the Executive Committee of the Council.[7] John Foster Dulles seemed the logical choice to act as the chairman. Years later Samuel M. Cavert, General Secretary of the Federal Council, recalled that the reason for inviting Dulles to assume the leadership role of the Commission was based on the recognition that he had distinguished himself as 'the person who had the contribution of both competence and experience and also of real orientation to the Christian approach.' Moreover, Dulles had consistently shown a keen interest in the Federal Council's activities. As Cavert noted, 'He was one of the people willing to be very generous with his time ... It sounds a little overly pious maybe, but I think he really had a sense of Christian vocation about this.'[8] But after being informed of his nomination, Dulles hesitated to accept the honour. Although he had supported the decision to establish the Commission, he had no desire to become involved in a study group which would be ineffectual in influencing the actual policy-making process of the American government. Instead of merely informing the Christian public about the intended shape of world order, he wanted to adopt a more activist posture. Simply to arouse public opinion on important social and political issues would not be enough to cause the changes he hoped would follow the conclusion of the World War. More had to be done in terms of exercising real political power to implement the liberal Christian vision of the Kingdom of God on earth, i.e., a world in which the concept of nationhood would be replaced by the ideal of an international community.

In October, 1939, while addressing a large audience at the National Council of the Y.M.C.A. in Detroit, he had already stated that 'the vitally important issue is the realization of a new world order which will put our political knowledge to work and end a system which makes these violent revolts both inevitable and recurrent.'[9] In his view, the churches had a distinctive contribution to make to international relations. He believed that, apart from the Christian community, no other group would succeed in creating 'a practical, workable system under which the barriers and restraints of sovereignty may be made yielding to the inevitable requirements of change.'[10] In one of his numerous addresses to the Federal Council he challenged his audience to translate their religious convictions concerning a better world order into a dynamic program of peaceful change. Presenting a statement on the world situation, he expressed himself as follows:

A few years ago, as a result of my thirty years of experience with international problems, I came to the conclusion that there was no hope of substantial progress toward peace unless there were in the world more people who would bring to bear upon international problems the type of Christian spirit which is reflected in the statement before you ... I have seen conference after conference fail because the participants felt that their task was to promote the welfare of their particular nation without regard to the general welfare.[11]

A few weeks after the official formation of 'The Commission to Study the Bases of a Just and Durable Peace' the Federal Council succeeded in persuading Dulles to accept the chairmanship.[12] Roswell P. Barnes, the Associate General Secretary of the FCC, remembered visiting Dulles in his office at Sullivan and Cromwell in New York City. In the ensuing conversation Dulles came immediately to the point by asking whether or not Barnes believed the Commission would be able to accomplish anything in the political arena.[13] Barnes convinced him that the churches were indeed in a position to go beyond merely discussing the finite status of the nation-state. They would be able to contribute significantly to the establishment of a world organisation powerful enough to guarantee the success of the postwar peace process. The main *modus operandi* would be the guiding of public opinion along the lines determined by the Commission. In an official statement Dulles gave two main reasons for accepting the chairmanship:

I have assumed this responsibility firstly, because I believe it is imperative that our nation should become generally conscious of the underlying moral and social forces which are at work and that we should come into harmony with them; secondly, because I believe that Christians, above all others, should be able to bring about this result.[14]

Marquis Childs, a well-known journalist, characterised Dulles' motivation to preside over the Commission as 'shrewd'.[15] This it certainly was. Richard M. Fagley, a Commission member, who knew Dulles intimately, confirmed the impression that John Foster's ambitions were more complex than simple religious vocation. 'Mr. Dulles - as all big men - was complex. There were many levels of motivation ... I think one could argue that his political future - he may have felt unconsciously, at least - was being advanced by his work in connection with the largest body of Protestant and Orthodox opinion in the country.' That did not mean, however, that the new chairman of the Commission lacked a genuine interest in furthering the internationalist cause of the FCC. Even Fagley noted that the Church leadership never questioned Dulles' sincerity. They had no reason to surmise that he worked solely to advance his own agenda.

> We knew that obviously he had political ambitions, and he wanted to have a responsible role in the making of peace and this group [was] in favour of conscientious laymen making their contribution in the secular sphere. But I would say that we had no particular feeling that he was trying to use the Commission to put forward points of view that were political in character vis-a-vis his political future.[16]

As a matter of fact, the Church leaders were outright flattered to have a man of Dulles' stature join their ranks. John C. Bennett affirmed that his colleagues, who had joined the Commission under Dulles' leadership, looked up to him as 'a big figure who had - I think, quite in a disinterested way - come to identify himself with the churches, and I think he made this for a time perhaps his major interest.'[17] Decades later, Henry Smith Leiper, a Commission member and Foreign Secretary of the FCC, still mused over the good fortune which had befallen them at that time. 'The thing that I have always thought was highly significant in a case of a man who was so engrossed in legal and financial matters was his sensitivity for the really key people in the religious world.'[18] John A. Mackay, another Commission member and president of Princeton Theological Seminary, maintained that Dulles' attitude in assuming the new leadership position was one of service, first of all to the churches, but also to the country as a whole. His involvement 'showed his very, very basic concern, at that time at least, not merely to win a war, but to see that the country would be worthy of its tradition and also worthy of the role which it would have to play in international affairs.'[19] It is thus not surprising, as Albert N. Keim observed, that Dulles was subsequently able to realign the purpose of the Federal Council's Commission on a Just and Durable Peace with that of the Council on Foreign Relations and other internationalist organisations:

> The decision to invite Dulles to serve as chairman of the proposed group was another factor which shifted the thrust of the Commission toward postwar peace aims. Dulles had been involved in forming both the Commission to Study the Organization of the Peace and the Council on Foreign Relations' task-forces. He eagerly grasped the opportunity to help create a church counterpart to these secular efforts. Ultimately he hoped to make the CJDP into a religious version of such blue-chip international affairs organizations as the Council on Foreign Relations, the Foreign Policy Association, the American Council of the Institute of Pacific Relations, and the Carnegie Endowment for World Peace.[20]

Under Dulles' leadership the Commission exercised great influence on the churches, but it also attracted wide public attention. One of its first tasks was to call for a reform of the economic system in western societies.

## 5.2    Demand for Economic Reform

Besides the promotion of a new world order, the primary concern Dulles and his co-workers addressed in all of their public addresses and publications was the dismal state of international economics. In Dulles' view, the Commission was morally obligated to denigrate sinful manifestations of pride and self-righteousness in the capitalist system of western democracies. This was in line with his understanding of the Protestant principle of prophetic protest; he felt that a word of judgment should be pronounced about sinful economic conditions in society. A memorandum was issued in May, 1941, which called for urgent economic reform. At the same time Dulles called for a well-informed Christian church capable of taking appropriate action on this reform.

> We do not believe that effective action is ever taken spasmodically. The Christians in this country will not exert an effective influence at critical moments unless through prior education and study they have background which enables them to appraise the significance and importance of some particular course of action.[21]

Dulles' appreciation of economic interdependence and his concern for its implications were quite prominent in the social and political circles of the 'American Establishment', to which he belonged. In a public address entitled 'The Church's Role in Developing the Bases of a Just and Enduring Peace', delivered on May 28, 1941, Dulles contended: 'As science and invention have overcome the separations which geography formerly imposed, what is done in one part of the world has repercussions which extend far beyond the national frontier. The world has become an interdependent economic machine.'[22]

In the same speech, Dulles portrayed other injurious aspects of a free enterprise system operating within the context of sovereign states. He explained that during 'the past century and a half the world had counted upon short-range material profit to arouse the effort required to drive our economic machine, to discover and develop natural resources, to market and manufacture them and to get them into consumption.'[23] This functioned fairly well 'so long as the world was one of open and constantly expanding opportunity.'[24] In time, however, this system showed symptoms of disintegration: 'We have seen during recent years extended periods during which millions of men were idle and facing misery and privation in the midst of potential plenty.'[25] Indeed, Dulles asserted, 'a solution of the problem of unemployment has been found only in armament programs.'[26]

The ability to alter the economic well-being of other states had grave consequences since, in Dulles' mind, economic instability was a principal cause of war. In a world of international interdependence such a factor needed to be controlled. Even before becoming chairman of the Commission, Dulles had suggested that, in reference to the economic realm, 'political power should be accompanied by a responsibility coextensive with power.'[27] He explained that 'this means in the economic sphere that those governments whose trade and monetary policies vitally affect millions beyond their borders should only exercise such power with [a] sense of responsibility toward these others.'[28]

A general dependence on the profit motive to run the international economy caused problems far beyond those in a capitalist domestic environment. As Dulles stated, 'the evil of dependence upon self-centred motivation is particularly acute in the field of international relations.'[29] The problem is largely produced by an unregulated system of international trade deprived of domestic checks on competition such as taxation and anti-trust laws. He explained that 'there is recognition of the principle that power involves a decent respect for all who are subject to that power. There exists no political mechanism to carry out the principle, even if it should be recognized.'[30]

The Church delegates at the National Study Conference at Delaware, Ohio, March 3-5, 1942 published a message[31] in which they declared that peace can only be established if economic problems are solved. 'We are deeply disturbed by the economic distress of millions of our fellow men and by economic conditions that threaten the extension of the kingdom of God on earth.' They insisted that the purpose of the conference was not to recommend a particular economic theory but to elevate human values above anything else. The Church delegates did not believe that they are 'limited to a choice between these two alternatives' of capitalism and communism. The 'manifest duty' of the Church was 'not to line up on the side of any economic system and certainly not to prescribe details or advocate panaceas. Its responsibility lies in a deeper moral realm.' As it turned out, however, most of the social and economic proposals advanced by the assembled clergymen were detailed applications of the Federal Council's Social Creed of 1932.

> The church must demand economic arrangements measured by human welfare as revealed by secure employment, decent homes and living conditions, opportunity for youth, freedom of occupation and of cultural activities, recognition of the rights of labor, and security in illness and old-age. To secure these arrangements it must appeal to the Christian motive of human service as paramount to personal or governmental coercion.

True to the tenets of the Social Gospel, the profit motive in economic transaction was castigated as the cause of 'grave defects' in society such as 'mass unemployment, widespread dispossession from homes and farms, destitution, lack of opportunity for youth and of security for old age.' These human tragedies, together with 'short range self-seeking trade policies,' produced the war. Economic instability had also engendered 'an atmosphere favorable to the rise of demagogues and dictators,' bringing 'in certain countries an alternative way of production which is based on complete management and control of all economic life by government.' This system of production curtailed individual freedoms and destroyed human dignity.

The delegates believed that a 'new ordering of economic life' was 'both imminent and imperative.' It would come about, 'either through voluntary cooperation within the framework of democracy or through explosive political revolution.' They therefore recognized 'the need to experimentation with various forms of ownership and control, private, cooperative and public.'

Dulles' article 'Towards World Order', in Francis J. McConnell, et al., *A Basis for the Peace To Come* (1942) elaborated on the practicality of implementing a central planning board for international trade.[32] This was only possible, if states would abandon the principle of sovereignty. Dulles argued that sovereignty means, 'by very definition ... the right to be free from change by outside forces. It is the essence of sovereignty that the sovereign can do as he pleases within his jurisdiction, no other nations having the right to interfere in any respect.'[33] If a sovereign state should decide to bring economic harm to one or any number of states, it could do so unrestrained and legally.[34] Dulles concluded that a system of sovereign states, being based on economic self-interest, was 'as obsolete as the unregulated public utility.'[35] He believed to have found 'overwhelming' evidence that the peoples of the world demanded a new 'international system' which would result in 'a transition to a new order'.[36]

Charles Taft, a member of the Commission, echoed the same sentiments in congressional hearings in 1946 to which he had been summoned to testify. His advocacy of establishing an international trade organisation parallelled Dulles' earlier belief that the churches had an important function to fulfil in blending of technical economics with religious moralism:

> Economically advanced nations constitute among themselves a community

in which no one can prosper through the disadvantage of others. Their policies can no longer intelligently follow the line of economic nationalism.

Barriers to world trade, whether in the nature of tariffs or of cartels, have become doubtful props of national welfare; and all of those acts, economic and political, in which one people affects the fortunes of another become subject both to the judgment of self-interest and of morality.[37]

Taft could count on Congress to give his views close attention. As the President of the Federal Council at the time, he expressed the official position of the mainline churches. Furthermore, Taft, a long-standing member of the Council on Foreign Relations, had previously been the Director of Wartime Economic Affairs for the Department of State, and as such, was privileged to formulate state policy.[38]

5.3     Dilution of National Sovereignty

In 'The Church's Contribution Towards a Warless World,' published in late 1939, Dulles suggested that 'any sound world order can be achieved only by a major operation upon [some dilution of] sovereignty.'[39] Such action would, however, meet a formidable challenge; it would 'operate upon an entity which is popularly deified.'[40] He thought that the best way to demystify the religious imagery of the nation-state in the public mind was to 'vitalize belief in a God who is the Father of us all, a God so universal that belief in him cannot be reconciled with the deification of Nations.'[41] The implication of Dulles' reasoning was that extreme patriotism was incompatible with the Christian faith.[42] As an act of true worship, adoring an 'universal God', the sovereignty system had to be exchanged for an 'International World Order'.[43] As reported in a *New York Times* article, on October 28, 1939, Dulles' proposition of a new world order would engender far-reaching consequences, which would diminish greatly, as a free act of national self-sacrifice, the excessive political, economic, and military power of the United States of America:

> Some dilution or levelling off of the sovereignty system as it prevails in the world today must take place ... to the immediate disadvantage of those nations which now possess the preponderance of power ... The establishment of a common money ... would deprive our government of exclusive control over a national money ... The United States must be prepared to make sacrifices afterwards in setting up a world politico-economic order which would level off inequalities of economic opportunity with respect to nations.[44]

In a number of other speeches and articles Dulles reiterated the same theme of diluting or abolishing the sovereignty system.[45] In 'The Churches and World Order', for example, he concurred with Philip Kerr's famous dictum that the society of nations is in a state of anarchy adding that this is an accurate description of the bankrupt system of national sovereignty.[46]

Nevertheless, Dulles harboured no illusions about the future set-up of the United Nations. Testifying before a Senate Committee in 1945, he asserted that the United Nations, far from being the desired expression of the guardian of world order, would merely be an international organisation, whose 'arrangement' under the Charter, 'was in the nature of a joint adventure'. He added that 'not one ... [of] the member states lost their independence of action in any respect by merging it and creating a new government, as was done under the Constitution of the United States.'[47] Thus Dulles, knowing the complex realities of international affairs, cautioned against prematurely instituting a fully functional world government. While highlighting the value of idealism and faith when addressing secular audiences, Dulles' habitually warned against a utopian approach in world politics before Christian assemblies:

> Practical political action is not often a subject for authoritative moral judgments of universal scope. Those who act in the political field must deal with the possible, not with the ideal; they must try to get the relatively good, the lesser evil; they cannot, without frustration, reject whatever is not wholly good; they cannot be satisfied with proclaimed ends, but must deal with actual means.[48]

He found that the criticism of Christian leadership to be 'too prone to rely upon high motivation without regard to practical limitations' was often valid.[49] To keep from falling into a quixotic trap, and to succeed as an agent in the 'ethical solution', Christians should learn to 'conform their daily conduct to their judgment of relative good and relative evil'.[50] They need to understand that Christianity was never a 'substitute for factual knowledge, practical experience and tested wisdom'.[51] It would be imperative, therefore, to 'take account of what men are, not what the Church thinks they ought to be'.[52]

At that time, Dulles did not overtly object to the Charter's provision of an international order still based on a sovereignty system.[53] Although expressing his hope that 'some day it ought to be different'[54], he simply accepted the political realities in the early 1940s which militated against the establishment of a functional world order system and opted for establishing an international organisation with effective but limited powers.[55] After all, the Second World War was fought to prevent Hitler's megalomaniacal grasp for world power. 'I've always said,' John C. Bennett recalled,

> that I thought it's very interesting that the American churches never went in heavily for world government, because of the influence of Reinhold Niebuhr and John Foster Dulles - Niebuhr providing, perhaps, the broader rationale, but Dulles also having this intuitive sense of the way things developed, that they didn't develop by fiat.[56]

199

What the United Nations represented was, however, still a matter of worthy contemplation. For Dulles it constituted a 'world organization that is prepared to break with past performance.' Alluding to the appalling performance of the League of Nations in the uncharted waters of a new international order, he predicted that 'within a few years the reality of [wartime] unity will have departed from the United Nations and new and now unpredictable national alignments will be in the making.'[57] If this situation were to materialise, as it did at the end of the Great War, it would be imperative to keep a sense of 'unity and fellowship' alive. This would require a recognition of the United Nations as 'a body to organize the nations to crusade together against intolerance, want, injustice and the denial to human beings of their fundamental rights and freedoms.'[58] Any such action, encouraging a united front on the part of sovereign nations, would eventually bring into being 'the store of trust and confidence which must precede any adequate delegation of power to a world organization.'[59] John F. Dulles was confident that, in due time, the United Nations would evolve into an institution which would exercise its comprehensive powers, not in order to deprive the world population of its rights and freedom, but to further its welfare and happiness.[60] In the meantime, a gradually increasing, but strictly voluntary, submission to the regulatory authority of the United Nations would engender that degree of trust necessary to facilitate the organisation's metamorphosis into a functional world government.

Dulles always seemed to equate the general welfare of humankind with the world-wide extension of the political powers of a new international organisation (calling it 'Executive Organ'). In an address in 1942 he defined the responsibilities of a world government thus:

> (1) I would have the Executive Organ create a Monetary or Banking Corporation ... empowered to provide monetary media through which needed exchange of goods between nations could be facilitated ... (2) I would have the Executive Organ authorized to charter commercial companies, as seemed to it desirable, to engage in the business of effecting international movements of goods from one country to another ... (3) I would have the Executive Organ authorize to negotiate compacts with the several nations whereby their tariffs and trade quotas would be fixed ... By these three initial steps we will have begun that dilution of sovereignty which all enlightened thinkers agree to be indispensable ... We will have avoided the mistake of assuming, at the beginning, tasks so vast, so difficult and so unexplored that failure is likely ...'[61]

During Dulles' work with the Commission, he identified another problem besides economic disparity and national sovereignty which contributed to volatile conditions in the world. He became very vocal on what he perceived to be 'spiritual inadequacies' in the international system. While these ideas were most thoroughly developed in the 1940s, they were present in embryonic form in his book *War, Peace and Change* (1939).[62]


## 5.4     War, Peace and Change

Dulles wrote *War, Peace and Change* presumably in response to the appeal of the Oxford Professor Gilbert Murray at the International Studies Conference on Peaceful Change in Paris, 1937. Professor Murray asked if 'some person, unofficially and on his private initiative, would be bold enough to try to summarize in a short volume the results to which he personally thinks the discussion point.'[63] Published in 1939, the book's message came to be recognized as Dulles' political manifesto, even though in some of its details, most notably on communism, he modified his position decisively during and after the Second World War.


### 5.4.1     Human Nature

Dulles observed that in an imperfect world conflicts would inevitably occur as a natural consequence of human selfishness. He saw people everywhere embroiled in a constant struggle to meet basic material and immaterial needs. They have to obtain food and clothing to sustain life, and create a safe and comfortable environment for themselves. As emotional and spiritual beings, they strive to satisfy their longings for love, beauty and religion. Reminded perpetually of the brevity of life, they seek self-exaltation by identifying with some external cause or being which bestows upon them a sense of nobility and immortality.[64]

The limitations imposed upon them as human beings, however, prevent them from satisfying these needs. In a state of social isolation their destitute state becomes even more noticeable and aggravating. Consequently, people form voluntary associations with others. Yet sooner or later they realise that such communal arrangements do not necessarily guarantee individual contentment. On the contrary, they engender another kind of dissatisfaction. The desires of some clash inexorably with those of others. Due to a material shortage of goods relatively few obtain sufficient means to gratify their desires.[65] Every perceived deficiency motivates those less fortunate to deprive others of their possessions.[66] Dulles aptly identified these two opposing groups as the static and dynamic elements of society. Pitched against each other, they tend to produce volatile conditions, even war, if left unrestrained.

Dulles believed this phenomenon is easily explained from a psychological point of view. As rational beings, humans in general devise mechanisms of settling conflicts when they arise. They seek to defuse tension peacefully before it erupts into violence. Experience has shown them that the exercise of brute force is a legitimate but primitive solution, since it does not produce a perfect sense of satisfaction. Instead, it creates inconveniences and difficulties without guaranteeing a predictable outcome. Thus, on the small group level two procedures are applied successfully in averting physical confrontation: the ethical and the political. The ethical solution directs its efforts 'to states of mind.'[67] As a result,

.... desires are spiritualized and selfishness in its crude form is transmuted into a sense of duty to fellow man and the attaining of a satisfaction by performance of that duty.[68]

The defining purpose of the ethical solution is, therefore, its potential to eliminate the psychological barriers which oppose the formation of an orderly society. Commenting on this aspect, Michael Guhin noted,

The "ethical solution" aimed at individuals and public opinion. It represented a slow process of enlightenment through education, emphasizing interrelatedness and interdependence. This process would, by design, eventually erode the foundations of isolationism and extreme nationalism and generate the growth of a functional substratum of international community interests.[69]

In contrast, the political solution relies on a governmental authority to determine by law which of the conflicting desires within a society will be allowed to prevail. Under the rule of law differences are first recognised and then channelled into non-violent forms:

... the setting up by social groups some arbiter who creates rules of conduct designed to create a society wherein a fair balance is established between the static and dynamic.[70]

The essence of the political solution in Dulles' mind is, therefore, its ability to set in motion legislative mechanisms which, while protecting the underlying principles of society and stabilizing its dynamic elements, allow peaceful change to occur and thus produce constructive governmental transformations.

Contrary to the propitious effects which these two solutions bring to the resolution of conflicts within nations, they tend to obstruct the settlement of international quarrels. Dulles believed that the ethical solution, although able to curb the selfish nature of humans in general, was inadequate to deal with disputes between nations, because of its failure to control nationalistic emotions.

In only a small segment of our lives are our acts dictated by reason. In the main we act unthinkingly under the impulses of emotional and physical desires or in accordance with tradition or the customs of the social group of which we happen to form a part.[71]

The ethical solution cultivated a receptiveness for mass emotional appeals to sacrifice one's best for the supposed good of the nation. Capitalising on this psychological disposition, governments have begun to employ successfully modern means of mass communication, particularly radio, movies, and loudspeakers, in an effort to stir up extreme nationalistic feelings. This, in turn, gave the nation the licence to conduct wars which usually led to total disaster. Nationalism is thus essentially a combination of irrational emotions stirred up by power-seeking governments solely interested in guarding their own privileged position.

Dulles identified still another reason for the nation state's success in securing the loyalty of its citizens. He described it as the idolisation of the nation.


## 5.4.2    The Idol of Nationalism

In attempting to solve rationally the problem of war, political institutions were formed and authorised to reconcile conflicts. The nation system has evolved, according to Dulles, in response to external stimuli of perceived physical danger. In the primitive stages, the father of the family assumed the role of protector. Soon this proved to be inadequate, '[a]s families came into contact and association with each other, and larger social groups came into being, a new authority was established such as a chief or mayor.'[72] Eventually this process, once it gained momentum in the formation of larger societal units, gave rise to 'a world of nations each of which has a supreme authority superimposed upon a multitude of subordinate and more localized authorities.'[73]

In seeking to explain the abrupt discontinuance of this development at the national level, Dulles suggested that the answer must be found in the nature and role of government. Any nation is governed by a supreme authority which seeks to maintain a delicate balance between the static and dynamic elements of society. In discharging its duty it must define the rules and enforce them. As long as the group is small, the governmental task remains manageable. The authority concerns itself primarily with the protection of life and property. Difficulties arise, however, when the society expands in scope and complexity.

> The task of appraising relative satisfaction and dissatisfactions, of diagnosing cause and effect and of prescribing rules calculated to achieve the greatest good for the greatest number becomes a task of great difficulty.[74]

Dulles contends that the preferred course of action which a government chooses to hide its own inadequacies and to keep its citizenry under control is to employ two human emotions: fear and pride.

> 1. Those who possess power invariably seek to enlarge and perpetuate their power. They do this by picturing external difficulties which necessitate large

concentrations of power in their hands.[75]

> 2. [The] individual tends to personify the group authority and to identify therewith to such an extent that they derive vicarious pride from the power of the group authority.[76]

The people's feeling of excitement, drama and romance is further aroused by their penchant to personify the nation and transform it into a living being endowed with heroic qualities 'who lives bravely and dangerously in a world of inferior and even villainous other nation personalities.'[77] Dulles argued, therefore, that one of the causes of totalitarian war is the tendency to give the state a fictional personality of the 'hero-nation'; essentially to deify its image[78] and portray it in constant struggle with the 'villain-nation'.

In the attempt to satisfy the innumerable wants of its citizenry, which cannot all be met within the national domain, the group authority seeks to extend its dominance in the international realm. In the quest to obtain trade, economic or territorial advantages for the group, it resorts to power politics[79] in an ostentatious display of its national will which derives its impetus from a high degree of national unity and patriotism.[80]

> It is thus natural that the group authority should seek to maintain and identify the nation-hero and the nation villain concepts and to accentuate in group members a sense of identification with and dependence upon their own nation personification.[81]

As soon as the personification of the nation has been accomplished, the individuals can be called upon to make great sacrifices in the context of modern warfare. Under the impulse of emotions, if sustained by a noble cause (real or imagined), human beings are willing to endure great hardship. These inclinations of the human nature contribute to the formation of a radical nationalism which militates against the establishment of any effective world authority. Dulles claimed the hidden cause for this development was the decline of traditional religion:

> There have been many times when religious concepts dominated human emotion and the action that springs therefrom. This has primarily been at times when such concepts involved the dramatic contrasting of God and Devil, of Heaven and Hell, of Believer and Infidel. But such ideology, doubtless beneficent at its inception, became exaggerated to a degree that led to widespread destruction and suffering, as during the period of religious wars. A reaction and dilution occurred. But such dilution involved religion becoming more universal and abstract. When this occurred, religion became less gripping and vital. It became inadequate to satisfy the mass need of a clear-cut, vivid object of adoration and sacrifice.[82]

Religious ideals, having become 'vague and uninspiring', deprived religion itself of its essential moral power over the mind of its adherents. Religion left these ideals 'to the false gods of patriotism to evoke the self-sacrificial qualities in mankind.'[83] In other words, as religions became less real in the eyes of individuals, they began to lose some of their potency to promote devotion and loyalty. But as the moral force of religions began to wane, the deified state became a substitute to fill the void. 'At this point', Dulles alleged, 'the gods of nationalism were imagined to fill the want which most men feel.'[84] Consequently, people shifted their allegiance away from the supernatural to the very human, but now deified, state. They embraced the 'nation-ideology'.[85] Dulles thus contended that one of the main causes of international conflict grew out of a distorted form of nationalism which assumed a religious ambience. 'We have been rendering unto Caesar that which is God ... The personified nation has to a marked degree preempted the role of that higher spiritual entity with which every man desires to feel some identification.'[86]

A spiritual revival would be needed to correct the perversion of the spirit of self-sacrifice by diluting the concept of the national hero-deity benefactor. It would also kindle the veneration of a truly universal ideal, namely the building of God's kingdom on earth. 'The finest qualities of human nature are at once too delicate and too powerful to be put blindly at the disposal of other humans who are primarily concerned with their own kingdom – not the bringing into being of the Kingdom of God.'[87]

## 5.5    Critic of Spiritual Deficiencies

During the course of World War II, Dulles argued, spiritual deficiencies were appearing on both sides of the conflict. The appropriate means to prevent armed conflicts in the future would be contingent on a thorough appraisal of the spiritual conditions in the warring countries. The problem which at first was brought on by the economic deprivations in Europe was further aggravated by the spiritual deficiency of National Socialism and Communism as atheistic ideologies.

When Dulles wrote *War, Peace and Change* in 1939, he recognized that the development of ideologies such as Communism and Fascism might alter slightly his analysis of violence on the international level. Without intending to minimise the potentially contentious nature of competing philosophies of government, he nevertheless believed that historically international conflicts were rooted in nationalistic causes, not in ideological abstractions. In his eyes, the ideologies of Fascism, Communism, or Democracy did not transcend nationalism. They were, rather, 'adjuncts to nationalism, representing causes which the nation-hero espouses ... Even where they tend to become more marked it would not invalidate the general principles which we come ... [to believe].'[88]

In the May 1941 speech at the Chicago Temple, Dulles modified his opinion, however, concerning the possible role of ideologies in causing war.

He drew the attention of his audience to the fact of the revolutionary character of both the German and Russian aggression:

> Germany and Russia today pose problems which are more than economic. Their designs are broadly revolutionary and they seek to overthrow not merely the old economic order, but also its political and moral ideologies. Just as the French Revolution, which grew out of economic distress, became atheistic, so the German and Russian revolutions are atheistic. Undoubtedly the world is now faced not merely with economic issues, but with moral and political issues of the utmost gravity.[89]

Although he expressed the opinion that National Socialism might eventually collapse as a consequence of its moral or spiritual problems, he believed that Germany would find 'her peace again' if she accepts 'the Christian concept that every human being has value as a person, irrespective of nationalities, color or class.'[90]

Dulles also observed spiritual defects on the Allies' side. He warned his countrymen that 'we also will never achieve our peace if we seek to perpetuate a world system which we believe to be to our immediate economic advantage because it legalizes the irresponsible use of our power. That, too, is immoral and un-Christian and bound to fail.'[91] He thus concluded that 'our great national weakness today is not physical, but spiritual', explaining that 'we lack a constructive power which is inspiring and contagious. We appear to be purely on the defensive and to be supporting the *status quo* of a national sovereignty system which has become vitally defective and which is inevitably productive of just such convulsions as the present World War.'[92] It is interesting to note that Dulles interpreted America's 'economic irresponsibility', as a form of spiritual weakness equal to that of totalitarian states. These remarks echoed earlier statements of Dulles in Spring, 1939, which blamed Great Britain, France and the United States for their immoral fixation on consolidating their position of power at the expense of other nations. This misguided policy, expressed in clichés such as 'sanctity of treaties', 'law and order', 'resisting aggression', and 'enforcing morality'[93], had, in Dulles' view, brought about volatile conditions of chaos and revolt in world affairs. A few months later, he deprecated the behaviour of the same countries in similar terms:

> For fifteen years following the World War, Great Britain and France dominated Europe. They, with the United States, achieved a power so overwhelming that their political and economic policies vitally affected all other peoples of the world ... Yet that power was exercised purely selfishly to the end of perpetuating in their own people a monopoly of advantage. We see in Japan, Italy and Germany the fruits of such a system.[94]

These remarks drew mild criticism from quarters which had previously supported Dulles in his drive for a new world order. Henry L. Stimson, a former Secretary of State[95] and a fellow member of the Council on Foreign Relations, took issue with Dulles' rhetoric about the morally reprehensible behaviour of western democracies. 'I am not sure,' he wrote in a letter, 'that you have not oversimplified your analysis.'[96]

Following the Japanese attack on Pearl Harbor in December, 1941, Dulles began to concentrate his efforts primarily on influencing the planning of the Allies for a postwar world, in which the reality, if not the concept, of national sovereignty would be significantly modified. To further that purpose, he cautioned at the National Study Conference of the FCC on March 3, 1942, against an irrational hatred of the Axis powers. He explained that 'we realize that to attain our end [in the war] requires a national purpose forged by hearts and minds that are comprehending and free from the evil emotions which Christ condemned.'[97] He objected to any notion that would make allowance for emotions of 'hatred, vengefulness and self-gratification' in the face of victory.[98] While these emotions may be natural reactions of a soldier in combat, they end up by 'fouling his mind and soul'.[99] These evil emotions 'burn up the moral fiber of a people; they do not produce a type of will which is persistent; they build up external resistances which make victory more difficult to obtain, and they render victory illusory if it is finally achieved.'[100] To reinforce his thesis that hatred would be detrimental to the cause of peace, Dulles referred to Christ and Abraham Lincoln as the protagonists of forgiveness and healing.

Dulles also argued that the victors should not merely be satisfied with the 'negative task'[101] of defeating the enemy on the battlefield. He asserted that 'victory is not itself the end. It is a means to an end, namely the organizing of a better world'.[102] Consequently, the United States needed a sense of mission beyond ending the war. It needed a 'national purpose which conforms to great human needs, a purpose', Dulles explained, 'that is responsive to the insistent demand of suffering humanity that a way be found to save them and their children and their children's children from the misery, the starvation of body and soul, the violent death, which economic disorder and recurrent war now wreak upon man.'[103] Dulles argued that it was the duty of Christians to help show the world how to accomplish these positive tasks. It would be necessary to counter the immoral tendency of re-establishing the corrupt nation-state system after the war. In the process of restructuring the international order according to the ideals of the Christian faith the mission of the church should be defined as the building of the Kingdom of God on earth, a community of nations living in peace and prosperity. The churches, as the moral repositories in society, were charged to embark on an educational campaign to propagate the gospel of reconciliation and unity among nations.

Dulles was praised by many of his co-workers for his ability in leading the Commission on a Just and Durable Peace. His devotion to the cause of world peace enabled him to work diligently to achieve the objectives of the Commission.[104] Dulles possessed an extraordinary organisational talent and resourceful agility. John Coleman Bennett assessed him as a man who was 'not dominating in an objectionable sense. He always did his homework, he always had drafts, he always knew the line he wanted to take.'[105] Dulles constantly drove the Commission members to higher productivity. At regular intervals Dulles convened a meeting of the Committee of Direction, a specially organised core group of the Commission, consisting of twenty-five members.[106] At times he invited the members of the Committee to his home on Long Island to discuss pressing issues, which they did in day-long sessions.[107] At these meetings, he exhibited a remarkable gift for reconciling contrary views by fusing them into a coherent statement of public policy. Always eager to listen to the comments of his colleagues,[108] and, if necessary, to modify his views, Dulles nevertheless imposed his own agenda on them. Henry P. Van Dusen recollected that the Commission was 'really a one man show ... a rubber stamp for John Foster Dulles' ideas.' When Dulles left the organisation in 1948[109], Van Dusen and others felt that 'the keystone [had] dropped out of the structure.'[110] The Commission was subsequently merged with the larger Department of International Justice and Goodwill. The Federal Council then persuaded Dulles to continue his service as chairman of the Department's newly formed Committee on Policy.[111]

At the Committee meetings most of the discussions were initiated by a roughly drafted pronouncement of Dulles which he felt the Commission should adopt.[112] Once the Committee of Direction was satisfied with the proposed statement, it was issued for critical assessment to the other members of the Commission. The outer circle of Commission members was limited to about one hundred and included the most prominent theologians and professors of the social sciences of the day.[113] After a consensus of opinion had been reached, the Commission published its pronouncements for popular consumption.[114] This was, indeed, the primary service Dulles intended the Commission to perform. 'Where its chairman had usually directed earlier efforts at limited audiences,' writes Ronald W. Pruessen,

> the Commission on a Just and Durable Peace aimed for stimulation of a vast segment of American public opinion. Indeed, publicity efforts and public relations campaigns became the dominant ingredient in Dulles's church-related work during World War II. The lion's share of his energy in this sphere, and no doubt that of other Commission members, was channelled more often than not in one direction: toward taking a few basic ideas that were agreed upon very early and elaborating and publicizing them in such a way that would have maximum popular appeal.[115]

The educational campaign was intended to 'clarify the mind' of the churches 'regarding the moral, political and economic foundations of an enduring peace', and to 'prepare the people' of the churches and nation 'for assuming their appropriate responsibility for the establishment of such a peace'.[116] The effectiveness of the Commission in influencing public opinion in favour of international co-operation as the basis of world peace was anticipated by Dulles immediately after he had become the Commission's chairman. In a letter to his English friend Lionel G. Curtis he expressed himself as follows:

> I have just agreed to become the Chairman of a Committee being organized by the Federal Council of Churches to study the basis for durable peace. This now seems a long way off. But some day it will come and I am fearful that this country will be the greatest obstacle in the way of then doing what ought to be done. On this account I am anxious to start some work of education which will permit the church's influence to be mobilized effectively when the moment comes.[117]

As chairman of the Commission Dulles began at once to persuade the churches to support his educational efforts.[118] It would be their responsibility, he told them, to teach the public to be 'willing that their political leaders should exercise the powers of sovereignty for ends loftier than the achievement of some immediate sectional advantage.'[119] The Christian community in the United States and elsewhere could 'and should create the underlying conditions indispensable to the attainment of a better international order'. The Commission itself would assist the Church leaders in preparing 'the hearts and minds of Christian people for fair and objective dealing with all international situations.' To achieve a reasonable degree of success in this venture would require 'a willingness to accept, in certain areas, a surrender or pooling of the exclusive perquisites of national sovereignty and a sharing of economic advantages; a learning of the techniques whereby men come to accord through processes other than those of military and economic warfare.'[120]

To be most effective in gaining publicity the Commission engaged the Institute of Public Relations, Inc. of New York City in 1943 to handle its public relations efforts. The Institute utilized sophisticated methods of reaching vast numbers of people in distributing the Commission's message. Its task was facilitated by the Commission's impressive array of information channels extending from the national headquarters to the local church assemblies. The most important of these channels were the social actions secretaries of the twenty five denominations associated with the Federal Council. The state and city councils of churches also served a vital role in disseminating Commission materials and concerns to the local levels. They regularly sponsored 'world order' seminars in the hope to promote an interest in world order issues. The educational effort of the Commission was an essential component to influence government policy. Dulles believed that a strong Protestant voice in support of a world organisation would give the Commission a firm position to lobby for its representations to the government.[121]

In the 1940s the religious press commanded an estimated readership of 18,500,000. The publication and distribution of printed materials played a vital role in the educational campaign. A handbook entitled 'A Just and Durable Peace', published in April and May, 1941, along with a 'Memorandum on Preliminary Views', was the first of many similar publications.[122] Its primary purpose was to collect and summarise important statements by different Church bodies concerning the peace issue. Among other declarations it included an account of the Federal Council's Biennial Meeting (1940), the American Council of the World Alliance for International Friendship, and the Oxford Conference.[123] One of the most striking aspects of the handbook was a summary of secular proposals dealing with the establishment of a new world organisation. It also contained a syllabus of discussion questions. More than 450,000 copies found their way to the American public 'in this first effort at large-scale publicity'.[124]

Since 1938, Dulles was involved in a personal crusade to propagate the message of world peace in the United States. Between the period of 1941 to 1945 his fervency grew and his message was reaching larger and more diversified audiences. World peace was contingent, he asserted, on a general willingness to accept the 'basic thoughts which Christ himself expressed - humility, repentance, avoidance of personal hatreds and hypocrisies, [and] recognition of the spiritual supremacy of God rather than of the state.'[125] Great statesmen in the past had implemented these Christian ideals. The greatest of them, Dulles claimed, was Woodrow Wilson. It was this president, his former professor at Princeton University, who had

conceived a peace founded upon a dilution of national sovereignty. No nation could claim a legal or moral right to perpetuate its own status, but treaties and international conditions would be subject to change, on the initiative of an international body ... The colonial areas would be wholly withdrawn from the operation of the sovereignty system. There would be "freedom of the seas" and provision of the levelling of the trade barriers.[126]

Invited to speak to countless church and business groups, college clubs, civic and political organisations, he relished the fact that his growing popularity allowed him to influence a wide cross-section of society. The number of speaking engagements increased steadily, finally averaging between fifty and sixty speeches per year in the early 1940s. At the same time he demonstrated a seemingly inexhaustible resourcefulness in producing a constant stream of articles, which were published in both secular and religious magazines. In writing or speaking, Dulles usually emphasised different aspects of his internationalist theme.[127] Three years after Dulles' resignation as chairman of the Commission on a Just and Durable Peace, the Executive Committee of the Federal Council stated that 'he became a creative leader in formulating the international policies expounded by the Council ... His insights and experience were invaluable in the drafting of .... [many] notable statements.'[128]


5.7     Political Pronouncements

Political changes in the world at large frequently evoked a reaction from the Commission. The first opportunity came in the wake of the eight-point joint declaration of Roosevelt and Churchill, the famous Atlantic Charter (as it became later known). Shortly after the pronouncement of the Charter the Commission published the booklet entitled *Long Range Peace Objectives*[129], a detailed analysis of the Charter's claim to constitute the basis 'for a better future world' and a set of postwar proposals. Its wide distribution was guaranteed, after it became known that Dulles himself was responsible for its content. Originally, it was one of his addresses delivered to all Commission members. Again, a detailed study guide was prepared with questions about the Atlantic Charter's provisions for economic sanctions, the issue of national sovereignty, and the future of a world organisation.

        After its publication on September 18, 1941 the statement startled many citizens, for in it Dulles criticised the Atlantic Charter as being 'inadequate'; its noble purpose 'tentative and incomplete', without provisions to safeguard against a repetition of the Versailles failure. Although recognising that Roosevelt and Churchill offered 'their conception of a new world order', their statement was deficient in its provisions for a long-range perspective of lasting peace. 'Unless we propose concrete measures', he argued, 'statements of good intentions ... will be looked upon with grave and warranted skepticism'. It would not be enough to strive towards 'a single, unifying conception, namely, that the postwar world should reproduce and stabilize the political organization of the prewar world.' Although completely overlooked in the Charter, Dulles contended that there was ample room for improvement in the organic interdependency among the peoples of the world. The goal, he proposed, was a change in world order rather than a regressive stabilisation of prewar arrangements and organisations. 'It is not enough to envision lofty ends,' Dulles told the press. 'Such ends are not self-realizing.' For that reason the Atlantic Charter, though an important 'starting point' in the quest for a lasting peace, was 'not enough'. The Churchill-Roosevelt war objectives, as stated in this Charter, fell 'far short of the conceptions of the great worldwide religious conferences of recent years', Dulles declared, adding that there would be 'danger' in thinking that it alone could be the basis for an enduring peace. 'The end of the present war, if it is fought through to military victory, will find an overwhelming concentration of power in one or two nations,' the report stated.

        The easy way will be for the victors to assume that the power they possess is so concentrated that peace can be assured by informal processes, not

requiring international machinery. The hard way will be for the victors to
create international organs having the power to make decisions in which
others will participate as a matter of right. Yet only this latter can be
expected to produce a durable peace.

Dulles was pragmatic enough to accept, as an inevitable 'reality', the
concentration of power in the hands of 'the Anglo-American architects of a
new military victory'.[130] Yet he argued that this could only develop into a
'beneficent reality', if the Anglo-American power were prepared to forgo its
advantage. This would involve consenting 'not to perpetuate itself, but to
create, support and eventually give way to international institutions drawing
their vitality from the whole family of nations.' A new world order could only
be achieved if the Allied war leaders took seriously the possibilities of a
'regional', 'continental', or 'hemispheric' integration of nations. In this respect
'a federated commonwealth of some type' in Europe would be particularly
desirable.[131] Most important of all, a lasting peace settlement would have to
include a procedure for creating a world federation, in which colonial areas
would be placed under the authority of an international mandate system.
Committed to the principle of 'interdependence' rather than independence,
especially in economic areas, the universal federation of nations would be
governed by an executive organisation, presided over by the most
distinguished statesmen in the world. The first duty of these global
administrators would be to advance the ideals of peace and welfare for the
entire human race. To precipitate the formation of a functional world
government, the new federal administration would initially incorporate the
existing machinery of the League of Nations, particularly such useful
departments as the International Labour Organisation. On the national level
each state would be required to establish governmental agencies to implement
the directives of the executive organisation. Answerable to both the national
and international authorities, these agencies would monitor the harmonisation
of the various domestic economic policies and report on any violation of
executive regulations by a given state.

Thus Dulles' criticism of the Atlantic Charter was based upon the
document's failure to call for an international organisation to keep the peace
after the war was won. According to news reports, this omission was insisted
upon by President Roosevelt. In 1920, F.D.R. had campaigned for the Vice
Presidency of the United States on a program calling for ratification of the
Versailles Treaty - and he remembered how public opposition to the League of
Nations had led to the defeat of the Democratic Party in the voting booths.
'American public opinion is not ready to accept another League of Nations,'
Roosevelt reportedly told associates.

At any rate, the Atlantic Charter omitted reference to a postwar
international organisation - and it was this omission which Dulles and the
Commission on a Just and Durable Peace sought to remedy by 'building a
ground swell of public opinion' in the United States for the establishment of a

postwar organisation to keep the peace - and for American participation in it. Michael A. Guhin describes the rationale behind Dulles' almost frantic insistence on mobilising the American Christians to bring about conditions of world peace:

> Actually, Dulles' approach to the "political solution" was best exemplified in his campaign for international organization and his views on international law. During World War II his campaign against isolationist tendencies and for international organization with American participation was characterized by a call to "idealism", in the sense of future possibilities, and a demand for "realism", in recognition of necessary gradualness and imperfections. To avoid repetition of the American refusal to ratify the Versailles Treaty and participate in the League of Nations, Dulles reasoned that with a resolute public opinion favoring participation in international organization, there would be less likelihood of squabbles in the Senate and intergroup conflicts reaching a peak where the baby would be thrown out with the bath water.[132]

Years later Dulles referred back to the publication of the *Long Range Peace Objectives* and recounted the success of his Commission (without actually mentioning it) in mobilising public support for a world organisation:

> When the Atlantic Charter was drawn up in August, 1941, to define the hopes for a better world, it was decided to omit reference to the creation of a world organization. It was judged that our people did not want to repeat the League of Nations experiment. That point of view was carried forward into the United Nations Declaration of January 1, 1942. The religious people then came to see their responsibility and opportunity. In this country they organized and campaigned widely to develop a public opinion favorable to world organization. The political leaders quickly responded on a bipartisan basis. I recall that history in order to remind ourselves that under a representative system of government it is private persons and organizations that must themselves make it possible to move ahead to develop great new institutions.[133]

Although there is no conclusive evidence, it is still plausible to believe that the Commission's campaign showed its first fruits of success when the so-called 'B2-H2' resolution was introduced in the Senate, deriving its name from its four co-sponsors, Senators Ball, Burton, Hatch, and Hill. The 'B2-H2' resolution demanded that the United States government initiate immediately the creation of a permanent international organisation. It was the political response of the legislators on Capitol Hill to the desires of the American people to participate in an international organisation of some form after the war. The organisation would have power to carry on the war, occupy territory liberated from the Axis, administer relief and economic aid, and provide the machinery for negotiating a peace settlement. The resolution also called for the creation of an international police force to 'suppress ... any future attempt at military aggression by any nation'.[134] When this development was brought to the attention of President Roosevelt, he was taken by surprise. He had not expected that public opinion would so quickly abandon its isolationist position, and turn towards an internationalist solution of the war issue. Capitalising on this opportune moment, he called for Secretary of State Cordell Hull and instructed him to draw up plans for a United Nations organisation.

5.8    The Informal Agenda Group

Acting on Roosevelt's instructions, Secretary Hull established a steering committee in January 1943 to coordinate the planning of the United Nations. This committee, later to be known as the Informal Agenda Group, included Cordell Hull, Leo Pasvolsky, Myron C. Taylor, Isaiah Bowman, John W. Davis, and Sumner Welles (until his resignation as Undersecretary of State in August 1943).[135] It is significant that Hull selected the committee members exclusively from the roster of the Council on Foreign Relations. In frequent meetings the Agenda Group exchanged ideas, formulated policy recommendations, and, generally, guided the activities of the State Department's Advisory Committee in all stages of postwar planning.[136] This group was, according to Harley A. Notter, largely responsible for the final shape of the United Nations Organization.[137]

Beginning in February, 1943 President Roosevelt met with members of the Agenda Group regularly, calling them 'my postwar advisers'.[138] Their influence reached not only into the planning stages of the United Nations Organization, but also into the final decision-making process.[139] One of the group's first assignments was to prepare drafts for the four-power agreements at the Quebec and Moscow conferences.

By December, 1943 the new Undersecretary of State, Edward K. Stettinius, Jr., joined the Agenda Group. Stettinius was a member of the Council on Foreign Relations and former chief executive of United States Steel. At that time the original group of six had been expanded to eleven members, of which eight - Leo Pasvolsky, Isaiah Bowman, Benjamin V. Cohen, John W. Davis, James C. Dunn, Stanley K. Hornbeck, Edward K. Stettinius, and Myron C. Taylor - were either present members of the Council or involved in the Council's War and Peace Studies Project.[140] Green H. Hackworth and Harley A. Notter, two government officials who, though not directly associated with the Council, were sympathetic to its internationalist orientation, had been added to the Agenda Group as well.[141] In mid-March, 1944 Joseph C. Green, another Council member, joined the group. Almost immediately he became involved in its armament studies.[142] Green invited five military officers to gatherings of the Agenda Group during March, April, and May of 1944. At least one of these, Admiral Hepburn, was a Council member. The others had close ties to the Council. General Strong and Rear Admiral Roscoe E. Schuirmann of naval intelligence, for example, had been active in the Council's War and Peace Studies Project.[143] Although John Foster Dulles was not officially part of the Informal Agenda Group, he stood in frequent communication with its principal members. For several years he had participated in different study groups which were either sponsored by or in some other ways connected with the Council on Foreign Relations.[144] Ronald W. Pruessen notes:

> In January 1940, for example, he [John F. Dulles] became a member of the Commission to Study the Organization of Peace, a new offshoot of the League of Nations Association. Through radio broadcasts and published reports, the Commission hoped to motivate the American public to a mature concern for the shaping of the postwar world. At about the same time, Dulles also agreed to participate in a secret Council on Foreign Relations project involving studies of postwar issues for the Department of State. Earlier ties with the National Council for the Prevention of War were maintained too.[145]

Dulles was one of the original members of the Commission to Study the Organization of the Peace, established under the chairmanship of James T. Shotwell, another founding member of the Council on Foreign Relations, in 1939. It is interesting to note that this Commission was made up primarily of scholars rather than churchmen. It had an investigative-educational task conceived in much the same spirit as was the task of the Commission on a Just and Durable Peace.[146]

Following the Moscow conference in late 1943, in which Great Britain and the Soviet Union had agreed to the American plan to set up a new world organisation, Secretary Hull, still revelling in his personal success, asked the Agenda Group to draft the American proposal for a United Nations Organisation. Its primary purpose was to maintain international peace and security at the end of war. In the period from December, 1943 to July, 1944 the group worked out the details of a plan which finally materialised in the Dumbarton Oaks conference (August 21 - September 27, 1944) and eventually led to the United Nations founding conference in San Francisco in April, 1945. The group also played a decisive role in establishing the International Monetary Fund and the World Bank at the Bretton Woods Conference.

In formulating the Charter of the United Nations the question of constitutionality was at the forefront of the discussions within the State Department. It was clear from the beginning that the American public would not approve of an organisation which was not based on democratic principles. Secretary Hull was particularly concerned about the apparent incompatibility of the provisional UN Charter with the American Constitution. To abate his doubts, he consulted three distinguished lawyers - Myron C. Taylor, John W. Davis, and Nathan L. Miller. Myron C. Taylor, a director of the Council on Foreign Relations, acted as a liaison between Hull and Charles Evan Hughes, a retired chief justice of the Supreme Court and member of the Council. John W. Davis, Democratic presidential candidate in 1924, had served as president of the Council from 1921 to 1933 and as a director from 1921 to 1955. Nathan L. Miller, a former Republican governor of New York, was not a member of the Council, but, like the others, was interested in world government schemes. As was expected, the three advised that the provisional UN Charter was constitutional, and on June 15, 1944, Hull, Stettinius, Bowman, Davis, and Pasvolsky discussed the draft with Franklin D. Roosevelt. The President gave his unreserved approval and immediately released a public statement to that end.[147]

At the Dumbarton Oaks and San Francisco conferences the United Nations Charter was modified in some details to accommodate the wishes of other participating nations. In its essential provisions, however, the final product showed clearly the Agenda Group's fingerprints.[148]

Always ready to strike a compromise to placate the opponents of world federation, as long as the ultimate goal was not lost out of sight, the members of the Agenda Group knew that the political realities in the mid-1940s militated against the concept of world order they had in mind. Thus they agreed to support the United Nations Organization, while simultaneously refining plans for regional federations, such as the European Union, which would eventually lead to a world federation.


5.9     Advocacy of Federalism

In 1940, even before the United States had entered the Second World War, the Carnegie Endowment for International Peace published *The New World Order*, which was a select list of references on regional and world federation, together with some special plans for a new world order after the war. This interesting list of references focussed on books and addresses published in 1939 and 1940[149] including Ralph Page's article, 'Designs for a World Order' (July, 1940), originally printed in the *Annals of the American Academy of Political and Social Science*. The author quotes John Foster Dulles as saying:

> The fundamental fact is that the nationalist system of wholly independent, fully sovereign states is complete in its cycle of usefulness ... Today, more than ever before, are the defects of the sovereignty system magnified, until now it is no longer consonant with either peace or justice. It is imperative that there be a transition to a new order. This has, indeed, become inevitable for the present system is rapidly encompassing its own destruction. The real problem is not whether there will be a transition, but how can transition be made, and to what.[150]

Page then goes on to state: 'That the peace of the world depends upon some surrender of national sovereignty has been stated by the leaders, past and present, of most democratic countries in Europe ... One purpose, one interest, one loyalty, the brotherhood of man, is the only goal that enlists the life forces

216

of the youth of the world.'

In 1944, while remaining chairman of the Commission on a Just and Durable Peace, John Foster Dulles became a trustee of the Carnegie Endowment For International Peace.[151] Two years later, he was elected chairman of the board and chairman of the executive committee, and held all those posts until 1952, the year he was appointed as U.S. Secretary of State. That Dulles occupied these strategic posts in one of the most influential and wealthiest foundations must be seen against the background of international policies pursued by the Endowment since its inception in the early twentieth century. In 1941, this institution published the following statement, which is fairly representative of its general policy:

> It is this kind of planning for a new world order on a cooperative basis which furnishes the constructive program of the peace movement at the present time. It is therefore important to ensure the preparation of careful and thoughtful monographs in the various fields covered by these surveys in order to prevent a recurrence of the superficiality which marked so much of the peace movement of the 1920's ...[152]

The formation of a new world order on a co-operative basis was the essential task to which Dulles had pledged himself. Like his English friends, Lionel G. Curtis and Philip Kerr, he became a vocal advocate of federalism.

### 5.9.1    European Federalism

In *War, Peace and Change*, Dulles dealt with international organisation on the universal level only, but as time progressed he also discussed some forms of regional organisation. Although his thoughts on regionalism were tentative at first, he defined it as a supra-national organisation in which certain nations merge their economic, political, or military functions to some degree but not entirely.

As Dulles' views on regional organisation began developing in the late 1930s and early 1940s, he vacillated between support and scepticism. In a letter to Quincy Wright, dated December 19, 1939, he endorsed the concept of regionalism. At that time he felt that 'an effort should be made to achieve some form of world organisation which, however, would be merely consultative and the meeting place of the chiefs of state or the ministers of foreign affairs.'[153] But, 'within the framework of this central organisation it might be possible to work out a series of stronger international arrangements, no one of which, however, would attempt at this stage to be world-wide in its scope, but each of which should preferably be 'open-ended' and capable of extension.'[154] These tight organisations could then be stepping stones to larger organisations. Dulles explained that those arrangements would be organised on several different levels.

There might, for instance, be some arrangements which would be regional, others which would be based upon a community of financial and commercial interests, and others which might be based upon a similarity of political institutions. The subject matter of such various agreements might be different. For instance, as illustrative of the first category, there might be an effort to develop the Federal system in Europe. As illustrative of the second category, there might be some monetary agreements as between such countries as the United States, England and France - something like the tripartite monetary agreement formalized. As illustrative of the third type, certain countries, such as some of the "democracies", might make a tentative beginning at some form of political collaboration through a central organisation, the members of which would be elected by the peoples and which might have at least a certain advisory capacity or even veto power with respect to matters of common interest.[155]

These three types of organisation could conceivably have overlapping membership, with some countries belonging to only one and others belonging to several. But these organisations, in Dulles' opinion, would probably not have enforcement mechanisms. He explained that he doubted 'very much if it is feasible or desirable to endow any of these organisations with military or even economic sanctions, and much less do I believe, at this stage, in an international police force.'[156] A few years later, however, Dulles vigorously advocated the desirability of an international police force.[157]

In 1940 a sensational book appeared in the United States under the title, *America and a New World Order*. Its author, Graeme Keith Howard, the vice-president of General Motors, sent an advance copy to his friend, John Foster Dulles, for review and criticism. Subsequently Dulles heartily endorsed the book. Apparently, he thought its thesis had much to recommend itself to an American audience at the height of the war.[158]

Howard asserted that it would be wrong to follow the reasoning of world federalists to establish a global federation by appropriating the same strategy which was successfully used by the original American states to join forces under one federal government: 'It is idealistic nonsense to assume that states will voluntarily surrender their power. The analogy so often employed, that the American colonies surrendered portions of their power in 1789 in order to form a federation of states, is entirely fallacious.'[159] Howard argued that 'the American colonies consolidated their power in order to achieve aggregate power in the international community commensurate with other eighteenth century nations. It is one thing for a group of states with low power ratios to consolidate their power and quite another for all states to sacrifice their power.'[160] Thus it would be better to propose that a new world order should be based on a co-operative regionalism:

It is power, morality, and sound economic foundation that must form the framework for support of the new world order ... The new international order must provide equality of economic opportunity as a moral factor, for

218

political freedom without social and economic freedom is a mere empty gesture ... [But] promising both a more ethical and a more realistic solution is the formation of regional economic entities ... Cooperative regionalism [will] bring about a better world order through internationally balanced economic and political Regional Blocs.[161]

While sympathetic to Howard's views, Dulles was not yet fully convinced of the practicality of a regional approach. In his 'Draft on Peaceful Change', he expressed fears that a federal system that developed on a less than universal basis could present problems. He explained that if the federal system can thrive only where there is a homogeneous population, 'the federal system may merely develop the world into groups which, while larger than any present nation, will still, as between themselves, be exclusive and resistant to change.'[162] Instead of a stepping-stone to globalism, a regional federal system might thus be nothing more than a superstate that would behave just like a conventional state but on a larger scale.

Yet despite his reservations, Dulles advocated European federalism on numerous occasions as chairman of the Commission on a Just and Durable Peace. One of his criticisms of the Atlantic Charter was that it contained provisions that could be interpreted as restricting the possibility of European union. In his discussion following the critique of the Atlantic Charter, Dulles explained:

We should seek the political reorganisation of continental Europe as a federated commonwealth of some type. As stated above, there must be a large measure of local self-government along ethnic lines. This can be assured through federal principles which in this respect are very flexible. But the reestablishment of some twenty-five wholly independent sovereign states in Europe would be political folly.[163]

Dulles' concerns about Europe were also, as would be expected, reflected in his religious publications. When the 'Statement of Political Propositions', commonly known as 'The Six Pillars of Peace'[164], was published by the Commission in March of 1943, the idea of regional collaboration, particularly European collaboration, was included. In the Comment to Pillar One, which provides for an overall political organisation, it was explained that this would not preclude regional arrangements:

The degree of collaboration can properly be related to the degree of interdependence and thus any universal scheme may contain within its framework provision for regional collaboration. To continue there the uncoordinated independence of some twenty-five sovereign states will assure for the future that, as in the past, war will be a frequently recurrent event.[165]

Although neither the Commission nor Dulles developed the specifics of how other regional arrangements should be set up, in principle they endorsed such organisations. This explains why Dulles soon became involved in efforts to establish regional organisations and developed a firm commitment to the idea of European federation. He advocated this union not purely for the interest of Europe, but for those of the United States as well. He argued:

> Twice within the last twenty-five years the United States has become deeply involved in the wars originating between the independent, unconnected sovereignties of Europe. It has been demonstrated that the world has so shrunk that European wars can no longer, as during the last century, be confined to Europe. Therefore, it is not merely of self-interest to Europe, but of vital concern to us, that there be not restored in Europe the conditions which inherently give rise to such wars. From a purely selfish standpoint any American program for peace must include a federated continental Europe. From the standpoint of the peoples concerned, their economic interdependence calls for political mechanisms to assure that their resources and markets be coordinated for maximum peaceful utility.[166]

It is interesting to see here, once again, Dulles' belief that war results from a system that is factually interdependent but yet composed of legally independent, politically unconnected, sovereign states.

In the early 1940s Dulles joined a number of movements specifically aimed at establishing some sort of regional organisation. The most important of these was the Federal Union movement.

### 5.9.2    Federal Union Movement

After Hitler annexed Czechoslovakia in late 1938, three Englishmen, Derek Rawnsley, Charles Kimber, and Patrick Ransome, came to the conclusion that Chamberlain's appeasement policy, despite its elusive promise of peace, had ended in failure.[167] They were convinced that the only realistic chance of preventing war would lie in a federated Europe. Kimber later recalled: 'Europe held the key to war and peace and we were thinking only of European democracies. Our hope was that the idea [European federation] would appeal to enough of the citizens of Germany and Italy to enable them eventually to join.'[168] Thus they decided to launch a movement whose sole purpose was to work towards a United States of Europe. In January, 1939, they published their first manifesto which bore the title, 'Federal Union'. Widely publicised, the idea to federate the European nations found a positive response in Great Britain immediately before and during the early years of the war.

In early July, 1939, Federal Union, as the movement became known, organised a conference at Besant Hall, Baker Street. Some 300 sympathisers from many parts of the British Isles participated at that event. C.E.M. Joad, Lionel G. Curtis, and Henry Wickham Steed gave spirited addresses. Several years later, Curtis recalled his earnest plea to the assembled federalists that they should concentrate their efforts 'on the task of getting into the heads of ordinary people the idea that an international federation was the only way to prevent world war'.[169] The editor of the *New Statesman*, Kingsley Martin, newly recruited by Charles Kimber, also joined the chorus, calling for a federal Europe in his public utterances. A few weeks later a number of local groups, which had been organised in the meantime, sent thirty-seven delegates to a meeting which appointed a provisional National Council.

From the outset, Patrick Ransome asked Lord Lothian to advise the Council on policy issues. Lothian, in turn, approached Lionel G. Curtis and both agreed to help in whatever form they could.[170] Commenting favourably on Ransome's 'Memorandum', which detailed the purpose of Federal Union, Curtis expressed his hope in a letter to Lord Lothian (2 April 1939) of associating the organisation with the Round Table Group:

> I have received the enclosed from Ransome which strikes me as really first-rate. I suggest that we should model our attitude towards these young men on the way in which Lord Milner treated us when we were founding the Round Table. One of our difficulties at the present moment is that everyone connected with the Round Table, especially those who see eye to eye with you and me, are up to their necks and over with war work; besides I have so preached to Ransome and his friends the importance of not starting separate organizations that I should hate not to carry them along with us. I dare say you will be able to improve this draft a lot, especially the three points on the past page but one; but they seem to have got the root of the matter in them.[171]

Lord Lothian was equally elated about the possibility of influencing the policy makers of the Federal Union movement.[172]

In lending their personal prestige and expertise to the rapidly expanding Federal Union movement, Lothian and Curtis became invaluable supporters of Ransome and his group. They concentrated their efforts in drafting policy statements, raising funds, and recruiting new members.[173] They also inspired the idea of founding the Federal Union Research Institute which attracted many of Britain's leading intellectuals and statesmen. During the course of one year, a number of prominent names were added to the membership list of Federal Union. These included among others William Temple, Archbishop of York (later Archbishop of Canterbury), Bishop Bell of Chichester, Lord Astor, Sir Herbert Barker, Arnold J. Toynbee, Captain B. H. Liddell Hart, Canon C. E. Raven, even J. B. Priestley and Dr Ralph Vaughan Williams. Other outstanding members of Federal Union were Lancelot Hogben, then a Professor at Aberdeen, Friedrich von Hayek, then a Professor at the London School of Economics, E. M. W. Tillyard of Jesus College, Cambridge, and A. L. Goodhard, Professor of Jurisprudence at Oxford.[174] In April, 1940 the membership exceeded 10,000 and was increasing at the astonishing rate of 2,000 per month. By that time 253 local chapters had spontaneously sprung up throughout the country, co-ordinated by a 'travelling organiser'; in London alone there were a dozen public meetings a month.[175]

Federal Union gained wide publicity through its high-quality publications and public lectures.[176] One of the early publications which received broad acclaim was Charles Kimber's 'Statement of Guiding Principles' which he had authored in April 1939 at a meeting of the 'Panel of Advisers' in Gordon Square. Besides Kimber the 'Panel' consisted of Curtis, Kingsley Martin, Lothian, Barbara Wootton, Wickham Steed, Rawnsley and Ransome. They decided to ask friends and likely sympathisers to endorse the statement and thus assure its wide circulation. Among others, the Astors and Ernest Bevin appended their signatures at once. Encouraged by the positive response from representatives of the political establishment, Lord Lothian also approached Church dignitaries to canvass support for the statement. William Temple did not hesitate to add his name to the list of signatories. The Archbishop had thrown his support behind the Federal Union movement in deference to Lionel G. Curtis whose lead in political matters he usually followed. 'Temple warmly admired Curtis,' writes Gerald Studdert-Kennedy, 'and pitched in without hesitation behind the movement.'[177] The staggering success of Federal Union as a popular movement, which had come to national prominence only a short while ago, was largely attributable to Temple's endorsement. As a well-respected Church leader and a highly influential personality, he commanded the attention of both the ruling class and the common people in Great Britain at the time.

> No doubt many supporters of Federal Union were grasping at straws, but that was not the message of Temple, who was to become the last archbishop with real national standing as a public figure, or of the political scientists, such as Curtis, whose "Christian" insight he welcomed and whose technical expertise he deferred to.[178]

In a letter of 5 May 1939, William Cosmo Gordon Lang, the Archbishop of Canterbury, expressed his sympathy with the federal idea, but declined to promote the movement publicly:

> During my cruise on the Mediterranean I have been reading parts of Lionel Curtis's treatise on the Commonwealth of God and Streit's book on Union Now. I am quite sure that things must move or rather be moved in that direction and that the dominance of national sovereignty must be abated, but I cannot as yet persuade myself that the steps can be anything more than tentative, and that responsible statesmen must think out these steps before people like me can advocate the constitutional change which would be involved.[179]

Another notable publication was a small pamphlet entitled 'The End of Armageddon'. On 13 June 1939 Lord Lothian, the pamphlet's author, gave the manuscript to Patrick Ransome along with a gift of £100 to defray the cost of printing. As in many of his earlier works, Lothian argued that national sovereignty had to be overcome and that federation must replace it. By preparing belligerent and neutral opinion for federation, he hoped to obtain a favourable response from the nations at war which would shorten the armed conflict and ensure a peace with hope for the future.[180]

During the early stage of the Federal Union movement, its members proposed a federation of free peoples without any suggestion as to which of these peoples might be likely to join. In the autumn of 1939 their thinking began to crystallise around the project of a European federation centred in Britain and France, to be joined as soon as possible by a democratic, postwar Germany. It was this assumption which formed the philosophical basis of a number of high-level conferences organised by Sir William Beveridge and Patrick Ransome, bringing together 'the best talent available outside the Government service to plan the constitutional and economic aspects of a federation.'[181] It was also the specific policy laid down by a Federal Union conference in February 1940, and confirmed by the National Council in March. Public figures such as Richard Law MP (son of the former Prime Minster Bonar Law) and Henry Wickham Steed officially endorsed the policy by publicly identifying themselves with the objectives of the Federal Union movement.

On February 28, 1940, the provisional National Council, acting as a steering committee, discussed a special 'Beveridge report', in which Sir William had outlined the purpose and direction of the Federal Union movement. In March, an Executive Committee was appointed to put Beveridge's proposals into practice. Thus officially established, the National Council became permanently located at Gordon Square in London. The Council also approved an optimistic budget, including five annual salaries which together totalled nearly £2000. Members of the Council, including C.E.M. Joad, Lionel Robbins, W.B. Curry, R.W.G. Mackay, Alan Sainsbury, Barbara Wootton and the distinguished constitutional lawyer W. Ivor Jennings (later Sir William Ivor Jennings and Vice-Chancellor of Cambridge University), drafted a democratic constitution for the whole movement, which was unanimously adopted by all local chapters.[182]

The statement of aims of Federal Union, based to a large degree on Jennings' book, *A Federation for Western Europe*[183], read in part as follows: 1.) To obtain support for a federation of free people under a common government, directly or indirectly elected by and responsible to the people for their common affairs, with national self-government for national affairs.[184] 2.) That any federation so formed shall be regarded as the first step towards ultimate world federation. 3.) Through such a federation to secure peace, based on economic security and civil rights for all.

To this end the present policy of Federal Union is: 1.) To work for an Allied statement of Peace Aims challenging the idea of race superiority with a declaration of the rights of man, and the method of aggression with a declaration of readiness to federate with any people whose government is prepared to recognise these rights. 2.) To welcome any steps towards such a federation of the Allies or any other groups of peoples, provided that at the time of its formation the federation is declared open to accession by other nations, including Germany.[185]

Following the publication of its constitution and statement of aims, Federal Union received favourable press coverage in many newspapers, including *The Times*, *The Guardian* and the *New Statesman*.[186] Politicians, public officials and even political parties aligned themselves with the movement. British and French cabinet minsters spoke of the wartime association of Britain and France as the beginning of a permanent union which would form the nucleus of general federalisation in Europe. The Parliamentary Labour Party in Great Britain dedicated itself to the establishment of a new commonwealth of states whose collective authority must transcend, within its proper sphere, the sovereign rights of separate states.[187] It became a commonplace in Great Britain that the Second World War must clear the way for some kind of federal union of Europe.[188]

After Lord Lothian's untimely death in 1940, differences of opinion soon surfaced between Kimber and Curtis on important policy issues. The most serious conflict centred in their different views about the final objective of Federal Union. Kimber believed that the creation of a United States of Europe was an end in itself, while Curtis was committed to the idea of a united Europe as an essential building block of a world commonwealth.[189] In 1943 Curtis left the movement to pursue his chimerical dream of an Atlantic federation, only to return to it again after the war when a union of European states had lost its attraction to many in Great Britain.[190] He remained a member until his death in 1955.[191]

### 5.9.2.1  Peace Aims Committee

In 1941, leading members of Federal Union, including C.E.M. Joad, Miss Josephy and Konni Zilliacus, organised the Peace Aims Committee. Acting primarily as a lobbying group, this Committee tried to persuade the Allied governments to put the establishment of a world federation at the top of the agenda at the forthcoming peace conference. At a board meeting on October 3, 1941, it was suggested that the most essential prerequisite for an international order would be the formal acceptance of a Charter of Rights and a Federal Constitution which would be binding upon all nations.[192] Each individual citizen would then pledge allegiance exclusively to that constitution. It was further suggested that, for the duration of war, the British propaganda service should continue its 'political warfare' by offering a Democratic Union, World Confederation, and a Charter of Rights in Europe in order to induce revolt against the Nazis. In addition to that, an allied Reconstruction Commission should be set up to plan the transition from war to peace. This would require two separate initiatives. First, joint machinery found essential in wartime should be carried forward into peacetime; and secondly, an international Consultative Parliament should prepare the way for a new world organisation. Instead of fighting each other, Kimber concluded, the nations of the world should rather concentrate their energy on waging 'a world war on want', and undertake measures which would guarantee freedom and prosperity for all.[193]

In early 1942, the Peace Aims Committee produced its first report of some 25,000 words. After being approved by the Annual General Meeting of Federal Union at Easter of the same year, it was published under the title *Federation: Peace Aims - War Weapon*.[194]

The report's main contribution to postwar planning was a proposal to establish a 'Confederate Council'. In its recommendations to set up a new world order the Peace Aims Committee went further than was politically feasible at the end of war. It urged the Allied governments, for example, to invest special powers in the 'Confederate Council', providing it with a near-monopoly of military power to maintain peace in the world. The Council would also be put in charge of forming an International Parliament, which, in its basic concept, resembled the later UN Assembly, differing only in its proposal to elect national representatives in proportion to their countries' population. The report projected that a number of democratic nations would form a nucleus within a wider global confederation. It intentionally selected 'a political rather than a geographical test for membership'. To allow a certain degree of flexibility, the Peace Aims Committee offered a number of alternative scenarios to achieve a federal Europe, one of which included the United Kingdom and Ireland, as part of a wider United States of Europe. Despite its adaptability to changing political realities, the report could not entirely conceal the fact that a divergence of views existed about the future of a European federation. This problem complicated the process of unification in the years immediately following the war. Great Britain's reluctance to become totally integrated in a European Union repeatedly surfaced and hampered the realisation of Federal Union's far-sighted proposals.[195]

The report's consideration of world government was palpably deficient. It merely quoted Field Marshal Smuts to the effect that there was a need for some form of world organisation more ambitious than the old League of Nations: 'We want a league which will be real, practical, effective as a system of world government.' Concurring with Smuts' opinion in its premise, the Peace Aims Committee noted, however, 'that no such government can be established within any foreseeable period after the war'. It perceived in the existing 'United Nations' - the name given to the Allied nations at war with the Axis powers - a first supranational alliance capable of crystallizing into a 'Federation of Democracies' directing the affairs of a 'World Confederation'. Describing the difference between confederation and federation, the report recognised that 'to found a world government whilst the States which it is to govern retain their sovereignty is a contradiction in terms'; but it expressed the hope that the proposed 'World Confederation' would evolve in a federal direction.

The report of the Peace Aims Committee was realistic enough to make an immediate impact on public opinion in Great Britain. William Temple, then Archbishop of York, representing the voice of the Anglican Church establishment, said in December, 1939 that 'the whole scheme of Federal Union has made a staggeringly effective appeal to the British mind.'[196] William Paton was elated about the internationalist program of the Peace Aims Committee. He decided to promote federalism among the churches, and thus emulate the efforts of Federal Union in his own sphere of influence. It was relatively easy for him to convince William Temple of the need to establish an ecumenical organisation which would facilitate co-operation between Church and State on public policy issues affecting the postwar world:

> When Paton wrote to Temple to explain how a relationship could be forged between government's advisers in Oxford (the so-called Chatham House Group), he said that they wanted to use the link to help bring international Christian thinking to bear upon the problem of war and peace. Paton responded to the cordial reception he received from Lindsay, Sir John Hope Simpson, Arnold Toynbee, H.J. Paton and Sir Alfred Zimmern by suggesting an international group with separate sub-groups kept in touch by visitation.[197]

Paton's suggestion was taken up enthusiastically by Archbishop Temple. In early 1941, the leading officers at Chatham House, in co-operation with Paton, Temple, and other ecclesiastics in Great Britain and America, set up a new organisation later known as the Peace Aims Group.

### 5.9.2.2 The Peace Aims Group

The original purpose of the Peace Aims Group was to work out a practical program to establish a new world order after the war and thus lay the foundation of lasting peace. Since the Church had already formulated its position on international organisation at the ecumenical conferences in Oxford (1937) and Tambaram (1938), it seemed appropriate to use the respective reports as the basis of discussion. Paton, even more so than Temple, realised that to translate these ecumenical proposals into concrete government policies it was imperative to call on people with sufficient power and influence in society. He would need to accommodate the views of government advisers at Oxford and London, if the Peace Aims Group were ever to become a force in international politics. Temple did not object to Paton's plan to forge links between ecclesiastical leaders and secular experts on international relations. To Paton's delight, the Archbishop relished the fact that some of the most congenial spirits of public and church life began to frequent the meetings of the Peace Aims Group which were held in London and Oxford towards the end of

1942 and in 1943. The most advantageous arrangement, considering its strategic importance, was the establishment of a Peace Aims Group section at the Foreign Research and Press Service (F.R.P.S.), a quasi-governmental agency directly connected with the Royal Institute of International Affairs.[198] The spacious halls of Balliol College, Oxford, served as the headquarters of the new organisation which was instructed to formulate the official British policy on postwar settlements.[199] This was hardly surprising. The experts at Chatham House had already begun 'planning a wartime role for the Royal Institute of International Affairs more than a year before hostilities started.'[200] Sir John Hope Simpson, who supervised the day-to-day affairs of the organisation, was eager to assist the Peace Aims Group in mastering highly technical material on foreign policy.[201] Simpson always 'seemed to value a specifically Christian contribution, believing that outside the common Christian bond there is no hope for the renewal of European civilization.'[202] This attitude meshed perfectly with the intentions of the ecclesiastical establishment to conceptualize the sociological structure of a new world order. Their preferred methods of disseminating their ideas was the written word.

> Beyond the question of the sensitivity of the group members to public opinion, their desire to educate it in respect of seeking a post-war settlement in accordance with Christian principles, and the way in which the reflected values proven in the ecumenical movement rather than national sentiment, there is the high quality of the study documents produced. One cannot read them quickly, nor are they cliché-strewn, even though it is clear from "The Church and the New Order" and the similar books produced by Bell, Temple, Beales, Baker and van Kirk, that their authors are aiming at a popular audience (see e.g., "Towards a Christian Britain" by Temple 1940, or the best sellers written by Dr. Parkes under the pseudonym "John Hadham"). Temple's famous words concerning his attitude as a churchman to the men in the street: "I do not ask: What will Jones swallow? I am Jones demanding what there is to eat", could well apply to the Peace Aims Group.[203]

Maintaining the framework of Christian world fellowship during the war the ecumenical leadership in Great Britain decided to articulate their public statements on peace in partnership with similar ecclesiastical organisations in America. To present a united front the churches were asked to forgo their particular denominational distinctives in favour of a policy of integration. An authentic judgment on international disorder could only be pronounced by a Church which had overcome its own divisiveness.[204]

In October 1941 an American delegation of ecclesiastics arrived in Oxford to open the dialogue with Toynbee and the Peace Aims Group. Alfred Zimmern, A. D. Lindsay, and William Temple, the Archbishop of York, were among those gathered to listen to Van Dusen's presentation about American attitudes towards a postwar settlement.[205] This event marked a fortuitous turn in Toynbee's career. For the first time he met Henry P. Van Dusen, who one year later would introduce him to Henry Luce, the American publisher of the *Time*, *Life*, and, *Fortune* magazines. At a social gathering set up by Van Dusen, Toynbee impressed Luce with his vision of a new world order.[206] The tremendous publicity accorded to Toynbee in the United States several years later was therefore not coincidental. '[I]t is easy to infer,' states McNeill, 'that the 1947 cover story in *Time*, which established Toynbee's American fame, had its genesis at the Van Dusen dinner party in October 1942 when Henry Luce encountered him for the first time.'[207]

At the outset there was nothing to indicate that the Peace Aims Group would succeed so brilliantly in its mission of bringing together the representatives of the spiritual and secular domains. It was doubtful whether Paton would be able to attract a large number of influential public figures. Yet the Group rapidly gained a degree of popularity among ecumenical leaders and government officials, both in Great Britain and in the United States, which can only be described as phenomenal.[208] The hearing it received from the general public was equally impressive. This is all the more astonishing, if it is kept in mind that the Group always maintained a distinct élitist style of operation: 'Although meetings and conferences in Britain and America tended to be semi-private, affairs arranged by invitation with limited members allowed, much of the "Peace Aims" group's best thought was disseminated in popular lectures and broadcasts, the Christian Newsletter, and subsidiary regional conferences.'[209] The success of the Peace Aims Group was even more remarkable, since Joseph H. Oldham had already organised a similar group, called 'The Moot', three years earlier in 1938.

Possibly in a conscious effort to perpetuate the ideals of the Round Table Group, which was also known by its members as 'The Moot'[210], Oldham sought to engage participants of the Oxford Conference in an on-going discussion of international issues. He was able to enlist such notables as Karl Mannheim and T. S. Eliot, but deliberately excluded Paton and Temple from membership. It still remains a mystery why Oldham slighted his former colleagues in such an overt manner, although they might have been of much use to him. There was certainly no doubt that they were in complete agreement with the general purpose of 'The Moot'. Paton's biographer, E. M. Jackson, suggests that Eleanora Iredale, the financial officer of the 'Council for the Christian Faith and the Common Life' and a key figure in 'The Moot', persuaded Oldham, who had fallen under her spell at that moment in his life, to distance himself from the church establishment in Great Britain, which she disliked intensely. She apparently held a grudge against Paton in particular, although there is still some uncertainty about the circumstances surrounding that episode. Jackson simply states that 'no-one knows when her feud with Paton began'.[211]

When Paton and Temple realised they would not be invited to the meetings of 'The Moot', they were deeply offended and, after a period of indecisiveness, decided to promote the ideals of Federal Union among the churches by setting up their own organisation in 1941. In competing with

Oldham's organisation for the patronage of the same kind of people, the prospects of the Peace Aims Group seemed anything but bright. All depended on who would prefer Paton's more practical approach to international affairs to Oldham's abstract and theoretical style of discussion.[212] Opposed to any unrealistic idealism, John Foster Dulles joined the Peace Aims Group almost immediately. His brother, Allen W. Dulles, who was later to become the director of the CIA and president of the Council on Foreign Relations, was also drawn to the Group, realising how closely its program coincided with his own advocacy of a new world order. In 1946, for example, Allen co-authored a publication called *The United Nations*, in which he stated the following:

> There is no indication that the American public opinion, for example, would approve the establishment of a super state, or permit American membership in it. In other words, time - a long time - will be needed before world government is politically feasible ... This time element might seemingly be shortened so far as American opinion is concerned by an active propaganda campaign in this country.[213]

In July, 1942, during a period of violent air raids, the Peace Aims Group convened an ecumenical conference in Oxford under the chairmanship of Archbishop William Temple. While participating at the Ohio Wesleyan Conference a few months earlier, William Paton had asked Dulles to come to war-torn England and deliver a keynote speech on the spiritual basis of peace. Intrigued by the possibility of extending his influence across the Atlantic, Dulles was more than pleased to accept Paton's offer. Soon thereafter he received a formal invitation from the organising committee of the Peace Aims Group, signed by Archbishop Temple, Arnold J. Toynbee, Professor Zimmern, Lord Hailey, Canon Cockburn, Professor Lindsay, and William Paton.[214] Accompanied by William W. Van Kirk, a leading member of the Commission, Dulles flew to England by military plane on July 3, 1942.[215] After arriving in London, Van Kirk visited many clergymen in different parts of the country, while Dulles renewed his contacts with individuals whom he had met at the Oxford and Geneva Conferences. The two Americans hoped to establish a good rapport with the representatives of the newly formed British Council of Churches. Perhaps, indicative of his real intention in coming to England, Dulles also spent considerable time with British Cabinet ministers, such as Anthony Eden, Stafford Cripps, Clement R. Attlee, and Ernest Bevin.[216]

The two-day conference of the Peace Aims Group was held at Balliol College, Oxford.[217] The primary purpose was to discuss a future postwar settlement which would be agreeable to both the American and the British leaderships of the ecumenical movement.[218] In addressing delegates from Catholic, Anglican, and non-conformist churches, Dulles contended that unless Great Britain and the United States recaptured a dynamic sense of purpose they would certainly 'lose the Third World War', even though they might emerge as victors in the present conflict. He argued that there were several reasons why the western democracies had in the past failed to take the just and durable road to world peace. They had been enamoured with nationalism and had erected economic barriers against other countries. By selfishly seeking their own advantage, without regard to the suffering and injury they caused to others, the democracies contributed to the outbreak of the Second World War. The only sensible way to bring about peace, he believed, was to establish agencies endowed with sufficient authority to deal with supranational issues. This approach would assure the most satisfactory results by breaking down the boundary lines between nations and eliminating the trappings of national sovereignty, without violating their citizens' sense of nationhood as such.[219] He cautioned, however, that an attempt to invest supreme power in a number of international institutions would fail to produce the desired results, unless their tasks were clearly outlined in advance. With these remarks, he captured the imagination of certain members of the Royal Institute of International Affairs who happened to be present at the conference.[220] His thoughts, for example, were further elucidated by Arnold J. Toynbee, another conference speaker. Toynbee asserted in his speech that there were several possibilities to end war and each of them would come at a different price. He stated that the most practical and workable offer, but also the least desirable, was extended to the Allies by Hitler. His price would be Nazi domination of the world, condemning its population to abject misery. Toynbee asserted that Hitler would never have risked the attack on Poland, had it not been for the deplorable thraldom permeating the western democracies during the years of peace. Since Nazi Germany had started the war, the only feasible road to peace would be to defeat the Axis powers as quickly as possible. Toynbee insinuated, however, that Hitler might have had his offer accepted, had he been as generous in his terms as the Romans of old.[221]

Devoid of diplomatic subtleties, Dulles and Van Kirk created a furore at the plenary session of the conference. Van Kirk later recalled that the American position on the possibilities of a new world order was more advanced than the British stance: 'Perhaps Mr. Dulles and I were more insistent than were our British colleagues that international collaboration after the war should look beyond the United Nations toward a more inclusive fellowship of nations.'[222] The Americans were implying that the Axis Powers, though eventually defeated militarily, should be invited to join the 'fellowship of nations' on equal terms. To reach a consensus among the Church delegates was put beyond reach when Dulles began to reproach British colonialism. A number of patriotic English clergymen took offence at Dulles' remarks and threatened to obstruct the conference proceedings. At that critical moment Arnold J. Toynbee stepped into the breach and declared himself in sympathy with Dulles' viewpoint. Subsequently, he and Dulles convinced the majority of the Protestant leaders that the British Empire should be brought to an end.[223] Yet for the time being, the advocates of world federation had to learn how to deal with set-backs such as those imposed upon them by the volatile conditions of wartime. As so often in the past, they saw propaganda as the best means to advance their political agenda:

> Originally the Americans [Dulles and Van Kirk] had hoped to create an
> Anglo-American world order commission to coordinate activity and present
> a united front to the British and American governments on world order
> questions. Given the difficulties of wartime communication, it was decided
> to abandon the idea as impractical. The conferees agreed that for the duration
> of the war the national churches would focus on creating public opinion
> within their own nations in support of Christian world order ideals. (Dulles
> and Van Kirk undertook to publish two British statements on world order in
> the United States. They were entitled The Christian Church and World Order
> and Social Justice and Economic Reconstruction).[224]

Three years earlier, in March, 1939, the Federal Union movement had
extended its influence across the Atlantic with the appearance of Clarence K.
Streit's book, *Union Now*. Acting on behalf of the Round Table Group, Lord
Lothian had asked Streit to direct the affairs of Federal Union in the United
States. In time it became clear, however, that Streit's ideas expressed in his
books *Union Now* (1939) and *Union Now with Britain* (1941)[225] diverted from
those of the British Federal Union movement.


5.9.2.3   Union Now

Clarence K. Streit, the *New York Times* correspondent at the League of Nations
(from 1929 to 1938), gave a series of three lectures at Swarthmore College in
February, 1939. It is significant that the president of Swarthmore College at the
time was Dr Frank Aydelotte. As one of the original Rhodes Scholars, he had
studied at Brasenose College, Oxford, from 1905 to 1907. In 1918 he became
the American secretary of the Rhodes Trust and in 1930 president of the
Association of American Rhodes Scholars.[226] His presidency at Swarthmore
College began in 1921 and lasted until 1940. Since 1922 he had been a trustee
of the Carnegie Endowment for International Peace and a long-standing
member of the Council on Foreign Relations. In 1937 he was awarded the
honorary degree of Doctor of Civil Law at Oxford University. More
importantly, Aydelotte became a member of the Commission on a Just and
Durable Peace in 1941.

In his lectures at Swarthmore College, Clarence K. Streit, also a former
Rhodes Scholar[227], urgently proposed a federal union of western democracies.
His ideas were subsequently published in the book, *Union Now*.[228] Almost
immediately after its publication, the book was publicised in an article of *The
Round Table* (June 1939), which described Streit's thesis to the journal's
audience as follows:

There is, indeed, no other cure ... In The Commonwealth of God Mr. Lionel

Curtis showed how history and religion pointed down the same path. It is one of the great merits of Mr. Streit's book that he translates the general theme into a concrete plan, which he presents, not for the indefinite hereafter, but for our own generation, now.

The reviewer concluded that 'it is the only way' for a successful world federation. Subsequently, the book was recommended to educational institutions by the Carnegie Foundation which generously financed its wide distribution. Again, in its September issue, the *Round Table* discussed the proposals of *Union Now* in an article entitled, 'Union: Oceanic or Continental', which compared Streit's federal union scheme with the plan of Count Coudenhove-Kalergi for a European union. The arguments of both were presented in a positive light. Favourable reviews also appeared in the *Christian Science Monitor* written by Lord Lothian and in the Council on Foreign Relations' journal, *Foreign Affairs*. In his review and in numerous personal letters[229] Lothian, who was a Rhodes Trustee at the time, made the most extravagant claims for the book. He wrote to Streit that it stood 'in the direct succession from Washington and the Fathers of the American Constitution, the writers of *The Federalist* and Abraham Lincoln'.[230] On another occasion he expressed his conviction that *Union Now* was destined to be an epoch-making work, comparable to *The Wealth of Nations* or *The Origin of Species*. In a letter of 28 February 1939, commending Jonathan Cape for publishing the book, he wrote the following:

> The importance of Union Now is that in it Mr Streit has penetrated through the jungle of political confusion and economic compromise which have befogged the word since 1920 to the only principle which can solve the problem of war and prosperity in the modern world. Only when the democracies grasp the profound nature of that principle and begin to give effect to it will they resume their leadership of mankind.[231]

Excited about Streit's proposal to assign to the United States a central role in federating the democracies of North America, North-west Europe and Australasia, he described Streit's proposal in 'The End of Armageddon'[232] as being 'by far the most original and complete plan for a federal union.' Intended as a short synopsis of his views on national sovereignty, international anarchy and the federal solution, he expressed his general concurrence with the objectives of the Federal Union movement. Despite the fact that the general thesis of *Union Now* was entirely to his own liking[233], he took issue with certain details of the Federal Union programme. The first practical difficulty, he perceived, was Streit's naïveté in assuming that the fifteen democracies would voluntarily limit their own national sovereignty. Lothian also noticed a number of problems regarding Streit's concrete proposals. He feared that the fifteen democracies might soon regard themselves as an exclusive club, and not allow other nations to enter the circle. Other non-totalitarian states in Asia,

Latin America and the rest of Europe would equally be qualified to join the federation from the beginning. The admission procedure should include provisions to admit colonies as full members as soon as they graduated to self-government and proved their ability 'to assume full responsibility'. Lothian appreciated Streit's unique idea of combining a Parliamentary and a Presidential system in a constitution 'otherwise based on the American model'. In his view, however, it was far too soon to project what kind of constitution a federal union would need to have in order to be fully functional. He declared that 'the real task today is to develop a sense of community and common patriotism among nations, rising above but in no way undermining the difference and independence of nationality itself.' In a letter to Henry V. Hodson[234], the editor of *The Round Table*, in April 1939, he frankly admitted that he did not expect a federal union of nations to be formed on the basis of a constitution modelled on the American system. The merit of Streit's plan was the suggestion of pooling the sovereignty of an increasing number of nations, rather than in his attempt to formulate a constitution.[235]

Generally, Lothian was interested in *Union Now* as 'a piece of leaven' which offered a sounder basis for the organisation of peace than had the League of Nations. In a letter to Frank Aydelotte, on 6 March 1939, he appealed to the President of Swarthmore College for his direct participation in promoting Streit's federal plan:

> Curtis has collected a gathering of enthusiasts at Blickling ten days hence to consider how we are to launch a "Union Now" movement on this side ... I have no doubt that "Union Now" will have an immense press welcome, but unless my judgement of American public opinion is wrong, within a week or two it will be pushed out of people's minds by some new sensations unless there is a pretty solid piece of organization possessed of some funds to keep the idea in front of the public mind and to build up support for it. I hope you will see your way to taking an active hand in the game.[236]

Writing to Lothian in May 1939, Streit summarised the essential ideas of the Federal Union movement, which had already gained some public attention:

> The Union will come about with miraculous speed when it does come ... My reasoned belief is that we shall none of us be able to stay out of war for two years more unless we make this Union, and that if war does come without it, the USA will not enter it except on the Union basis. As I said in my talks, if we do let the war come on we shall be faced by the same problem: how we organize our relations with the democracies and what shall we fight or organize for? For our own Union system? or the Old World system of leagues and alliances? ... This issue rouses the deepest feeling in the American people, it is no ephemeral matter as is so often the case with you, and those who are not already astonished at the way this idea has spread and roused enthusiasm in this country will be before six months are gone ... The union has been rolling on for the past few months as a snowball – and you

know what that means for the coming weeks and months. Believe me, to work for a Union is no longer a forlorn hope ... Even if we didn't have Hitler to help us, once we get a good many leaders shaken from their natural first assumption that of course this can't be done now and afraid to express belief in its remoteness, for fear of being ridiculous through all future ages, why, the battle is half won.[237]

In his exuberance Streit seemed to have lost perspective of what could be accomplished in the short run. Despite its considerable following, the Federal Union movement could not overcome the political reality of isolationism in America which was diametrically opposed to the federal idea in unifying the democracies. The revolutionary implications of abolishing the national sovereignty system were also too radical for the taste of the other democratic governments, especially on the European continent. They were much more concerned about strengthening their national identity as a bulwark against the thread of totalitarian ambitions of conquest.

In 1940, while British Ambassador to the United States, Lord Lothian admitted that no organic union between Great Britain and the United States, such as demanded by Streit, was in the sphere of practical politics. But he undoubtedly believed that the first step towards world government was ever closer partnership between the British Commonwealth and the United States. Such partnership constituted in his view the right aim of statesmanship for the present and near future and was the most hopeful means of preserving peace when the war was over. It was a policy which maintained the essentials of the ideals of the Round Table Group, and was entirely in line with Lothian's own political aspirations.[238]

Lionel G. Curtis hailed *Union Now* as an independent affirmation of his federalist views. While staying in New York City in January 1939 to give a lecture at the Council on Foreign Relations he had met Streit who told him of his disenchantment with the League of Nations. His reporting on the League's performance as a *New York Times* correspondent in Geneva had convinced him of the instability of a collective security system based on agreements between sovereign nations. Inspired by reading *The Federalist* papers, Streit began to understand the League's main problem which Curtis had already analysed in *Civitas Dei*. It was the formidable task, perhaps the most difficult of all, to convince sovereign nations of the benefits of forgoing their independence and submit willingly to the dictates of a world government.[239]

Curtis was thrilled to discover that Streit had articulated an even more comprehensive vision of a world federation than he had dared to conceive. In 'World Order', an article published in the May-June issue of *International Affairs* (1939), he summarized briefly the thesis of *Union Now* as follows:

Mr. Streit shows how restricted and how precarious is the freedom which peoples enjoy under national commonwealths. He proves with unanswerable force what an increase in personal freedom, material prosperity and national security the democracies would gain by joining one international commonwealth. He has brought to bear on the subject a better grasp and also an incomparably fuller knowledge of the social and economic factors than I can command. I have dealt more fully with the moral and religious foundations of freedom than was possible in the length to which Mr. Streit has wisely limited his work.[240]

In February 1939, Arnold J. Toynbee, commenting on a discussion paper submitted by Curtis to Chatham House, fully endorsed Streit's plan. Toynbee concurred with Curtis on blaming national sovereignty as the reason for the failure of the League, and noted that 'the clash between political parochialism and cultural and economic interdependence, which you bring out in the present case, has happened in the histories of other civilisations and has been the death of them'.[241] Taking his cues from passages in *Union Now* Toynbee asserted that the political unification of the world into a single state is likely to happen sooner rather than later. The challenge is to find enough time to construct a culturally homogeneous federalism and guard against previous mistakes in short-circuiting the process of unifying the nations by force which had always ended in failure. Curtis' plan would not be sufficient to overcome this dilemma. Yet the more 'ambitious' though still 'practical' plan proposed by Streit would bode well. Disregarding Toynbee's slight of hand, Curtis replied that this is 'indeed good news. I had no idea that you could take this constructive view'.[242] Expressing his excitement about the upcoming discussions at Chatham House, he pleaded with Toynbee to 'go for me hell for leather' over his own timidity and Streit's better judged daring.[243]

In Union Now Clarence Streit advocated a gradual approach through regional unions to final world union[244], urging the immediate federation of fifteen democracies: Australia, Belgium, Canada, Denmark, Finland, France, Great Britain, Ireland, Netherlands, New Zealand, Norway, Sweden, Switzerland, Union of South Africa, and United States. The choice of democracies to be federated is based on three aspects which are of great value if combined with each other: (1) great economic power; (2) strong existing bonds of community; and (3) mature political experience.[245] The prime objective of world government, Streit argued, was to preserve and, if possible, increase freedom among the citizens of federated nations.[246] For this reason he selected only democracies as suitable candidates for his federal union. Totalitarianism, which negates the principles of democracy, is incompatible with the ideals of freedom and justice, and thus unable to contribute to the realisation of a world federation.[247] Moreover, it was Streit's firm conviction that the establishment of a world government could not be based on the co-operation of states as single political units, but only on the combined efforts of citizens in these states. This meant that nationals of different states should be encouraged to be loyal to, and participate in, an organisation which would eventually replace the sovereignty of each individual state with its own centralised authority.[248] According to Streit, these measures would militate against the essential philosophy of dictatorship in its emphasis on national autonomy. Consequently, he required each state seeking admission to the union to adopt democratic forms of government. The author predicted that the Union would be financially secure, economically prosperous, and militarily invincible.[249] As a result of such ideal conditions, the federalised peoples would enjoy perfect stability in many areas of society at minimal expense to themselves. Federation would create a situation which would surpass in every aspect their present imperfect and costly national systems of military defence. The relief from the dead burden of armaments, combined with the removal of trade barriers, would raise the standard of living to heights never yet attained.[250]

The Union would, however, impose by necessity the following measures on its citizens. The federal government would: (1) have the power to tax the people directly, as voluntary state contributions are too unreliable to finance its programs[251]; (2) raise and command its own armed forces[252]; (3) have its own machinery of law enforcement[253], and (4) enact laws bearing directly upon the citizen, not merely upon the federated nations.[254]

The federal organs of the Union would be a bicameral Legislature, an executive Board, a Prime Minister and Cabinet, and a High Court.[255] The government of the Union would have power in those matters in which common administration would best serve the cause of freedom. Such matters would include citizenship, trade, defence, postal and other communications. All matters which could best be regulated by local administration would be left to the national governments. This distribution of powers, according to Streit, would guarantee the freedom of each federated state to experiment in its political, economical and social sphere of influence.[256]

The House of Deputies would be elected by the people of the federated democracies, that is to say by the citizens of the Union. One deputy would be chosen for every million of a member state's citizens. Hence the United States would be represented by 129 deputies, Great Britain by 47, France by 42, Canada by 11, the Netherlands by 8, and Australia by 7, to mention only the states with the largest percentage of deputies. In the Senate there would be a minimum representation of each state by two, with an additional two Senators for every twenty-five million of population after the first twenty-five. The United States would have ten Senators, Great Britain and France four each, and all the other members two each.[257]

The Board would consist of five persons - three elected directly by the citizens of the Union, one by the Senate and one by the House of Deputies. These individuals would rotate as Presidents of the Board. The President would be authorised to appoint diplomatic agents and consuls, make treaties with the assent of Congress (the House and Senate) and the Premier. He would also be the commander-in-chief of the armed forces of the Union.[258]

The Premier would be appointed by the Board, which would delegate to him all the executive powers not expressly retained by it in this Constitution. He would be assisted by a Cabinet of his own choice and remain in office so long as he could retain the confidence of Congress.

The High Court, whose judges would be appointed for life to a number not less than eleven, would have jurisdiction in all controversies between states of the Union, between the citizens of different states, between a state and citizens of another state, and between states or citizens of the Union and foreign states.[259]

Streit devoted part of his book to the effort to persuade his fellow Americans that the Union which he planned was urgently necessary for the United States.[260] It is safe to say that when he wrote it the majority of his countrymen in America would have refused to follow him into this close association with the warring states of Europe. Yet even if the people of the United States were willing to make this drastic break with their tradition of aloofness, there would be strong resistance in Europe to many features of the Constitution. Representation by population, for instance, though it is a principle difficult to fault, would probably be unpalatable to the British and French. They would have forty-seven and forty-two deputies respectively, in the Federal House, against one hundred and twenty-nine from the United States. Even if the people themselves could be persuaded to accept what would look like government by the United States (though in fact the American deputies would represent their citizens and not their country), their political leaders would almost certainly reject such an erosion of their present power and prestige.

Another serious objection, based this time on the desirability rather than the practicability of Streit's plan, is that by its exclusion of the totalitarian states it would sharpen and perpetuate the division of the world into democracies and dictatorships. The opposition thus created would hardly be persuaded to adopt democratic forms of government by the standing invitation to join the Union. On the contrary, the tendency in the totalitarian states would be to draw more closely together and to compete for the adherence of unattached political units. Thus the world would still be divided into armed camps juggling an unstable balance of power.

Despite its deficiencies, Streit's federal union movement found many devoted disciples and more partial adherents. Numbers of commentators accepted the principles laid down in his book, but rejected the plan of execution and concentrated on advocacy of the federal union of European states. The outbreak of war in September, 1939, only increased the volume of oral and written support for such a project.

In 1940, Clarence K. Streit, together with Percival F. Brundage, later a Director of the Budget for Eisenhower, and Melvin Ryder, publisher of the *Army Times*, founded the Federal Union, Inc., to work for the goals outlined in *Union Now*. A number of leading members of the Commission on a Just and Durable Peace joined Streit's organisation immediately, among them Frank Aydelotte, Mary Woolley, Francis J. McConnell, G. Ashton Oldham, H. S. Leiper, C. J. Frederick, and Ralph Sockman.[261]

In 1941, Streit published another book, calling it *Union Now With Britain*.

He claimed that the union he advocated would be a step toward a 'formation of free world government'. The following passage is descriptive of the book's main thesis:

> It is proposed here that we create now the nucleus of that free world republic that must be formed some day by men like you and me and the neighbours. It is proposed that we seize the present opportunity to start this Union of the Free as a United States of Man constituted to secure eventually, and in an ever-growing degree, the freedom, peace and prosperity of every man and woman.[262]

In 1939 John F. Dulles began a lively correspondence with Streit. This contact developed into a lasting friendship, culminating in Dulles' recommendation of Streit for the Nobel Prize of 1950. In March of 1940, Dulles became an official consultant to Federal Unionists on legal and constitutional matters pertaining to the concept of federalisation across national boundaries.[263] Recognising the significance of Streit's federal concept, Dulles began to attend many of the Union Now meetings and gave substantial financial support to the movement. On November 4, 1940, he assisted Streit in drafting a joint resolution that would give the President of the United States extraordinary powers, not explicitly granted by the American constitution, to form a 'Provisional Federal Union' with the United Kingdom, Australia, New Zealand, and South Africa.[264] This resolution also contained provisions that would authorise the President 'to join with the other members of the Union to achieve their common defence and to perfect some common military organisation as seems appropriate.'[265] Dulles intended to create a military organisation endowed with a supranational structure that would effectively limit the national sovereignty of participating states. The president was thus empowered to 'enlist and issue commissions to any person owing allegiance to any Member Democracy, it being the intent hereof that the perfection of an effective military, naval and aerial organisation shall not be impeded by any distinctions flowing from differences in nationality or allegiance between the Members of the Union.'[266] This statement makes it clear that the military organisation was not restricted to function merely as a defence alliance. The resolution also contained provisions calling for reciprocal lifting of immigration quotas and the establishment of a Supreme Economic Council 'to promote the economic welfare of the Union.'[267] In 1941, Dulles even asserted that, if the United States were to attempt to preserve the practice of self-centred sovereignty, the nation would and should succumb in the long-run.[268]

On January 5, 1942, the Federal Union, Inc., published an advertisement in major newspapers urging Congress to adopt a joint resolution favouring immediate union of the United States with several specified foreign countries. The signatories of the petitions were dignified members of government or officers of closely aligned government agencies, including Harold L. Ickes, Roosevelt's Secretary of the Interior[269], Owen J. Roberts[270], and John Foster

Dulles. In fact, it was mainly Dulles who had written the joint resolution to Congress. The advertisement, published by the *Washington Evening Star* on January 5, 1942, read in part as follows:

> Resolved: That the President of the United States submit to Congress a program for forming a powerful union of free peoples to win the war, the peace, the future. That this program unite our people, on the broad lines of our Constitution, with the people of Canada, the United Kingdom, Eire, Australia, New Zealand, and the Union of South Africa, together with such other free peoples, both in the Old World and the New, as may be found ready and able to unite on this federal basis ... We gain from the fact that all the Soviet republics are already united in one government, as are also all the Chinese-speaking people, once so divided. Surely, we and they must agree that union now of the democracies wherever possible is equally to the general advantage ... Let us begin now a world United States ... The surest way to shorten and win this war is also the surest way to guarantee to ourselves, and our friends and foes, that this war will end in a union of the free. The surest way to do all this is for us to start that union now.

The American Congress was also urged upon (1) to form a 'union' government of a number of federated nations; (2) to impose a common citizenship; (3) to tax citizens directly; (4) to make and enforce all laws; (5) to coin and borrow money; (6) to have a monopoly on all armed forces; and (7) to admit new member countries; etc.

The American Congress resolutely rejected the petition *in toto*, as incompatible with the United States Constitution. This set-back of the most realistic world government proposals presented to Congress signalled to Dulles the impracticality of the *Union Now* project in its existing form.[271] While continuing his friendship with Streit[272], Dulles became increasingly sceptical about the scheme.[273] In June of 1941, he stated his concerns in a private letter to Hugh Wilson as follows: 'I think the educational value of what he [Streit] is doing is very great, but I doubt very much that it is practical or perhaps desirable to attempt a political union as close as he suggests.'[274] In the same letter, Dulles even criticised Clarence Streit for accentuating immediate political union of western democracies, while neglecting more effective approaches, like functionalism: 'I would favor economic and financial union, letting the political union work out of them if and when this became a natural development.'[275]

### 5.9.3    World Federalism

Disappointed by the slow progress of the Federal Union movement to establish a functional world government, Dulles developed a renewed interest in world federalism, a concept he had first expounded in a speech before the Conference on Canadian-American Affairs at St. Lawrence University in June 1939. On that occasion he hailed the federal system as the ideal model for a future international organisation, describing it as the best 'North American contribution to world order'.[276] He contemplated the viability of a form of world federation under which certain strictly defined powers are transferred to an international authority, while in all other respects the individual countries remain responsible for their internal affairs. In this regard he echoed the same ideas which had been propagated by officials of the FCC much earlier. In 1919, Samuel Z. Batten of the FCC had propagated world federalism as the only practical foundation of a new world order.

> The only alternative is World Federation. It is useless to talk about a return to the old order. The attempt to break up the race into distinct and independent nationalities, some small, others large, would be a reversal of history. It is certain that the races will more and more tend toward consolidation and cooperation. Mankind that has once tasted the advantages of combination, is not likely to throw those advantages away. That would destroy progress, limit trade, bring no benefit to any one, and deny the unity of the race. The process of consolidation must go on if the race is to advance. But it cannot be promoted by the formation of imperialistic groups; it cannot come through the world dominion of one power. There is only one way out for the nations, and that is a genuine federation of all peoples. This is just and fair. It recognizes the right of each people, however small, to live its own life and develop its own institutions; but it recognizes the interdependence of all. It provides for the union of all for the sake of all; and so it provides a basis upon which there can be a real community of life and interchange of gifts.[277]

It was Dulles' firm conviction that the principle of federation offered the best form of association of different peoples which would create an international order without putting an undue strain on their legitimate desire for independence.[278] The federal concept which appealed to Dulles' mode of thinking at that time was once defined by Lord Acton in this way:

> Of all checks on democracy, federation has been the most efficacious and the most congenial ... The federal system limits and restrains the sovereign power by dividing it and by assigning to Government only certain defined rights. It is the only method of curbing not only the majority but the power of the whole people.[279]

Under such an arrangement, states lose most or all of their sovereignty over matters of international concern and the centralised body becomes the governing authority, although keeping some, if not most, of their domestic affairs in the realm of self-governance.

Dulles differentiated between two kinds of 'federalism'. In his earlier writings he favoured a more comprehensive definition of federalism, while changing his perspective in his later works to a more limited 'classical' definition. Dulles' first use of federalism, which appeared in an article written in 1939, was still quite tentative in its application to specific situations. He explained:

> The federal system recognizes that sovereignty is a bundle of powers which do not necessarily all have to be vested in the same entity or exercised with regard for the same group of people. Certain powers, for example those relating to trade, immigration, and money, operate upon a far wider circle of persons than do those relating to sanitation, education, etc. It, therefore, vests the first set of powers in a body having responsibility to a large group of people, while it leaves the second group of powers in bodies responsible only to smaller groups of persons. Our own Constitution is, of course, the best known example of the federal system, but the federal principle is subject to indefinite expression and many possible variations. For instance, any number of states might agree that a matter of trade between them was a matter of common concern and, therefore, that authority over trade between these nations should be vested in a body which derived its authority from and had responsibility toward all the peoples concerned. In this way power and responsibility tend to become coextensive, and we do away with a condition whereby certain persons are restrained and restricted by power exercised without regard for their welfare.[280]

In this statement Dulles describes a federal system in which national sovereignty can be given up by groups of states to deal with particular issues that extend beyond their boundaries. It is not the standard description of a general abandonment of sovereignty by a set number of states or the transfer of specific powers to an established authority. Instead, Dulles seemed to be suggesting a functional abandonment of sovereignty, with bodies organised to be co-extensive with the particular problem. He corroborates this interpretation by explaining that 'under the federal system, power is divided up as between different bodies having different jurisdictions. There is no single entity which has the majesty of full power.'[281] As an example, he suggests that 'the establishment of a common money might be vested in a body created by and responsible to the English, French, German, and American people.'[282] Dulles may have realized, however, that his particular views of federalism were not widely held.


## 5.9.4   Collective Security

Within the Commission on a Just and Durable Peace, the issue of collective security was very controversial. In response to portions of the September, 1941 paper on *Long Range Peace Objectives*, in which Dulles expressly omits any discussion of sanctions because 'they are at the present time highly disputable and I do not consider them essential to inaugurating an era of peace,'[283] the members of the Commission fell into several camps. Some individuals felt that sanctions would be necessary to any peace plan.[284] Others agreed with Dulles' emphasis on first securing a stable political order. Finally, some seemed to have believed that sanctions, under any conditions, were incompatible with Christian ethics.[285]

In December, 1942, when the Commission issued the 'Statement of Guiding Principles', there was no mention of sanctions; but by March, 1943, when the 'Six Pillars of Peace'[286] were published, mention was made of collective enforcement. Pillar Six provided that 'the peace must establish procedures for controlling military establishments everywhere'.[287] In the related comment, it was explained that this principle meant two things. First, and most obvious, it meant that procedures for general arms control should be established; but second, it meant that there must be a system of collective security:

> A positive purpose of control is to bring such military establishments as remain into the affirmative service of international order. International agencies, such as those we contemplate, will primarily need to depend upon the moral support of the great body of mankind. That is their only reliable source of permanent power and unless they can commend such moral backing they are not entitled to other forms of power. But any society will produce minority elements who are not subject to moral suasion and who, if they feel able, may defy the general interest to advance their own. Therefore, the economic and military power of the world community should be subject to mobilization to support international agencies which are designed to, and do in fact, serve the general welfare.[288]

This statement is very much in keeping with Dulles' thought. Moral support must first be built to establish an international community, but in order to protect the great majority of society from those few that would not respect political authority an enforcement system is needed. Thus, police power has to be given to an international organisation. Dulles was convinced that only by equipping its enforcement mechanisms with supreme military and economic power would it be effective to deal with recalcitrant nations.[289] In his thoughts collective security played a major role, since he wanted to create a world which would be ruled by a centralised global government to preserve peace.[290]

### 5.10    The Statement of Guiding Principles

On March 28, 1941, the Greater New York Federation of Churches submitted a resolution to the Federal Council's Executive Committee to appoint 'the ablest possible individuals' who would formulate the 'basic principles which the consensus of Christendom would feel should be the foundation of any peace emerging from this war.' It stated further that these principles should 'be made as succinct as possible' and followed by a concerted effort 'to make these

242

principles, once established, familiar to the whole Christian community in the United States.'[291] The Executive Committee of the Federal Council turned the responsibility to conduct this study over to Dulles' Commission. With unusual vigour the Commission undertook this assignment. The sheer magnitude of the task, however, delayed any real progress for several months.

After a year of preliminary work, the Commission convened a National Study Conference on the Churches and a Just and Durable Peace at Delaware, Ohio, March 3-5, 1942. The campus of Ohio Wesleyan University was chosen to accommodate the 375 appointed representatives of some 30 denominations who convened to discuss the Council's postwar policy. The Methodist bishop Ivan Lee Holt of Texas[292] described the conference as 'the most distinguished American church gathering I have seen in 30 years of conferencing'. Four sections produced findings on 'Political Aspects of a Just and Durable Peace', 'Economic Aspects of a Just and Durable Peace', 'Social Aspects of a Just and Durable Peace', and 'The Relation of the Churches to a Just and Durable Peace'. *Time* magazine (March 16, 1942) called the final report of the conference 'U.S. Protestantism's super-protestant new program for a just and durable peace after World War II' and summarised its propositions thus:

> Ultimately, a world government of delegated powers; complete abandonment of U.S. isolationism; strong immediate limitations on national sovereignty; a universal system of money ... so planned as to prevent inflation and deflation; worldwide freedom of immigration; progressive elimination of all tariff and quota restrictions on world trade; autonomy for all subject and colonial peoples (with much better treatment for Negroes in the U.S.); no punitive reparations, no humiliating decrees of war guilt, no arbitrary dismemberment of nations; democratically controlled international bank to make development capital available in all parts of the world without the predatory and imperialistic aftermath so characteristic of large scale private and governmental loans.[293]

The article went on to affirm that 'every local protestant church in the country will now be urged to get behind the program.' The conference's organisers were quoted as saying: 'As Christian citizens, we first seek to translate our beliefs into practical realities and to create a public opinion which will insure that the United States shall play its full and essential part in the creation of a moral way of international living.'

John Foster Dulles, in his function as chairman of the conference, submitted a set of thirteen principles for peace, calling for the establishment of 'a true community of nations ... ordered by agencies having the duty and power to promote and safeguard the general welfare of all peoples'. In these principles, the Commission stated that Germany and Japan were not to blame for the prosecution of war. It further asked the United States government to rethink seriously the 'shortsighted selfishness of its own policies after World War I', if the world is to enjoy lasting peace. The principles themselves were summarised succinctly in the *Federal Council Bulletin*. Again, the churches were told that their purpose, indeed their foremost obligation, is to fulfill the objectives of progressive internationalism which in the end would bring God's kingdom to this earth:

> Moral law undergirds our world; disregard of the moral law brings affliction; revenge and retaliation bring no relief; we must find a way to bring into ordered harmony the interdependent life of the nations; this requires that economic resources be looked upon as a trust to promote the general welfare; also, because the world is living, and, therefore, changing, there must be ways of effecting peaceful change; colonial governments, too, must be administered in the interests of the colonial peoples; military establishments should be internationally controlled; there must be personal freedoms and liberties, without discrimination against nation, race or class; the power of the United States carries with it a special responsibility which we have neglected; a supreme responsibility rests upon the church of Christ; Christians should, as citizens, seek to translate their beliefs into realities; they must seek that the Kingdom of the world become the Kingdom of Christ.[294]

The *Christian Century* expressed its hope that 'the substance and significance of this document may be borne in on those who head the government of the United States, for it speaks a word which they can ignore only at the nation's peril.'[295]

Dulles' concepts of interdependence and the problem of state arrogance are reflected in Principle Four, which refers to the 'interdependent life of nations'. It advocates the institution of a system of co-operation, as opposed to one based on absolute state sovereignty, stating that 'a world of irresponsible, competing and unrestrained national sovereignties whether acting alone or in alliance or in coalition, is a world of international anarchy.' Principle Five explicitly cautioned against economic arrogance, contending that 'the possession of such natural resources should not be looked upon as an opportunity to promote national advantage or to enhance the prosperity of some at the expense of others.' Principle Six recognised that the world is 'living and therefore changing'. Consequently, the dynamic must be allowed to express itself: 'Any attempt to freeze an order of society by inflexible treaty specifications is bound, in the long run, to jeopardize the peace of mankind.' The principle continues: 'Nor must it be forgotten that refusal to assent to needed change must be as immoral as the attempt by violent means to force such change.'

Since the Commission was most concerned with spiritual problems, these are discussed at the beginning of the Guiding Principles. The underlying premise of the peace settlement is the reality of the Fatherhood of God and the brotherhood of humankind. Principle One proclaims that there was, in fact, a 'moral law' that 'undergirds the world'. According to Principle Two, 'the sickness and suffering which afflict our present society are proof of indifference to, as well as direct violation of, the moral law.' Furthermore, 'all share in responsibility for the present evils. There is none who does not need forgiveness. A mood of genuine penitence is therefore demanded of us - individuals and nations alike.' Principle Three echoes Dulles' injunction against hatred of enemy, arguing 'that it is contrary to the moral order that nations should be motivated by a spirit of revenge and retaliation'. This approach would only be self-defeating, since 'such attitudes will lead, as they always have led, to renewed conflict'.

These Guiding Principles based, as can clearly be seen, largely on Dulles' thought, underlay the more specific proposals that the Commission developed for the establishment of a new international order.[296] 'It might be noted,' states E. Raymond Platig, 'that if these principles were really to have been embodied in law and government that the result would have been a surrender of so much power to a central authority as to result in a "dilution" of sovereignty to the point that the essence of sovereignty itself would have been surrendered.'[297]

An interesting side-show of the conference were the Merrick-McDowell Lectures, an annual event at Ohio Wesleyan University. The university asked Dulles to choose the lecturers from among the conference participants. Thus it happened that the student body came to enjoy the lectures of such distinguished public figures as William Paton, Secretary of the International Missionary Council, Leo Pasvolsky, Special Assistant to the Secretary of State[298], and C. J. Hambro, President of the Assembly of the League of Nations. All of the discourses dealt with some aspect of the conference motto, 'A Basis for the Peace to Come'.[299]

After the conference, Dulles sent copies of the Guiding Principles to the White House, the State Department, and to numerous other government agencies. The Commission embarked on an 'evangelistic campaign' (a phrase frequently used by Van Kirk) to educate local churches about world order issues. The Commission also organised regional conferences in Houston, Detroit, Syracuse, and St. Louis to spread its message across the country. Countless copies of the Principles were distributed to all the organisations listed in George Galloway's *Postwar Planning in the United States*.

In the summer of 1942, the Rockefeller Foundation of New York asked Arnold J. Toynbee to come to the United States 'to consult on post-war problems'.[300] The Royal Institute of International Affairs willingly complied with this request, since it came from an organisation which had generously financed some of its projects in the past.[301] Toynbee was immediately released from his responsibilities at the Institute and spent nearly two months, from 23 August to 20 October, in America, primarily travelling from city to city as a propagandist for world order. According to his biographer, William H. McNeill, he was also urged to gather intelligence from influential policy groups in the heartland of the country.

> The Rockefeller Foundation, which financed the trip, wanted him to circulate and sample opinion outside official Washington, and undertook, with help

from the Council on Foreign Relations in New York, to assemble 'worthwhile groups'; for him to talk with all across the country. After spending two weeks in Washington with Pasvolsky and the State Department, Toynbee therefore started on a grand tour that took him to more than a dozen American cities, including Houston, Los Angeles, Chicago, and many smaller cities, like Louisville, Des Moines, and St. Paul. At each stop he discoursed on the conditions for a just and durable peace as he saw them to small groups of editors, lawyers, educators, and other professional people interested in international affairs. The burden of his message was that a durable peace would require the United States to take an active part in world affairs, repudiating the isolationism of the 1920s and 1930s and subordinating national sovereignty to some sort of world government.[302]

The most memorable event on Toynbee's speaking tour was a lecture he gave at Princeton University on 7 October 1942.[303] Addressing John Foster Dulles and other leaders of the Commission on a Just and Durable Peace, Toynbee passionately presented his case for world government. In a letter to William Paton, the chairman of the British Committee on a Just and Durable Peace, Henry P. Van Dusen succinctly summarised the speaker's thesis:

> Toynbee followed, to both Dulles' and my surprise, by insisting that there were no adequate solutions of the main problems of world order apart from world government. His specific proposal was a reconstruction of a World Association of Nations, to which all the United Nations would initially belong, and the Axis powers as soon as possible; and the allocation to the four major powers of responsibility for police.[304]

Although sympathetic to the idea of world government in general, the Commission members hesitated to endorse it openly as a workable solution, being aware of the political realities of the time. In the end, however, the group at Princeton gave in to Toynbee's logic and agreed that 'there is no reasonable likelihood of avoiding either a third world war or chaos, except through organized and effective world government.'[305] Dulles, still holding on to the notion of a piecemeal approach to achieve global governance was, according to Van Dusen, 'reluctantly compelled to concede the validity of this conclusion.'[306] As a first step, Toynbee suggested the preparation of a joint Anglo-American statement, which would contain a concise summary of the Guiding Principles, followed by some concrete foreign policy proposals.[307]

In the weeks following, Dulles, Van Dusen, Toynbee, and Kenneth Grubb, who visited the United States at that time, drafted the statement which was subsequently sent to Archbishop Temple and William Paton for approval. The statement urged the governments of the United States, Great Britain, China and the Soviet Union to merge at the earliest possible moment into a world organisation. Emphasising the internationalist aspects of the Principles, the authors argued that, since the world had 'factually' become an interdependent political and economic community, 'its constituent members no longer have the moral right to act without regard to the harm done to others.' The final words of the statement, reminiscent of utopian chimeras throughout the centuries, called for the formation of a military force so strong that no other nations would be able to challenge its supremacy. Thus empowered, the world organisation would use its authority for the common good.[308]


## 5.11 World Order and Peace

December 7, 1941, marked the end of an era. With the Japanese attack upon Pearl Harbour, isolationism was virtually eliminated in the United States. The European conflict became worldwide. With the United States once more involved in war, the anguished hearts of Americans turned to thoughts of the peace that would follow victory. The democracies had proved several decades earlier that they could win a world war, but they had failed to win the peace. As the Second World War drew closer to its end, intelligent people everywhere were anxious to think and talk about the problems of peace. They were anxious to listen and learn. Discussion materials, reports, studies were issued by the Commission on a Just and Durable Peace. These found an eager reception from many American church people. Every Protestant church in the United States was urged to get behind the Commission's program calling for an end to U.S. isolationism and for the establishment of a world organisation to keep the peace. 'All of the major injunctions,' writes Ronald W. Pruessen,

> which became central to the work of the Commission on a Just and Durable Peace emerged directly from his [Dulles'] analyses and recommendations. Immediately after the group began functioning, it took up his emphasis on the need for "some new world order", some "better world order" ... Dulles's Commission also accepted his earlier conclusion that the logical way to produce a new and better world order was to alter the established system of totally independent nations-state.[309]

In October, 1942 the Commission published a booklet entitled *A Righteous Faith for A Just and Durable Peace*. It contained fourteen articles of distinguished Americans which were presented in the form of a symposium.[310] The titles of the first six indicated something of the general thinking which occupied the minds of their authors in formulating general propositions of peace: (1) The American people need now to be imbued with a righteous faith; (2) In time of war the spiritual task of the churches becomes one of peculiar urgency; (3) The ecumenical (world-wide) character of the Church enables it and its members to make a unique contribution toward world order; (4) Christian motivation supplies an essential prerequisite to effective action; (5) Christians must seek the cooperation of other faiths; (6) the churches do not have primary responsibility to devise the details of world order. But they must proclaim the enduring moral principles by which human plans are constantly to be tested. The following seven articles expounded directly the *Guiding Principles* and the *Message* of the Delaware Conference. They were expositions of some of the moral principles which could serve as a standard to test the future world order. The final article elaborated on the primary responsibility of Christians, as citizens, to seek a postwar order which would reflect such truths as those articulated in the previous essays. The contribution of Albert W. Beaven, the former president of the Federal Council, was especially noteworthy. Among other things it recognized that the concepts of a new world order and the kingdom of God on earth were nearly identical in meaning:

> If we are to get the lift today from the vision of the things toward which we are working, we need to try to see the outline of the world ahead which we desire ... We want also the chance to influence to that same end the new world order which we believe will follow this war. If our enemies win, we know we will have little to say ... Christianity portrays men as children of one Father who is the universal God above nation, race, color, or social condition ... Power which comes to men is given in order that they may serve the common welfare, this power is not for exploitation but to be used toward the way of society which accords with God's purpose, a way which religion calls the kingdom of God on earth; its motive is goodwill not hatred, its object construction and not destruction, and the requirements of that God are binding on every race and nation.[311]

The high point of Dulles' work with the Commission came with the issuing of the famous 'Six Pillars of Peace' report in March, 1943. It became the greatest publicity effort of the Federal Council since its inception in 1908. Dulles, 'deeply impressed by the critical nature of this hour', expressed in a letter to the Commission members his apprehension about the long-range commitment of the Allies to international collaboration after the war.[312] On March 18, 1943, he urged the churches in a public address to become involved in a major campaign to 'force' an affirmative response from the American government in favour of world organisation.[313] A decision on this crucial issue could no longer be postponed.

5.11.1    The Six Pillars of Peace

The guiding principles were not as warmly received by the churches, as had been expected. Dulles was the first to recognise and acknowledge their deficiencies. At the Executive Committee meeting of the Federal Council of 23 January, 1943, he proposed to rephrase the last five principles in order to change them 'from a "credo" to policies which people could support'.[314] The new version of guiding principles was issued soon afterwards under its original title: 'Statement of Political Propositions. The Spiritual Foundation of World

Order.'[315] Dulles claimed authorship of what became popularly known as 'The Six Pillars of Peace'.[316] Unlike the Guiding Principles, the 'Six Pillars' gained immediate approval by the Christian public. In a letter to the Commission dated March 12, 1943, Dulles deliberated further on the purpose of this statement: 'In the statement we describe six "pillars of peace" that are needed to support a just and durable world order and to the establishment of which this nation ought now to be committed. We have stated our propositions in simple terms which can effectively unite all those who favour organized international collaboration.'[317] At the following Executive Meeting, on 16 March, the leadership of the Federal Council gave a 'hearty approval' of the 'Six Pillars' and recommended them to the churches.[318] This document is remarkable for two reasons: (1) it was the clearest pronouncement of the Commission to create a nationwide demand for American participation in the United Nations, rather than a 'go it alone' policy such as that adopted after World War I; and (2) it provided an incisive insight into Dulles' thinking - a clear forecast of his future attitudes as Secretary of State.

The 'Six Pillars', although based on the Guiding Principles, constituted a collection of general political statements concerning the peace issue. In a meeting with President Roosevelt on 26 March 1943, one week after the publication, Dulles explained that, by issuing the 'Six Pillars of Peace', the Commission intended to create strong public support for a new international organisation.[319] To gain Roosevelt's approval, he added that the United States would certainly take a preeminent position within that organisation. The first step towards that end would be to assure an ongoing coalition of the fighting United Nations after the war. This would require 'the willingness of the American people this time to go the way of organized international collaboration.'[320] Coinciding with his own aspirations, the President promised to study the 'Six Pillars' in detail. In parting Dulles expressed his confidence that the statement would be thoroughly discussed by Christian ministers and laymen alike.[321]

What did Dulles intend to accomplish by promulgating the statement at the highest levels of the American government? In an article entitled 'Six Pillars of Peace', published in *Christianity and Crisis* 3 (May 31, 1943), he revealed that the primary objective of the statement was 'to provide thinking and action along realistic lines' by 'outlining six areas within which national interdependence is demonstrated, and where, accordingly, international collaboration needs to be organized.'[322] In issuing the statement on 'The Spiritual Foundation of World Order' Dulles acted shrewdly in exploiting the idealism of his fellow-Americans for his own purposes. He proposed, according to Leonard Mosley, 'a charter for a postwar future by which nationalism would be subordinated to One World, united for peace and mutual development, living under the canopy of a more practical yet more idealistic League of Nations, to be called the United Nations, this time with the United States as a charter member.'[323]

The essential elements of the 'Six Pillars' were: (1) continuation of Allied collaboration after the war, to be joined by neutral and enemy nations as soon as possible; (2) provision for international economic agreements; (3) compatibility of treaty structures with a changing world situation; (4) national autonomy for subject peoples; (5) control of military establishments; and (6) recognition 'in principle' of the right to religious and intellectual liberty for peoples everywhere.[324]

These six principles constituted the essence of Dulles' aspirations in guiding public opinion towards the recognition of the need to establish political mechanisms that would facilitate the co-operation between nations in an interdependent world. He wrote in the cover letter accompanying the first mailing of the statement to all Commission members, that the 'nation has now entered upon the critical period where public opinion must be crystallized in favour of organised international collaboration.'[325] Dulles, in a moment of unusual perceptiveness, realised that the United States stood at the crossroad of being the torch-bearer of a new world order or the champion of a dysfunctional system of nation-states. His latent fear was that it would once again refuse to play its part and postpone the fledgling development of international co-operation indefinitely.[326]

Dulles explained himself in unmistakable terms in his 'Six Pillars of Peace' speech before a meeting of religious, financial, labour and educational leaders[327] at the Rockefeller Center Luncheon Club in New York on March 18, 1943.[328] In this speech, Dulles reviewed the work of the Commission:

> In 1940, the Federal Council of Churches voted to set up a commission to study the bases of a just and durable peace ... Up until now we have primarily emphasized spiritual factors. We have urged upon the churches that they inculcate in men the qualities that Christ taught. We have pointed out that Christ's way was not to tell men what to do in relation to worldly matters, but to give them qualities of vision, of mind and of soul so that they would be enlightened and filled with a righteous faith. We have not sought, indeed we have opposed, the preaching from the pulpits of economics and politics. We have said to the churches, give us men and women possessed of Christian qualities, and then our citizenry can be counted on to take enlightened action.

Now the time had come for action, not words, declared the future Secretary of State: 'Faith will shrivel unless it is made manifest by works. The Commission seeks to bring the Christian approach into our lives as citizens.' The Commission was now entering on 'a second phase of its work', Dulles emphasised.

> We are about to address ourselves to the citizens of this country and say to them that, in our judgment, considerations of morality and enlightened self-interest combine to require our nation now to commit itself to a future of organized international collaboration. There are those who say: Let us get on with the war; when it is won will be time enough to talk about the peace. To

an extent, I agree with that viewpoint. It would be folly to divert our effort and imperil our unity by forcing debate on the details of hypothetical future problems. But there is a decision which must be made now, both from the standpoint of winning the war and winning the peace. That decision is: Will the American people now commit themselves to a future of organized international collaboration within the areas of demonstrated world interdependence?

'The decision must be made at once,' Dulles said, emphasising that the opportunity might disappear. In that event, the world would be doomed to the continuance of the 'war system'. 'The last war was fought to victory and the peace was made on the assumption that this nation was committed to organized international collaboration,' he asserted. 'It was a profound and unforgettable shock when we rejected that collaboration and decided to go it alone. Will history repeat itself? That question raises a fundamental doubt, and until we conclusively resolve it, it will plague us at every turn.' Yet paradoxically he also expressed some doubt about the desirability of the pillars' influence on, or even acceptance by, the churches. He remarked that 'we do not pretend to speak with divine sanction; nor is there anything exclusively Christian about our proposals. We do not want them preached from our pulpits.'

'The Six Pillars of Peace' speech is important in understanding the life and thinking of John Foster Dulles. It also expressed the opinion of many churchgoers that the United States should abandon isolationism and take an active role in international affairs.

### 5.11.2   The Public Campaign

To avoid a repetition of the same dilemma which at the end of the First World War sealed the fate of the League of Nations, Dulles set all levels of mass propaganda in motion to publicise the idea of American participation in some form of world organisation.[329] The 'Six Pillars of Peace' seemed to be the ideal instrument for that purpose. The Federal Council used every conceivable avenue to increase its circulation among the churches, not only in the United States itself, but also in foreign countries. For example, 60,000 copies of the Commission's statement were sent to Protestant ministers, denominational leaders, social action secretaries, city and state councils of churches. These recipients were urged to make the 'Six Pillars' available to the average church member. An additional 2000 copies were mailed to newspapers and Christian magazines. They contributed to its wide distribution by making its basic precepts known in favourable articles and front page coverage.[330] An article in the New York *Herald Tribune* reflected accurately the consensus among American journalists about the statements:

These propositions are broad in concept; nevertheless they are definite enough, as the Commission says, "to force the initial and vital decision on the direction in which the nation will move." Can the American people seriously decide for less than the minimum ends as the Commission poses them[?][331]

To improve public awareness of the 'Six Pillars' the Commission published a series of eight weekly articles which expounded the concepts of the statement in great detail. These articles, which were subsequently circulated in ninety-six daily newspapers with combined circulation of 5,400,000, were written by prominent figures in public life such as Governor Thomas E. Dewey, Senator Joseph Ball, and Undersecretary of State Sumner Welles.[332] Sixteen religious publications also published them.[333] Dulles promoted the 'Six Pillars' assiduously. In a series of letters, addressed to Franklin D. Roosevelt, Senator Connally, Harold Stassen, Supreme Court Justice Felix Frankfurter, Wendell Willkie, Lord Halifax, Joseph H. Oldham, and many more, he encouraged them to study the statement diligently and, if possible, mention it in public addresses. When Anthony Eden stayed at the British Embassy in Washington in the summer of 1943, Dulles gave him the 'Six Pillars' personally.[334]

In a note to a friend, Dulles stated that the statement has made 'a very profound impression' on countless editorials in newspapers across the country; even in Europe the press coverage was 'more favorable and sympathetic than I could have expected'.[335] Reinhold Niebuhr described the 'Six Pillars' as one of those 'increasingly realistic' statements made by the Commission.[336] This realism was actually the result of a compromise between two different perspectives. Henry P. Van Dusen, in an editorial published in *Christianity and Crisis*, commented on that aspect of the statement:

> But its greater importance lies in the fact that, in our judgment, it furnishes the briefest, clearest and soundest agenda for post-war order which has yet been forthcoming from any source, within or outside the churches ... Thus it stakes a middle course between the two main schools of thought on the organisation of peace - those who espouse a single over-all instrument of world order and those who favour a policy of "muddling through" by piecemeal solutions of separate problems ... The Commission's political propositions offer median ground with some hope of winning adherence from both parties.[337]

The historian Winthrop S. Hudson, in *Religion in America*, observes that 'probably no report ever received more serious consideration among church people'.[338] In his address before the biennial meeting of the FCC on November 28, 1944, John F. Dulles remarked that the 'Six Pillars' had a great effect upon the country at large and upon the State Department in particular. He was convinced that it actually influenced the Dumbarton Oaks Conference in Washington, D.C., which laid the groundwork for the United Nations. In this speech, as quoted in the 1944 *Biennial Report*, he said: 'In looking back to appraise the influences which led to the Dumbarton Oaks Conference, it can fairly be said that the Protestant churches have played a decisive part.' Addressing the congregation at the First Presbyterian Church in Watertown, New York, on August 28, 1949, Dulles reflected again on the churches' success in influencing government policy:

> It is the churches that have missionary affiliations that spread great spiritual truths throughout the world. They have central agencies ... that provide studies of world problems by qualified Christian statesmen. These, if used, can create an enlightened public opinion that will directly influence the acts of government and of the United Nations. That has been proved.'[339]

Although it is still a matter of conjecture whether or not Dulles lost his sense of realism in assessing the actual influence of the statement on public opinion, the 'Six Pillars' remain a landmark that brought 'the thinking of the nations in harmony'.[340] Townsend Hoopes affirmed that this pronouncement made a decisive impact on shaping the attitude towards international organisation in America: 'The Federal Council of Churches, in company with like-minded groups throughout the country, then waged an intensive public campaign for the United Nations organization - an effort that was crowned with success when both houses of congress passed supporting resolution.'[341]

The Commission followed meticulously the directives set out by the Executive Committee of the Federal Council both in its publications and in its political activities. One effective course of action which the Commission chose, to inform the American public more directly about its objectives, was the organisation of local Pillars of Peace Committees. In these committees the Commission invited the public to deliberate about the prospects of a new world order.[342] Dulles estimated that more than 20,000 people participated at these events which also received wide publicity.[343]

Dulles himself recognised the enormous possibilities of the mass media to reach an audience in the tens of millions. He bought time on the radio to broadcast interpretative addresses on the 'Six Pillars' and other internationalist pronouncements of the FCC. To present the proposal of a world organisation to the public he authorised the distribution of a four-page, tabloid-size paper, entitled *Post War World*. Its purpose was to analyse the progress in international relations according to the principles formulated in the 'Six Pillars'. As a means to monitor better the developing new world order, Dulles began to write several appraisals of the changing world situation. The common theme which runs through these public statements was a repetitious elaboration of the 'Six Pillars'.[344] The Commission also produced an eighty page discussion outline entitled *Six Pillars of Peace – A Study Guide*. The pamphlet was designed, in Van Kirk's words, to be 'simple, readable, informative and provocative.'[345] Later an *Instruction Manual for Use With 'Six Pillars of Peace'* was published to help ministers in leading discussion groups.[346] In 1942

Walter W. Van Kirk had already expressed the intentions of Dulles in seeking maximum publicity of the Commission's pronouncements when he declared that 'the American churches are the only group in American life with an adequate training in thinking in international terms.' The task of the churches must be to 'create a public opinion which will ensure that the United States shall play its full and essential part in the creation of a moral way of international living.'[347]

In January 1944, the Commission published an essay by Dulles entitled 'World Organisation - Curative and Creative: A Statement to Our Public Leaders and Our People'. It was basically a public plea that the postwar international structure should not be limited to preserving any *status quo*. The Federal Council's *Biennial Report* of 1944 summarised the salient points of the essay:

> Very early in the year, the commission turned its mind to the problem of world organization. Interest in this subject had been enormously increased by the declaration of the Moscow Conference which stressed the necessity of creating at the earliest possible moment a general international organization. The Commission formulated and the Executive committee of the Federal Council approved a statement entitled "World Organization - Curative and Creative." The attention of the churches was called to the need of choosing between "international organization designed merely to perpetuate by repression the particular structure of the world which will emerge from the war, and international organization which, in addition to such use of force under law as is a requisite of order, discharges tasks that are curative and creative." People in and out of the churches were urged to "remain united and vigorous to achieve such international organization and American participation therein."[348]

The report further stated that the Commission had publicly appealed to the President, the Congress, and the people of the United States to implement the ecumenical proposals of a world government. The ecclesiastical establishment declared that 'if international organization is to achieve a durable peace, it must be planned from the beginning to become universal in membership and redemptive in purpose.' More than 1,000 Protestant leaders appended their signature to that appeal. It was also immediately released to the national press.[349] In addition, the Commission produced 'A Guidebook for Action' which was mailed to many local pastors. It was hoped that this document would enlist even more churches in support of the Commission's pronouncements, especially of the 'Six Pillars'.

In June, 1944, the magazine Christianity and Crisis printed an important article of the Commission concerning an appeal of a committee of clergymen headed by John C. Bennett and Reinhold Niebuhr relating to a draft of the future peace agreements in Europe and Asia. This committee of clergymen actually proposed the same ideas which had been formulated in 1940 by Reinhold Niebuhr and other famous intellectuals, including Herbert Agar[350] and Lewis Mumford, in the book, *The City of Man. A Declaration on World Democracy*. The authors called for a 'new order' where 'all states, deflated and disciplined, must align themselves under the law of the world-state ... when the heresy of nationalism is conquered and the absurd architecture of the present world is finally dismantled.'[351] 'Universal peace', these socialist philosophers asserted, 'can be founded only on the unity of man under one law and one government.'[352] The *City of Man* contains many concepts[353] which have found their way into the terminology of the Unity-in-Diversity Council (subsequently Unity-and-Diversity World Council) and the speeches of former President George H. W. Bush, who popularised the concept of a new world order in recent times.

Despite the positive public response the 'Six Pillars' met with some criticism. Mortimer Adler was disappointed with Dulles' opinion that a world government could only be introduced after gradually substituting nationalism with internationalism. 'Dulles', writes Adler, 'included the notion of world government,' but it 'is regarded as a remote objective to be approached through stages of progressively mitigated nationalism.' A direct approach to world government was more to Adler's liking. Thus he sympathised with Michael Straight who, in the book, *Make This The Last War*, calls for an immediate political and economic unification of the world.[354] Adler notes that Straight 'does not regard nationalism in all its forms as an insuperable obstacle to the institution of world government'. Historical developments, however, have vindicated Dulles' approach of gradualism. Nationalism had not yet run its course. Despite proof to the contrary, Adler continued to believe that world federation was not merely possible, but highly probable and could be attained within the twentieth century.[355]

Dulles and his colleagues felt a great sense of satisfaction in their efforts at communicating the ecumenical vision of a World State[356] to countless individuals, in and outside the Church.[357] Nearly every statement of the Commission published until the time of the signing of the United Nations Charter in late 1945 referred in some way to the 'Six Pillars'. The general acceptance of this pronouncement by the American churches motivated the Commission to extend its efforts across the Atlantic in persuading closely aligned ecumenical bodies to adopt a similar position concerning the reconstruction of the postwar world.[358]


5.11.2.1 A Christian Basis for Reconstruction

In late 1942, Henry P. van Dusen, a director of the Commission on a Just and Durable Peace, became chairman of the Peace Aims Group in America. Since John Foster Dulles had already joined the Peace Aims Group, a close co-operation between this group and the Commission was assured from the beginning. Both organisations co-ordinated their efforts in persuading the secular and ecclesiastical authorities to call for a new world order. British and

American Christians were urged to counter any sentiments in their countries which threatened to sabotage the establishment of a world government once victory had been won. By correspondence and occasional visits, the principal officers of the two ecumenical bodies stayed in close contact. Several members of the British Peace Aims Group – among them A. D. Lindsay, Arnold J. Toynbee, Hugh Martin, and Kenneth Grubb[359] – travelled intermittently to the United States. William Paton visited America at least twice before his death in 1943. Henry P. Van Dusen, Reinhold Niebuhr and other members of the American Peace Aims Group went to England on various occasions. Eleanor M. Jackson states that the purpose of these visits was, in most cases, to influence government policy on postwar planning. She writes:

> It is significant that when Paton's "opposite number" in the American Peace Aims Group, H. R. Van Dusen, came over in October 1941, he was able to spend two evenings with the Minister of Information, Brendan Bracken, to have a prolonged interview with Sir Stafford Cripps and Anthony Eden (Colonial Office and Foreign Office) and was given red carpet treatment for his B.B.C. broadcast. "Influence", especially on governments, is something very difficult to measure, but it is significant that the Peace Aims Group had this intimate connection with the government planning.[360]

After the Commission on a Just and Durable Peace published the 'Six Pillars of Peace' in March, 1943, John Foster Dulles urged Archbishop Temple and William Paton to issue a similar statement to the churches in Great Britain. In June, 1943 the British Peace Aims Group released its first manifesto, entitled 'A Christian Basis for Reconstruction', which followed minutely the lines of the 'Six Pillars of Peace' and was released simultaneously in the United States and Great Britain.[361] Dulles recognized the great significance of the statement and saw it as an indication of Christian unity. In an article, which appeared in the October issue of the *Federal Council Bulletin*, he stated the following:

> Its spirit will uplift, and its content will inform, the Christian people of America. Of equal importance is the fact that the British and American statements, taken together, strikingly manifest the power of Christianity to unite national groups in practical programs of common purpose. Each of the two statements was prepared by loyal citizens, in one case British, in the other case, American. But they were Christian citizens and they believed that the welfare of their own nation would best be served by righteous policies. The net result is substantial agreement upon the fundamentals of a post-war order.[362]

Paton later admitted that he was mainly responsible for drafting the text of the British statement. He explained, however, that the final version reflected the consensus of the whole group, since he had to revise his original statement repeatedly to accommodate different views.[363]

Paton recognised selfishness as a basic impediment in achieving 'universal fellowship' among the peoples of the world. He believed that war revealed a deeper reality than merely a struggle between nations; it was a conflict of faiths. Hence he postulated that real victory can only be achieved on two conditions. Firstly, the allied powers would need to define specific war objectives which went beyond the military defeat of the enemy; and, secondly, they would have to dedicate themselves in all sincerity to those objectives. After the war the world would be confronted with a number of pressing needs, the most demanding of which would be the feeding of hungry people and the restoration of world order. The statement further emphasised the urgent need for 'a vigorous dealing with the question of security'. It would be necessary to restore conditions of peace which would liberate all nations from fear of repeated wars. Paton asserted that, unless the nations were set free from that fear, other peace objectives would remain illusory. If this would not be achieved, future wars would plunge them again into the abyss of carnage and destruction. Following his discussion on political security, he embraced the view, advanced in the 'Six Pillars', that 'the peace must make provision for bringing within the scope of international agreement those economic and financial acts of national governments which have widespread international repercussions'. To assure peace, however, a further step needed to be taken:

A permanent aim of the nations of the world ... should be to develop and to mobilize the resources of the earth with a view to achieving for all peoples freedom from want. In the case of industrial nations, and especially Great Britain and the United States, this must include the avoidance of widespread unemployment ... Such a task corresponds to the Christian belief that all men and all nations are members of the family of God, who created the world and its resources for the benefit of all.

In the next paragraph the author challenged the churches to look beyond their immediate concerns to fulfil the vision of a new world order: 'Nothing but dedication to a great ideal, with the readiness for sacrifice which true dedication involves, will be enough. It is at least doubtful whether that dedication can endure without religious inspiration.'

In seeking to be sensitive to public opinion, Paton claimed to have observed that Christians, both in Great Britain and in the United States, would be ready to pledge their allegiance to some form of world government. Thus he concluded (in the section on treaty revision) that 'on major issues it is essential that the decision should be arrived at by the supreme world agency, whatever that may be.' It would also be imperative to place the production and sale of weaponry under international control. Concerning the administration of colonies an international colonial commission should be instituted. This commission

would have the right to inform itself upon the condition of subject territories, to report to whatever world political organization is created upon breaches of international undertakings, to supervise the application of pooled international resources in carrying forward economic and social development and to watch over the development of self-government.

In projecting the situation immediately following the cessation of war, Paton argued for a fair treatment of vanquished enemies. Although acknowledging the need to destroy the means of aggression, he advocated a lenient approach in dealing with the conquered nations:

> At the same time we must take care that there is open to their citizens the same opportunity as other people enjoy of an equal share in all that conduces to the good life ... The settlement following on their defeat must be militarily and politically severe ... but it must be such that coming generations, in those countries, looking back with fuller knowledge on the events of those years, can accept it as just.

The statement went on to support the right of all individuals to intellectual liberty and religious freedom, especially in the light of the refugee problem. The latter was likely to remain a matter of international concern for years to come: 'We think that no world settlement which does not give reasonable security and freedom to the religious, cultural and other minorities, and especially to the most ancient of all, the Jewish people, can be said to have succeeded.'

In its concluding paragraph, Paton faced the immensity of the task involved in realising the ideals implied in this manifesto:

> We shall be very weary, and fatigue is a selfish mood. There will be great temptation to relax, to shirk responsibility and to gather for our own advantage the fruits of victory. If we do that, the interval between this war and the next may be less than the twenty years of restless truce that ended in 1939. We need still the spirit of dedication and of sacrifice for the general good, which now means no less than the good of all the peoples upon the earth. For the tasks, though immense, are those which arise out of the historical situation in which we stand, and this situation, to those who believe in the Living God, is with all its vast responsibilities and difficulties still within the providence and purpose of God. It is he who had given us at this time the opportunity to serve in a manner new in history the interests of all mankind.

Fourteen British church officials and the moderator of the Church of Scotland endorsed heartily the statement as an expression of their own ecclesiastical policy. In America, John Foster Dulles openly declared his agreement with the manifesto of the Peace Aims Group and recommended it to the American churches.[364] Due to its close correspondence with the theme of the 'Six Pillars', the British statement found ready acceptance by the Christian public in the United States. In a letter to the members of the Group, written in July, 1943, Paton expressed his delight about the statement's wide circulation and its positive reception. He also underlined the value of transatlantic co-operation between different ecumenical bodies in achieving changes in the political and social structure of the world.

At about the same time Paton recorded a message on 'Some Principles of Reconstruction' at the BBC in London. His purpose was to interpret the 'Six Pillars of Peace' to a British audience and to elucidate further his position on 'a Christian Basis for Reconstruction'. He especially emphasised the right of the Church, or its ecclesiastical leaders, to deal with the issue of war and peace. In his concluding remarks he advocated the establishment of a world government as the only realistic solution to the problems of the world. Had he lived to see the founding of the United Nations Organisation, he would have been pleased with the determination of the churches to bring his vision of an international community one step closer to reality, even though he may have been disappointed about the limitations of the UN Charter. Yet by the time the program was broadcast in different countries overseas, his frail body had succumbed to disease.

Despite the immense loss which Paton's death brought to the ecumenical movement, the Peace Aims Group and the Commission on a Just and Durable Peace continued their public campaign. Encouraged by the resounding success of their previous efforts to inform the churches about world order, they turned their attention increasingly to the non-English-speaking world with the same message of international co-operation.

### 5.11.2.2 Round Table of Christian Leaders

In mid-1943 Dulles began to promote an 'international Christian approach to the establishment of world order.' As an executive of the FCC, he contacted the Canadian United Church Commission on Church, Nation and World Order and suggested the convening of an ecumenical conference prior to the conclusion of the war. His intention was to gather representatives of different national Church bodies and give them the opportunity to study the peace issue. This was in accordance with the mandate of the Commission on a Just and Durable Peace which stipulated: '... to consider the convening, as soon as possible, of an assembly of Christian leaders, lay and clerical to mobilize the Christians of all lands in support of a peace consonant with Christian principle.'[365] An organising committee was selected and charged with the task to lay the groundwork for a future World Council of Churches. Recognizing the impediments of wartime to convene a truly ecumenical assembly,[366] every effort was made to guarantee that the deliberations 'were entered upon with a clear consciousness of the Church's ecumenical character and function.'[367] The committee named Bishop G. Bromley Oxnam as general chairman, and accorded Dulles the honour of giving the opening address.

Representative Church leaders and Christian laymen from twelve countries participated at the 'International Round Table of Christian Leaders', at Princeton, N.J., on 8-11 July 1943, including the General Secretary of the British Council of Churches and ecclesiastical executives from Canada, New Zealand, and Australia.[368] They were joined by the former president of Doshisha University in Kyoto, the president of Ginling College, China, as well as government representatives from the United States, Switzerland, and the Netherlands.[369] Their primary purpose was to formulate an agenda for peace by insisting on the need to institute a world government.[370]

In his speech Dulles reminded the ecumenical leaders at the beginning of the conference that the isolationists in America had been forced to go on the defensive. 'They can be kept there if our efforts are unremitting. We plan that they shall be.'[371] Then he remarked further that '[o]ur task will be greatly helped if we can feel that what we are urging upon our nation parallels that which Christians of other lands are prepared to urge upon their nations. It is most important that we be in step with each other.'[372] With great enthusiasm he pointed to the 'Six Pillars' as an example of how the Christian public can effectively influence foreign policy. 'If today the leaders of both political parties are with virtual unanimity expressing themselves in favour of a future international collaboration much as we outlined, that is due in no small part to our timely intervention.'[373] Now it would be the task of the churches to warn the Allies not to succumb to 'the very devils [of nationalism] against which they fought.'[374] He was dismayed that a new 'Holy Alliance' based on military force was being created and stood as a formidable obstacle to a just and durable peace in its 'demand for vengeance on whole peoples many of whom have risked more than we in standing steadfast for the right.'[375]

In order to assure an atmosphere of openness and free discussion journalists and visitors were not allowed to participate at the conference. Since the group of delegates was relatively small, it was possible to meet in general session as a body, and discussion and dialogue took the place of formal presentations during the four-day conference. The Round Table selected a Guiding Committee of six men from five nations to identify the points of discussion which had met substantial agreement in previous study papers, and to draft and submit for consideration of the Round Table statements relating to these issues.[376] The results of the proceedings were summarised and released for publication to the Associated Press, United Press and International News Service, and the three principal press associations. In addition, dispatches were sent to the Standard News Association, New York (servicing the New York metropolitan area), Religious News Service, Canadian Press, Australian Associated Press, *New York Times, New York Herald Tribune* and the *Christian Science Monitor*, Boston.

The conference concluded that the 'Six Pillars' afforded goals towards which they could all work and issued a joint declaration to that effect, entitling it, *A Christian Message on World Order*:

Concern for world order, then, is for us an imperative obligation inherent in the Christian world view. A weary and frustrated world needs and desires a clear statement of a goal toward which to strive. Therefore there is demanded of us a positive affirmation of our faith and purpose as directed toward the problem of world order. Such an affirmation should arouse a spirit more dynamic than that which impels other movements seeking universal acceptance. Our faith and purpose derive from the conviction that they are in conformity with God's purpose in history and are therefore required by Divine mandate. To support us we have the guidance and power of the Holy Spirit. We are committed to the goal of world-wide political order, and thus to the establishment of the institutions or organizations best suited to serve this end. The need for action is urgent. We recognize, however, that our objective may not be fully attainable at a single step but may have to be evolved through intermediate developments.[377]

In typical fashion, the assembled ecumenical leaders proclaimed that the 'Christian church is potentially the chief instrument of world order' for 'the desperate needs of the people are for moral and spiritual light, for relief from fear, for faith and courage, for forgiveness and the grace to forgive. It is the responsibility of the Church to meet those needs.'[378] They believed that the first hopeful sign of a coming era of peace was the 'new access of power in unity' of the churches.[379]

The political propositions which had been pronounced by the Commission on a Just and Durable Peace were identified as the basis of what the people of all nations should 'study, understand and accept in relation to the conditions by which they are confronted' and 'seek through appropriate channels to have accepted by their governments.'[380]

The Round Table set forth a table of ten requirements for advancing its agenda of a new world order. These were the following:

1) That national isolationism, the monopolization of political power by a few nations, and the balance of power which hitherto have failed to maintain peace, be repudiated as policies which contravene the purpose of establishing world order and the institutions requisite thereto. 2) That temporary collaboration among the United Nations should, as quickly as possible, give way to a universal order and not be consolidated into a closed military alliance to establish a preponderance of power or a concert of power. 3) That drastic reduction in armaments be undertaken as steps toward the goals envisaged in the Atlantic charter of the "abandonment of the use of force" and lifting from the peoples of the world "the crushing burden of armaments." 4) That immediate international collaboration such as is involved in (a) conferences dealing with specific problems and in (b) the administration of relief and reconstruction be guarded against exploitation for purpose of power politics. 5) That if regional organizations arise, they be part of an inclusive world order and shall not threaten the interests of world organization. 6) That a larger measure of discipline and sacrifice for the good of the whole world community be practice by each nation as necessary to the

good of that nation as a part of the community. 7) That individual citizens recognize their responsibility for their collective decisions as reflected in national policies. 8) That ethical and moral standards recognized as applying to individual conduct be recognized as applying also to group, corporate, and national conduct. 9) That cultural and social collaborations be established, along with political collaboration, as essential for the achievement of world order. 10) That an adequate motivation be developed in the will of the peoples of the world to support the agencies and arrangements for cooperation, so that the sense of national destiny which has hitherto led nations to seek national aggrandizement, shall hereafter find its expression in works that promote the general welfare of mankind.[381]

The Round Table perceived the war not just as an armed struggle between nations, but as a clash of ideologies. Germany had prostrated itself to the 'demonic forces of racialism and perverted nationalism'.[382] These forces were being opposed 'not only in the free countries of the United Nations and in occupied lands, but also among growing groups in Germany itself.'[383] Moreover, 'the very same forces find support in some sections of opinion, and even in certain governmental policies, within the United Nations, free and occupied'.[384] To guard against being infected by the nefarious ideology of Naziism, Christians 'should beware of thinking solely on nationalistic lines.'[385]

The problem of Germany must be seen in a world-wide context. The only adequate solution would be to establish as soon as possible a world organisation 'embracing all nations. Our object should be to help Germany take her place within this organization assuming all the responsibilities and rights which membership implies.' In a conscious attempt to apply the lessons learned from the Versailles Peace Conference, the following suggestions were made with regard to the treatment of Germany:

> ... Christian principles must prevail. Controls and safeguards will be necessary. But it would be folly to attempt to apply repressive measures so vindictive and harsh that public opinion in the victor nations themselves will later revolt against them. This will inevitably bring about a breakdown of the peace structure and lead to renewed conflict.[386]

The mere fact that the international delegates expressed such advanced views was certainly remarkable. The most significant aspect of the Round Table conference, however, was that it took place at all. In the foreword to the conference *Message*, Dr Nolde stated that the 'very fact that it was held, with its international representation, testified that the life and concern of the Christian Church transcend national lines even at a time when the greater part of the world is torn by war.'[387]

262

5.11.2.3 Popular Support

In the autumn of 1943 an American interfaith *Declaration on World Peace*, commonly known as *Pattern for Peace*, was published by Richard M. Fagley of the Church Peace Union and Father Edward A. Conway, SJ, of Regis College. Fagley, who was later to become a secretary of the Commission on a Just and Durable Peace, took his inspiration from a similar pronouncement, the *Letter to the Times*, issued earlier and signed by the Archbishops of Canterbury and York, by the Cardinal-Archbishop of Westminster and by the Moderator of the Free Church Federal Council.[388] The *Letter* basically contained the Five Peace Points of the 1939 Christmas Allocution of Pope Pius XII and the Message of the 1937 Oxford World Conference on Church, Community, and State. Given the British precedent Fagley was convinced that an American interfaith statement would counter any confusion which may have arisen in the minds of many by a steady stream of pronouncements on world order coming from diverse religious groups.

The *Pattern for Peace* was signed by 146 prominent religious leaders, approximately fifty from each faith, who were associated either with the National Catholic Welfare Conference, the Synagogue Council of America, or the FCC. The list of signatories included the leaders of twenty-two national interdenominational agencies, twenty-one Protestant and three Orthodox communions, ten Catholic archbishops, fourteen bishops, well-known priests and leaders of lay organisations, the executives of ten rabbinical and congregational organisations and other representative rabbis. John Foster Dulles signed the statement on behalf of the Federal Council. In a national radio address he commented favourably on the statement and urged its widespread study, stating that the principal representatives of different faith communities intended to convey to the American public the importance of establishing a new international organisation at the end of war.[389]

The publicity effort to disseminate the message of the *Pattern for Peace* was most impressive. On the release date of 7 October 1943, the secular and religious media accorded it full press and radio coverage. Editorial comments lauded the statement almost unanimously for its well-articulated principles. At once each of the three faith communities launched an educational campaign among the millions of their followers. Joint sessions were held in a number of cities to arouse public opinion in favour of the principles.[390] The meeting in Syracuse on 15 February 1944, for example, proved extraordinarily successful. The organisers convened a 'Civic Gathering' to discuss the foundations of a just peace and a better social order, sponsored by the Roman Catholic Diocese of Syracuse, the Syracuse Jewish Welfare Federation, and the Syracuse Council of Churches. The entire program was focussed on the *Pattern for Peace*. On the three Sundays preceding the event the three nationally prominent speakers were featured in the newspapers. A few days before the event the local radio station discussed favourably the purpose of the 'Civic Gathering'. The Sunday papers contained full-page advertisements making emotional appeals to the community to attend the public meeting.

The message of the *Pattern for Peace* was reinforced by actions of numerous denominational bodies across the country and by other agencies of the various faith communities. The statement even found its way to Central and South America in Spanish and Portuguese translations. In a Christmas Day NBC broadcast representatives of the three faiths explained its meaning to a national audience.

The *Pattern of Peace* was also circulated in Great Britain. The British Council of Christians and Jews headed by the Archbishop of Canterbury, the Archbishop of Westminster, the Moderator of the Free Church Federal Council, the Moderator of the Church of Scotland and the Chief Rabbi of Great Britain received it favourably. In a statement published simultaneously in Great Britain and the United States on 2 June 1944 they endorsed it in part as follows:

> The Council of Christians and Jews in Great Britain warmly welcomes the statement on the conditions of world peace signed by Protestant, Roman Catholic and Jewish religious leaders in America on October 7th, 1943, and finds itself in general agreement with the principles therein laid down.[391]

In the Fall of 1943, the *Pattern of Peace* featured prominently in congressional debates, especially in the US Senate. Following the summer recess, the House passed a resolution on world organisation presented by Representative J. William Fulbright. In September the Republican Postwar Advisory Committee went on record with its own declaration favouring the United States' integration 'in a post-war cooperative organization among sovereign nations'.[392] Both legislative initiatives led eventually to the passing of the Connally Resolution which read in part:

> Resolved, That the war against all our enemies be waged until complete victory is achieved.
>
> That the United States cooperate with its comrades-in-arms in securing a just and honourable peace.
>
> That the United States, acting through its constitutional processes, join with free and sovereign nations in the establishment and maintenance of international authority with power to prevent aggression and to preserve the peace of the world.[393]

For some Senators the resolution was not precise nor comprehensive enough in expressing the intent of the US government to join a world organisation and, under the leadership of Senator Pepper of Florida, introduced an amendment, referring directly to the *Pattern of Peace* statement.

> What are the teachers, what are the preachers, what are the bishops, what are the rabbis, what is the clergy of America saying about an effective international organization after the war?

> Mr. President, I am confident that every Senator would like to know the solemn and elaborative opinion – let me add, the reverent sentiment – of 146 of the principal religious leaders of the United States, as embodied in a declaration made within the last month, entitled 'Catholic, Jewish, and Protestant Declaration on World Peace,' issued by representatives of the Catholic, Jewish and Protestant faiths ...
>
> Mr. President, the program of the religious leaders of the United States is contained in seven points. They are brief and they are pertinent, and I shall read them to the Senate.

Stressing the political importance of the religious declaration, Senator Hatch read extracts from fifteen editorials into the *Congressional Record*.[394] A spirited debate ensued lasting ten days which sought to clarify two essential questions. The first was to ascertain information concerning the approval of the religious leaders of either the Connally Resolution or the proposed Pepper amendment. In his reply Senator Pepper used the *Pattern of Peace* as supporting evidence. He rightly claimed that it would be possible to prove that 'the minimum requirements of the religious leaders' went 'far beyond the resolution reported by the Senate Foreign Relations Committee [i.e., the Connally Resolution]' and were indeed 'far more in accord' with his amendment. The second question addressed the significance of the interfaith statement itself. After reading the *Pattern of Peace* to the Senate, Pepper stated that it was apparent that 'public opinion has formed behind a purpose for peace through an effective international organization'.[395] Senator Hatch made even more extravagant claims for the statement, at least by implication, when he stated, 'It is important that the principle endorsed by men representing, as I understand some 16 million citizens[396] ... be well considered by the Senate of the United States.'[397] These statements were quickly challenged by some Senators. Wherry, for instance, wanted to know if the religious signers 'were speaking for the churches or were voicing the opinion of the churches they represent.'[398] Pepper replied somewhat elusively, 'I can say that I believe these eminent men – approximately fifty from each of the faiths mentioned – represent the sentiment of the leadership of the ministry of those three faiths.'[399] At the time this was all what could be said in favour of the *Pattern of Peace* which had been released only three weeks earlier. The concerted effort to propagate its principles was still in its initial stage, but would gather steam quickly. Recognizing the historical moment, officers of the Commission on a Just and Durable Peace tried to rally behind Senator Pepper and his senatorial allies. First, they tried to get a hearing before the Senate Foreign Relations subcommittee which had issued the Connally Resolution. When this petition was declined, Dulles wrote a letter to Chairman Connally, which stated in part:

> The Federal Council of Churches of Christ in America and its Commission to Study the Bases of a Just and Durable Peace sincerely hope that the Senate will adopt a clear and comprehensive resolution favoring United States collaboration with other nations in the now demonstrated areas of national

interdependence. In its "Six Pillars of Peace" statement, the Federal Council's Commission advocated continuing and broadening collaboration within the six areas there mentioned. The Inter-Faith statement recently read into the Congressional Record by Senator Mead,[400] reflects in our judgment the prevailing mind of American Christians as to the goals toward which we should work.[401]

The debate ended abruptly when the Moscow *Declaration of Four Nations on General Security* was announced on October 30, 1943. The executive branch of the US government went on record for the first time seeking to establish a postwar international organisation.

Another platform, the pulpit, was utilised to great effect for the cause of world order and peace. At the opening of the Federal Council's National Mission on World Order, on October 28, 1943, John F. Dulles was invited to preach at the Cathedral of St. John the Divine in New York City.[402] His sermon called on the American Christians to revive the vision of the Founding Fathers and assume that same 'sense of destiny in the performance of a great work of creation'.[403] In penetrating prose, Dulles developed his theme of a righteous faith, which 'senses the power of creation and [provides] a satisfaction which far surpasses that of possession'; a faith that discovers the purpose of the American nation to bring peace to a war-torn world.

> We shall hear the cry of multitudes that a way be found to save them and their children from the death, the misery, the starvation of body and soul which recurrent war and economic disorder now wreak upon man. We shall be so moved by that cry that we shall resolutely dedicate ourselves to find that way.[404]

America, he continued, was not only destined by divine providence to discover that way, but also to lead the world into a new dispensation of world history. This grand vision will be realised, if the Church and the nation begin to act decisively 'to resume a creative role in world affairs'. 'Without that', he warned, 'we are doomed'.[405] Yet this dire prospect would not materialise. The American nation would, indeed, rise to the occasion and triumph. It will not shrink back from its God-given mission to create a new society, 'the like of which men never saw before'. With such confidence, Dulles assured his audience that the day would come when

> we will not merely see the challenge, feel the sympathy, think out the way. We will act. We will embark, in company with others, on the next great adventure, that of building a fellowship that is world-wide in scope. Out of the perils, the difficulties, the accomplishment of that task, will come again the joy that is reserved to those who seek here to create in God's image.[406]

The Commission on a Just and Durable Peace engaged the Institute of Public Relations to organise the Mission in co-operation with five of the major denominational agencies concerned with world order.[407] Walter W. Van Kirk was appointed director of a committee of seven Church executives to supervise the operation. During the campaign he fell ill and had to be replaced by Paul Macy. Fifteen teams of well-known ministers and Christian laymen held one-day conferences in 100 cities across the nation. The aim was to swell the number of partisans in the camp of the internationalists.[408] Labour and business groups, women's clubs, luncheon clubs, high schools and colleges were all invited to contribute their share to the success of the mission.[409]

In January, 1944, G. Bromley Oxnam, a director of the Commission and presiding bishop of the Methodist Council of Bishops, launched a 'Crusade for a New World Order', generally known as the 'Bishop's Crusade'. On January 10, mass rallies were organised in major cities across the country. Under the slogan, 'The Peace May be Won by a Three-Cent Stamp' local ministers encouraged eight million Methodists to write to the United States government, demanding a repudiation of isolationism and the establishment of a world organisation. As a result, Washington was inundated by letters and postcards. The Bishop's Crusade amounted to the greatest public petition drive in history.[410] President Franklin D. Roosevelt sent a letter to the leaders of the Crusade thanking them for 'transforming public opinion, and making it more receptive to the idea of a United Nations organization.'

During March, when the endeavour of the Methodists had reached its climax, the Northern Baptist Convention initiated a World Order Crusade. A second massive outpouring of mail reached the White House, calling for a universal world organisation to maintain the peace.[411] Two months later, in May 1944, the Congregational Church started a 'personal commitment' campaign on behalf of international organisation. On Sunday, May 21, Congregational ministers invited their parishioners to sign a World Order Compact. The document closely followed the format of the Mayflower Compact. The signatories committed themselves 'to work for a just and cooperative world order', and to help establish 'an international organization for the better ordering of the inter-dependent life of nations'.[412]

In anticipation of 'World Order Day', November 12, 1944, the Federal Council's Department of International Justice and Goodwill distributed a six-page folder entitled 'The Churches and World Order'. This publication recommended that the day 'be observed in a spirit of utter obedience to Jesus Christ and with the one thought of rededicating our lives and our treasure to the winning of a peace universal in scope and redemptive in purpose'.[413] On that particular Sunday the churches were asked to reflect upon the possibilities of a world order of peace and to pray for its realisation. Countless sermons were preached by participating clergymen on international reconstruction and peace. A memorable precedent was set for future 'World Order' days. Only a few months later, the Commission influenced Bishop Oxnam, by then the acting president of the Federal Council, to call for the dedication of Sunday, April 22, 1945, and Wednesday, April 25, 1945, 'as occasions for special intercession' on behalf of the San Francisco United Nations Conference. A prayer specially written for the occasion was signed by moderators and presidents of thirty-four denominations: 'Let us confess that we have been concerned too much with our own affairs, at times indifferent to the needs of others and unready to make sacrifices to prevent war and insure peace.'[414] On Sunday, April 22, 1945, the Oakland Council of Churches invited Dulles to speak about the proceedings of the first United Nations conference to a crowd of approximately eleven thousand people.[415] Reflecting on all these diverse activities of the Commission, E. Raymond Platig paid tribute to Dulles in orchestrating a greatly significant public campaign:

> Dulles himself considered this national educational work of the Commission as its most important task – especially in the war years. It is clear from many of his statements that he looked upon the Commission as one of the prime leaders and moulders of public opinion which did much to foster public acceptance of (if not actually created a public demand for) the United Nations.[416]

On November 6, 1945, President Harry Truman, the signer of the UN Charter, wrote in a personal letter to Dulles that the Commission reflected 'the highest values in American life'. 'If today we Americans have a clearer understanding of our place in the world community – as I believe we have – it is due, in no small part, to the advanced position in international thinking taken by the Federal Council.'[417]

### 5.11.3   The United Nations, 1945

The activity of the Commission reached its zenith in the months immediately preceding the San Francisco Conference for the drafting of the Charter of the United Nations. From January 16 to 19, 1945, a national study conference was held in Cleveland, Ohio, chiefly focussing on the provisional proposals which had been put forward in the previous fall by the Dumbarton Oaks consultation of four major powers. The churchmen at Cleveland greeted the Dumbarton Oaks outline for the United Nations with reserved enthusiasm. Although the proposals did not meet the high expectations expressed in religious publications, such as the 'Six Pillars of Peace', political realism demanded that they be accepted as an imperfect expression of a desired end. It was recognised that the original draft of the UN Charter had some merit in laying the ground work of a collective security system which could be further improved in the future.[418] The ecumenical leaders suggested nine concrete amendments of policies deemed deficient. These included a plea that the Charter clearly specify that all nations would be eligible for membership, that more adequate provision should be made for the protection of small nations, and that there should be greater stress on 'human rights and fundamental freedoms'.[419]

During the San Francisco Conference, which convened on April 25, 1945,

Secretary Stettinius invited 42 national non-governmental organisations in the United States each to name one delegate and two associates to be officially related to the Conference. One hundred and twenty-six representatives of religious organisations such as the American-Jewish Committee, American Jewish Conference, Catholic Association for International Peace, Church Peace Union, and National Catholic Welfare Conference, served as consultants to the American delegation. The State Department made all the arrangements for travel and hotel accommodations, and gave the delegates official credentials. Comparison of the UN Charter with the major statements of various religious groups indicates the important contribution made by these organisations. According to Charles S. Macfarland, the conference laid the foundations for a new world order.[420] Stettinius publicly acknowledged the debt of the emerging United Nations to the interest and activity of these ecclesiastics and Christian laymen.[421] John Foster Dulles and Walter W. Van Kirk served as consultants to the American delegation, with Bishop Baker and O. Frederick Nolde[422] as associate consultants. They were in frequent touch with the other non-church members of the delegation. That the representatives of the FCC were partially instrumental in framing the UN Charter[423] was further proof of the close co-operation between the Federal Council and the Council on Foreign Relations, for representatives of both councils constituted a large segment of the American delegation to the UN Founding Conference.[424] Over forty of these delegates belonged to either or both of these councils including Alger Hiss, the General Secretary[425], John J. McCloy, Julius C. Holmes, Nelson A. Rockefeller, Adlai Stevenson, Joseph E. Johnson, Ralph J. Bunche, Clark M. Eichelberger, and Thomas K. Finletter.

This Conference equally marked a momentous occasion in the history of the Federal Council's Commission on a Just and Durable Peace.[426] In 'The Faith of Our Fathers', John Foster Dulles described how important it was to direct and co-ordinate the efforts of the Commission and other secular organisations while organising the United Nations:

> Most of all I worked with the Commission on a Just and Durable Peace of the Federal Council of the Churches of Christ in America. During these same years I helped organize the United Nations and attended its meetings and those of the Council of Foreign Ministers. Serving at the same time in both religious and political groups made ever clearer the relationship between the two. I saw that there could be no just and durable peace except as men held in common certain simple and elementary religious beliefs.[427]

At the San Francisco Conference Dulles served as an advisor to the American delegates on Commission I, which dealt with the general provisions of the Charter, and Commission II, which dealt with provisions for the General Assembly.[428] He is generally credited for his significant contributions to the provisions for regional arrangements, to the issue of domestic jurisdiction, and to the broad definition of powers of discussion for the General Assembly.[429]

After his return from San Francisco, Dulles reported on the conference to the Federal Council's executive committee. He asserted that no one could read the United Nations Charter as a whole without realising that it could be a magnificent charter of human liberty. The committee then adopted 'The Churches and the Charter of the United Nations', a statement written by Walter W. Van Kirk. It read in part:

> The Charter ... offers mankind an important means for the achievement of a just and durable peace. The new organization ... can help governments to join their moral and material resources in support of a system of world order and justice. The churches of Christ in America have long held that the nations can better serve God's purpose for the world as they are brought into organic relationship with one another for the commonweal. The Charter signed at San Francisco marks a genuine advance toward this end ... We believe it is the clear duty of our government promptly to ratify the Charter and thus to assure cooperation by the United States in the task of making the organization an effective agency for the maintenance of international peace and security.[430]

In San Francisco the international system Dulles had envisioned seemed to become a potential reality. Although the United Nations Organisation, in 1945, was still far from being a world federation, he relished the thought that America had finally accepted the responsibility to take its leading position in the world. He was convinced that, given the continuous expansion of an incipient international community, the ideal of a unified world would eventually come to fruition. Yet he realised that the fulfilment of the vision of the 'Commonwealth of God', as formulated by his close associate, Lionel G. Curtis, lay still in the distant future. In a letter to Curtis he wrote that the United Nations Organisation, despite its positive aspects, was still beset by obvious short-comings: 'I am rather skeptical as to whether much can be done [at the present time] on the global level beyond consultation.'[431]

Eight years later Walter W. Van Kirk confidently brushed aside any lingering doubts about the versatility of the United Nations Organisation to develop into a world government at some point in time. On February 4, 1953, he delivered a speech before the Southern California ministers' annual convocation at the University of California (Los Angeles) on the subject, 'The Church and World Government'. According to a press release, he concluded his message as follows:

> The surest way ultimately to achieve some form of world government is through the United Nations. A super-world with constitutional authority and with sufficient police force to impose its judgments on sovereign nation states may come some day ... It is because Christians have dared dream of a political and social order that would transcend the absolute sovereignty of the nation state that they have given whole-hearted support to the United Nations.[432]

The churches had superbly discharged their responsibility, as defined by the FCC, of shaping public opinion in favour of international co-operation[433] based on the principle of the brotherhood of humankind.[434] The Church leaders and their associates expectantly looked forward to the future when the Kingdom of God on earth would be a reality.

Notes

[1] Dulles' address, 'The Churches and the International Situation,' February 1940, *JFD Papers*; as cited in FCC Pamphlet, *The United States and the World of Nations* (February, 1940), New York, 8.

[2] Letter, Henry P. Van Dusen to JFD, with enclosure, January 11, 1940, *JFD Papers*. The date of the letter indicates that Dulles had received an advance copy of the public statement weeks before he addressed the delegates at the National Study Conference. Thus the joint statement of Coffin and Van Dusen was not really a spontaneous declaration in support of Dulles' internationalist position at the National Study Conference, as it was made out to be.

[3] See Federal Council of Churches, 'Developing a Positive Peace Policy,' *Federal Council Bulletin* 23, no. 5 (May, 1940), New York.

[4] See Federal Council of Churches, 'The American Churches in Time of War,' *Federal Council Bulletin* 24, no. 1 (January, 1941), New York.

[5] The Commission to Study the Bases of a Just and Durable Peace [John F. Dulles], *A Just and Durable Peace. Data Material and Discussion Questions*, New York, 1941, 3; see also Federal Council of Churches, *Annual Report* (1941), New York, 94. In an early memorandum the Commission defined its purpose as trying to 'educate and crystallize public opinion' about the problems inherent in the realisation of 'a just and durable peace'. This would be done by 'providing background without which none of our major problems can be solved', and also by formulating 'certain broad moral principles' on which the future policy decisions of governments could be based. See 'A Just and Durable Peace. Memorandum of preliminary views on certain basic questions of the Committee of Direction of the Commission to Study the Bases of a Just and Durable Peace', undated, *JFD Papers*.

[6] On 16 November 1943 the name was shortened to 'Commission on a Just and Durable Peace'; see Federal Council of Churches, *Annual Report* (1943), New York, 153.

[7] See 'A Just and Durable Peace. Memorandum of preliminary views on certain basic questions of the Committee of Direction of the Commission to Study the Bases of a Just and Durable Peace,' undated (probably drafted in May 1941), *JFD Papers*; and also Federal Council of Churches, *Biennial Report* (1940), New York, 214.

[8] Samuel McCrea Cavert, '*Oral History Collection*', 1965, 12.

[9] John F. Dulles, 'America's Role in World Affairs', 28 October, 1939, *JFD Papers*; see also *New York Times*, October 29, 1939.

[10] *Ibid.*

[11] Federal Council of Churches, *Federal Council Bulletin* 24, no. 1 (January 1941), New York, 6.

[12] See The Commission to Study the Bases of a Just and Durable Peace (John F. Dulles), *A Just and Durable Peace. Data Material and Discussion Questions* (1941), New York, 3-4.

[13] See transcripts of interviews with Roswell P. Barnes and Henry P. Van Dusen, *Oral History Collection*; also Federal Council of Churches, *Biennial Report* (1940), New York, 214; and John M. Mulder, 'The Moral World of John Foster Dulles,' 165.

[14] John F. Dulles, 'Christianity in This Hour ,' 21 April 1941, 19, *JFD Papers*, Box 20. This speech was delivered before a meeting of the Federation of Churches and Council of Church Women, held at Rochester, New York.

[15] Marquis Childs, *Oral History Collection*, 1966, 2.

[16] Richard M. Fagley, *Oral History Collection*, 1964, 29-30.

[17] As cited in Richard D. Challener and John M. Fenton, 'Recent Past Come Alive in Dulles "Oral History,"' *University: A Princeton Quarterly* (Spring 1967), 6.

[18] Henry Smith Leiper, *Oral History Collection*, 1965, 2.

[19] John M. Mackay, *Oral History Collection*, 1965, 8.

[20] Albert N. Keim, 'John Foster Dulles and the Federal Council of Churches of Christ, 1937-1949,' 59.

[21] Federal Council of Churches, *Federal Council Bulletin* 24, no. 6 (June 1941), New York, 9.

[22] John F. Dulles, 'The Church's Role in Developing the Bases of a Just and Enduring Peace', *When Hostilities Cease*, Addresses and Findings of the Exploratory Conference on the Bases of a Just and Enduring Peace, Chicago Temple, May 27-30, 1941, Commission on World Peace of the Methodist Church, Chicago, 1941, 17.

[23] *Ibid.*, 13.

[24] *Ibid.*, 17.

[25] *Ibid.*

[26] *Ibid.*

[27] Letter, JFD to Professor Eugene Staley, January 3, 1940, *JFD Papers*.

[28] John F. Dulles, 'The Church's Role in Developing the Bases of a Just and Enduring Peace', 13.

[29] *Ibid.*, 14.

[30] *Ibid.*, 15.

[31] 'A Message from the National Study Conference on the Churches and a Just and Durable Peace' (Pamphlet, New York, 1942).

[32] See John F. Dulles, 'Towards World Order,' in Francis J. McConnell, et al., *A Basis for the Peace To Come* (New York: Abingdon-Cokesbury Press, 1942).

[33] John F. Dulles, *Peaceful Change within the Society of Nations*, an address delivered at Princeton University on March 19, 1936, as one of the Stafford Little Foundation Series (n.p., n.d.), 9; see also John F. Dulles, 'The Church's Role in Developing the Bases of a Just and Enduring Peace', 15: 'Sovereignty means, by very definition (Webster), "independent of, and unlimited by, any other". It implies the right to do what one pleases, irrespective of the effect elsewhere.'

[34] See John F. Dulles, 'The Church's Role in Developing the Bases of a Just and Enduring Peace,' 15-16.

[35] *Ibid.*, 19.

[36] *Ibid.*, 22.

[37] *Reciprocal Trade Agreements Program*, Hearings before the Committee on Ways and Means, House of Representatives, 80th Congress, 1st Session (Washington, D.C.: Government Printing Office, 1946), 1173, as cited in Kenneth Nelson Vines, *The Role of the Federal Council of the Churches of Christ in America in the Formation of American National Policy*, unpublished Ph.D. thesis, University of Minnesota, 1953,

171.

[38] See Kenneth Nelson Vines, *The Role of the Federal Council of the Churches of Christ in America in the Formation of American National Policy*, 171-172.

[39] John F. Dulles, 'The Churches's Contribution Toward a Warless World', *Religion in Life*, IX (Winter, 1939) 39.

[40] John F. Dulles, 'The Churches's Contribution Toward A Warless World', 40.

[41] *Ibid.*

[42] See letter, John F. Dulles to John Hightower, December 22, 1954, *JFD Papers*: Dulles believed that 'anybody who is truly a Christian person cannot very well be ultra-nationalistic.'

[43] Dulles article in Federal Council of Churches, *Biennial Report* (1944), New York, 26-28; see also John F. Dulles, 'Statement of the Committee of Direction of the Commission on a Just and Durable Peace,' *Post War World*, I (February 15, 1944), 1, 4; John F. Dulles, 'Law Needed in an International World Order,' *Post War World*, I (April 15, 1944), 3; John F. Dulles, 'International Institutions to maintain Peace with Justice must be organized,' *World Affairs*, CVII (March, 1944), 34-37.

[44] 'Dulles Outlines World Peace Plan,' *New York Times*, on October 28, 1939.

[45] See, e.g., John F. Dulles, 'Peaceful Change within the Society of Nations' (1936), *JFD Papers*; 'The Problem of Peace in a Dynamic World' (1937), *Religion in Life*; John F. Dulles, 'The American Churches and the International Situation,' December 1940; 'Christianity in this Hour' (April 21, 1941), *JFD Papers*; John F. Dulles, 'Address at Union Theological Seminary,' (May 19, 1941), *JFD Papers*; John F. Dulles, 'Peace without Platitudes,' *Fortunes*, XXV (January 1942), 42-43, 87-88, 90; John F. Dulles, 'Towards World Order' (March 5, 1942), in Francis J. McConnell, et al., *A Basis for the Peace To Come*; John F. Dulles, 'The Churches and World Order,' Address delivered to the graduating class of Princeton Theological Seminary on May 16, 1944, published in *Theology Today*, October, 1944, in Henry P. Van Dusen, ed., *The Spiritual Legacy of John Foster Dulles*.

[46] John F. Dulles, 'The Churches and World Order,' Address delivered to the graduating class of Princeton Theological Seminary on May 16, 1944, published in *Theology Today*, October, 1944, in Henry P. Van Dusen, ed., *The Spiritual Legacy of John Foster Dulles*, 29; see also Lord Lothian, 'The End of Armageddon,' Federal Union, June 193, 3-5, reprinted in Patrick Ransome, ed., *Studies in Federal Planning* (London: Macmillan, 1943) 1-3.

[47] U.S. Congress, Senate Hearings before the Committee on Foreign Relations, *The Charter of the United States*, 79th Congress, 1st Session (Washington, D.C.: Government Printing Office, 1945) 647.

[48] John F. Dulles, 'The Christian Citizen in a Changing World,' in The World Council of Churches, *Man's Disorder and God's Design*, Vol. IV: *The Church and the International Disorder* (New York: Harper and Brothers, 1948) 73.

[49] John F. Dulles, reprint from *Social Progress*, January, 1943, 2, JFD *Papers*.

[50] John F. Dulles, 'The American Churches and the International Situation' (1940), 6, *JFD Papers*.

[51] Dulles' article sent to the International Council of Religious Education (April 29, 1942), 5, *JFD Papers*.

[52] Dulles address at Episcopalian Diocesan dinner (May 19, 1942), 4, *JFD Papers*.

[53] See U.S. Congress, Senate Hearings before the Committee on Foreign Relations, *The Charter of the United States*, 79th Congress, 1st Session (Washington,

D.C.: Government Printing Office, 1945) 641: 'Actually, the document before you charts a path which we can pursue joyfully and without fear. Under it we remain the masters of our own destiny. The Charter does not subordinate us to any supergovernment. There is no right on the part of the United Nations Organization to intervene in our domestic affairs. There can be no use of force without our consent. If the joint adventure fails, we can withdraw.'

[54] John F. Dulles, 'The General Assembly', in Hamilton Fish Armstrong, ed., *The Foreign Affairs Reader* (New York: Harper and Brothers, 1947) 421. This article was first published in 1945. Armstrong was a leading member of the Council on Foreign Relations.

[55] See *ibid.*, 420.

[56] John C. Bennett, *Oral History Collection*, 1965, 5-6.

[57] John F. Dulles, *The New York Times Magazine* (August, 19, 1945), 12.

[58] *Ibid.*, 35. See also John F. Dulles, 'The General Assembly', 422.

[59] John F. Dulles, 'The General Assembly', 422.

[60] John F. Dulles, 'Towards World Order' (March 5, 1942), in Francis J. McConnell, et al., *A Basis for the Peace To Come*.

[61] In September, 1945 Dulles detailed his ideas about functional activities of an international organisation which he deemed to be necessary: 'The Assembly ... must take into account not merely the relative merits of the goals themselves but the degree to which the pursuit of them will produce the by-products of increased fellowship between the member nations ... It is very important, for example, particularly during the first years when the war coalition will tend to disintegrate, that the Assembly choose projects which are likely to succeed ... It is important, too, that the goals ... should include some which will arouse popular interest and backing ... The Assembly should seek psychological substitutes for military warfare. It must do some things that will be dramatic ... The Assembly should utilize its grant of authority and act to ameliorate the economic and social conditions which help to breed war ... The Assembly can contribute to the accord between ... [the Great Powers] ... It can refrain from using its privileges, notably that of discussion, in a way to exploit and magnify the minor differences which will inevitably arise among the Great Powers ... Since the smaller nations control the Assembly, there will be a natural tendency for them to organize its social and economic activities so as to benefit themselves at the expense of the larger members ... The Assembly should consciously sponsor activities which bring the larger powers to like an international way of life and thereby promote harmony between themselves and the smaller powers. It will succeed in this if it chooses activities of a kind which will be affirmatively advantageous to all.' John F. Dulles, 'The General Assembly', 422-424. Dulles then suggested that there were primarily three areas in which functional tasks for the Assembly would be appropriate. These were: (1) the development and codification of International Law, (2) examination of the conditions of international trade and finance, and (3) co-operation in the field of health.

[62] John F. Dulles, *War, Peace and Change* (New York: Harper and Brothers, 1939).

[63] International Institute of Intellectual Cooperation, *Peaceful Change, Procedures, Population, Raw Materials, Colonies*, 608-609.

[64] John F. Dulles, *War, Peace and Change*, 6.

[65] *Ibid.*, 7.

[66] *Ibid.*

274

[67] *Ibid.*, 9.

[68] *Ibid.*, 52.

[69] Michael A. Guhin, *John Foster Dulles. A Statesman and his Times* (New York: Columbia University Press, 1972) 72.

[70] John F. Dulles, *War, Peace and Change*, 52.

[71] *Ibid.*, 56.

[72] *Ibid.*

[73] *Ibid.*, 29.

[74] *Ibid.*, 30.

[75] *Ibid.*, 34.

[76] *Ibid.*

[77] *Ibid.*, 58.

[78] See also John F. Dulles, 'As seen by a Layman,' in Henry P. Van Dusen, *The Spiritual Legacy of John Foster Dulles*, 14.

[79] *Ibid.*, 62.

[80] *Ibid.*

[81] *Ibid.*, 63.

[82] *Ibid.*, 115-116.

[83] *Ibid.*, 63, 64.

[84] *Ibid.*, 116.

[85] *Ibid.*, 64-65.

[86] *Ibid.*, 63.

[87] *Ibid.*, 117.

[88] *Ibid.*, 105.

[89] John F. Dulles, 'The Church's Role in Developing the Bases of a Just and Enduring Peace,' May 28, 1941, 11-12.

[90] *Ibid.*, 25.

[91] *Ibid.*

[92] *Ibid.*, 24-26.

[93] Dulles address at the Foreign Policy Association, March 18, 1939, *JFD Papers*. Dulles added 'such phrases have always been the stock in trade of those who have vested interests which they wish to preserve against those in revolt against a rigid system.'

[94] John F. Dulles, 'America's Role in World Affairs,' address to Detroit YMCA, October 28, 1939, *JFD Papers*.

[95] Stimson was Coolidge's Secretary of War and Hoover's Secretary of State, until he became Roosevelt's Secretary of War. He remained in this position throughout the duration of war.

[96] Letters, Henry L. Stimson to JFD, January 5, 1939, *JFD Papers*.

[97] John F. Dulles, 'Opening Address Delivered at the National Study Conference', March 3, 1942, 1, *JFD Papers*.

[98] *Ibid.*, 3.

[99] *Ibid.*

[100] *Ibid.*, 5.

[101] *Ibid.*

[102] *Ibid.*, 2.

[103] *Ibid.*, 5.

[104] Frederick Nolde, then a professor at Lutheran Theological Seminary and a

member of the Commission, related that 'there's no question that he exercised the top leadership.' See Frederick Nolde, *Oral History Collection*, 1965, 1.

[105] John Coleman Bennett, *Oral History Collection*, 1965, 6.

[106] In 1941 the members of the Committee of Direction were: Dr Henry A. Atkinson, General Secretary, Church Peace Union; Dr E.E. Aubrey, Professor, Christian Theology and Ethics, University of Chicago Divinity School, Dr John C. Bennett, Professor, Christian Theology, Pacific School of Religion; Dr Russel Clinchy, Center Church, Hartford, Conn., Dr Albert B. Coe, First Congregational Church, Oak Park, Ill.; Dr James H. Franklin, President, Crozer Theological Seminary; Dr Georgia Harkness, Professor of Applied Theology, Garrett Biblical Institute; Harold A. Hatch, Vice-President, Deering-Williken Co.; Dr Kenneth S. Latourette, Professor, Yale University; Dr Henry Smith Leiper, Foreign Secretary, FCC; Dr Elmore M. McKee, St. George's Episcopal Church; Dr Harold Nicely, Brick Presbyterian Church, Rochester, New York; Dr J.W. Nixon, Professor of Christian Theology and Ethics, Colgate-Rochester Theological Seminary; Bishop G. Bromley Oxnam, Methodist Church; Dr Albert W. Palmer, President, Chicago Theological Seminary; Rev. Almon R. Pepper, Secretary of Department of Christian Social Relations, Protestant Episcopal Church; Dr Harold Cooke Phillips, First Baptist Church, Cleveland; Dr William E. Hocking, Professor, Harvard University; Dr Albert W. Beaven, President, Colgate-Rochester Theological Seminary; Dr C.H. Tobias, Secretary, Colored Men's Division, National Council, YMCA; Dr A.L. Warnshuis, Secretary, International Missionary Council; Dr Luman J. Shafer, Secretary, Board of Foreign Missions, Reformed Church of America; Dr Ernest F. Tittle, First Methodist Church, Evanston, Ill.; Dr Henry Pitney Van Dusen, Professor, Systematic Theology, Union Theological Seminary; Dr Mary Woolley, President Emeritus, Mount Holyoke College, see Federal Council of Churches, *Bulletin*, June 1941, 9; *A Just and Durable Peace. Data Material and Discussion Questions*, [FCC Pamphlet], 1941, 3-4.

[107] See Ronald W. Pruessen, *John Foster Dulles*, 199.

[108] Henry Smith Leiper recalled, 'I don't think ... that there was any preponderant influence, let's say, coming from Mr. Dulles, which pushed the other views aside and persuaded people against their will to accept his views.' See Henry Smith Leiper, *Oral History Collection*, 1965, 25. John C. Bennett added: 'He was the leader of this effort for about a decade ... He was, in dealing with church groups, open, and he listened.' See John Coleman Bennett, *Oral History Collection*, 1965, 6.

[109] Dulles served as chairman of the Commission only until 1946, except for a brief interval when he asked for a leave of absence during the founding conference of the United Nations Organization; see Ronald W. Pruessen, *John Foster Dulles*, 190.

[110] Henry P. Van Dusen, *Oral History Collection*, 1965, 37-38, 53; see also the transcript of Roswell P. Barnes' interview in the *Oral History Collection*. The mass media frequently referred to the Commission as the Dulles Commission.

[111] See Federal Council of Churches, 'Department Reorganization Is Announced,' *Federal Council Bulletin* 21, no. 2 (February, 1948), New York, 19; and also Federal Council of Churches, 'International Justice and Goodwill,' *Biennial Report* (1948) 105-106; Federal Council of the Churches, *Annual Report* (1949), New York, 141-142.

[112] Henry P. Van Dusen, a member of the Committee of Direction, described the procedure at the discussion meetings of the Commission and the origin of many of its public statements: 'It was really his [Dulles] Commission. It produced a series of documents ... Every one of them originated on one of his yellow lawyer's pads, on

which he wrote his memoranda ...' Henry P. Van Dusen, *Oral History Collection*, 1965.

[113] The Commission membership included Reinhold Niebuhr, John McNeill, William W. Van Kirk, Charles Clayton Morrison, John R. Mott, and Harry Emerson Fosdick.

[114] In a letter to John Bassett Moore, dated January 21, 1941, Dulles wrote that the Commission had decided to establish 'definite lines of communication running from the Committee [of Direction] ... through the full Commission and then on to churches and Christian groups throughout this country.'

[115] Ronald W. Pruessen, *John Foster Dulles*, 192, 193.

[116] Federal Council of the Churches, *Annual Report* (1941), New York, 94.

[117] Letter, JFD to Lionel G. Curtis, 28 February 1941, Box 20, *JFD Papers*.

[118] See Federal Council of Churches, *Biennial Report* (1942), New York, 109.

[119] John F. Dulles, 'The American Churches and the International Situation', (1940), 6, *JFD Papers*.

[120] *Ibid.*, 8.

[121] See Albert N. Keim, 'John Foster Dulles and the Federal Council of Churches of Christ, 1937-1949,' 71-72

[122] 'A Just and Durable Peace: Data Material and Discussion Questions'; 'A Just and Durable Peace: Memorandum of Preliminary Views' (April and May 1941), *JFD Papers*.

[123] The complete list of statements included also accounts of the National Study Conference in Philadelphia, of the Malvern Conference (7-10 January 1941) held in England under the auspices of the International Christian Fellowship and presided over by the Archbishop of York, and of the Madras Conference.

[124] Ronald W. Pruessen, *John Foster Dulles*, 193.

[125] Report to the Federal Council of Churches after returning from England, August 1942, *JFD Papers*.

[126] Dulles memorandum, 'The Aftermath of the World War,' February 1940.

[127] See, for example, John F. Dulles, 'Analyses of Moscow Declaration in the Light of the Six Pillars of Peace,' *Post War World*, Vol. I (December 15, 1943), 1.

[128] Federal Council, *Annual Report* (1949), New York, 142; see also 'John Foster Dulles', *The Christian Century*, LXI (October 25, 1944), 1224.

[129] The Commission to Study the Bases of a Just and Durable Peace (John Foster Dulles), *Long Range Peace Objectives. Including an Analysis of the Roosevelt-Churchill Eight Point Declaration*, September 18, 1941, New York.

[130] See *ibid.*

[131] See John F. Dulles, 'Peace Without Platitudes,' *Fortune*, XXV (January 1942), 42-43, 87-88, 90.

[132] Michael A. Guhin, *John Foster Dulles*, 79, 80.

[133] John F. Dulles, 'The Moral Foundation of the United Nations,' in Henry P. Van Dusen, *The Spiritual Legacy of John Foster Dulles*, 128, 129.

[134] See Robert A. Divine, *Second Chance. The Triumph of Internationalism in America* (New York: Atheneum, 1967) 88-92.

[135] See Harley A. Notter, *Postwar Foreign Policy Preparation, 1939-1945* (Temecula, CA: Reprint Service Corporation, (1949) 1993, 169) 170; entry for January 4, 1943 in Harley A. Notter 'Recollections: Notes January 1942 - December 1943,' Records of the Department of State, Harley A. Notter File, Box 1, Record Group 59,

National Archives, Washington, D.C. (henceforth cited as Notter File).
    [136] See memorandum, Leo Pasvolsky to staff members of the Division of Special Research, December 22, 1942 in Notter File, Box 4, R.G. 59.
    [137] See Harley A. Notter, *Postwar Foreign Policy Preparation, 1939-1945*, 171.
    [138] *Ibid.*, 10f, 172; memorandum, Franklin D. Roosevelt to General Watson, February 20, 1943, Official File 4351 (January-March 1943), Franklin D. Roosevelt Library, Hyde Park, New York (FDRL); memorandum, Sumner Welles to Roosevelt, March 18, 1943, President's Personal File 5575, FDRL.
    [139] See Harley A. Notter, *Postwar Foreign Policy Preparation, 1939-1945*, 226-227; Robert A. Divine, *Second Change*, 136-137.
    [140] See Council on Foreign Relations (CFR), *The Council on Foreign Relations. A Record of Fifteen Years* (New York: Harold Pratt House, 1937) 46-53; CFR, *Annual Report of the Executive Director* (New York: Harold Pratt House, 1940); CFR, *The War and Peace Studies of the Council on Foreign Relations, 1939-1945* (New York: Harold Pratt House, 1946) 19-24.
    [141] See Harley A. Notter, *Postwar Foreign Policy Preparation, 1939-1945*, 248.
    [142] See CFR, *Annual Report of the Executive Director* (New York: Harold Pratt House, 1940).
    [143] See CFR, *Annual Report of the Executive Director* (New York: Harold Pratt House, 1940); CFR, *The War and Peace Studies of the Council on Foreign Relations, 1939-1945* (New York: Harold Pratt House, 1946) 20.
    [144] Written in the midst of the Second World War, the Council's annual report for 1943 described the organisation's pervasive influence on many institutions, including the State Department, which were involved in postwar planning: 'For over twenty-five years the Council - one of a handful of such institutions in this country - has devoted itself to a study of the role of the United States in the world. Now, quite suddenly, almost every group, no matter what its normal purpose, is devoting prime attention to the problems of international affairs, and to America's postwar position. Naturally they depend upon the Council for light and guidance; and the Council, within the limits of a modest budget and an overburdened staff, is doing its best to meet its increased responsibilities.' CFR, *Annual Report of the Executive Director* (New York: Harold Pratt House, 1943) 4.
    [145] Ronald W. Pruessen, *John Foster Dulles*, 186; see also Albert N. Keim, 'John Foster Dulles and the Federal Council of Churches of Christ, 1937-1949,' 70: 'Tactically the Commission perceived its role on three levels: as a deliberative or research body; as an agency for educating the public; and as a pressure group speaking to government on behalf of the churches. The Commission performed its deliberative and research functions in a number of ways. Once in 1942, and again in 1945, it held national study conferences where a broadly representative group of Protestant churchmen met to discuss world order issues and make public recommendations on policy. Another project was an arrangement between the Commission and the State Department whereby the Commission accredited four of its members to the State Department in order to keep the Commission abreast of new developments. The Commission also had three study groups -- task forces modelled on those established earlier by the Council on Foreign Relations -- dealing with specific peace-making problems.'
    [146] See 'Preliminary Report of the Commission To Study the Organization of Peace,' *International Conciliation*, No. 369 (April, 1941) 195-196.

[147] See Harley A. Notter, *Postwar Foreign Policy Preparation, 1939-1945*, 247; Robert A. Divine, *Second Chance*, 192.

[148] See Ruth B. Russell, *A History of the United Nations Charter. The Role of the United States, 1940-1945* (Washington, D.C.: The Brookings Institute, 1958) 21-22, 205.

[149] The list of references included the following: 1. Lothar von Wurmb, 'The World Federal State,' *World Order* (January 1939 edition). 2. Campaign for World Government, *World Federation Is Begun*, April 1939. 3. American Campaign for World Government, 'Plan for an Unarmed World Federation, Democratic, Non-Military, and All-Inclusive,' *Peace News* (London), May 19, 1939. 4. The speech delivered by John Foster Dulles on October 28, 1939. He suggested that America lead the transition to a new order of less independent, semi-sovereign states bound together by a league or federal union. 5. The address given by Pope Pius XII on December 24, 1939. He outlines five points considered essential for setting up a new world order. 6. E.C. Brunauer, *Building the New World Order*, League of Nations Association, 1939; Brunauer proposes to build on the foundations of the League of Nations for a union of democracies and peace system in the western hemisphere. 7. Lionel Curtis, *Civitas Dei* (1939). Ralph Page, in 'Designs for a World Order', calls Curtis's 985-page work the foundation of all thought upon the design of a new order, and says, 'Curtis's thesis is that to engender in man a desire to serve each other is the end and object of human existence.' 8. Duncan and Elizabeth Wilson, *Federation and World Order* (1939); the authors examine how federalism has already worked in the British Empire, the United States, and elsewhere, and from this deduce how it might be adopted on a worldwide scale. 9. Iwao Ayusawa, 'The New World Order: A Japanese View,' *Contemporary Japan*, July 1940. 10. Ralph Page, 'Designs for a World Order,' *Annals of the American Academy of Political and Social Science*, July 1940. 11. A preliminary report issued by the Commission to Study the Organization of Peace (November 1940), setting forth elementary principles essential to a lasting peace. It recommends world federation. 12. John G. Alexander, 'A New World Order,' *Congressional Record*, December 12, 1940. An article, similar to Alexander's declaration to federate the world, was also in the November 3, 1939 *Congressional Record*.

[150] Page quoted from Dulles' address, 'America's Role in World Affairs,' October 28, 1939, *JFD Papers*.

[151] See Carnegie Endowment for International Peace, *The Year Book 1947*, Washington, D.C., 1947. O. Frederick Nolde, the director of Commission of the Churches on International Affairs, an agency of the World Council of Churches, which carried on the work of the Commission on a Just and Durable Peace, was also a trustee and member of the executive committee of the Endowment; see Carnegie Endowment, *The Yearbook 1950-1951*, Washington, D.C., 1951; and *Annual Report*, Washington, D.C., 1949. In 1948 CFR member and future president Dwight D. Eisenhower had also become a trustee of the Carnegie Endowment; see Carnegie Endowment, *Annual Report*, Washington, D.C., 1948, iv.

[152] Carnegie Endowment, *Yearbook 1941*, 117.

[153] Letter, JFD to Quincy Wright, December 19, 1939, 1, *JFD Papers*.

[154] *Ibid.*

[155] *Ibid.*, 1-2.

[156] *Ibid.*, 2.

[157] See below: 'Collective Security'.

[158] See 'Author's Note', at the beginning of the book.

[159] Graeme Keith Howard, *America and a New World Order* (New York: C. Scribner's Sons, 1940) 61.

[160] *Ibid.*

[161] *Ibid.*, 73-74, 76.

[162] John F. Dulles, 'Peaceful Change', Draft of January 23, 1940, *JFD Papers*, 9; cf. John F. Dulles, 'Peaceful Change', *International Conciliation*, No. 369, April 1941, 493-498.

[163] The Commission to Study the Bases of a Just and Durable Peace (John Foster Dulles), *Long Range Peace Objectives. Including an Analysis of the Roosevelt-Churchill Eight Point Declaration*, September 18, 1941, New York, 12.

[164] See John Foster Dulles, 'Statement of Political Propositions. The Spiritual Foundations of World Order', in Henry P. Van Dusen, *The Spiritual Legacy of John Foster Dulles*, 107-110.

[165] Commission to Study the Bases of a Just and Durable Peace (edited with an introduction by John Foster Dulles), *Six Pillars of Peace. A Study Guide Based on A Statement of Political Propositions*, New York, 1943, 8.

[166] Commission to Study the Bases of a Just and Durable Peace (John Foster Dulles), *Long Range Peace Objectives*, 12-13.

[167] Referring to the Federal Union movement (without mentioning it directly), Lord Lothian wrote the following in a letter to Aga Khan: 'In the last few months I have been driven to the conclusion that the organization of resistance to Hitler is the necessary preliminary to a real settlement ... The organisation of resistance has already begun to have effect. It has detached Japan for the European end of the Axis. It has made Italy extremely doubtful and extremely cautious. It has caused heart searchings in Germany itself.' Letter, Lord Lothian to Aga Khan, 16 May 1939, SRO, *Lothian Papers*, GD40/17/388/14; as cited in Andrea Bosco, 'Lothian, Curtis, Kimber and the Federal Union Movement (1939-40),' *Journal of Contemporary History*, Vol. 23, 1988, 501.

[168] Richard Mayne & et al., eds., *Federal Union: The Pioneers. The History of Federal Union* (London: Macmillan, 1990) 21.

[169] Letter, Lionel Curtis to Miss M.M. Wingate, 24 October 1944.

[170] See Andrea Bosco, 'Lothian, Curtis, Kimber and the Federal Union Movement (1939-40),' 477ff.

[171] As cited in Andrea Bosco, 'Lothian, Curtis, Kimber and the Federal Union Movement (1939-40),' 479. See Henry V. Hodson, 'The Round Table 1910-81,' *The Round Table*, no. 284 (October 1981), 308-333.

[172] In a letter of 4 April 1939 to Lionel G. Curtis, Lord Lothian replied: 'I have read Ransome's paper and think it is very good, though not adequate as a basic statement of principles. He rang me up this morning and I told him that I thought that next step was to agree upon a few basic principles which could be printed on a half sheet of notepaper to which we could ask adherents to subscribe, and to publish behind it a series of pamphlets written by different people from different points of view in support of the general thesis but to which nobody would be asked to agree in all their details. I am going to see him tomorrow afternoon ... One of the things we shall have to do is to convince people that the problem is not solved merely by creating a new alliance for defence, even if we avoid war.'

[173] Curtis, for example, secured the participation of Professor Lionel Robbins, in

May 1939.

[174] See Richard Mayne & et al., eds., *Federal Union*, 10, 11, 19. Other members were Sir Montagu Burton, Sir Richard Gregory, Sir Thomas Beecham, Sir John Marriott, Lord Marley, Sir Walter Napier, Sir John Orr, Lady Rhondda, Professor Norman Bentwich, Dr H. Hamilton Fyfe, Julian Huxley, Ramsay Muir, Seebohm Rowntree, J. K. Hammond, Storm Jameson, and E. McNight Kauffer.

[175] See *Federal Union News*, no. 31, April-May 1940.

[176] *Ibid.*, 25.

[177] Gerald Studdert-Kennedy, 'Christianity, Statecraft and Chatham House. Lionel Curtis and World Order,' 485.

[178] *Ibid.*

[179] See SRO, *Lothian Papers*, GD380/182; as cited in Andrea Bosco, 'Lothian, Curtis, Kimber and the Federal Union Movement (1939-40),' 483-484.

[180] Philip Kerr (Lord Lothian), 'The End of Armageddon,' Federal Union pamphlet, London, 1939; it was reprinted, with the omission of a section from pp. 12-14 concerning Streit's *Union Now*, in Patrick Ransome, ed., *Studies in Federal Planning* (London: Macmillan, 1943) 1-15. See also *Federal Union News*, no. 31, April-May 1940, 24-25.

[181] Lionel Robbins, *The Economic Causes of War* (London: Jonathan Cape, 1939); see also W.B. Curry, *The Case for Federal Union* (Harmondsworth: Penguin Books, 1939); and W. Ivor Jennings, *A Federation for Western Europe* (London: Cambridge University Press, 1940) viii.

[182] See Richard Mayne & et al., eds., *Federal Union*, 12.

[183] W. Ivor Jennings, *A Federation for Western Europe*. Jennings' book appeared in print shortly after the statement of Federal Union's aims was made public.

[184] The Federation would control foreign policy, armed forces and armaments. It would exercise substantial control over tariffs, currency, migration, communications and similar matters. It would also have power to ensure that colonies and dependencies were administered in the interests of the inhabitants and not for the benefit of any particular country.

[185] See Richard Mayne & et al., eds., *Federal Union*, 48.

[186] See Sir Charles Kimber, 'Federal Union,' *The Federalist* (Pavia), Year XXVI, No. 3, December 1984, 199-205.

[187] In *Federal Union* there are numerous references to the Labour Party's internationalist program; see e.g., Richard Mayne & et al., eds., *Federal Union*, 56-57: '... and the Labour leadership was often explicit in its support for world government. Thus, in 1946, Sir Stafford Cripps declared that : 'World federation has hitherto been looked upon as a very long-term objective, but the atomic bomb has telescoped history and made it impossible for us to wait long years of acute danger of war, because from that war civilisation and mankind cannot survive.' Quoted from Cripps' speech in Newcastle, February 1946, in *Federal News*, no. 149, August 1947, 6. In the following year Harold Laski, Chairman of the Labour Party, said: 'We cannot rest content until we have a genuine World Government expressing, through the direct choice of peoples, in a parliament responsible to them, the will of the common folk, instead of being dependent, like the United Nations, upon the sovereign wills of nation states which express, in all vital matters, the purposes of their ruling classes and subordinate to those purposes the interests of the common peoples' (Laski's statement, *ibid.*, 9).

[188] See Richard Mayne & et al., eds., *Federal Union*, 80, 94: 'The idea of uniting

Europe as a first step towards better order in the world had deep roots in Federal Union's short history. In 1939-40, the Federal Union Research Institute (FURI) had seen it as a way to prevent the war, then as a development of the alliance with France but open to accession by post-Nazi Germany, then as a peace aim offering the Germans an equal place in a post-war federal Europe ... By 16 January 1947, Churchill was chairing the first meeting of a "provisional British Committee to further the cause of a United Europe", which unanimously approved a short declaration. The twenty-one members of the Committee included four representatives of Federal Union: Jo Josephy, Evelyn King, MP, Gordon Lang, MP, and Commander Stephen King-Hall ... Lionel Curtis was also a member ...'

[189] See Sir Charles Kimber, 'Federal Union,' 203-204.

[190] See Andrea Bosco, *Federal Union*, 59.

[191] See Richard Mayne & et al., eds., *Federal Union*, 11.

[192] See *ibid.*, 46; quoting from Board Minutes, 3 October 1941.

[193] See *ibid.*, 46-47; quoting from Board Minutes, 2 January 1942.

[194] Printed in full in *Federal Union News*, no. 88 (June 1942), 1-16.

[195] See Richard Mayne & et al., eds., *Federal Union*, 47-48.

[196] *Federal Union News*, no. 14, 23 December 1939.

[197] Eleanor M. Jackson, *Red Tape and The Gospel. A Study of the Significance of the Ecumenical Missionary Struggle of William Paton (1886-1943)* (Birmingham: Phlogiston Publishing, 1980) 266; Jackson refers to a letter from Paton to Temple (23 November 1939), in *Paton Papers* VIII; and another to Demant (21 December 1939), in *Paton Papers* VIII. There are a number of passages in Jackson's book indicating Paton's close relationship with most leading members of the Royal Institute of International Affairs, such as Sir Alfred Zimmern, Philip Kerr, and Arnold J. Toynbee; see e.g., *ibid.*, 141, 243, 244, 257, 266, etc.

[198] See William H. McNeill, *Arnold J. Toynbee. A Life*, 180: 'On 4 August 1939 the Foreign Office agreed to pay most of the costs of transferring the staff of Chatham House, together with its collection of press clippings, to Balliol College, Oxford, where the group would have the task of providing accurate information on foreign affairs to any branch of the government on demand. Oxford University was a party to the arrangement also, for the Foreign Research and Press Service, as the new outfit was officially called, was expected to add university experts to its staff.'

[199] See Eleanor M. Jackson, *Red Tape and The Gospel*, 266: The Peace Aims Department of the Royal Institute of International Affairs 'collected all such information as may be of value to the British government at the time of the eventual peace conference whenever it takes place.'

[200] William H. McNeill, *Arnold J. Toynbee. A Life*, 179.

[201] See Eleanor M. Jackson, *Red Tape and The Gospel*, 266.

[202] *Ibid.*

[203] *Ibid.*, 268.

[204] See Samuel McCrea Cavert, 'When Is the Church Free?' *Christian Century*, LIV (May 26, 1937) 676; and Henry P. Van Dusen, *What Is the Church Doing?* (New York, 1943) 94-95.

[205] See 'Report of Peace Aims meeting, Balliol College, 2-3 October 1941,' Toynbee Papers, Bodleian Library, Oxford, as cited in William H. McNeill, Arnold J. Toynbee. A Life, 302.

[206] See William H. McNeill, *Arnold J. Toynbee. A Life*, 184: 'Luce had become a

powerful shaper of American opinion through his publications. He had grown up in China, the son of a Presbyterian missionary, and his extraordinary success as a publisher rested partly on the fact that he remained accessible to missionary ideas such as the new world order that Toynbee was preaching, and was ready to use his magazines to back them.'

[207] *Ibid.*

[208] See Eleanor M. Jackson, *Red Tape and The Gospel*, 267: 'Paton succeeded in forging such good relations with a wide cross-section of government advisers, that when eventually signatories were needed for a Peace Aims statement in 1943, to match a declaration issued by the Federal Council of Churches entitled "The Six Pillars of Peace" in March 1943, it proved very difficult to find lay people who were members of the Peace Aims Group in Britain, but not connected to government, and therefore obliged to be anonymous. At the inception of the Peace Aims Group in Britain, Paton was gratified to receive encouragement from Halifax's preferential treatment in the granting of travel facilities to the U.S.A., if they had not had a considerable amount of governmental support. According to Bishop R.R. Williams, who negotiated many of these visas when he was in the Ministry of Information, a person of Paton's convictions moving independently in America, but undermining isolationism with almost every word he spoke, was very useful precisely because of this fine balance of independence from and support for the British Government which he achieved in America. His church contacts in Sweden were also useful to the Ministry of Information trying to cultivate public opinion in Sweden.'

[209] *Ibid.*, 268.

[210] See e.g., John Marlowe, *Milner, Apostle of Empire*, 212.

[211] Eleanor M. Jackson, *Red Tape and The Gospel*, 266.

[212] See *ibid.*, 265.

[213] Allen W. Dulles and Beatrice Pitney Lamb, *The United Nations* (New York: Headline Series, No. 59, The Foreign Policy Association, September-October, 1946) 44, 86.

[214] Letter, William Paton to JFD, May 27, 1942, *JFD Papers*, Box 8.

[215] See 'Notes taken by Bob as Foster recounted to the family his trip to England, July 1942,' *JFD Papers*; 'Confidential Memorandum Prepared by John Foster Dulles and Walter Van Kirk on Their Recent Visit to England,' summer 1942, *JFD Papers*; and Walter W. Van Kirk, 'British and American Post-War Aims,' *Federal Council Bulletin* 25, no. 9 (September, 1942), New York, 10.

[216] See Ronald W. Pruessen, *John Foster Dulles*, 198.

[217] See Albert N. Keim, 'John Foster Dulles and the Federal Council of Churches, 1937-1949,' 102.

[218] See Federal Council of Churches, *Federal Council Bulletin* 25, No. 9 (September, 1942), New York, 10. The ecumenical leaders at the conference included Archbishop Temple, William Paton, Associate Secretary of the Provisional Committee of the World Council of Churches; Bishop Bell of Chichester; Rev. J. Hutchinson Cockburn, former Moderator of the Church of Scotland; Rev. J. Pitt Watson, Chairman of the Church and Nation Committee, Church of Scotland; Rev. Eric Fenn, Assistant Director of Religious Broadcasting, BBC; Kenneth Grubb, Controller of the Ministry of Information; A. D. K. Owen, secretary to Sir Stafford Cripps; Chairman of the Christian Council of Refugees; Rev. R. D. Whitehorn, Professor of Church History, Westminster College, Cambridge; Margaret Wrong, Secretary of the International

Committee on Christian Literature; Dr. Lindsay, the Master of Balliol; Mr. Dennis Rough, Fellow of All Souls Church, Oxford, for Department of Ministry of Information; Sir John Hope-Simpson, Chairman of Christian Council of Refugees; Professor Arnold Toynbee, head of the Foreign Research Department of the Royal Institute of International Affairs; Sir Alfred Zimmern, Royal Institute of International Affairs; John Foster Dulles; George Steward, Pastor of the First Presbyterian Church, Stamford, Connecticut; and Dr. William W. Van Kirk.

[219] See John R. Beal, *John Foster Dulles*, 92-93.

[220] The British participants at the conference included Arnold J. Toynbee; Sir Alfred Zimmern, both of the Royal Institute of International Affairs; Dr. Lindsay, Master of Balliol; Dennis Routh, Fellow of All Souls College, Oxford; Sir John Hope-Simpson.

[221] See John R. Beal, *John Foster Dulles*, 92-93.

[222] Federal Council of Churches, *Federal Council Bulletin* 25, no. 9 (September, 1942), New York, 10.

[223] See Albert N. Keim, 'John Foster Dulles and the Federal Council of Churches of Christ, 1937-1949,' 102: 'Dulles' rather tactless criticism of British colonialism occasioned some defensive reaction from several churchmen, although most agreed that the time was at hand for the liquidation of the British Empire.'

[224] Albert N. Keim, 'John Foster Dulles and the Federal Council of Churches of Christ, 1937-1949,' 102. The two statements were originally issued by the British Commission of the Churches for International Friendship and Social Responsibility.

[225] Clarence K. Streit, *Union Now with Britain* (London: Jonathan Cape, 1941). The book was also published in New York by Harper & Bros. in the same year.

[226] Aydelotte's book, *The American Rhodes Scholarships. A Review of the First Forty Years*, was published by Princeton University Press, Princeton, New Jersey in 1946 (the same book appeared in Great Britain under the title, *The Vision of Cecil Rhodes. A Review of the First Forty Years of the American Scholarship* (London: Geoffrey Cumberlege, Oxford University Press) 1946.

[227] Clarence K. Streit received a Rhodes Scholarship at the University of Oxford in 1920.

[228] Clarence Streit, *Union Now. A Proposal for a Federal Union of the Democracies of the North Atlantic* (New York: Harper & Bros.,1939). Jonathan Cape published the same book in London.

[229] See e.g., letter, Lothian to Patrick Ransome, 8 March 1939, SRO, *Lothian Papers*, GD40/17/376/714, as cited in John Pinder & Andrea Bosco, ed., *Pacifism is not enough. Collected Lectures and Speeches of Lord Lothian (Philip Kerr)*, Lothian Foundation Press, London, 1990, 21. In this letter, Lord Lothian urged Patrick Ransome to read Streit's book.

[230] Letter, Lothian to Clarence Streit, March 1939, SRO, *Lothian Papers*, GD40/17/386/747-51, as cited in John Pinder & Andrea Bosco, ed., *Pacifism is not enough*, 21.

[231] As cited in Andrea Bosco, 'Lothian, Curtis, Kimber and the Federal Union Movement (1939-40),' 478.

[232] Philip Kerr (Lord Lothian), 'The End of Armageddon,' Federal Union pamphlet, London, 1939; it was reprinted, with the omission of a section from pp. 12-14 concerning Streit's *Union Now*, in Patrick Ransome, ed., *Studies in Federal Planning* (London: Macmillan, 1943) 1-15.

[233] That Lothian appreciated Streit's thesis is not difficult to understand, since Streit quoted favourably from Lothian's publications and lectures in his books. The following quotations are representative of several others: 'The importance of the Federalist papers is that they expose, from experience and with unanswerable argument, why sovereignty is an insuperable obstacle to the organization of peace, and why the federal principle is the only way forward' - Lord Lothian, July 30, 1938. Clarence K. Streit, *Union Now*, 98: 'No thinking person can seriously dispute that it is State sovereignty and the anarchy it creates in a shrinking world which is the basic cause of our main troubles to-day ... It is what prevents the League, for all that it represents the first attempt to organize the world for law and peace, from accomplishing its noble purpose' - Lord Lothian, July 30, 1938. *Ibid.*, 105.

[234] Henry Vincent Hodson; fellow of All Souls 1928-35; on the staff of the Economic Advisory Council 1930-1; Ministry of Information 1939-41; assistant editor of *The Round Table* 1931; editor of *The Round Table* 1934-39; reforms commissioner, Government of India 1941-2; assistant editor of the *Sunday Times* 1946-50; provost of Ditchley since 1961.

[235] Lothian made the following comments to Hodson's draft review of Streit's book for the journal: 'The essence of this book is not the draft constitution but the argument that the democracies have no choice between war, possible defeat and the loss of liberty and union. He told me that he put in the draft scheme simply because so many people had told him that it was impossible to formulate a scheme so he had produced the best he could as something to be shot at ... I have never thought that Federal Union of Nations would take the same form as the American constitution. Nationality is too vigorous and valuable a plant to allow itself to be treated like statehood in USA or Australia or a province in Canada. What matters is making it clear that cooperation between sovereign nations cannot be made to work and that they must find some system for organic union which will pool the sovereignty of all their people for certain purposes without losing the national individuality of the parts. Your article in its present form will strike the reader as being a theoretical approval and then a blasting criticism of Streit's plan, as if that plan was really the essence of this proposal.'

[236] As cited in Andrea Bosco, 'Lothian, Curtis, Kimber and the Federal Union Movement (1939-40),' 475.

[237] As cited in *ibid.*, 476.

[238] In response to Streit's proposal to form a federal union between fifteen democracies, Professor George Catlin, in *One Anglo-American Nation*, reviewed the idea of a world federation, which he had promoted several years before Streit's book, *Union Now*, became popular. Stating his case for establishing a new world order - 'we must be sure that we lay the right foundations for "a new order"' (p. 39) - he wrote: 'Federation is, of course, no very new idea ... Cecil Rhodes' whole life was devoted to the notion of an Anglo-Saxon federation of nations ... Mr. Lionel Curtis, in the direct succession of Rhodes and associated with the *Round Table* group, in his three volumes *Civitas Dei* (1934-37) brought us back again to the notion of federation in the Anglo-Saxon world. President Aydelotte developed the idea. Mr. Clarence Streit, Geneva correspondent of the *New York Times*, set out to federate fifteen democracies, as explained in his *Union Now* (1937-38) .... In November, 1939, Lord Lothian, late British Ambassador in Washington, and also a member of the *Round Table* group, said: "Some form of federation ... at any rate for part of Europe, is a necessary condition of

any stable world order." He added an admirable pamphlet, advocating Federation, called *The End of Armageddon.*' George Catlin, *One Anglo-American Nation. The Foundation of Anglo-Saxony as Basis of World Federation. A British Response to Streit* (London: Andrew Dakers Ltd., 1941) 37, 38; see also Richard Mayne & et al., eds., *Federal Union*, 13.

[239] Lionel G. Curtis, 'World Order,' *International Affairs* (May-June, 1939), Vol. XVIII, No. 3 (London: Royal Institute of International Affairs) 11: '... the transition from the national to the international State is perhaps the most difficult step in political construction that man will ever attempt.'

[240] *Ibid.*, 11.

[241] Letter, Toynbee to Curtis, 16 Feb. 1939, *Curtis MSS*, Box 13, ff.190-192, as cited in Gerald Studdert-Kennedy, 'Christianity, Statecraft and Chatham House: Lionel Curtis and World Order, 479.

[242] Letter, Curtis to Toynbee, 17 Feb. 1939, *Curtis MSS*, Box 13, ff.190-192, as cited in Gerald Studdert-Kennedy, 'Christianity, Statecraft and Chatham House: Lionel Curtis and World Order, 479-480.

[243] *Ibid.*

[244] See Clarence K. Streit, *Union Now*, 33: 'Clearly democracy bids us now unite our unions of free men and women in one world Union of the free.'

[245] See *ibid.*, 24-25, 129-130: 'These few democracies suffice to provide the nucleus of world government with the financial, monetary, economic and political power necessary both to assure peace to its members ...' (p. 25).

[246] See, e.g., *ibid.*, 22-23, 285-320 ('Of Freedom and Union').

[247] See *ibid.*, 154-156.

[248] See *ibid.*, 163-172.

[249] With the advent of nuclear weapons Streit's proposition of military invincibility could not be sustained by later advocates of his scheme. Yet they argued that this very fact made the establishment of a world government even more urgent: 'The possibilities of atomic and bacteriological warfare, which the world began to conceive in 1949 have brought the prospect of an international commonwealth nearer than they were before the last war. We are now overshadowed by a sense of impending calamities which, if they befell, might plunge us back into centuries darker than those that followed the fall of ancient civilisation in Europe. I believe that these dangers are inherent in a world united by mechanisation, but divided into sovereign states, and can only begin to abate when men have learned to pass from the national to the international commonwealth.' Lionel G. Curtis, *Civitas Dei*, 735. The Federal Council of Churches argued along the same lines: 'Therefore we need to study and support all feasible social controls of all destructive atomic power ... Atomic bombs and rockets in the separate hands of competing states would tend to precipitate total war because of the mutual fears of annihilating aggression. Consequently the establishment of single world control of destructive atomic power is an urgent necessity ... We urge our government to state its intention to place the new discovery under a worldwide authority as soon as all the states will submit to effective controls. We also urge the government to press without delay for the creation of such controls.' Federal Council of Churches, *Annual Report* (1945) 172.

[250] See Clarence K. Streit, *Union Now*, 218-230 ('How the Union Remedies Our Ills').

[251] See *ibid.*, 226-229.

[252] See *ibid.*, 338-341.

[253] See *ibid.*, 221-214.

[254] See *ibid.*

[255] See *ibid.*, 325-335 ('Illustrative Constitution').

[256] It might be interesting to note that money, as H. G. Wells in *New World Order* (New York: Alfred A. Knopf, 1940) points out, can only become a common medium of exchange between communities which are willing to adopt the same principles of economic organisation. It would probably also be impossible to maintain free trade and a common currency between political units following divergent social policies, for these would almost inevitably involve profound differences in economic practice. The history of federations demonstrates that a federal union, if it functions properly, does not tolerate profound social and economic differences. The underlying causes of the Civil War in the United States speak eloquently in this regard.

[257] Clarence K. Streit, *Union Now*, 331.

[258] See *ibid.*, 332-333.

[259] See *ibid.*, 333-334.

[260] See *ibid.*, 83-97 ('Urgent Most For Americans').

[261] Over 100 ecumenically minded clergymen and Christian laymen supported the Federal Union movement in 1960. Naturally, this movement was very attractive to scores of CFR members as well.

[262] Clarence K. Streit, *Union Now with Britain*, 20. Streit highly recommends Lionel Curtis' book, *Civitas Dei*: 'I take this occasion to pay tribute to the work done by all the other authors who have cultivated this field, not only those in the distant past but such recent ones as Lionel Curtis (*World Order*, Oxford University Press; in a footnote Streit adds the following: 'The book by Lionel Curtis published in England by Messrs. Macmillan under the title of *Civitas Dei* or, in its popular edition, *The Commonwealth of God*, was republished in the U.S.A. by the Oxford University Press under the title of *World Order*), and W.B. Curry (*The Case for Federal Union*, Penguin) - to mention but two of the British champions of Federal Union of the democracies (p. 12). On page 217 Streit states: 'Lionel Curtis's *World Order*. A monumental recent work by the statesman who for a generation has been the outstanding British champion of federal union.'

[263] See letter, Clarence Streit to JFD, March 21, 1940; this letter is contained in the 'Clarence Streit-Union Now, 1939-1944' folder, *JFD Papers*, Box 7.

[264] Letters, JFD to Clarence Streit, January 23, 1939, *JFD Papers*, Box 7; and same to Hugh Wilson, June 13, 1941, *JFD Papers*, Box 138.

[265] John F. Dulles, 'Memorandum', undated, 1, *JFD Papers*.

[266] *Ibid.*

[267] *Ibid.*, 1-2.

[268] Dulles address, March 12, 1941, 17, *JFD Papers*.

[269] Besides being Secretary of the Interior, Harold L. Ickes held 30 other positions in the New Deal Administration; see *Chicago Tribune*, 24 January 1935.

[270] Supreme Justice, Owen J. Roberts, a member of the Council on Foreign Relations, became famous for chairing the Roberts Commission investigating the causes of the Pearl Harbor catastrophe. Later he presided over the Atlantic Union Committee. In July 1971 he testified before the House Committee on Foreign Affairs that 'in joining the Atlantic Union, the U.S. government would have to surrender its rights and powers to coin money, to levy taxes and tariffs, to regulate immigration, to

enact citizenship laws, to declare war, and to maintain standing armies.' O. J. Roberts' statement to Myra Hacker in July 1971 to the House Committee on Foreign Affairs regarding House Concurrent Resolutions 163 and 164, 'Atlantic Union Delegation'.

[271] Immediately after the formation of NATO in 1949, Clarence K. Streit created the Atlantic Union Committee, Inc. The charter of AUC stated its purposes as follows: 'To promote support for congressional action requesting the President of the United States to invite the other democracies which sponsored the North Atlantic Treaty to name delegates, representing their principal political parties, to meet with delegates of the United States in a federal convention to explore how far their peoples, and the peoples of such other democracies as the convention may invite to send delegates, can apply among them, within the framework of the United Nations, the principles of free federal union.'

[272] See Clarence K. Streit, 'An Open Letter to John Foster Dulles,' *Freedom and Union*, III (October, 1948), 1-3.

[273] Dulles expressed his doubts about a regional approach thus: 'The fact that various national groups are "democratic" is not determinative of interdependence. That, we have seen, is world-wide ... A federation of the so-called democracies would, to others, appear as the banding together of the well-to-do to maintain the *status quo*. A natural reaction would be a banding together of the dissatisfied peoples in a counter alliance, somewhat comparable to the present Axis. Such peoples as the Russians and the Chinese who are reasonably satisfied with their present national domains, but who are not democratic by our standards, would occupy an ambiguous position and perhaps hold the balance of power.' John F. Dulles, 'Towards World Order,' in Francis J. McConnell, et al., *A Basis for the Peace To Come*, 47; see also John F. Dulles, 'Ideals Are Not Enough,' *International Conciliation*, No. 409, Section I (March, 1945), 133. See also Ronald W. Pruessen, *John Foster Dulles*, 186-187.

[274] Letter, JFD to Hugh Wilson, June 13, 1941, *JFD Papers*, Box 138.

[275] *Ibid.*

[276] Dulles address, 'The North American Contribution to World Order, June 20, 1939, *JFD Papers*, Box 138.

[277] See Samuel Z. Batten, *New World Order* (New York: American Baptist Publishing Society, 1919) 123-124.

[278] See W. Ivor Jennings, *A Federation for Western Europe* (London: Cambridge University Press, 1940). As indicated earlier, Jennings was a prominent member of the Federal Union movement.

[279] Lord Acton, *The History of Freedom and other Essays* (London: Macmillan, 1907) 98.

[280] John F. Dulles, 'The Church's Contribution Toward a Warless World,' in Henry P. van Dusen, ed., *The Spiritual Legacy of John Foster Dulles*, 144-145. It might be interesting to quote at this point an exchange between Dulles and Congressman Bloom before a House Committee in 1948: 'Mr Dulles: The United States should be ready to take the lead in surrendering its sovereignty to the extent necessary to establish peace through the ordering of just law ... Chairman Eaton: I note that you say that our great Nation is ready to take the lead in surrendering its sovereignty. What do you mean by "sovereignty?" Mr Dulles: Perhaps "surrendering sovereignty" can be misunderstood. It may be better to say "exercising sovereignty" by agreeing to certain rules of procedure by which we would be bound. I believe we can agree that in fact we have agreed under the Charter of the American States to certain rules of procedure by

which we are bound and to that extent we have given up our complete freedom of action. As a matter of fact, every treaty involves to some extent a surrendering of sovereignty because by the treaty a nation foregoes its complete freedom to do whatever it will that is contrary to the terms of the treaty. Mr Bloom: Is sovereignty divisible, Mr. Dulles? Mr Dulles: In my opinion, it is. Mr Bloom: Either you have sovereignty or you do not have it. I do not see how you can divide sovereignty. Mr Dulles: I think we divided it here in the United States. Some of our sovereignty resides in the States and some of our sovereignty resides in the Federal Government. Mr Bloom: ... That is a new interpretation to me ... Mr Dulles: I believe that sovereignty consists of a bundle of rights and you can dispose of the contents of that bundle in different places, but it represents a metaphysical question we are discussing; that is not of great practical significance. Mr Bloom: ... Either you have a sovereignty or you have no sovereignty at all. You have given your sovereignty away. However, I do not see how you can divide it. That is all' (U.S. Congress, House Hearings before the Committee on Foreign Relations, *Structure of the United Nations and the Relations of the United States to the United Nations*, 80th Congress, 1st Session (Washington, D.C.: Government Printing Office, 1948) 279, 282-283. It should be obvious that if any entity has the real power to determine the distribution of powers then that entity is supreme or sovereign and the units with which it is willing to share power are no longer sovereign.

[281] John F. Dulles, 'The Church's Contribution Toward a Warless World', in Henry P. Van Dusen, ed., *The Spiritual Legacy of John Foster Dulles*, 146.

[282] *Ibid.*

[283] Commission to Study the Bases of a Just and Durable Peace (John Foster Dulles), *Long Range Peace Objectives* (1941), 17, *JFD Papers*.

[284] *Ibid.*, 19.

[285] *Ibid.*

[286] See John Foster Dulles, 'Statement of Political Propositions. The Spiritual Foundations of World Order' ('Six Pillars of Peace'), in Henry P. van Dusen, *The Spiritual Legacy of John Foster Dulles*, 107-110.

[287] *Ibid.*, 107.

[288] *Ibid.*, 107-108.

[289] John F. Dulles, 'Comments on the Fifth Statement; Pattern for Peace; 5. International Institutions to Maintain Peace with Justice Must Be Organized,' *World Affairs*, CVII (March, 1944), 34-35.

[290] See e.g., John F. Dulles, 'Discussion of Greek Problem,' *The Department of State Bulletin*, XIX (November 14, 1948), 607-609.

[291] Federal Council of Churches, *Annual Report* (1941), New York, 122.

[292] Ivan Lee Holt (1886-1967), ordained as a minister by the Methodist Episcopal Church South, was pastor of St. John's Methodist Church in St. Louis, 1918-1928, and then elected bishop. He was president of the Federal Council of Churches, 1934-1936. He also served as chairman of the Methodist Ecumenical Council.

[293] *Time* magazine, 39 (March 16, 1942), 44-45.

[294] See Federal Council of Churches, 'Conference on the Bases of Peace,' *Federal Council Bulletin* 25, no. 4 (April 1942), New York, 9.

[295] 'The Churches and the Peace,' *Christian Century* 59 (18 March 1942) 342.

[296] The preamble to the 'Guiding Principles' clearly reveals Dulles' guiding influence in drafting the principles: 'From [their] faith Christians derive the ethical

principles upon which world order must be based. These principles, however seem to us to be among those which men of goodwill everywhere may be expected to recognize as part of the moral law. In this we rejoice. For peace will require the cooperation of men of all nations, races and creeds. We have therefore first set out (points 1 to 9) those guiding principles which, it seems to us, Christians and non-Christians alike can accept. We believe that a special responsibility rests upon the people of the United States. We accordingly (point 10) express our thoughts in that regard. Above all, we are impressed by the supreme responsibility which rests upon Christians. Moral law may point the way to peace, but Christ, we believe, showed that way with greatest clarity. We therefore, in conclusion (points 11 and 12) address ourselves to Christians.' John F. Dulles, 'Moral and Spiritual Bases for a Just and Lasting Peace,' in Henry P. Van Dusen, *The Spiritual Legacy of John Foster Dulles*, 101; see also Federal Council of Churches, *Biennial Report* (1942), New York, 42; and John Mulder, 'The Moral World of John Foster Dulles,' *Journal of Presbyterian History* 49 (Summer 1971) 170.

[297] E. Raymond Platig, 'John Foster Dulles', 287.

[298] As noted earlier, Leo Pasvolsky, a leading member of the Council on Foreign Relations, was a guiding hand in the Informal Agenda Group.

[299] See Federal Council of Churches, *A Basis for the Peace to Come,* New York, 1942. The other lecturers were Methodist Bishop Francis John McConnell, Hu Shih, Chinese Ambassador to the United States, and John Foster Dulles.

[300] Royal Institute of International Affairs, Archives, 4 Toynbee Carton 8, letter, Walter Mallory to Arnold J. Toynbee, 6 July 1942, as cited in William H. McNeill, *Arnold J. Toynbee. A Life*, 182.

[301] See William H. McNeill, *Arnold J. Toynbee*, 166 (cf. Bodleian Library, Toynbee Papers, 'Plan for Chatham House Research' by AJT, dated February 1932).

[302] William H. McNeill, *Arnold J. Toynbee. A Life*, 183.

[303] See 'Report of Peace Aims meeting, Balliol College, 6 July 1942,' Toynbee Papers, Bodleian Library, Oxford, as cited in William H. McNeill, *Arnold J. Toynbee. A Life*, 302.

[304] Letter, H. P. Van Dusen to William Paton, 15 October, 1942, Toynbee Papers, Bodleian Library; as cited in William H. McNeill, *Arnold J. Toynbee. A Life*, 183, 184.

[305] *Ibid.* See also the following quotation from a typescript of the conclusions reached at this meeting which exists among Toynbee's papers confirming Van Dusen's report, in William H. McNeill, *Arnold J. Toynbee. A Life*, 184: 'The new [world] government must thenceforth be independent of any nation or group of nations, and those who determined from time to time its powers and personnel must come to include those who are now neutrals and enemies. "Some may feel that our proposals are overbold, others that they are ill-timed. We have not acted without profound reflection on both these matters. "As Christians we must proclaim the moral consequences of the factual interdependence to which the world has come. The world has become a community and its constituent members no longer have the moral right to exercise "sovereignty" or "independence" which is now no more than a legal right to act without regard to the harm which is done to others. The time has come when nations must surrender the right to do that which is immoral."'

[306] *Ibid.*, 184.

[307] See Albert N. Keim, 'John Foster Dulles and the Federal Council of Churches, 1937-1949,' 106. Commission members in attendance were Frank Aydelotte, Raymond L. Buell, Harold W. Dodds, Clyde Eagleton, Frank Graham, William A. Neilson,

Francis P. Sayre, Charles P. Taft, Kenneth S. Latourette, John Mackay, Reinhold Niebuhr, William Scarlett, Henry P. Van Dusen, Luther Weigle, Bishop McConnell, Roswell P. Barnes, Dulles; see Memoranda, October 9-11, 1942, Box 139, Federal Council of Churches, Manuscripts, in National Council of Churches Archives, The Inter-church Center, New York.

[308] See *British-American Statement on World Order*, October, 1942; letter, Dulles to Van Dusen, October 28, 1942, Box 139, Federal Council of Churches, Manuscripts, in National Council of Churches Archives, The Inter-church Center, New York.

[309] Ronald W. Pruessen, *John Foster Dulles*, 191.

[310] The contributors were: John Foster Dulles, William Ernest Hocking, Henry P. Van Dusen, Luther A. Weigle, Everett R. Clinchy, John A. Mackay, John C. Bennett, Alfred W. Beaven, Pitirim A. Sorokin, G. Bromley Oxnam, Francis B. Sayre, Clyde Eagleton, William Scarlett and Harry Emerson Fosdick. See also Federal Council of Churches, *Federal Council Bulletin* 25, no. 10 (October, 1942), New York, 2-3.

[311] Commission to Study the Bases of a Just and Durable Peace, *A Righteous Faith for A Just and Durable Peace* (October, 1942), 53, 55.

[312] See letter, JFD to members of the Commission on a Just and Durable Peace, January 6, 1943; see also letter, JFD to same, February 9, 1943.

[313] See Dulles' address, March 18, 1943, *JFD Papers*: 'It is that decision which our proposals are designed to force, and it must be made *now* or the opportunity for such collaboration will inevitably disappear ... Will the American people now commit themselves to a future of organized international collaboration within the areas of demonstrated world interdependence?' (His emphasis). Dulles' remarks were read into the appendix of the *Congressional Record* at the request of Senator Joseph Ball; see U.S. Congress, *Congressional Record*, 78th Congress, 1st Session (Washington, D.C: Government Printing Office, 1943) Appendix, 1589.

[314] Federal Council of Churches, *Annual Report* (1943), New York, 97.

[315] See John Foster Dulles, 'Statement of Political Propositions. The Spiritual Foundations of World Order', in Henry P. van Dusen, *The Spiritual Legacy of John Foster Dulles*, 107-110.

[316] See Townsend Hoopes, *The Devil and John Foster Dulles*, 56.

[317] Letter, JFD to all members of the Commission, 12 March 1943, *JFD Papers*, Box 22.

[318] Federal Council of Churches, *Annual Report* (1943), New York, 108.

[319] See *ibid.*, 63. At the meeting with Roosevelt, Dulles was accompanied by the Presiding Bishop of the Protestant Episcopal Church, the Reverend Henry St. George Tucker, and Dr Roswell P. Barnes.

[320] Louis L. Gerson, *John Foster Dulles*, 25.

[321] See John F. Dulles, 'Confidential Memorandum of Conference with the President,' 26 March 1943, *JFD Papers*, Box 22; and also Memorandum of Conversation with Sumner Welles, March 4, 1943.

[322] John F. Dulles, 'Six Pillars of Peace', *Christianity and Crisis* 3 (31 May 1943) 5.

[323] Leonard Mosley, *Dulles*, 151. Several pages earlier Mosley had already stated that Dulles' 'idea was to turn the Charter into a "beneficent reality" by stripping away the big power conceptions on which it was based and replacing them with a more egalitarian sharing of world government. The plan went through many stages and was eventually published as a manifesto called *Six Pillars of Peace*. As such it was backed

by the Federal Council of Churches, which organized an intensive campaign to promote public interest in it.' *Ibid.*, 120.

[324] Federal Council of Churches, *Annual Report* (1943), New York, 62-63; see also John F. Dulles, 'Political Propositions,' in Henry P. van Dusen, *The Spiritual Legacy of John Foster Dulles*, 110.

[325] Letter, JFD to the Commission membership, 12 March 1943, *JFD Papers*, Box 22.

[326] In the 'Introductory Statement by the Commission,' prefacing the 'Six Pillars of Peace', John F. Dulles clearly expressed his fears regarding the potential withdrawal of the United States from participating in a world organisation at the conclusion of the Second World War: 'The American people again find themselves in an era of critical decision ... Now, more than ever, a wrong choice of the part we shall act will involve us in the general misfortune of mankind. In anticipation of this critical period, the Federal Council of Churches, over two years ago, set up this Commission to Study the Bases of a Just and Durable Peace ... Military peril has dramatized, for all to see, the need for international cooperation. But as military victory becomes more certain and draws more near, that need will be less obvious. As we come to grips with the appalling moral, social, and material aftermaths of Axis rule, transitory issues will arise to perplex and divide the United Nations. These may loom large and obscure the fundamentals and incline us to relapse into reliance only upon our own strength. Thus, if our nation does not make the right choice soon, it may never be made in our time ... If the six Propositions we enunciate become an official program of this nation, we will be committed to move, by definite steps, to bring ourselves into an ordered relationship with others. Only if the nations join to do this, can we escape chaos and recurrent war. Only if the United States assumes a leadership, can it be done now. For we, more than any other nation, have the capacity to influence decisively the shaping of world events .... [signed] John Foster Dulles, *Chairman.*' John F. Dulles, 'Political Propositions,' in Henry P. van Dusen, *The Spiritual Legacy of John Foster Dulles*, 107-109.

[327] Among those present at the luncheon were: John D. Rockefeller, Jr.; Dr Harold Dodds, President of Princeton University; Professor William Hocking of Harvard University; Mrs Dwight Morrow; Dean Virginia Gildersleeve of Barnard College; Thomas Lamont, partner at J. P. Morgan & Co.; Bishop Henry St. George Tucker, President of the FCC; and Bishop G. Bromley Oxnam of the Methodist Church.

[328] The idea to hold a luncheon for 'leading civic leaders' came from Dulles. He asked John D. Rockefeller, Jr., with whom he had been working at the Rockefeller Foundation, to organise the meeting. Dulles' intention in selecting Rockefeller as host was to give maximum publicity to the launching of the 'Six Pillars of Peace'. See letter, JFD to John D. Rockefeller, Jr., March 3, 1943. Rockefeller's letter of invitation was actually written by Donald Bolles, Vice President of the Institute of Public Relations, Inc., a New York advertising agency, which was employed by Dulles to conduct the Commission's public campaign. Rockefeller appended his signature under the following text: 'I understand that Mr. John Foster Dulles had invited you to lunch with him on Thursday, March 18. He had also invited me. The basis for a just and durable peace, there to be presented and discussed, which Mr. Dulles has set forth in six brief, ably drawn paragraphs, has impressed as of such profound significance to the future of civilization that I am setting aside all other plans in order to attend the luncheon and I greatly hope you will do the same. (signed) John D. Rockefeller, Jr.' Rockefeller letter, March 9, 1943, *JFD Papers*, Box 180.

[329] Dulles told a group of churchmen early in 1943 that unless the United States committed itself without reservation to the creation of a world organization during the war it would never become a reality. Postwar power rivalries between the United States and the Soviet Union over the disposition of Eastern Europe, and the United States' monopoly of world power, would destroy any possibility of creating such a body after the war. The United States would be tempted to repeat its experience after World War I. He was committed to preventing this from happening again; see Discussion at 5th Avenue Presbyterian Church, February 24, 1943, *JFD Papers*, Box 21.

[330] *Christianity and Crisis* 3 (17 May 1943) 3, reported that the 'Six Pillars' were 'greeted by favourable editorial comments not only in this country but abroad'. The *Times* of London printed the statement on the front page with the following commentary: 'They [the six pillars] are admirably comprehensive; they cover the economic as well as the political field; and, while avoiding all unnecessary detail, they constitute a definite programme, the adoption of which would be an immense step forward.' Quoted in the same issue of *Christianity and Crisis* 3. Both the *New York Times* and the *New York Herald Tribune* of March 19 carried two-column front page stories. The statement was given one column of the principal newspage of the London papers and it was conspicuously reported in the Swiss press.

[331] *Ibid.*

[332] Commission on a Just and Durable Peace Notes, Federal Council of Churches, Manuscripts, Box 195, in National Council of Churches Archives, The Inter-church Center, New York. Other contributors included Harold W. Dodds, President of Princeton University; Arthur H. Sulzberger, publisher of the *New York Times*; Francis B. Sayre, special assistant to the Secretary of State and former High Commissioner to the Philippines; Dr Harry Emerson Fosdick of Riverside Church, New York City; and, of course, John Foster Dulles.

[333] Cf. *Christianity and Crisis* 3 (31 May 1943) 5-6; *ibid.* (28 June 1943) 6-8; and *ibid.* (12 July 1943) 6-7.

[334] Correspondence, March, 1943, Box 8, *JFD Papers*.

[335] See Ronald W. Pruessen, *John Foster Dulles*, 196.

[336] Reinhold Niebuhr, 'American Power and World Responsibility,' *Christianity and Crisis* 3 (5 April 1943) 40.

[337] Henry P. Van Dusen, 'The Six Pillars of Peace,' *Christianity and Crisis* 3 (22 March 1943) 1.

[338] Winthrop S. Hudson, *Religion in America* (New York: Charles Scribner's Sons, 1965) 388.

[339] John F. Dulles, 'The Faith of Our Fathers', in Henry P. Van Dusen, ed., *The Spiritual Legacy of John Foster Dulles*, 11.

[340] See Mark G. Toulouse, *The Transformation of John Foster Dulles*, 70 (quoting from John F. Dulles, 'The Beginning of a World Order,' 22 April 1945, *JFD Papers*, Box 27).

[341] Townsend Hoopes, *The Devil and John Foster Dulles*, 56.

[342] See 'A Just and Durable Peace: Discussion of Political Propositions (Six Pillars of Peace),' March 1943, *JFD Papers*.

[343] See letters, JFD to Arthur Ballantine, September 22, 1943; same to Wendell Willkie, September 28, 1943; same to Herbert Hoover, October 5, 1943; same to Sumner Welles, October 26, 1943; same to Walter Yust, December 27, 1943. All these letters are contained in the *JFD Papers*.

[344] The first of these was Dulles' 'Analysis of the Moscow Declaration'.

[345] Letter, Walter W. Van Kirk to Social Action secretaries, April 20, 1943, Federal Council of Churches - Manuscripts, Box 195, in National Council of Churches Archives, The Inter-church Center, New York.

[346] Federal Council of Churches, *Federal Council Bulletin* 26, no. 10 (October, 1943), New York, 9.

[347] *Christian Century*, March 11, 1942, 330.

[348] Federal Council of Churches, *Biennial Report* (1944), New York, 135-137. In this context Richard Fagley made the following remarks about Dulles' intentions concerning these publications: 'He really enjoyed looking forward to setting goals which were grounded in real possibilities, but pointed towards something more creative and curative. In fact, these were two of his favourite words - curative and creative - something that was healing and something that was forward looking, dynamic, constructive. These were two words we always associated with him.' See Mark G. Toulouse, *The Transformation of John Foster Dulles*, 72, fn. #35.

[349] See Federal Council of Churches, *Biennial Report* (1944), New York, 135-137.

[350] Herbert Agar was the former editor of the *Louisville Courier-Journal*.

[351] Reinhold Niebuhr, Lewis Mumford, et al., *The City of Man. A Declaration on World Democracy* (New York: Viking Press, 1940) 25. By 1949 Reinhold Niebuhr was one of the most influential American Protestant theologians, renowned for his analysis and criticism of the American capitalist system. Following his tour of Germany in 1946 he became a government consultant, meeting regularly with the State Department's Advisory Commission on Cultural Policy in Occupied Territories. That same year Allen W. Dulles, president of the Council on Foreign Relations (1946-1950), nominated him for membership in the Council. Co-authors Lewis Mumford and Herbert Agar of *The City of Man* were also members of the Council on Foreign Relations. *Ibid.*, 102, 122, 128.

[352] Reinhold Niebuhr, Lewis Mumford, et al., *The City of Man*, 23.

[353] See *ibid.*: 'Diversity in unity and unity in diversity will be the symbols of federal peace in universal democracy ... Society may be likened to a triangular pyramid with its three faces representing the constitutional order, the economic order, the international order. None of them stands alone; each of them leans on the other. All three together converge toward the common apex ... A positive plan for world legislation ... cannot be assigned any longer to pure theoretical thinking ... even if as August as Mazzini's ... And there must be a common creed ... or ethico-religious purpose.'

[354] Michael Straight, *Make This the Last War,* Harcourt (New York: Brace and Company, 1943).

[355] Mortimer J. Adler, *How to Think about War and Peace* (New York: Simon and Schuster, 1944) 16-17.

[356] See Ronald W. Pruessen, *John Foster Dulles*, 191-192.

[357] See especially, the 'Commission on a Just and Durable Peace - 1943' file, containing numerous documents on mass media and publicity efforts in relation to the issuance of the 'Six Pillars of Peace', *JFD Papers*. A subsection, entitled, 'International Understanding', in the Federal Council pamphlet, 'Furthering Christian Unity', reads as follows: 'The Council's Commission on a Just and Durable Peace, made up of thoughtful leaders of special competence in international affairs, under the chairmanship of the distinguished lawyer, Mr. John Foster Dulles, has shown that a

united influence is possible. National study conferences have been held for the purpose of formulating programs on which the churches can stand together. Study groups in local churches have been formed in order to develop an informed conscience on international problems, throughout the nation. Such influential statements as the "Six Pillars of Peace", "Soviet-American Relations", and "Crossroads of Foreign Policy" have given a sense of direction to Christian thinking. Christian missions on World Order have been held in cities across the continent. A mobilization of the churches for support of the European Recovery Program (The Marshall Plan) has been conspicuously effective.'

[358] John F. Dulles, 'The Beginning of a World Order,' 22 April 1945, *JFD Papers*, Box 27.

[359] Kenneth Grubb would later become a director in the Commission of the Churches on International Affairs.

[360] Eleanor M. Jackson, *Red Tape and the Gospel*, 267.

[361] See 'A Christian Basis for Reconstruction,' August 1943, *JFD Papers*.

[362] Federal Council of Churches, *Federal Council Bulletin* 26, no.10 (October, 1943), New York, 12.

[363] Albert N. Keim indicates that certain British government officials collaborated in drafting the statement: 'As it turned out the statement, entitled *A Christian Basis for Reconstruction*, became a fairly good representation of the official position of the British government, for Dulles learned that several high officials of the government had helped to write the statement, although they declined to sign it.' Albert N. Keim, 'John Foster Dulles and the Federal Council of Churches of Christ, 1937-1949,' 125.

[364] See Federal Council of Churches, *Federal Council Bulletin* 26, no.10 (October, 1943) 12.

[365] Federal Council of Churches, *Biennial Report* (1942), New York, 108.

[366] Minutes of the meeting of the Commission at Bronxville, N.Y., September 16-17, 1942, Commission MSS; as cited in Jessie June Burroway, 'Christian Witness Concerning World Order, The Federal Council of Churches and Postwar Planning 1941-1947,' unpublished Ph.D. thesis, University of Wisconsin, 1953, 67.

[367] National Council of Churches of New Zealand (John Foster Dulles), *A Christian Message on World Order from the International Round Table of Christian Leaders, July 1943, Princeton*, 8.

[368] The two Australian delegates flew across the Pacific in a bomber furnished with special orders from General Douglas MacArthur; see Manuscript of broadcast by Dr. Van Kirk from CBS New York, July 9, 1943.

[369] Other delegates who lived in exile in the United States represented their national Church organisations in Norway, Japan, Poland, and Russia.

[370] See 'Purposes, Agenda, Personnel of the International Round Table of Christian Leaders, Princeton, July 1943,' *JFD Papers*. See also the ten requirements for progress toward world order stipulated by the International Round Table in National Council of Churches of New Zealand (John Foster Dulles), *A Christian Message on World Order from the International Round Table of Christian Leaders, July 1943, Princeton*, 173 Cashel St., Christchurch, 1943, 15-16.

[371] Dulles' address at the International Round Table, July 8, 1943, Upright File, Federal Council of Churches, Manuscripts, National Council of Churches Archives, The Inter-church Center, New York.

[372] *Ibid.*

[373] *Ibid.*

[374] *Ibid.*

[375] Press release, Princeton, July 8, 9, 1943; files of the Commission on a Just and Durable Peace.

[376] The Committee consisted of John Foster Dulles, New York, Chairman of the Commission on a Just and Durable Peace; Dr. A.C. Craig, London, General Secretary, British Council of Churches; Dr. Gordon A. Sisco, Toronto, Ontario, General Secretary of the United Churches Commission on Church, Nation and World Order; Very Reverend Alwyn Keith Warren, Dean of Christchurch Cathedral, New Zealand; Dr. H.J. Gezork, Newton-Andover Theological Seminary; and Dr. Timothy Lew, Dean of the Department of Theology of Yenching University and Member of the Chinese Yuan (Senate). See press release, Princeton, July 8, 1943.

[377] National Council of Churches of New Zealand (John Foster Dulles), *A Christian Message on World Order from the International Round Table of Christian Leaders*, 12-13.

[378] *Ibid.*, 16.

[379] *Ibid.*

[380] *Ibid.*, 14.

[381] *Ibid.*, 15-16.

[382] *Ibid.*, 21.

[383] *Ibid.*

[384] *Ibid.*, 22.

[385] *Ibid.*

[386] *Ibid.*, 23.

[387] *Ibid.*, 8.

[388] The letter was published in the London *Times* on December 21, 1940.

[389] Commission on a Just and Durable Peace memoranda, 1943, Upright File, Federal Council of Churches, Manuscripts, National Council of Churches Archives, The Inter-church Center, New York.

[390] Among these were Syracuse, New York; Gary, Indiana; Toledo, Ohio; San Antonio, Texas; and Los Angeles, California.

[391] Pattern's Progress, Bulletins 1-9, *Fagley MSS.* See the *New York Times*, June 1, 1944, for an editorial comment on the British statement.

[392] *Editorial Research Report* II (Washington, D.C., 1943), 396-397.

[393] United States Congress, *Congressional Record*, 78th Congress, 1st Session (Washington, D.C.: Government Printing Office, 1944) 8620.

[394] *Ibid.*, 8732-8733.

[395] *Ibid.*, 8731.

[396] Senator Hatch actually said '60 million citizens', which the reporter writing the Congressional Record mistook for 16 million. Rev. Edward A. Conway, SJ, made mention of this fact at the seventeenth annual convention of the Catholic Association for International Peace, Washington, D.C., April 11, 1944; see *Pattern's Progress*, Supplement 3, *Fagley MSS.*

[397] United States Congress, *Congressional Record*, 78th Congress, 1st Session (Washington, D.C.: Government Printing Office, 1944) 8733.

[398] *Ibid.*, 8737.

[399] *Ibid.*

[400] The *Pattern of Peace* was read into the *Congressional Record* three different

times; by Senator Mead, October 14 (one week after its publication), by Senator Pepper on October 26, and by Senator Guffey on November 3, 1943. See United States Congress, *Congressional Record*, 8322-8323, 8729-8730, 9045.

[401] Letter, JFD to Senator Connally, October 26, 1943, *Commission on a Just and Durable Peace MSS.*

[402] The other speaker at the Cathedral on that day was Senator Joseph Ball, who called the Mission the 'greatest crusade since Jesus sent His twelve disciples out to preach the brotherhood of man.' Ball criticised the Connally Resolution for its elusive commitment to create a world organisation and urged support for his own B2-H2 bill; see *Time* magazine, November 8, 1943, 34.

[403] John F. Dulles, 'The American Vision,' in Henry P. Van Dusen, *The Spiritual Legacy of John Foster Dulles*, 57. Dulles' address was subsequently printed in the *Congressional Record*, at the behest of Senator Ball, U.S. Congress, *Congressional Record*, 78th Congress, 1st Session, Appendix (Washington, D.C.: Government Printing Office, 1944) 4649-4650. See also John F. Dulles, 'Christian Message Address,' delivered in Newark (November 4, 1943), Macon (November 8, 1943), Birmingham (November 9, 1943), and Mobile (November 10, 1943), *JFD Papers.*

[404] John F. Dulles, 'The American Vision,' in Henry P. Van Dusen, *The Spiritual Legacy of John Foster Dulles*, 63.

[405] *Ibid.*, 62.

[406] *Ibid.*, 63.

[407] These were the Foreign Missions Conference of North America, the Home Missions Council of North America, the International Council of Religious Education, the Missions Education Movement, and the United Council of Church Women; see *Post War World*, December, 1943, 3.

[408] The Commission on a Just and Durable Peace sought to accomplish three tasks through the National Mission on World Order: 1) equip leaders to carry on education and action programs (each conference included at least one methods session, where study materials were introduced); 2) 'develop a strong body of public opinion alive to the need for keeping America in peace,' which translated meant support for an international collective security organisation at the end of the war; 3) educate the public regarding the principles which Christians believed necessary for a viable world order. See Federal Council of Churches, *Federal Council Bulletin* 26, no. 9 (September, 1943), New York, 8.

[409] See *Post War World*, December, 1943, 3.

[410] See Robert Divine, *Second Chance*, 161.

[411] See *Fellowship*, April, 1944, 78.

[412] *Christian Century*, March 22, 1944, 356.

[413] Federal Council of Churches, *Biennial Report* (1940), New York, 92.

[414] Federal Council of Churches, *Annual Report* (1945), New York, 130-32.

[415] In 1945, John F. Dulles was a senior member of the American delegation to the founding conference of the United Nations in San Francisco. Even before becoming Secretary of State, he regularly represented the United States at innumerable United Nations affairs (see e.g., John Foster Dulles, 'The North Atlantic Pact,' *Vital Speeches of the Day*, Vol. 15, No. 20, August 1, 1949, 617). Also in 1945, he attended the first meeting of the Council of Foreign Ministers, as legal counsel to Democratic Secretary of State James Byrnes. Two years later he was at the Moscow and London meetings to advise Democratic Secretary of State George Marshall. Later he regularly accompanied

Marshall's successor, Dean Acheson to international conferences.
[416] E. Raymond Platig, 'John Foster Dulles,' 36; see also John F. Dulles, 'Analyses of Moscow Declaration in the Light of the Six Pillars of Peace,' *Post War World*, Vol. I (December 15, 1943), 4; John F. Dulles, 'Ideals Are Not Enough,' *International Conciliation*, No. 409, Section. I (March, 1945), 131; John F. Dulles, *War or Peace*, 33-38.
[417] Letter, Truman to JFD, November 6, 1945, in 'Truman and Dulles Exchange Letters', *Post War World*, Vol III (December 15, 1945) 2. For some other examples of secular recognition extended to Dulles' Commission, see the following: Cordell Hull, *The Memoirs of Cordell Hull*, Macmillan Co., New York, 1948, 1625-1626; Robert Divine, *Second Chance*, 252ff.; and Robert Divine, *Foreign Policy and the United States President Elections, 1940-1948* (New York: New Viewpoints, 1974) 91-92.
[418] See Federal Council of Churches, *Biennial Report* (1944) 185-186: 'With all of these defects, the proposals do, however, have the great merit of providing for a continuing and virtually constant consultation of representatives of the great powers, and of selected lesser powers under conditions which will subject what is done to the moral judgment of mankind ... If the proposals envision much that partakes of a military alliance, at least that military alliance is to be put into a setting which will permit public opinion to influence its revolution toward a more adequate general organization ... We believe that the proposed organization with such beneficial modifications as ought to result from further considerations by the prospective members can be developed into one that will commend itself to the Christian conscience.'
[419] In reference to the Dumbarton Oaks Proposals the conference *Message* stated: 'Accordingly, we recommend that the churches support the Dumbarton Oaks Proposals as an important step in the direction of world cooperation but because we do not approve of them in their entirety as they now stand, we urge the following measures for their improvement: 1) *A preamble* -- to state the purposes of justice set forth in the Atlantic Charter; 2) *Development of International Law* -- to ring the actions of the world organization under law; 3) *Voting power* -- to prevent a nations from voting if and when its case is being judged according to predetermined international law; 4) *Colonial and Dependent Areas* -- to establish a Commission to promote the well-being of colonies with the goal of their independence in view; 5) *Human rights and Fundamental freedoms* -- to establish a Commission to promote human rights; 6) *Universal membership* -- to admit all nations willing to accept the obligations of membership; 7) *Limitation of armaments* -- to speed the reduction of armaments; 8) *Smaller powers* -- to protect more fully the rights of smaller nations; 9) *Amendment* -- to make it possible to amend the Charter without the consent of all the permanent members.' Federal Council of Churches, *Annual Report*, 1945, 143.
[420] See Charles S. Macfarland, *Pioneers for Peace through Religion. Based on the Records of the Church Peace Union 1914-1945* (Westwood, N.J.: Fleming H. Revell Co., 1946) 232.
[421] See Federal Council of Churches, *Federal Council Bulletin* 28, no. 6 (June 1945), New York.
[422] O. Frederick Nolde, United Lutheran clergyman, became professor of religious education in the Lutheran Theological Seminary in Philadelphia in 1931 and dean of the graduate school, 1943-1962. He was a trustee of the Carnegie Endowment for International Peace and a member of its executive committee along with five others,

including chairman John Foster Dulles. After the creation of the World Council's Commission of the Churches on International Affairs in 1946, he became its executive director.

[423] In an address at the 'Festival of Faiths' of the San Francisco Council of Churches, June 19, 1955, Dulles stated that the representatives of the Federal Council and other religious organisations played a decisive role in framing the UN Charter. See John F. Dulles, 'The Moral Foundation of the United Nations,' in Henry P. Van Dusen, *The Spiritual Legacy of John Foster Dulles*, 129.

[424] In *Post War World* Dulles interpreted the meaning of the UN Charter to the churches, stating that it was 'a great document of human rights' which 'largely gives effect to the political propositions which our Commission [on a Just and Durable Peace] enunciated.' John F. Dulles, 'The Charter -- A Great Document of Human Rights,' *Post War World*, Vol. II (July 10, 1945) 1-3.

[425] It should be noted that Alger Hiss, the first Secretary General of the United Nations and member of the Council on Foreign Relations, became a member of the Federal Council's Committee on Policy in 1948; see Federal Council of Churches, 'International Justice and Goodwill,' *Biennial Report* (1948), New York, 105, 106.

[426] See e.g., Dennis L. Tarr, 'The Presbyterian Church and the Founding of the United Nations,' *Journal of Presbyterian History* 53 (Spring 1975) 3-32.

[427] John F. Dulles, 'The Faith of Our Fathers,' in Henry P. Van Dusen, ed., *The Spiritual Legacy of John Foster Dulles*, 7.

[428] See United Nations Information Organizations, *Documents of the United Nations Conference on International Organization, San Francisco, 1945*, Vol. XV, New York, 1946, 579-580.

[429] See Arthur H. Vanderberg, Jr. & Joe Alex Morris, eds., *The Private Papers of Senator Vanderberg* (Boston: Houghton Mifflin Co., 1952) 187-193; *New York Times*, June 16, 1945, 9; statement of Herbert Evatt before Commission II on June 21, 1945 in *Documents of the United Nations Conference on International Organization, San Francisco, 1945*, Vol. VIII, New York, 1946, 209.

[430] Federal Council of Churches, *Annual Report*, 1945, 151-152.

[431] Letter, JFD to Lionel G. Curtis, September 19, 1944, *JFD Papers*. See also Lionel G. Curtis, *Civitas Dei*, 743-744.

[432] Walter W. Van Kirk, *A Christian Global Strategy* (New York: Willett, Clark and Co., 1945) 76.

[433] The 'Foreword' of the report issued by the 'International Round Table of Christian Leaders' states: 'During the early stages of the war, Christian activity in behalf of a just and durable peace moved most intensively within separate nations. National church bodies instituted commissions, convened study conferences, issued statements of Christian principles, contributed to the enlightenment of public opinion, and established contacts with governmental officials. As the churches throughout the world thus assigned themselves to an international task, it seemed imperative that more definite international consultation, ultimately collaboration, be effected. In order to promote this international Christian approach to the establishment of world order, sixty-one Christian leaders met for four days in an International Round Table at Princeton in July, 1943.' National Council of Churches of New Zealand, *A Christian Message on World Order from the International Round Table of Christian Leaders, July 1943, Princeton*, Christchurch, 1943, 5.

[434] See *ibid.*, 17, 18: 'The Churches in their corporate relationships, wherever they

themselves are a part of the world order, and in their programmes of evangelism, education and social action, locally, nationally and internationally, should practice in their own life the principles which they recommend to others, and create new patterns and expressions of brotherhood which will be an example to the secular community.'

# 6

# CONCLUSION

In 1919, the perennial dream of many philosophers, the dream of creating an international community, seemed finally to have become a political reality. Woodrow Wilson, standing at the helm of the victorious Allied Powers, made the proposal to establish the League of Nations the cornerstone of his policy at the Peace Conference. He had come to France in December of 1918, and was received triumphantly, as an 'angel of peace'. On 25 January 1919 the Peace Conference established a special committee to draft the Charter of the League. President Wilson presided over this committee which presented its findings on international co-operation to the Peace Conference on 29 April 1919. The League of Nations was finally established on 10 January 1920.

Yet only a few brief years after the League appeared on the international scene, the initial excitement had markedly declined in the face of its appalling failure to enforce an international system of collective security. The 1930s had refused to confirm the bright hope of a new world order built on the foundation of the first international organisation in human history. The promises of peace and security were challenged by political ideologies which seemed to offer people an identity more concrete than the 'world citizenship' which the League bestowed upon them. As the essential impotence of the League (devoid of any independent means to function on its own authority) emerged, Woodrow Wilson's assurance that national purposes had been replaced by the common purpose of enlightened mankind rang increasingly hollow.

Anticipating that the future League of Nations would succeed neither in preventing violations of the sanctity of nations, nor prevail in challenging the national sovereignty system, a group of American and British delegates at the Peace Conference founded the Institute of International Affairs at the Hotel Majestic on May 30, 1919. The Institute later evolved into two separate, but closely affiliated, organisations: the Royal Institute of International Affairs (London) and the Council on Foreign Relations (New York).[1]

In the foregoing pages it has been shown that the main instigator of the Institute of International Affairs was also the founder of the Round Table Group, namely Lionel G. Curtis. In order to understand Curtis' motivation and objectives it became advisable to revert back in time and come to grips with the imperial ambitions of Lord Alfred Milner.

The Round Table Group, the off-shoot of 'Milner's Kindergarten', represented a combination of many facets of British society. In various ways it displayed a dual concern for socially uplifting the English working class and colonialising the non-Western world. Most importantly, it reflected the imperial traditions of the British ruling classes. The Group's formation at the latter part of the nineteenth century indicated that the ideal of imperial federation had become a dominant factor for the wealthy upper class in Great Britain.

Although suspicious of party politics as such, the Round Table Group embraced a positive view of the state's role in economic and social life. Milner and his associates were convinced that the British Empire was the highest moral achievement of humankind, but an achievement yet imperfect and still developing. In persuading others to accept this viewpoint, they dreamt of a greatly enlarged British Empire. Their efforts were focussed on creating a common outlook among English-speaking nations by using mass propaganda in support of a wide range of specific social and imperial projects. The Round Table Group, both in its public and its private aspects, served to spread knowledge about the Empire. What marked out this organisation was its emphasis upon organic union, first of the British Empire, but then of the world as a whole. In the persons of Lord Alfred Milner, Philip Kerr, and Lionel G. Curtis, it represented the leadership of the imperial federation movement during the years, 1910-1918.

In short, there were three ideas which were regarded by the Group as basic to its philosophy. These ideas were: (1) the creation of a common ideology and world outlook among the peoples of the United Kingdom, the Empire, and the United States; (2) the creation of instruments and practices of co-operation among these various communities in order that they might pursue parallel policies; and (3) the creation of a federation on an imperial, Anglo-American, and finally world basis.

The Round Table Group expected that many of the great convulsions of the future would be caused by dysfunctional relationships between different races and civilisations. The issue of war and peace would thus hinge on the question of racial and national interaction and integration. Although the Round Table advocated no overt form of racism, it conveyed an assumption of British superiority, elevated to a high idealistic level in Lionel Curtis's discussion of the principle of the Commonwealth. This ethnocentrism was balanced by a dawning interest in the welfare of non-Western nations of the Commonwealth. Concerning these peoples, they displayed, at times rather paternalistically, the traditional British upper-class concept of duty and the legal and social concept of trusteeship.

Two world wars testify to the correctness of Milner's fear that the growth of national power on the Continent posed a serious threat to the Commonwealth and the English-speaking world. More broadly, the seriousness of the problems of war and peace in an age of great empires was also recognised in its historical significance. As one analyses the writings of Kerr and Curtis after 1918, it becomes obvious that they were most deeply concerned about the prevention of war, even though they were never pacifists as such. They supported the national war efforts, when armed conflict became inevitable. The primary purpose of their literary works was to demonstrate that the national sovereignty system with its underlying economic and political conditions was the culprit which makes wars not only possible, but unavoidable. The solution they passionately proposed was the federalisation of the world's nations under a central authority. This became strikingly evident in Curtis' *Civitas Dei* and in his writings on world federalism and Anglo-American union after 1939.[2] Curtis believed that anarchy was the antithesis of individual freedom, and thus (by logical inference) that international anarchy, as exemplified by the national sovereignty system, was the antithesis of political freedom. Interpreting the Sermon on the Mount in his own unique way, Curtis equated the vision of a world society, in which the problem of nationalism would be a thing of the past, with the realisation of the kingdom of God on earth. Its political manifestations can be seen in the Federal Union movement and in the promotion of Clarence K. Streit's *Union Now* campaign.

The postwar years brought out a vigorous internationalism in some of the more cosmopolitan members of the Round Table Group, but also a growing scepticism about the collective security system put in place after the First World War. They felt justified in their belief that the League of Nations in which they had placed such great hopes prior to its inception seemed to breed only jealousy and chaos in international relations. Disillusioned to the core, they suspended further support of the League in the aftermath of the refusal of the United States Senate to ratify the Versailles Peace Treaty. American constitutionalists were unwilling to bow before the international coterie of high-spirited idealists who had hoped to place the military and economic might of America under the authority of the League. For some time individual members of the Round Table, most notably Alfred E. Zimmern, continued to work within the parameters of the League, but the Group as a whole set out to substitute the international organisation with a world federation in which the United States would be firmly integrated.[3] They found their most fervent allies among the prominent ecumenical leaders of their day.

The importance of channelling the forces of change through instruments of international co-operation became the theme of papers prepared for the World Conference of Life and Work at Oxford in 1937. Joseph H. Oldham, the organising secretary of the Conference, stressed the importance of study, research, and propaganda, even calling these aspects the main responsibility of the churches. Adequate factual knowledge of the international situation was needed if Christians were to work effectively for a policy of peaceful change on the part of their governments. When the preparatory work for the ecumenical conference was begun, the theologians, church leaders and Christian laymen found it necessary to find a consensus about Christian concepts of the Church, society and the state. Only then could they discuss such things as the limits of state responsibility, state power, or the limitations on Christian obedience to the state and concur on specific lines of action. The involvement of distinguished scholars and men experienced in international affairs, such as Philip Kerr, Alfred Zimmern, and John Foster Dulles, guaranteed a note of proportion and reality in its pronouncements.

The Christian participants at the Conference were keen analysts of the pace and direction of contemporary history. Since the turn of the century Protestant clergymen tried to give the Church a stronger voice in matters affecting the moral and social condition of the world. By establishing a worldwide 'fellowship of churches', they wanted to halt the division of the Church into denominational factions and to counteract their own declining strength in western countries, a decline which was becoming all too evident in the period after the First World War. The goal of uniting the churches was not an end in itself, but rather a realistic approach to enlarge the base of supporters and thus exert greater influence in the public arena. Thinking primarily in political and sociological terms, the ecumenical leaders set out to 'Christianise' the world and introduce a new social order. The task envisaged was the radical modification of the world's economic system according to the principles of the Kingdom of God supposedly gleaned from the Sermon on the Mount, the gospels, and Christ's teaching of His coming.

The Oxford Conference was more than an attempt to create a social ethic; it indicated a new chapter in the ecumenical movement. The simple motto 'Dogma divides, service unites' had been sufficient for the Stockholm Conference in 1925. It mobilised the resources of the churches for social action. In 1937, however, it was palpably inadequate to deal with the challenge of a world staggering at the brink of chaos and social disintegration.

The Church leaders had witnessed the unification of the world through science, trade, modern transport and communications. Eager to usher in a millennium of peace, the churches sprang into action at the end of the Great War to promote international co-operation. The growing awareness of an interdependent world, in which nationalism had become an obsolete phenomenon, was welcomed as a sign that God was leading humankind towards an international society. Yet in 1937, the Church delegates at Oxford noticed disconcerting developments in the community of nations. Any progress towards an international order always seemed to be accompanied by outbursts of national rivalry and the rise of secular ideologies. Mussolini's fascist take-over of Italy and Hitler's repudiation of the Versailles Treaty demonstrated drastically that mechanisms for change in the international order were urgently needed. The delegates recognised that the national sovereignty system was the greatest obstacle to the formation of a world society. The predominance of the state in international society was perceived as the main impediment to a peaceful world community. The ecumenical leaders hoped to bring political mechanisms into play to precipitate the demise of the nation-state system. It was resolved that the state, as a human construct, should lose its main role in international affairs. The abandonment of the claim of each nation-state to be judge in its own cause, and the abrogation of absolute national sovereignty, were deemed imperative. The Church was called upon to lead the nations into a new dispensation of history. The causes of war, it was pointed out, must be attacked by promoting peaceful change and the pursuit of justice. Power politics (and the attitude of mind it represents) was held to lie at the root of international conflict. In the absence of a superior political authority only voluntary action could pre-empt the use of force (or the threat of force) to bring the international order into conformity with changing realities. The universal body of Christians was ideally constituted to put pressure on national governments to establish a new world order. Only thus could the foreign policies of individual nations be moderated by the acceptance of international law administered by supranational institutions.

Reviewing areas of possible Christian action, the Oxford Conference did not fail to note the efforts of those movements which were working for the cause of international understanding through the churches. It was the deep conviction of the ecumenical leadership that the Church could only speak with authority if it spoke in unity. It was an ingenious idea to form a universal council of churches as the nucleus of a world society reaching beyond racial, social, and national barriers. This idea had been the driving force behind the ecumenical movement from its beginning; it was particularly important in formulating the policy of the Federal Council of Churches of Christ in America.

In December 1908 the overwhelming majority of Protestant Churches in the United States had formed the Federal Council of Churches. The policies of this Council were determined by representatives of the twenty-five constituent Protestant denominations, who met in biennial plenary sessions and in bi-monthly meetings of the Executive Committee of the organisation. An administrative secretariat, divided into departments representing major areas of church concern, and headed by a general secretary, carried out the actual work of the Council. For the first two decades of its existence, the Federal Council, though moving on the periphery of the wider Christian community, encouraged co-operation between the churches. However, although it spread the ecumenical spirit among the churches, the Council exerted minimal influence in the formation of organic unions between different denominations before 1932. During the New Deal era this situation was to change drastically.

The ready acceptance of liberal theology in the mainline churches stimulated a new desire to find common ground between various Christian traditions. To improve interdenominational relations the ecumenical leadership began to downplay the importance of doctrinal distinctives, thus contributing significantly to the growing number of Church mergers in the 1930s. The largest of those unions occurred in 1939, when three different denominations of the Wesleyan tradition formed the Methodist Church. By that time the Federal Council of Churches had become the leading force within the ecumenical movement in the English-speaking world.

Bishop Francis J. McConnell, the president of the Federal Council, told his audience at the Indianapolis quadrennial in 1932 that the best means of encouraging Church unions was to allow the ecumenical ethos to permeate the Christian community gradually from within. Thus he rejected the imposition of artificial designs from the outside. By steadily increasing its influence among the churches, the Council would function as a catalyst to stimulate a co-operative program.

Despite its growing popularity, in 1933 the Federal Council was still severely limited in its unifying efforts by the prevailing denominationalism of its twenty-eight constituent churches. To overcome these limitations E. Stanley Jones, in 1935, proposed the formation of a confederation of Baptist, Methodist, Episcopalian and Presbyterian churches. Answering his critics, Jones explained that he took the U.S. Constitution of 1787 as his model for the Church of Christ in America. He wished to establish a federal union, not a federation, of united churches. This approach would allow each denominational branch of the Church of Christ to retain its distinctive features and liturgical practices. The larger organisational structure thus realised would, however, facilitate efforts to translate Christian charity into practical social action.

To reach a consensus among the churches, Jones flagrantly disregarded doctrinal questions. Unity was declared to be the over-riding principle. Any divisive issues were excluded from the agenda. His whole plan was characterised by a general indifference to the development of Christian theology since the Council of Nicea. Some of the creedal churches, like the Lutherans and Presbyterians, were asked to relinquish the heritage of the Reformation.

In response to Jones' proposal, the executive committee of the Federal Council set up the Commission on Christian Unity in 1937. A report published by the Commission in March 1938 dampened the optimism of many ecumenical leaders concerning the achievement of actual unity among the churches in the foreseeable future. Analysing the various proposals for Church union, the Commission concluded that the plans submitted to the Federal Council were all deficient in some way and that the right moment for implementation in the United States had not yet arrived. One year later, in 1939, a second report of the Commission expressed a more positive view, especially in connection with plans to form a World Council of Churches.

At the Indianapolis quadrennial in 1932 the Federal Council of Churches presented its revised version of the Social Creed of 1908. The new Creed outlined the Council's program for transforming American society into a Christian collectivism. By applying the principles of socialism, as expounded by Walter Rauschenbusch, the kingdom of God on earth would be set up according to the ecumenical ideal. A unified Church would represent a collectivist Protestantism modelled on the pattern of the medieval guild system.

Establishing its public profile through an address delivered on Labour Day 1932, the Commission on the Church and Social Service stepped into the forefront of the campaign for Christian collectivism. It demanded a redistribution of wealth in the United States and other countries of the world. Decisive action would be required in regulating and managing finance, credit, and industry, for only then could the kingdom of God be made to benefit the global population. The Commission's political and social program foreshadowed many features of the New Deal legislation. The Social Creed of 1932 revealed the Federal Council's disposition to support the radical policies of the Roosevelt administration. It met with much acclaim from the general public, because the economic conditions of 1932 were more conducive to social reform than they were before the depression. The Federal Council believed that the establishment of a collectivist society in America would be the particular form in which the kingdom of God would appear on earth. A new emphasis on communicating the social gospel to the church-going public was deemed necessary by the Council, in order to mobilise a grassroots movement of socially active Christians in support of the Social Creed. Although couched in biblical terminology, the Council's social appeals were based on a reinterpretation of Scriptural concepts. A new social order in its emphasis on the class war was considered of much greater relevance to the majority of economically oppressed Americans than the message of the cross which was hardly, if ever, mentioned. In 1934 the Federal Council realised that, in order to become a force of renewal in America, it needed to spread the message of the social gospel among its constituent churches. Beginning in the autumn of 1935 and continuing throughout most of the following year, the ecumenical leadership conducted national preaching missions across the country. It engaged some of the most renowned theologians and preachers in America. All in all, it was a resounding success. The final statistics revealed that over twenty-three thousand ministers had preached to a total of about twenty million people in twenty-eight cities. Nearly thirty university and college campuses were visited by representatives of the Federal Council. Although intended to serve the same purpose, this ministry among students was not organically connected with the preaching missions. It was continued for more than five years reaching its climax in 1939. To capitalise on the acceptance of the social gospel among the broad masses in America, presented in a Christian context, the missions were extended into 1937 with an even greater number of officiating ministers. To consolidate the gains in popularity, the Federal Council initiated a new approach to propagate its message in 1940. Known as the National Christian Missions program, the propaganda campaign, led by more than two hundred Christian orators, received again a good hearing in twenty cities over seven months, ending in Los Angeles in March 1941.

The great preaching campaigns of the churches during the 1940s represented the culmination of the liberal Protestant social gospel movement which had begun shortly after the turn of the century. John Foster Dulles' work as a Christian layman and executive officer of the Federal Council of Churches coincided with an era of unusual activism by American Protestantism in the field of social and international affairs. Under his leadership the ecumenical movement became a dominant force in spear-heading the intended radical transformation of Western society at large. The Protestant churches in the United States were to be an active element in the process of establishing a new social order, even on a worldwide scale. Much of the activity of those years was centred in the work of the Commission on a Just and Durable Peace, established under the chairmanship of John F. Dulles in 1941. For most of the decade of the 1940s the Commission defined the issues, formulated its positions, and lobbied the American government on behalf of the approximately thirty million Protestants affiliated with the Federal Council of Churches. The general purpose was to bring moral and religious judgments to bear on international policy. This, it was thought, could be accomplished by influencing public opinion. Thus Dulles concentrated on setting forth a Protestant policy which would generate a broad consensus on world-order issues among the churches.

With extraordinary efficiency, Dulles presided over the Committee of Direction, a select group of Church leaders which co-ordinated the affairs of an outer circle of commission members. This wider circle consisted of about one hundred renowned theologians and professors of the social sciences. His colleagues maintained that the greatest service Dulles rendered to the ecumenical cause was that of fusing conflicting views of commission members into a coherent whole. Directing the affairs of the Commission with a strong hand, Dulles embarked on a public campaign to inform the churches about the postwar arrangements deemed necessary to ensure the development of a peaceful world community. Convinced that the root cause of war was the division of the world in numerous sovereign nation-states, Dulles and his associates proposed a new system in which the affairs of humankind would be directed by an international organisation endowed with sufficient authority to guarantee perpetual peace. In all his efforts, Dulles tried to persuade the churches to embrace this vision of a unified world. It was clear to him that such a proposition would be readily accepted by the general public, if it had first gripped the imagination of the Christian community in America. Consequently, the Commission reminded the churches of their unique responsibility to bring a Christian spirit to bear on questions of international co-operation.

During the 1940s, Dulles inspired American Protestantism to fulfill its destiny of being one of the primary agents of change in world affairs. Quite naturally, the Church leaders followed closely the lead of a man who repeatedly reassured them that they ought to make their voices known in the public arena. Dulles' membership at the Council on Foreign Relations, his intimate friendship with the leading members of the Round Table Group, and his access to the instrumentalities of power in American politics, afforded an opportunity to ambitious ecclesiastics to bring their influence to bear on international policy issues. Putting his prestige at the disposal of the Federal Council of Churches, Dulles served simultaneously as spokesman for Protestant world-order concerns and as a leader of the American foreign policy establishment. His dual role as Christian layman and statesman created a unique chapter in the annals of American church-state relations.

Dulles brought about an important change in the posture of the churches on international affairs. The inherent realism of the Commission's pronouncements was largely due to the moderating influence of Dulles on the thinking of normally over-idealistic clergymen. The real significance of his chairmanship of the Commission on a Just and Durable Peace seems to be that he outlined the extent to which the churches could influence public opinion in favour of an internationalist American foreign policy. To be credible when speaking to the government, the Commission had to adopt positions which were broadly shared by the President and his cabinet. Thus, while Dulles received official sanction for most of his statements made on behalf of the Commission, he also limited the churches' ability to express an independent viewpoint critical of current government policies. The most celebrated exception to this was Dulles' assessment of the Atlantic Charter, the famous eight-point joint declaration of Roosevelt and Churchill, which, in his view, was palpably deficient as a stimulus to the establishment of 'a better world order'. Following the publication of the Charter, the Commission prepared a detailed critique of its proposals. This document was called *Long Range Peace Objectives* (October 9, 1941). Dulles, the principal author of the declaration, was disenchanted with Roosevelt's reluctance to state in unmistakable terms his support for a world organisation as the basis of a durable peace. Since the Atlantic Charter omitted any mention of a postwar international authority, Dulles and the Commission on a Just and Durable Peace resolved to influence public opinion in the United States and abroad in favour of such an organisation whose membership would be inclusive of all nations.

Public mailing campaigns organised by different mainline denominations apparently verified the claim that thirty million Protestants opposed American isolationism as irresponsible when confronted with Hitlerian totalitarianism. Despite the fact that opinions were shaped by the Federal Council's leadership and then filtered down to the rank and file of the local churches, the Christian world-order efforts grew into a massive, co-ordinated, and highly influential crusade in support of American involvement in an international organisation. The Commission of a Just and Durable Peace outdid more narrowly based secular movements of the time to force a decision on the President to come out in favour of a world organisation as the expressed war-aim of the United States and its allies.

The Commission also recognised the dismal state of international economics. The capitalist system in the Western hemisphere was, it claimed, particularly responsible for the international chaos of the twentieth century, culminating in two world wars. Dulles pronounced a word of prophetic protest

309

against sinful structures in society. In May 1941 he issued a memorandum on economic reform reflecting the consensus among commission members that the principles of a new social order should be introduced into global trade agreements. It was asserted that an international community could only be sustainable in an environment of regulated economic processes. A sense of responsibility for the welfare of all countries would be required to assure peaceful co-existence and co-operation among the peoples of the world. In a speech following the publication of the memorandum, Dulles defended this proposition by stating that science and invention had moulded the nations into an interdependent organism. If a nation decided to assert its economic independence at the expense of other nations, it would reap only short-term material benefits, while incurring severe penalties in the long-run.

Dulles argued that the principle of national sovereignty is a liability in the modern world, for it impedes the central planning of international trade, and the global co-ordination of the exchange of goods and services. He wanted to see a special Board set up to oversee these matters. Dulles was conscious of the fact that a managed international economy was contingent on the establishment of a politically unified community of nations, able to restrain the more powerful countries from seeking economic advantages over weaker nations. Without a world organisation, each nation would continue to maintain conditions advantageous to its own interests and not willingly subject itself to the dictates of a centralised authority interested in the general welfare of the world's nations. Disruption of the delicate equilibrium of the world economy would be unavoidable. The cost of such disruption would fall on all parties involved, and would be similar to that exacted by the Great Depression and its aftermath, namely high unemployment, social unrest, and war.

Dulles also mentioned that the depression of the early 1930s had given rise to totalitarianism in different European countries, where dominant groups sought to implement atheistic ideologies by revolutionary means. He was confident, however, that National Socialism and Communism would eventually run their course and collapse under the weight of their own spiritual deficiencies. Yet Dulles also reminded the western democracies that they would do well to take account of their own spiritual shortcomings before condemning those of totalitarian regimes. The United States, he believed, showed signs of moral decay in preserving the *status quo* of a system of national sovereignty which had become dysfunctional and had led to the devastations of the Second World War. Similarly, it would be wrong to depend on armament production to stimulate the national economy. Dulles continuously warned his audience on various occasions that to depend on America's economic potential to preserve its privileged position among the nations would be irresponsible, immoral and un-Christian. To combat the growing threat of totalitarianism the western democracies, foremost of all the United States, were called upon to surrender the right to determine their own political and economic affairs. Only then would they follow the course of self-denial which Christ had set before them.

310

Dulles inferred that the declining influence of religion in the industrialised countries left a spiritual vacuum which was being filled by the personified state, elevated to the status of a quasi-deity. The churches should resist the re-establishment of the corrupt nation-state system after the war. They should, for example, denounce such perversion of religious sentiments as the concepts of 'hero-nation' and 'villain-nation'.

As long as the fighting continued, America would need to find a positive purpose beyond merely defeating Nazi Germany and its allies, and thereby guard the moral integrity of its mission in the world. It would be wrong to let emotions of hatred and vengeance against a weakened enemy spoil the higher inclinations of soul and mind; such an attitude would be incongruent with Christian ethics. The churches were summoned to uphold the virtues of reconciliation and unity, thus following the examples of Christ and of Abraham Lincoln in proffering forgiveness and healing. Their message should be a clarion call to the nation. It should inspire the peoples on every continent to build a new world society based on the principle of the brotherhood of humankind. A spiritual rejuvenation would thus be initiated and usher in a new age. An incipient international community would be built on the ruins of the old world. For that purpose, printed material was distributed to the churches, containing reports from important ecumenical gatherings, like the Oxford Conference of 1937.

According to the Oxford prescription, taken over whole-heartedly by Dulles, the churches served the indispensable function of providing a common set of moral values upon which a system of international law could ultimately be built. It was Dulles' most fervently held belief that, until a satisfactory international legal system had been created, the ultimate objective of replacing the chaotic and dangerous nation-state system would be doomed.

Under the leadership of Dulles the Commission became an important adjunct of the internationalist crusade during the Second World War to end American isolationism and to create a new international organisation to replace the League of Nations. A central element in Dulles' perception of America's place in the world was a Wilsonian internationalism, devoted to assuring that the United States shouldered her world responsibilities. It was only a short and rather direct route from his crusade to end American isolationism, to the perception of the United States as the custodian of a new world order. Both demanded an activistic and assertive role for the United States, but that could only occur after the development of a common world ethos.

In March 1942 the Commission organised the National Study Conference at Ohio Wesleyan University. The conference was praised by some participants as the most distinguished church gathering in the past three decades. According to a *Time* magazine report its resolutions were primarily concerned with establishing a world government, regulating global trade, and creating an international bank.[4]

In his work with the Commission on a Just and Durable Peace, Dulles frequently encouraged European federalism. He repeatedly proposed a political reorganisation of continental Europe as a federated commonwealth, most notably in his analysis of the Atlantic Charter. As a consequence of his commitment to the idea of European federation, he advocated efforts to establish regional organisations of federated nations. These bodies could eventually be used as stepping stones to larger organisations, leading to the unification of all states under one centralised authority. At times, however, Dulles expressed doubts about the desirability of a regional approach. He feared that regionalism, if it failed to serve as a transitional phase to globalism, might simply create a superstate, which would retain all the negative features of a conventional state.

Despite his scepticism, Dulles became a fervent advocate of the Federal Union movement, which proposed regional unions as the building blocks of a world state. This concept, as delineated in Clarence K. Streit's book, *Union Now*, was similar to Lionel G. Curtis' thesis in *Civitas Dei*, namely to begin with a federation of Western democracies as the foundation of a future world commonwealth. In fact, it seems likely that Streit, a former Rhodes Scholar, adopted many of the ideas propagated by the Round Table Group to develop a realistic plan for world federation. Dulles offered his legal advice to Streit on questions of international law. A joint resolution written by Dulles and Streit and signed by high officials in the Roosevelt administration was published in the *Washington Evening Star* on January 5, 1942, calling upon Congress to create a union government with other countries, like Canada, the United Kingdom, New Zealand, Australia, and the Union of South Africa. The American government rejected the proposition to set up a 'world United States', since it violated fundamental principles of the Constitution.

Disillusioned by this unexpected set-back, Dulles turned his attention to world federalism. In 1919 Samuel Z. Batten of the Federal Council of Churches had already suggested the establishment of a world federation as the only feasible solution to the problems of social inequality, national sovereignty, and war. Echoing Batten's proposal, Dulles incorporated certain aspects of world federalism in the 'Statement of Guiding Principles', which was adopted by the Cleveland biennial meeting of the Federal Council in December 1942. These principles summarise Dulles' views on the state of world affairs in the early 1940s. They describe the international system as a conglomerate of static and dynamic nations, of those preserving the *status quo* and those encouraging change. The former would support the sovereignty system which allowed them to assert their independence against the best interest of all nations, whereas the latter would welcome a system of co-operation. Dulles branded the behaviour of the first as economic arrogance, revealing a deeper-seated spiritual malady and encouraging 'a world of international anarchy'.

After the Japanese attack on Pearl Harbor (December 7, 1941), the Commission produced numerous reports, studies and discussion manuals to cater for the receptive mood in the churches, which were seeking urgent answers to the questions of war and peace. In March 1943, the Commission published the 'Six Pillars of Peace' advocating enforcement mechanisms to keep the peace. Dulles intended to introduce procedures for general arms control that would be a preliminary measure to create a system of collective security.

The publication of this document became a landmark in the history of the Federal Council's Commission on a Just and Durable Peace. The 'Six Pillars' proved highly popular, in contrast to the poor reception afforded to the earlier 'Statement of Guiding Principles', for they provided the churches with a concise set of political propositions concerning the peace issue. Dulles described the 'Six Pillars' as a conceptual framework demanding America's participation in a future United Nations. It revealed also the Commission's general purpose in leading public opinion to support a world organisation. Dulles wanted to prevent a recurrence of America's refusal to participate in the League of Nations, which had created such a dilemma after the First World War for the advocates of world federation. As the end of the Second World War approached, he counted on the churches to promote the idea of a future world organisation in which the United States would play a major part.

The ready acceptance of the 'Six Pillars' encouraged the Commission to continue its public campaign with renewed vigour. It prepared a study guide and several other publications commenting on the theme of the 'Six Pillars'. Favourable editorials appeared in numerous Christian magazines and secular newspapers. Dulles later believed that the 'Six Pillars' were the most constructive contribution of the churches to the formation of a new world order.

Other means than the printed page were used by the Commission to promulgate its message widely. These included Church conferences, like the International Round Table of Christian Leaders at Princeton (1943), mailing campaigns, and various discussion forums. Pastors were encouraged to preach sermons on world order and international co-operation. In November, 1943, the Federal Council and other interdenominational agencies conducted 'Christian Missions on World Order' in one hundred cities. Special 'World Order Days' were designated so that prayer could be offered for the successful conclusion of the Dumbarton Oaks consultation of four major powers in the autumn of 1944.

The combined efforts of the Federal Council of Churches and the Council on Foreign Relations were crowned with a certain degree of success on April 25, 1945, when the founding conference of the United Nations Organisation convened in San Francisco. Although its Charter called for the establishment of an international organisation, it failed to meet the expectations of Dulles and others. However, the acceptance of its Charter by most nations in the world, especially by the United States of America, held out the promise that it would eventually evolve into a world federation. The postmillennial ambition of liberal Church leaders and Christian laymen to build God's kingdom on earth had indeed reached a pivotal point in its historic mission of promoting internationalism. It was clear, however, that the churches would need to continue their efforts with renewed vigour in pursuing the ecumenical vision of a united world of peace and justice until its final form would become reality.

Notes

[1] See Royal Institute of International Affairs, *Annual Report of the Council, 1955-1956*, London, 7.
[2] See Philip Kerr and Lionel Curtis, *Prevention of War* (1923); Lionel Curtis, *Civitas Dei; Decision and Action* (1942); *Faith and Works, or a World Safe for Small Nations* (1943); *World War. Its Cause and Cure* (1945); *World Revolution in the Cause of Peace* (1949); *The Open Road to Freedom* (1950).
[3] See 'The Practical Organisation of Peace,' *Round Table*, IX (1919), London, 217-248; 'The Peace of Versailles,' *ibid.*, 429-454; 'The Harvest of Victory,' *ibid.*, 645-671; 'The World in Conference,' *ibid.*, 21-29; 'Diplomacy by Conference,' *ibid.*, XI (1921), 287-311.
[4] *Time* magazine, 39 (March 16, 1942), 44-45.

# BIBLIOGRAPHY

**Works by John Foster Dulles**

*Books:*
Dulles, John F., *War, Peace and Change* (New York: Harper and Brothers, 1939).

----, *War and Peace* (New York: Macmillan, 1950).

National Council of Churches of New Zealand (John Foster Dulles), *A Christian Message on World Order from the International Round Table of Christian Leaders, July 1943, Princeton* (Christchurch, 1943).

The Commission to Study the Bases of a Just and Durable Peace (John Foster Dulles), *A Just and Durable Peace. Data Material and Discussion Questions* (New York, 1941).

----, *Long Range Peace Objectives. Including an Analysis of the Roosevelt-Churchill Eight Point Declaration*, (New York, 1941).

----, ed., *Six Pillars of Peace. A Study Guide Based on A Statement of Political Propositions*, New York, 1943; reprinted in Henry P. Van Dusen, *The Spiritual Legacy of John Foster Dulles* (Philadelphia: The Westminster Press, 1960).

*Articles & Addresses:*
Dulles, John F., Draft statement, 21 March 1918.

----, Address on 'Principles of Reparations,' in Commission on Reparation of Damages, 7 February 1919.

----, 'Criticisms of Mr. Hatch's Report on War,' 1924, 6, *JFD Papers*, Princeton University, Princeton NJ.

----, 'Conceptions and Misconceptions Regarding Intervention,' *The Annals of the American Academy of Political and Social Science*, CXLIV (July, 1929) 103.

----, 'The Road to Peace,' *Atlantic Monthly*, CLVI (October, 1935) 492-499.

----, 'Peaceful Change within the Society of Nations,' 1936, 9-11, *JFD Papers*.

---, 'The Problem of Peace in a Dynamic World,' *Religion in Life*, VI, No. 2 (Spring 1937).

----, 'As Seen by a Layman,' *Religion in Life*, VII (Winter 1938); reprinted in Henry P. Van Dusen, *The Spiritual Legacy of John Foster Dulles* (Philadelphia: The Westminster Press, 1960).

----, Address on 'The North American Contribution to World Order, 20 June 1939, *JFD Papers, Box 138*.

----, 'America's Role in World Affairs,' 28 October 1939, *JFD Papers*.

----, 'The Church's Contribution Toward a Warless World,' *Religion in Life*, VIII (Winter, 1939), 31-40; reprinted in Henry P. Van Dusen, ed., *The Spiritual Legacy of John Foster Dulles* (Philadelphia: The Westminster Press, 1960).

----, 'The American Churches and the International Situation' (1940), *JFD Papers*.

----, 'Peaceful Change,' Draft of January 23, 1940, *JFD Papers*.

----, 'The Churches and the International Situation,' February, 1940, *JFD Papers*.

----, 'Peaceful Change,' *International Conciliation*, no. 369 (April, 1941).

----, 'The Church's Role in Developing the Basis of a Just and Enduring Peace,' in *When Hostilities Cease*, Addresses and Findings of the Exploratory Conference on the Bases of a Just and Enduring Peace, Chicago Temple, May 27-30, 1941 (Chicago: Commission on World Peace of the Methodist Church, 1941) 15-17.

----, 'Memorandum,' undated, 1, *JFD Papers*.

----, 'Christianity in this Hour,' 21 April 1941, *JFD Papers*, Box 20.

----, Address at Union Theological Seminary, 19 May 1941, 7, *JFD Papers*.

----, 'The Church's Role in Developing the Bases of a Just and Enduring Peace,' *When Hostilities Cease*, Addresses and Findings of the Exploratory Conference on the Bases of a Just and Enduring Peace, Chicago Temple, May 27-30, 1941 (Chicago: Commission on World Peace of the Methodist Church, 1941).

----, Article sent to the International Council of Religious Education, 29 April 1942, 5, *JFD Papers*.

----, Address at Episcopalian Diocesan dinner (May 19, 1942), 4, *JFD Papers*.

----, Opening Address delivered at the National Study Conference, 3 March 1942, 1, *JFD Papers*.

----, 'Towards World Order,' in Francis J. McConnell, et al., *A Basis for the Peace To Come* (New York: Abingdon-Cokesbury Press, 1942).

----, Address, 18 March 1943, *JFD Papers*.

----, Discussion at 5th Avenue Presbyterian Church, February 24, 1943, *JFD Papers*, Box 21.

----, 'Confidential Memorandum of Conference with the President,' 26 March 1943, *JFD Papers*, Box 22.

----, 'Six Pillars of Peace,' *Christianity and Crisis* 3 (31 May 1943).

----, 'Comments on the Fifth Statement; Pattern for Peace; 5. International Institutions to Maintain Peace with Justice Must Be Organized,' *World Affairs*, CVII (March, 1944) 34-35.

----, 'The Churches and World Order,' *Theology Today*, I (1944), 3, 341-348; reprinted in Henry P. Van Dusen, *The Spiritual Legacy of John Foster Dulles* (Philadelphia: The Westminster Press, 1960) 23-30.

----, 'The Beginning of a World Order,' 22 April 1945, *JFD Papers*, Box 27.

----, Article, *The New York Times Magazine* (August, 19, 1945) 12.

----, 'The General Assembly,' in Hamilton Fish Armstrong, ed., *The Foreign Affairs Reader* (New York: Harper and Brothers, 1947).

----, 'The Task of World Peace,' *The Commercial and Financial Chronicle*,

CLXVI (August 21, 1947).

----, 'The North Atlantic Pact,'*Vital Speeches of the Day,* Vo. 15, No. 20, 1 August 1949.

----, 'Address before the Watertown Chamber of Commerce,' 30 April 1952, *JFD Papers,* Box 307.

----, 'The Churches and World Order'; reprinted in Henry P. Van Dusen, *The Spiritual Legacy of John Foster Dulles* (Philadelphia: The Westminster Press, 1960).

----, 'Faith of Our Fathers'; reprinted in Henry P. Van Dusen, ed., *The Spiritual Legacy of John Foster Dulles* (Philadelphia: The Westminster Press, 1960).

----, Report noting the events of his meeting with Roosevelt, 26 March 1943, *JFD Papers,* Box 22.

----, 'Analyses of Moscow Declaration in the Light of the Six Pillars of Peace,' *Post War World,* Vol. I (December 15, 1943).

----, 'The Charter -- A Great Document of Human Rights,' *Post War World,* Vol. II (July 10, 1945).

----, 'The Christian Citizen in a Changing World,' in The World Council of Churches, *Man's Disorder and God's Design,* Vol. IV: *The Church and the International Disorder* (New York: Harper and Brothers, 1948) 73-114.

----, 'Discussion of Greek Problem,' *The Department of State Bulletin,* XIX (November 14, 1948) 607-609.

----, Speech upon receiving the Peace Medal of St. Francis, 20 February 1952, 1, *JFD Papers.*

----, 'Can Freedom Win' (speech at St. Lawrence University), 8 June 1952, 7, *JFD Papers.*

**Biographies & Memoirs**

Addams, Jane, *Peace and Bread in Time of War* (New York: Garland Publishing Co., (1922) 1972).

Alexander, Eleanor, ed., *Primate Alexander. A Memoir* (London: Edward Arnold, 1913).

Allen, Frederick Lewis, *Lord of Creation* (New York: Harper & Brothers, 1935).

Baker, Ray Stannard, *Life and Letters of Woodrow Wilson*, 8 Vols. (New York: Garden City, 1927-1939).

Baruch, Bernard M., *The Public Years* (London: Odhams Press Ltd., [1960] 1961).

----, *My Own Story* (London: Odhams Press Ltd., (1957) 1958).

Beal, John Robinson, *John Foster Dulles.1888-1959* (New York: Harper and Brothers, 1957).

Brand, Robert H., ed., *Letters of John Dove* (London: Macmillan, 1938).

Brett, Reginald B, *Journals and Letters of Reginald, Viscount Esher*, 4 Vols., London.

Brown, John MacMilan, *Memoirs* (University of Canterbury, N.Z., Christchurch: Whitcombe & Tornbs, 1974).

Butler, J.R.M., *Lord Lothian (Philip Kerr) 1882-1940* (London: Macmillan,1960).

Century Association, *Elihu Root*, New York, 1937.

Chernow, Ron, *The House of Morgan* (New York: Simon & Schuster, 1990). ----, *The Warburgs. A Family Saga* (London: Random House, 1993).

Crankshaw, Edward, *The Forsaken Idea. A Study of Viscount Milner* (London: Longmans Green, 1952).

Dulles, Eleanor Lansing, *John Foster Dulles. The Last Year* (New York: Harcourt, Brace and World, 1963).

Flint, John, *Cecil Rhodes* (Boston: Little, Brown and Co., 1974).

Fox, Richard W., *Reinhold Niebuhr. A Biography* (New York: Pantheon Books, 1985).

Gauld, Alan, *The Founders of Psychical Research* (London: Routledge & Kegan Paul, 1968).

George, Alexander L. & Juliette L., *Woodrow Wilson and Colonel House*

(New York: The John Day Company, 1956).

George, David Lloyd, *Memoirs of the Peace Conference*, Vol. I (New Haven: Yale University Press, 1939).

Gerson, Louis L., *John Foster Dulles* (New York: Cooper Square Publishers, Inc., 1967).

Glyn, Elinor, *Romantic Adventure*, London, 1936.

Gollin, A.M., *Proconsul in Politics. A Study of Lord Milner in Opposition and in Power 1854-1905* (London: Anthony Blond, 1964).

Goold-Adam, Richard John Morton, *The Time of Power. A Reappraisal of John Foster Dulles* (London: Weidenfeld and Nicolson, 1962).

Guhin, Michael A., *John Foster Dulles. A Statesman and His Time* (New York: Columbia University Press, 1972).

Halpérin, Vladimir, *Lord Milner and the Empire. The Evolution of British Imperialism.* (With a foreword by The Rt. Hon. L.S. Amery, P.C., C.H.) (London: Odhams Press, 1952).

Harris, Frank, *My Life and Loves*, 5 Vol., New York, (1925,1953,1963) 1979.

Heaton, Herbert, *A Scholar in Action. Edwin F. Gay* (Cambridge, Mass.: Harvard University Press, 1952).

Heller, Deane & David, *John Foster Dulles. Soldier for Peace* (New York: Holt, Rinehart and Winston, 1960).

Hendrick, Burton J., ed., *The Life and Letters of Walter Hines Page*, Vol. III, London, 1925.

Hobson, J.A., *Confessions of an Economic Heretic* (London: George Allen & Unwin, 1938).

Hoopes, Townsend, *The Devil and John Foster Dulles* (Boston: Little, Brown, and Company, 1973).

Jackson, Eleanor M., *Red Tape and the Gospel A Study of the Significance of the Ecumenical Missionary Struggle of William Paton (1886-1943)* (Birmingham: Phlogiston Publishing, 1980).

Johnson, Alan Campbell, *Viscount Halifax. A Biography* (London: Robert

Hale, 1941).

Knock, Thomas J., *To End All Wars. Woodrow Wilson and the Quest for a New World Order* ( New York: Oxford University Press, 1992).

Lavin, Deborah, *From Empire To International Commonwealth. A Biography of Lionel Curtis* (Oxford: Clarendon Press, 1995).

Link, Arthur S., *Wilson. The New Freedom* (Princeton, N.J.: Princeton University Press, 1956).

Macdonald, Dwight, *Henry Wallace. The Man and the Myth* (New York: Garland Publishing., Inc., 1979).

Markowitz, Norman D., *The Rise and Fall of the People's Century. Henry A. Wallace and American Liberalism, 1941-1948* (New York: The Free Press, 1976).

Marlowe, John, *Milner, Apostle of Empire. A Life of Alfred George the Right Honourable Viscount Milner of St James's and Cape Town, KG, GCB, GCMG, (1854-1925)* (London: Hamish Hamilton, 1976).

Masters, Anthony, *Nancy Astor. A Life* (London: Weidenfeld and Nicolson, 1981).

McNeill, William H., *Arnold J. Toynbee. A Life* (New York: Oxford University Press, 1989).

Mosley, Leonard, *Dulles. A Biography of Eleanor, Allen, and John Foster Dulles and their Family Network* (London: Hodder and Stoughton, 1978).

Nimocks, Walter, *Milner's Young Men. The 'Kindergarten' in Edwardian Imperial Affairs* (London: Hodder and Stoughton, [1968] 1970).

Poulton, E.B., *John Viriamu Jones and other Oxford Memories* (London: Longmans & Co., 1911).

Pruessen, Ronald W., *John Foster Dulles. The Road to Power* (New York: The Free Press (Macmillan), 1982).

Rasmussen, Larry, *Reinhold Niebuhr. Theologian of Public Life* (London: Collins Liturgical Publications, 1989).

Scott, Nathan A., *The Legacy of Reinhold Niebuhr*, Chicago, 1975.

Seymour, Charles, *Letters From The Paris Peace Conference* (New Haven: Yale University Press, 1965).

----, *The Intimate Papers of Colonel House*, 4 Vols. (London: Ernest Benn, 1926-1928).

Sinclair, Andrew, *Corsair. The Life of J. Pierpont Morgan* (Boston: Little, Brown, 1981).

Sinclair, Margaret, *William Paton* (London: SCM Press Ltd., 1949).

Toulouse, Mark G., *The Transformation of John Foster Dulles. From Prophet of Realism to Priest of Nationalism* (Macon, GA.: Mercer University Press, 1985).

Vanderberg, Jr., Arthur H. & Morris, Joe Alex, eds., *The Private Papers of Senator Vanderberg* (Boston: Houghton Mifflin Co., 1952).

Visser 't Hooft, Willem A., *Memoirs* (London: SCM Press Ltd., 1973).

Wells, Herbert G., *Experiment in Autobiography. Discoveries and Conclusions of a Very Ordinary Brain (since 1866)* (London: Macmillan, 1934).

Wheatcroft, Geoffrey, *The Randlords. The Men who made South Africa* (London: Weidenfeld & Nicolson, 1985).

White, Theodor, *The Making of the President* (New York, Atheneum, 1964).

Whyte, Sir Frederick, *The Life of W.T. Stead*, 2 Vols. (London: Jonathan Cape, 1925).

Woodruff, Philip (pseud. [i.e. Philip Mason]), *The Men Who Ruled India* (London: Jonathan Cape, 1963).

Wrench, John Evelyn, *Alfred Lord Milner. The Man of No Illusiuons, 1854-1925* (London: Eyre & Spottiswoode, 1958).

----, *Geoffrey Dawson and Our Time* (London: Hutchinson, 1955).

**Secondary Works**

Adler, Mortimer J., *How to Think about War and Peace* (New York: Simon and Schuster, 1944).

322

Armstrong, Hamilton Fish, *Peace and Counterpeace* (New York: Harper & Row, 1971).

Aydelotte, Frank, *The American Rhodes Scholars* (Princeton: Princeton University Press, 1946).

Bailey, Thomas A. & Ryan, Paul B., *Hitler vs. Roosevelt. The Undeclared Naval War* (London: Collier Macmillan, 1979).

Bailey, Thomas A., *Woodrow Wilson and the Lost Peace* (New York: Quadrangle Books, 1963).

Baruch, Bernard M., *American Industry in the War. A Report of the War Industries Board* (March 1921), (New York: Prentice-Hall, 1941).

----, *The Making of the Reparation and Economic Sections of the Treaty* (New York: Harper and Brothers, 1920).

Batten, Samuel Zane, *The New World Order* (New York: American Baptist Publication Society, 1919).

Beard, Charles Austin, *President Roosevelt and the Coming of the War* (New Haven: Yale University Press, 1948).

----, *American Foreign Policy in the Making, 1932-1940* (New Haven: Yale University Press, 1946).

Bell, G.K.A., ed., *The Stockholm Conference of 1925. Official Report of the Universal Christian Conference on Life and Work held in Stockholm, 19-30 August 1925*, London, 1926.

Berding, Andrew H., *Dulles on Diplomacy* (Princeton, N.J.: Van Nostrand, 1965).

Bergson, Henri, *Creative Evolution*, trans. Arthur Michel (New York: Henry Holt and Company, 1911).

Birdsall, Paul, *Versailles Twenty Years After* (London: G. Allen & Unwin, 1941).

Bosco, Andrea, ed., *The Federal Idea,* Vol. 1, *The History of Federalism for the Enlightenment to 1945* (London: Lothian Foundation Press, 1991).

----, ed., 'The Lionel Curtis-Philip Kerr (Lord Lothian) Correspondence 1909-1940,' *Annals of the Lothian Foundation*, 1 (London: Lothian Foundation

Press, 1991).

---- and Navari, Cornelia, eds., *Chatham House and British Foreign Policy 1919-1945: The Royal Institute of International Affairs during the Inter-War Period* (London: Lothian Foundation Press, 1994).

Bryce, James, *The Ancient Roman Empire and the British Empire in India. The Diffusion of Roman and English Law throughout the World* (Oxford, Oxford University Press, 1914).

Burnett, Philip M., *Reparation at the Paris Peace Conference. From the Standpoint of the American Delegation*, 2 Vols. (New York: Columbia University Press, 1940).

Cargill, Oscar, *Intellectual America. Ideas on the March* (London: Macmillan, 1941).

Carnegie Endowment for International Peace, *The New World Order*, New York, 1940.

Carnegie, Andrew, *Triumphant Democracy* (New York: Charles Scribner's Sons, 1893).

Catlin, George, *One Anglo-American Nation. The Foundation of Anglo-Saxony as Basis of World Federation. A British Response to Streit* (London: Andrew Dakers Ltd., 1941).

----, *Church Cooperation and Unity in America. A Historical Review. 1900-1970* (New York: Association Press, 1970).

Cavert, Samuel McCrea, *The American Churches in theEcumenical Movement 1900-1968* (NewYork: Association Press, 1968).

Center for the Study of Democratic Institutions, *A Constitution for the World* (New York: The Fund for the Republic, 1965).

Clark, Kenneth, *Ruskin Today* (New York: Holt, Rinehart & Winston, 1964).

Comfort, Mildred H., *John Foster Dulles. Peacemaker* (Minneapolis: T.S. Denison, 1960).

Council on Foreign Relations, *Council on Foreign Relations. A Record of Fifteen Years* (New York: Harold Pratt House, 1937).

----, *Handbook*, New York, 1919.

----, *By-Laws with List of Officers and Members*, New York, 1922.

----, *The War and Peace Studies of the Council on Foreign Relations, 1939-1945* (New York: Harold Pratt House, 1946).

Crocker, George N., *Roosevelt's Road to Russia* (Chicago: Henry Regnery Co., 1959).

Curtis, Lionel George, *Dyarchy* (Oxford: Oxford University Press, 1920).

----, *Civitas Dei* (London: Macmillan, (1934) 1938); republished by George Allen & Unwin in 1950.

----, *Faith and Works* (London: Oxford University Press, 1943).

----, *The Way to Peace* (London: Oxford University Press, 1944).

----, *World War, its Causes and Cure: The Problem considered in view of the Release of Atomic Energy* (New York: Putnam, 1946).

Divine, Robert A., *Second Chance. The Triumph of Internationalism in America* (New York: Atheneum, 1967).

Drummond, Roscoe & Coblentz, Gaston, *Duel at the Brink. John Foster Dulles' Command of American Power* (Garden City, N.Y.: Doubleday, 1960).

Engelbrecht, H.C. & Hanighen, F.C., *Merchants of Death* (New York: Dodd, Mead, and Co., 1934).

----, *One Hell of a Business* (New York: Dodd, Mead, and Co., 1934).

Faunce, W.H.P., *Christian Principles Essential to a New World Order* (New York: Association Press, 1919).

----, *The Roosevelt Myth* (New York: The Devin-Adair Co., 1948).

Foundation Library Center, *The Foundation Directory* (New York: Russell Sage Foundation, 1960).

Gardner, Lloyd, *A Covenant with Power. America and World Order from Wilson to Reagan* (New York: Oxford University Press, 1984).

Gelfand, Lawrence, *The Inquiry. American Preparations for Peace, 1917-1919* (New Haven: Yale University Press, 1967).

Goodall, Norman, *The Ecumenical Movement* (London: Oxford University Press, 1961).

Headlam, Cecil, ed., *The Milner Papers*, I, (London, 1931, 1933).

Hicks, Ferderick C., *The New World Order* (New York: Doubleday, Page & Co., 1920).

Hogg, William Rickey, *Ecumenical Foundations. A History of the International Missionary Council and its Nineteenth-Century Background* (New York: Harpers, 1952).

Hoggan, David L., *The Myth of the 'New History'. Techniques & Tactics of the Mythologists of American History* (Torrance: Noontide Press, [1965] 1985).

House, Edward M. & Seymour, Charles, eds., *What Really Happened at Paris. The Story of the Peace Conference, 1918-1919* (New York: Charles Scribners' Sons, 1921).

Howard, Graeme Keith, *America and a New World Order* (New York: C. Scribner's Sons, 1940).

Hudson, Winthrop S., *Religion in America* (New York: Charles Scribner's Sons, 1965).

Hudson, Darril, *The Ecumenical Movement in World Affairs* (London: Weidenfeld & Nicolson, 1969).

----, *The World Council of Churches in International Affairs* (Leighton Buzzard: Faith Press for the Royal Insititute of International Affairs, 1977).

Hull, Cordell, *The Memoirs of Cordell Hull* (New York: Macmillan Co., 1948).

Hyde, H. Montgomery, *The Quiet Canadian. The Secret Service Story of Sir William Stephenson* (London: Hamish Hamilton, 1962).

Jenkyns, Richard, *The Victorians and Ancient Greece* (Oxford: Blackwell, 1980).

Jennings, W. Ivor, *A Federation for Western Europe*, London, 1940.

Johnson, Charles Henry, *One Common Purpose* (New York: Gettinger Press, 1937).

Kendle, J.E., *The Round Table Movement and Imperial Union* (Toronto: University of Toronto Press, 1975).

----, *Federal Britain. A History* (London: Routledge, 1997).

Kerr, Philip (Lord Lothian), *The End of Armageddon* (London: Federal Union pamphlet, 1939).

Keynes, John Maynard, *A Revision of the Treaty* (New York: Harcourt, Brace and Co., 1922).

King-Hall, Stephen, *Chatham House. A Brief Account of the Origins, Purposes and Methods of the Royal Institute of International Affairs* (London: Oxford University Press, 1937).

Kuitenbrouwer, J.B.W., *The New Capitalist World Order* (The Hague: Institute of Social Studies, 1981).

Lansing, Robert, *The Peace Negotiations. A Personal Narrative* (Boston: Houghton Mifflin, 1921).

*Lansing Papers*, Library of Congress.

Lossky, N. & Bonino, J.M. & Pobee, J. & Stranky, T. & Wainwright, G. & Webb, P., eds., *Dictionary of the Ecumenical Movement* (Geneva: WCC Publication, 1991).

Latourette, K.S., *Christianity in a Revolutionary Age. A History of Christianity in the Nineteenth and Twentieth Century*, Vol.5 (Devon: The Pater Noster Press, [1962] 1970).

Lord Riddell, *Lord Riddell's Intimate Diary of the Peace Conference and After, 1918-23* (London: Victor Gollancz, 1933).

Loucks, William N. & Hoot, J. Weldon, *Comparative Economic Systems* (New York: Harper & Brothers, 1948).

Lucas, Charles P., *Greater Rome and Greater Britain* (Oxford: Clarendon Press, 1912).

Macfarland, Charles S., *Pioneers for Peace through Religion. Based on the Records of the Church Peace Union (founded by Andrew Carnegie) 1914-1945* (Westwood, N.J.: Fleming H. Revell Co., 1946).

Mackie, Robert C. & West, Charles C., ed., *The Sufficiency of God. Essays on the Ecumenical Hope in Honor of W. A. Visser 't Hooft* (Philadelphia: The Westminster Press, 1965).

Madden, Frederick, & Fieldhouse, D.K., eds., *Oxford and the Ideal of Commonwealth* (London: Croom Helm, 1982).

Mayer, Arno, *Politics and Diplomacy of Peacemaking. Containment and Counterrevolution at Versailles, 1918-1919* (New York: Alfred A. Knopf, 1967).

Mayne, Richard & Pinder, John & de V. Roberts, John C., eds., *Federal Union: The Pioneers. A History of Federal Union* (London: Macmillan, 1990).

McGhee, George C., *World Community. A Goal for the New World Order* (New York: University Press of America, 1992).

McIntire, C.T. & Perry, Marvin (eds.), *Toynbee: Reappraisals* (Toronto: University of Toronto, 1989).

Meyer, Donald B., *The Protestant Search for Political Realism, 1919-1941* (Berkeley: University of California Press, 1961).

Milner, Alfred, *The Nation and the Empire. Being a Collection of Speeches and Addresses with an Introduction by Lord Milner, G.C.B.* (London: Constable and Co., 1913).

----, *Arnold Toynbee. A Reminiscence* (London: Edward Arnold, [1895] 1901).

----, *The British Commonwealth* (London: Constable & Co., 1919).

*Minutes of the Meeting of the Universal Christian Council for Life & Work*, Fanø, Denmark, 1934.

Nichols, James Hastings, *Democracy and the Churches* (Philadelphia: The Westminster Press, 1951).

Nicolson, Harold, *Peacemaking 1919* (London: Constable & Co., 1933).

Niebuhr, Reinhold & Mumford, Lewis & et al., *The City of Man. A Declaration on World Democracy* (New York: Viking Press, 1940).

----, *Man's Nature and Immoral Society. A Study in Ethics and Politics* (New York: Charles Scribner's Sons, 1932).

----, *Christianity and Power Politics* (New York: Charles Scribner's Sons,

1940).

----, *The Illusion of World Government* (Whitestone, N.Y.: The Graphics Group, 1949 - a reprint of Niebuhr's article by the same title in *Foreign Affairs*, April 1949).

Notter, Harley A., *Postwar Foreign Policy Preparation, 1939-1945* (Temecula, CA: Reprint Service Corporation, [1949] 1993).

Oldham, Joseph H., ed., *Church, Community, and State*, 8 Vols. (London: George Allen & Unwin, 1938).

----, ed., *Foundations of Ecumenical Social Thought. The Oxford Conference Report* (Philadelphia: Fortress, 1966).

Osborn, Andrew R., *Christianity in Peril. The New World Order and the Churches* (New York: Oxford University Press, 1942).

Paton, William, *World Community* (London: Student Christian Movement Press, 1938).

----, *The Church and the New Order* (London: Student Christian Movement Press, 1941).

Pinder, John & Bosco, Andrea, *Pacifism is not enough. Collected Lectures and Speeches of Lord Lothain (Philip Kerr)* (London: Lothian Foundation Press, 1990).

Ransome, Patrick, ed., *Studies in Federal Planning* (London: Macmillan, 1943).

Reade, William Winwoode, *The Martyrdom of Man* (London: Trübner & Co., [1872] 1874; reprinted by Pemberton Publishing Co., 1968 [1934 edition] ).

Roberts, Richard, *Schroders. Merchants & Bankers* (London: Macmillan, 1992).

Rothwell, Victor Howard, *British War Aims and Peace Diplomacy, 1914-1918*, Oxford, 1971.

Rouse, Ruth & Neill, Stephen Charles, eds., *A History of the Ecumenical Movement, 1517-1948*, Vol. 1 (Geneva: World Council of Churches, [1954] 1986).

Royal Institute of International Relations, *The Future of the League of Nations*

(London: Chatham House, 1936).

Ruskin, John, *Lectures in Art*, in *Collected Works*, Vol. 20, London, 1903.

Russell, Ruth B., *A History of the United Nations Charter. The Role of the United States, 1940-1945* (Washington, D.C.: The Brookings Institute, 1958).

Shepardson, Whitney H., *Early History of the Council on Foreign Relations* (Stanford, CA: Stanford University Press, 1960).

Shotwell, James T., *At the Paris Peace Conference* (New York: Macmillan, 1937).

Shulzinger, Robert D., *The Wise Men of Foreign Affairs. The History of the Council on Foreign Relations* (New York: Columbia University Press, 1984).

Stanley Jones, E., *The Next Greal Step* (Boston: The Association for a United Church, n.d.)

Stokes, R., *Political Ideas of Imperialism* (Oxford: Oxford University Press, 1960).

Straight, Michael, *Make This the Last War* (New York: Harcourt, Brace and Company, 1943).

Streit, Clarence, *Union Now. A Proposal for a Federal Union of the Democracies of the North Atlantic* (New York: Harper & Bros., 1939).

----, *Union Now with Britain* (New York: Harper & Bros., 1941).

----, *Freedom's Frontier Atlantic Union Now* (New York: Harper & Bros., 1961).

Tansill, Charles Callan, *Back Door to War. The Roosevelt Foreign Policy 1933-1941* (Chicago: Henry Regnery Co., 1952).

Tardieu, André, *The Truth About the Treaty* (Indianapolis: The Bobbs-Merrill Co., 1921).

Tawney, R.H., *Equality* (London: Allen & Unwin, [1931] 1938).

Temperley, H.W.V., ed., *A History of the Peace Conference of Paris* (London: Hodder & Stoughton, 1920).

Tillman, Seth P., *Anglo-American Relations at the Paris Peace Conference of*

*1919* (Princeton: Princeton University Press, 1961).

Todd, Lewis Paul & Certi, Merle, *Rise of the American Nation* (New York: Harcourt, Brace & World, 1966).

Toynbee, Arnold, *Lectures on the Industrial Revolution in England. Popular Addresses, Notes and other Fragments ... together with a short Memoir by B. Jowett.* [With a perfactory note by Charlotte M. Toynbee], (London: Rivingtons, 1884).

Toynbee, Arnold J., *Acquaintances* (London: Oxford University Press, 1967).
Turner, John, ed., *The Larger Idea. Lord Lothian and the Problem of National Sovereignty* (London: Intl. Specialized Book Service, 1988).

Universal Christian Council, *The Message and Decisions of Oxford on Church, Community and State*, New York, 1937.

Van Kirk, Walter W., *A Christian Global Strategy* (New York: Willett, Clark and Co., 1945).

Visser 't Hooft, Willlem A., *The Genesis and Formation of the World Council of Churches* (Geneva: World Council of Churches, 1982).

Walters, F.P., *A History of the League of Nations* (Oxford: Oxford University Press, 1986).

Wells, Herbert G., *The New World Order* (New York: Alfred A. Knopf, 1940).

Wolfskill, George, *The Revolt of the Conservatives* (Boston: Houghton, Mifflin, 1962).

The World Council of Churches, *Man's Disorder and God's Design*, Vol. V: *The First Assembly of the World Council of Churches* (New York: Harper and Brothers, 1949).

Zimmern, Sir Alfred, *The Greek Commonwealth. Politics and Economics in Fifth-Century Athens* (Oxford: Clarendon Press, 1911).

----, *The Third British Empire. Being a Course of Lectures delivered at Columbia University* (London: Humphrey Milford, 1926).

----, *Public Opinion and International Affairs* (Manchester: The Co-operative Union Limited, 1931).

----, *Spiritual Values and World Affairs* (Oxford: Clarendon Press, 1939).

----, *From the British Empire to the British Commonwealth* (London: Longmans' Pamphlets on the British Commonwealth, no. 3, 1941).


**Articles & Interviews & Unpublished Theses**

'The Malvern Conference,' *Time* magazine XXXIX (May 20, 1941).

'The World Church: News and Notes - Toronto Ecumenical Conference,' *Christianity and Crisis* (30 June 1941).

'The Churches and the Peace,' *Christian Century* 59 (18 March 1942).

'Notes taken by Bob as Foster recounted to the family his trip to England, July 1942,' *JFD Papers*.

'Confidential Memoradnum Prepared by John Foster Dules and Walter Van Kirk on Their Recent Visit to England,' summer 1942, *JFD Papers*.

'Report on Federal Council Conference on a Just and Durable Peace,' *Time* magazine (March 16, 1942).

'A Just and Durable Peace: Discussion of Political Propositions (Six Pillars of Peace),' March 1943, *JFD Papers*.

'John Foster Dulles,' *The Christian Century*, LXI (October 25, 1944), 1224-1225.

Bennett, John C. & Niebuhr, Reinhold & Nixon, Justin Wroe & Oxnam, G. Bromley, 'Concerning Mr. Dulles,' *The Christian Century*, LXI (October 25, 1944), 1231.

Bennett, John C., 'John Foster Dulles,' *Christianity and Society* 18 (Winter 1952-1953), 4-5.

Bonn, Moritz J., 'The New World Order,' *The Annals of the American Academy of Political and Social Science* (July 1941).

Bosco, Andrea, 'Lothian, Curtis, Kimber and the Federal Union Movement (1939-40),' *Journal of Contemporary History*, Vol. 23, 1988, 465-502.

[Brand, R.H.], 'Lionel Curtis, the Prophet of Organic Union,' *Round Table*, 46 (1956), 105-9.

Burgess, Michael, 'Empire, Ireland and Europe: A Century of British Federal Ideas,' in Michael Burgess, ed., *Federalism and Federation in Western Europe* (London: Croom Helm, 1986).

Burroway, Jessie June, 'Christian Witnes Concerning World Order, The Federal Council of Churches and Postwar Planning 1941-1947,' unpublished Ph.D thesis, University of Wisconsin, 1953, 27.

Cavert, Samuel M., 'When Is the Church Free?' *Christian Century*, LIV (May 26, 1937).

----, 'Moving toward the World Council,' *The Christian Century* (22 February 1939).

Challener, Richard D. and Fenton, John M., 'Recent Past Come Alive in Dulles "Oral History,"' University: A Princeton Quarterly (Spring 1967), 3-34.

Chamberlain, John, 'John Foster Dulles. A Wilsonian at Versailles, This Famous Lawyer May Be Dewey's Secretary of State,' *Life* XVII (21 August 1944), 84ff.

Conway, John, 'The Round Table. A Study in Liberal Imperialism,' unpublished Ph.D dissertation, Harvard University, 1951.

'Correspondence,' *The Christian Century*, 27 September 1939, 1172.

Curtis, Lionel G., 'World Order' (Address given at Chatham House on February 21, 1939), *International Affairs* (May-June 1939), Vol. XVIII, No. 3, Royal Institute of International Affairs, London.

Davis, Forrest, *The Saturday Evening Post*, CCXVII (September 9, 1944), 24ff.

Divine, Robert, *Foreign Policy and the United States President Elections, 1940-1948* (New York: New Viewpoints, 1974) 91-92.

Douglas, Paul H., Review of *War or Peace*, by John Foster Dulles, in *The Saturday Review of Literature* 32 (May 27, 1950), 14-15.

Dulles, Allen W. & Lamb, Beatrice Pitney, *The United Nations*, Headline Series, No. 59, *The Foreign Policy Association* (September-October 1946), New York.

Dove, John, 'The Round Table. A Mystery Probed. Notes for a History of the Round Table,' a typescript dated December 18, 1924, deposited in the archives of the *Round Table* editorial offices.

Eayrs, James, 'The Round Table Movement in Canada, 1909-1920,' *Canadian Historical Review*, XXXVIII (March 1957), 1-20.

Eliot, Charles W., 'The Next American Contribution to Civilization,' *Foreign Affairs* (September 15, 1922), New York.

Ellinwood, Jr., DeWitt Clinton, 'Lord Milner's "Kindergarten", the British Round Table Group, and the Movement for Imperial Reform, 1910-1918, unpublished Ph.D dissertation, Washington University, 1962.

Federal Council of Churches Pamphlet, *The United States and the World of Nations* (February, 1940), New York.

Fey, Harold E., 'News of the Christian World - Outline Policy for Crisis,' *The Christian Century*, 25 December 1940.

Garrett, Edmund, 'Milner and Rhodes,' in Charles S. Goldman, ed., *The Empire and the Century. A Series of Essays on Imperial Problems and Possibilities by various Writers. With an Introduction by C.S. Goldman ... and a Poem by Rudyard Kipling entitled 'The Heritage'* (London: John Murry, 1905).

Gilkey, Langdon, 'Niebuhr, Reinhold's Theology of History,' in Nathan A. Scott, Jr., ed., *The Legacy of Reinhold Niebuhr* (Chicago: The University of Chicago Press, 1975).

Hodson, Henry V., 'The Round Table 1910-81,' *The Round Table*, no. 284 (October 1981), 308-333.

Kerr, Philip (Lord Lothian), 'From Empire to Commonwealth,' *Foreign Affairs* (December 1922), New York.

----, 'The Demonic Influence of National Sovereignty,' in Joseph H. Oldham, *Church, Community, and State*, Vol. 7: *The Universal Church and the World of Nations* (London: George Allen & Unwin, 1938) 3-23.

Keim, Albert N., 'John Foster Dulles and the Federal Council of Churches of Christ, 1937-1949,' unpublished Ph.D thesis, Ohio State University, 1971.

----, 'John Foster Dulles and the Protestant World Order Movement on the Eve of World War II,' *Journal of Church and State*, 3 (1978), 73-89.

Kraft, Joseph, 'School for Statesmen,' *Harper's* (July 1958), 217: 64-68.

Leslie, Kenneth, 'Cable to Dulles,' *The Protestant*, VII (August-September 1946), 5-6.

----, 'John Cardinal Dulles?,' *The Protestant*, VII (August-September 1946), 6-8.

Leuchtenburg, William E., 'The New Deal and the Analogue of War,' in John Braeman, ed., *Changes and Continuity in Twentieth-Century America*, Columbus, Ohio, 1964, 88-144

Lukas, J. Anthony, 'The Council on Foreign Relations: Is It a Club? Seminar? Presidium? Invisible Government?,' *New York Times Magazine* (November 21, 1971), 129.

Menn, Wilhelm, 'The Church of Christ and the International Order,' in Joseph H. Oldham, *Church, Community, and State*, Vol. 7: *The Universal Church and the World of Nations*, George Allen & Unwin, London, 1938.

Morrison, Charles Clayton, 'Editorial,' *The Christian Century* (30 November 1938), 1453.

----, 'Editorial - Toward a World Converence,' *The Christian Century* (8 March 1939).

----, 'Editorial - Peace and Neutrality Sought by American Churches,' *The Christian Century* (20 September 1939), 1124-1125.

----, 'Editorial - The Federal Council's Message,' *The Christian Century* (18 October 1939), 1262-63.

Mulder, John, 'The Moral World of John Foster Dulles,' *Journal of Presbyterian History* 49 (Summer 1971), 157-182.

Nagorski, Zygmunt, 'A Member of the CFR Talks Back,' *National Review* (December 9, 1977), 1419.

Niebuhr, Reinhold, 'Leaves from the Notebook of a War-Bound American,' *The Christian Century*, 25 October 1939, 1298-99; 15 November 1939, 1405-6; 6 December 1939, 1502-3; 27 December 1939, 1607-8.

----, 'Plans for World Reorganization,' *Christianity and Crisis* 2 (October 19, 1942), 3-6.

----, 'The Moral World of John Foster Dulles,' *The New Republic* 139 (December 1, 1958), 8.

Nimocks, Walter, 'Lord Milner's "Kindergarten" and the Origins of the Round Table Movement,' *South Atlantic Quarterly*, LXIII (Autumn, 1964), 507-520.

Page, Ralph, 'Designs for a World Order,' *Annals of the American Academy of Political and Social Science* (July 1940).

Palmer, Albert W., 'Call a World Economic Conference!' *The Christian Century* (9 November 1938).

----, 'What Should the Churches Do Now?' *The Christian Century* (21 December 1938).

----, 'A Christian Fourteen Points,' *The Christian Century* (13 September 1939).

Platig, E. Raymond, 'John Foster Dulles. A Study of His Political and Moral Thought Prior to 1953 with Special Emphasis on International Relations,' unpublished Ph.D dissertation, University of Chicago, 1957.

Poulgrain, Greg, 'Dean Rusk. A Reflection,' *Australia & World Affairs* 26, Spring 1995, 27-39.

Quigley, Carroll, 'The Round Table Groups in Canada, 1908-38,' *Canadian Historical Review*, XLIII (September 1962), 204-224.

Reston, James B., 'John Foster Dulles and His Foreign Policy,' *Life*, XXV (October 4, 1948), 131-132.

Shafer, Luman J., 'The Christian in Politics,' *Post War World*, Vol. I (October 16, 1944), 2.

Shepardson, J.W., 'Lionel Curtis, Commonwealth Builder,' unpublished M.A. thesis (Cambridge, Mass.: Harvard University, 1949).

Special Correspondence, 'Emphasize War Responsibility,' *The Christian Century*, 31 January 1940, 152.

Stone, William T., 'The Munitions Industry,' *Foreign Policy Association Reports*, No. 20 (1935).

Streit, Clarence K., 'An Open Letter to John Foster Dulles,' *Freedom and Union*, III (October 1948), 1-3.

Studdard-Kennedy, Gerald, 'Christianity, Statecraft and Chatham House,' *Diplomacy and Statecraft*, 5 (1994).

Tarr, Dennis L., 'The Presbyterian Church and the Founding of the United Nations,' *Journal of Presbyterian History* 53 (Spring 1975), 3-32.

Toulouse, Mark G., 'Working Towards Meaningful Peace: John Foster Dulles and the F.C.C., 1937-1945,' *Journal of Presbyterian History* 61:4 (Winter 1983), 393-410.

Toynbee, Arnold J., 'Was Britain's Abdication Folly?,' *The Round Table* 60 (November 1970), London.

Van Dusen, Henry P., 'The Churches Speak,' *Christianity and Crisis* (6 April 1942).

----, 'The Six Pillars of Peace,' *Christianity and Crisis* 3 (22 March, 1943).

----, *What Is the Church Doing?* New York, 1943, 94-95.

Vines, Kenneth Nelson, *The Role of the Federal Council of the Churches of Christ in America in the Formation of American National Policy*, unpublished Ph.D. thesis (University of Minnesota, 1953).

Watt, David, 'The Foundation of the Round Table. Idealism, Confusion, Construction,' *The Round Table* 60 (November 1970), London, 425-433.

----, 'The Men of the Round Table: An American View of the Kindergarten,' *Round Table*, 59 (1969), 327-336.

Wilkerson, Doxey, 'Russia's Proposed New World Order of Socialism,' *The Journal of Negro Education*, (July 1941).

Whyte, F., 'The British Institute of International Affairs,' *The New Europe*, July 1920.

Zimmern, Sir Alfred, 'The Ethical Presuppositions of a World Order,' in Joseph H. Oldham, *Church, Community, and State*, Vol. 7: *The Universal Church and the World of Nations* (London: George Allen & Unwin, 1938), 27-56.


**Periodicals**

*American Oxonian* (April 1944), XXXI, 65-69; (July 1944), XXXI, 129-138; (January 1945), XXXII, 1-11.

*Capital Times* (Madison, Wisconsin: September 26, 1944), 20; (September 28, 1944); (September 29, 1944).

*Christian Becon,* (February 22, 1955).

*Christian Century,* (January 4, 1933); (November 23, 1933); (November 29, 1933); (October 9, 1935); (April 21, 1937); (March 22, 1944); (October 25, 1944).

*Christianity and Crisis* 3 (17 May 1943); (31 May 1943); (28 June 1943); (12 July 1943).

*Commonweal* (December 28, 1932).

Federal Council of Churches, *Federal Council Bulletin* 15, no. 1 (January 1932), New York.

    *Federal Council Bulletin* 15, no. 9 (September 1932), New York.

    *Federal Council Bulletin* 16, no. 1 (January 1933), New York.

    *Federal Council Bulletin* 16, no. 10 (October 1933), New York.

    *Federal Council Bulletin* 16, no. 11 (November-December 1933), New York.

    *Federal Council Bulletin* 17, no. 1 (January 1934), New York.

    *Federal Council Bulletin* 17, no. 2 (February 1934), New York.

    *Federal Council Bulletin* 17, no. 5 (May 1934), New York.

    *Federal Council Bulletin* 17, no. 6 (June 1934), New York.

'Federal Council Supports Munitions Inquiry,' *Federal Council Bulletin* 17, no. 11 (November-December, 1934) 21.

    *Federal Council Bulletin* 18, no. 1 (January 1935), New York.

    *Federal Council Bulletin* 18, no. 4 (April 1935), New York.

    *Federal Council Bulletin* 18, no. 10 (November-December 1935), New York.

    *Federal Council Bulletin* 19, no. 8 (October 1936), New York.

*Federal Council Bulletin* 20, no. 1 (January 1937), New York.

*Federal Council Bulletin* 20, no. 4 (April 1937), New York.

*Federal Council Bulletin* 20, no. 5 (May 1937), New York.

*Federal Council Bulletin* 20, no. 6 (June 1937), New York.

*Federal Council Bulletin* 21, no. 3 (March 1938), New York.

*Federal Council Bulletin* 22, no. 9 (September 1939), New York.

*Federal Council Bulletin* 23, no. 1 (January 1940), New York.

'Developing a Positive Peace Policy,' *Federal Council Bulletin* 23, no. 5 (May 1940), New York.

*Federal Council Bulletin* 24, no. 1 (January 1941), New York.

*Federal Council Bulletin* 24, no. 6 (June 1941), New York.

'Conference on the Bases of Peace,' *Federal Council Bulletin* 25, no. 4 (April 1942), New York.

(Walter W. Van Kirk), 'British and American Post-War Aims,' *Federal Council Bulletin* 25, no. 9 (September 1942), New York.

*Federal Council Bulletin* 25, no. 10 (October, 1942), New York.

*Federal Council Bulletin* 26, no. 9 (September 1943), New York.

*Federal Council Bulletin* 26, no. 10 (October 1943), New York.

*Federal Council Bulletin* 28, no. 6 (June 1945), New York.

'Progress Report by New Commission on World Affairs,' *Federal Council Bulletin* 30, no. 1 (January 1947), New York.

'Department Reorganization Is Announced,' *Federal Council Bulletin* 21, no. 2 (February 1948), New York.

*Fellowship*, (April, 1944).

*Fortune* IX, (March 1934).

*Newsweek*, (August 20, 1990).

*Oxford Magazine*, vol. 7 (June 19, 1889) 398.

*The Review of Reviews*, (May 1912).

*The Round Table* XV (June 1925), 427-430; (September 1935).

*Time* magazine, (January 20, 1936); (November 8, 1943).

**Annual Reports**

*Annual Report Of Federal Deposit Insurance Corporation for 1934* (Washington, D.C., 1934).

Carnegie Endowment for International Peace, *Annual Report of 1948* (New York, 1949).

    *Annual Report of 1949* (New York, 1950).

    *Yearbook of 1941* (New York, 1942).

    *Yearbook of 1950-1951* (New York, 1951).

Council on Foreign Relations, *Annual Report of the Executive Director* (New York: Harold Pratt House, 1924).

    *Annual Report of the Executive Director* (New York: Harold Pratt House, 1940).

Federal Council of Churches of Christ in America, *Annual Report* (New York, 1932, 1934, 1935, 1936, 1941, 1943, 1945, 1949).

Federal Council of Churches of Christ in America, *Biennial Report* (New York, 1938, 1940, 1942, 1944).

Federal Council of Churches of Christ in America, 'International Justice and Goodwill,' *Biennial Report* (New York, 1948).

Federal Council of Churches of Christ in America, *Quadrennial Report* (New York, 1932).

Rockefeller Foundation, *Annual Report* (New York, 1936).

**Letters**

Abraham Lincoln to William F. Elkins, 21 November 1864, in Archer H. Shaw, ed., *The Lincoln Encyclopedia. The Spoken and Written Words of A. Lincoln*, Macmillan Co., New York, 1950, 40.

Alfred Milner to George Parkin, 15 December 1893, in the *Private Papers of Sir George Parkin*, Public Archives of Canada, Ottawa.

Alfred Milner to George Parkin, 30 June 1896, in the *Private Papers of Sir George Parkin*, Public Archives of Canada, Ottawa.

Alfred Milner to Congdon, 23 November 1904, in Cecil Headlam, ed., *The Milner Papers. South Africa, 1899-1905*, Vol. 2, Cassell & Co., London, 1931-1933, 506.

Herbert Croly to Alfred E. Zimmern, 8 July 1915, *Zimmern Papers*, box 14, ff.198-199.

Walter Weyl to Alfred E. Zimmern, 5 May 1915, *Zimmern Papers*, box 14, f.175.

Walter Lippmann to Alfred E. Zimmern, 7 June 1915, *Zimmern* Papers, box 14, ff.180-181.

Alfred E. Zimmern to Walter Lippmann, 24 April 1917, *Zimmern Papers*, box 15, ff.60b-60c.

John Biddle, Secretary of War, to Vance McCormick, 12 March 1918, *JFD Papers,* Princeton University, Princeton, New Jersey.
John F. Dulles to Chief of Staff, 23 July 1918, *JFD Papers.*

'Mother' to John F. Dulles, December, 1918, *JFD Papers.*

Eustace Percy to Alfred E. Zimmern, 16 January 1919, *Zimmern Papers*, box 16, f.36.

Reginald B. Brett to Robert Smillie, 5 May 1919.

Woodrow Wilson to John Foster Dulles, 27 June 1919, *JFD Papers.*

J.H. Hall to Basil Williams, 5 July 1919, in Mss. Afr. s. 134 ( 39-40), Rhodes House, Oxford.

Robert E. Speer to John F. Dulles, 28 June 1921.

341

Tertius Van Dyke to John F. Dulles, 6 March 1922, *JFD Papers*.

Samuel McCrea Cavert to John F. Dulles, 29 December 1922, *JFD Papers*.

Henry Atkinson, general secretary of the Presbyterian Assembly, to John F. Dulles, 29 May 1923, Box 5, *JFD Papers*.

E.C. Carter to John F. Dulles, 12 December 1923.

John F. Dulles to E.C. Carter, 14 December 1923, Box 5, *JFD Papers*.

John F. Dulles to 'Father,' 2 June 1924, *JFD Papers*.

John F. Dulles to 'Foster,' 3 June 1924, *JFD Papers*.

Sidney L. Gulick to John F. Dulles, 30 November, 1925, Box 7, *JFD Papers*.

William Adams Brown to John F. Dulles, 8 January 1926, Box 7, *JFD Papers*.

Tertius Van Dyke to John F. Dulles, 25 January 1926, Box 7, *JFD Papers*.

Henry Sloane Coffin to John F. Dulles, 15 October 1926, Box 7, *JFD Papers*.
John F. Dulles to Helen Bramble, 24 October 1928, *JFD Papers*.

Memorandum from John F. Dulles to William Nelson Cromwell, 16 June 1931, Box 9, *JFD Papers*.

William Nelson Cromwell to John F. Dulles, 23 October 1931, Box 7, *JFD Papers*.

Edward M. House to Mrs. Randolph Tucker, 8 January 1933.

Henry Atkinson to Theodore R. Savage, 8 January 1933, Box 110, *JFD Papers*.

Philip Kerr (Lord Lothian) to Lionel G. Curtis, 6 May 1933.

John F. Dulles to William Nelson Cromwell, 19 February 1934, *JFD Papers*.

Hjalmar Schacht to Dulles, 27 September 1935, *JFD Papers*.

Tertius Van Dyke to John F. Dulles, 7 October 1935, Box 14, *JFD Papers*.

John F. Dulles to Heinrich F. Albert, 27 December 1935, *JFD Papers*.

John F. Dulles to George S. Brown, 29 January 1936, *JFD Papers.*

John F. Dulles to Hjalmar Schacht, 15 June 1937, *JFD Papers.*

Philip Kerr (Lord Lothain) to Pfarrer Wilhelm Menn, 27 July 1937.

Henry L. Stimson to John F. Dulles, 5 January, 1939, *JFD Papers.*

John F. Dulles to Clarence Streit, 23 January, 1939.

Philip Kerr (Lord Lothian) to Patrick Ransome, 8 March 1939, SRO, *Lothian Papers*, GD40/17/376/714.

Philip Kerr (Lord Lothian) to Clarence Streit, March 1939, SRO, *Lothian Papers*, GD40/17/386/747-51.

John F. Dulles to Heinrich F. Albert, 15 June 1939, *JFD Papers.*

John F. Dulles to Charles A. Lindbergh, November 1939, *JFD Papers.*

John F. Dulles to Quincy Wright, 19 December 1939, 1, *JFD Papers.*

John F. Dulles to Professor Eugene Staley, 3 January 1940, *JFD Papers.*

Henry P. Van Dusen to JFD, with enclosure, 11 Janurary 1940, *JFD Papers.*

John F. Dulles to Granville Clark, 4 March 1940, Box 138, *JFD Papers.*

John F. Dulles to Helen Miller, 7 March 1940, Box 138, *JFD Papers.*

John F. Dulles to Henry P. Van Dusen, 18 March 1940, *JFD Papers.*

Clarence Streit to John F. Dulles, 21 March 1940, *JFD Papers.*

John F. Dulles to Thomas Debevoise, 30 April 1940, Box 138, *JFD Papers.*

Walter Van Kirk to John Foster Dulles, 11 May 1940, Box 7, *JFD Papers.*

William Adams Brown to John Foster Dulles, 24 May 1940, Box 7, *JFD Papers.*

John F. Dulles to William W. Van Kirk, 13 June 1940, Box 19, *JFD Papers.*

William Van Kirk to John Foster Dulles, 28 June 1940, Box 7, *JFD Papers.*

John F. Dulles to America First Committee, 4 December 1940, Box 131, *JFD Papers.*

John F. Dulles to John Bassett Moore, 21 January 1941.

John F. Dulles to Lionel Curtis, 28 February 1941, Box 20, *JFD Papers.*

John F. Dulles to Arthur Sulzberger, 21 May 1941, Box 7, *JFD Papers.*

John F. Dulles to Hugh Wilson, 13 June 1941, Box 138, *JFD Papers.*

John F. Dulles to members of the Commission on a Just and Duarable Peace, 6 January 1943.

John F. Dulles to Robert E. Speer, n.d., Box 4, *JFD Papers.*

Memorandum, Franklin D. Roosevelt to General Watson, 20 February, 1943, Official File 4351 (January-March 1943), Franklin D. Roosevelt Library, Hyde Park, New York (FDRL).

Rockefeller letter, March 9, 1943, Box 180, *JFD Papers.*

John F. Dulles to all members of the commission, 12 March 1943, Box 22, *JFD Papers.*

Memorandum, Sumner Welles to Roosevelt, 18 March, 1943, President's Personal File 5575, FDRL.

Walter W. Van Kirk to Social Action secretaries, 20 April, 1943, Federal Council of Churches, Manuscripts, Box 195.

John F. Dulles to Arthur Ballantine, 22 September 1943, *JFD Papers.*

John F. Dulles to Wendell Wilkie, 28 September 1943, *JFD Papers.*

John F. Dulles to Herbert Hoover, 5 October 1943, *JFD Papers.*

John F. Dulles to Sumner Welles, 26 October 1943, *JFD Papers.*

John F. Dulles to Walter Yust, 27 December 1943, *JFD Papers.*

John F. Dulles to Lionel G. Curtis, 19 September 1944, *JFD Papers.*

Lionel G. Curtis to Miss M.M. Wingate, 24 October 1944.

Hall to Williams, in Mss. Afr. s. 134, Rhodes House, Oxford.

Harry S. Truman to John F. Dulles, 6 November 1945, in 'Truman and Dulles Exchange Letters,' *Post War World*, Vol III (December 15, 1945).

John F. Dulles to George C. Marshall, 10 March 1948, *JFD Papers*.

John F. Dulles to John Hightower, December 22, 1954, *JFD Papers*.

**Newspapers**

*New York Call*, October 8, 1917.

*New York Times*, December 20, 1922; October 4, 1938; June 16, 1945; February 25, 1946; July 30, 1946; August 4-8, 1946; December 6, 1950; November 11, 1957; October 21, 1987.

*New Yorker*, December 28, 1957.

*Times*, March 27, 1902; September 10, 1949; October 1, 1949.

Washington *Evening Star*, December 14, 1935.

**Public Documents**

Acting Secretary of State to the Commission to Negotiate Peace, December 19, 1919, in U.S. Department of State, *Papers Relating to the Foreign Relations of the United States. The Paris Peace Conference, 1919*, Vol. I.

*Report of the Federal Trade Commission on War-Time Profits and Costs of the Steel Industry*, June 25, 1924.

Notter, Harley A., 'Recollections: Notes January 1942 - December 1943,' in Records of the Department of State, Harley A. Notter File, Box 1, Record Group 59, National Archives, Washington, D.C.

Memorandum, Leo Pasvolsky to staff members of the Division of Special Research, December 22, 1942 in Records of the Department of State, Harley A. Notter File, Box 4, Record Group 59, National Archives, Washington, D.C.

United States Congress, *Congressional Record*, 78th Congress, 1st Session (Washington, D.C.: Government Printing Office, 1944).

United States Congress, Senate Hearings before the Special Senate Committee on the Investigation of the Munitions Industry, 78th Congress, 2nd session, Parts 1-17 (Washington, D.C.: Government Printing Office, 1944).

Speech of Senator Joseph F. Guffey of Pennsylvania, in United States Congress, *Congressional Record*, 78th Congress, 2nd Session (Washington, D.C.: Government Printing Office, 1944, XC, Part 6, 8058-8061).

Speech of Senator Arthur H. Vanderberg of Michigan, in United States Congress, *Congressional Record*, 78th Congress, 2nd Session (Washington, D.C.: Government Printing Office, 1944, XC, Part 6, 8061).

United States Congress, Senate Hearings before a Subcommittee of the Committee on Military Affairs, *Elimination of German Resources for War*. Report pursuant to S. Res. 107 and 146, July 2, 1945, Part 7, 78th Congress and 79th Congress (Washington, D.C.: Government Printing Office, 1945).

United States Congress, Senate Hearings before the Committee on Foreign Relations, *The Charter of the United States*, 79th Congress, 1st Session (Washington, D.C.: Government Printing Office, 1945, 647).

United Nations Information Organizations, *Documents of the United Nations Conference on International Organization, San Francisco, 1945*, Vol. XV, New York, 1946.

Statement of Herbert Evatt before Commission II on June 21, 1945 in *Documents of the United Nations Conference on International Organization, San Francisco, 1945*, Vol. VIII, New York, 1946, 209.

Speech of representative Adolph J. Sabbath of Illinois, in United States Congress, *Congressional Record*, 80th Congress, 1st Session (Washington, D.C.: Government Printing Office, 1947, XCIII, Part 4, 4607).

United States Congress, House Hearings before the Committee on Foreign Relations, *Structure of the United Nations and the Relations of the United States to the United Nations*, 80th Congress, 1st Session (Washington, D.C.: Government Printing Office, 1948, 279, 282-283).

Testimony by Dulles, in United States Congress, Senate Hearings before the Committee on Foreign Relations, *United States Assistance to European Recovery Program*, Part 2, 80th Congress, 2nd Session (Washington, D.C.: Government Printing Office, 1948).

Testimony by Milton Mayer, in United States Congress, Senate Hearings before the Committee on Foreign Relations, *North Atlantic Treaty*, 81st

Congress, 1<sup>st</sup> Session (Washington, D.C.: Government Printing Office, 1949, 825).

Testimony by Dulles, in United States Congress, Senate Hearings before the Committee on Foreign Relations, *North Atlantic Treaty*, 81$^{st}$ Congress, 1$^{st}$ Session (Washington, D.C.: Government Printing Office, 1949, 339-345).

United States Congress, Senate Hearings before a Subcommittee of the Committee on Foreign Relations, *Revision of the United Nations Charter,* 81$^{st}$ Congress (Washington, D.C.: Government Printing Office, 1950).

United States Congress, Special Committee to Investigate Tax-exempt Foundations and Comparable Organizations, House of Reps., *Tax-Exempt Foundations*, Report, 82$^{rd}$ Congress, 2$^{nd}$ Session (Washington, D.C.: Government Printing Office, 1953).

# INDEX

# D

Darwin, Charles · 37
*Descent of Man* (1871) · 37
Davis, John W. · 18, 32, 33, 186,
214-216
Dawson, Geoffrey *see also*
Robinson, Geoffrey · 16, 43, 45,
46, 50, 73, 74-76
democracy · xv, 39, 41, 57, 58, 66,
86, 109, 174, 197, 205, 235, 238,
240, 286, 294
divine commonwealth · 60, 64
divine kingdom · 61, 62, 63, 105
Dulles, Allen W. · 26, 92, 126, 142,
229, 283, 294
Dulles, Avery · 64, 79, 97, 116, 119,
131, 140
Dulles, Eleanor · 89, 90, 117, 123,
139, 141
Dulles, John Foster · x, 1-4, 6-11,
19, 21-28, 64, 65, 69, 79, 83-99,
102, 103, 105, 113, 115-135,
137-143, 170-173, 175-180, 186-
189, 191-213, 215-220, 229-231,
238-256, 258, 260, 263, 265, 266,
268-280, 283, 284, 287-299, 304,
308-313
'Statement of Political
Propositions' · 219, 249, 280,
289, 291
humanistic creed · 119
*Long Range Peace Objectives* ·
211, 213, 241, 277, 280, 289,
309
*War, Peace and Change* · 64, 65,
79, 89, 143, 172, 201, 205,
217, 274, 275
Dumbarton Oaks conference · 215,
252, 253

# E

ecumenical movement · ix, x, xiii,
63, 83, 84, 87, 99-102, 104, 106-
108, 115, 118, 121-123, 133, 135,
137, 146, 227, 229, 259, 304-306,
308
league of churches · 64
ecumenicity · 103, 104, 112, 134
ecumenism · x, 146
European federalism · 217, 219, 311
European federation · 87, 220, 223,
225, 312
European Union, *see also* United
States of Europe · 216, 219, 225,
232

# F

Fascism · 66, 88, 89, 92, 97, 158,
205
*Federal Council Bulletin* · 137, 142,
151, 154, 162, 181-184, 186, 188,
244, 256, 271, 272, 276, 283,
284, 289, 291, 294, 295, 297, 298
Federal Council of Churches (FCC) ·
1, 65, 69, 80, 83, 95, 102, 137,
141, 142, 145, 147, 177, 181-184,
186, 188, 209, 250, 253, 265,
268, 271-273, 276, 277, 283, 284,
286, 289, 290-299, 305, 306, 308,
309, 312, 313
'A Christian Message on World
Order' · 260, 295, 296
'Christian Missions on World
Order' · 295, 313
'The Churches and World Order'
· 97, 124, 132, 133, 137, 198,
267, 273
'The Spiritual Challenge of the
Economic Crisis' · 153
Atlantic City Biennial Meeting
(1940)· 150, 179, 192, 210
Christian collectivism · 151, 153,
154, 306, 307
National Study Conference · 180,
191, 196, 207, 243, 268, 271,
272, 275, 277, 278, 295, 311
Ohio Wesleyan Conference
(1942) · 229
Philadelphia conference (1908) ·
149
World Order Days · 267, 313

351

260, 262, 303, 304
nation-state system · 111, 207, 305,
311
Nazi Germany, *see* Germany
Naziism, *see* Germany
New Deal · 153, 158-162, 183, 185,
287, 305, 307
new international order, *see also*
international order · xv, 200, 218,
245
new international organisation · 200,
249, 263, 311
*New Republic* · 2, 53, 91, 92
new social order · 145, 151, 152,
159, 304, 307, 308, 310
new world order, *see also* world
order · xii, 4, 11, 12, 20, 53, 56,
69, 77, 79, 88, 95, 96, 101, 106,
107, 113, 121, 122, 134, 149,
159, 173, 174, 191, 193, 195,
198, 207, 211, 212, 216-218,
225-228, 230, 240, 247, 248, 250,
253, 257, 261, 267, 269, 279,
283, 285, 287, 301, 305, 311, 313
new world organisation · 210, 215,
225
new world society · 311
new world system · 85
Niebuhr, Reinhold · 92, 101, 127,
133, 174-176, 179, 199, 252, 254,
256, 277, 291, 294

# O

Oldham, Joseph H. · 64, 66, 80, 83,
84, 98-101, 123, 132, 228, 229,
252, 303
Oxford · vii, 35, 37-40, 43, 49, 58,
64, 65, 67-69, 73, 80, 83, 84, 88,
95, 97, 98, 100-104, 115, 118,
121-123, 131, 133-135, 143, 201,
221, 226, 227, 229, 231, 282,
284, 303, 304
Oxnam, Bishop G. Bromley · 92,
259, 267, 276, 291, 292

# P

Paris Peace Conference, *see also*
Versailles Peace Conference · 1,
6, 10, 20, 24, 26, 53, 56
Pasvolsky, Leo · 214, 216, 245, 246,
278, 290
Paton, William · 66-69, 99, 104, 112,
113, 134, 226, 228, 229, 245,
246, 256-259, 282, 283
'Some Principles of
Reconstruction' · 259
'The Church and World Order' ·
69
*The Church and the New Order*
(1941) · 69, 112, 134, 227
*World Community* (1938) · 66
patriotism · 198, 204, 205, 233
Pattern for Peace · 263, 264
Peace Aims Committee · 224-226
Peace Aims Group · 226-229, 255,
256, 258, 259, 283
'A Christian Basis for
Reconstruction' · 255, 256,
259
Pearl Harbor · 162, 168, 177, 186,
207, 287, 312
Plato · 36, 39, 70
Pre-Armistice Agreement · 5-8, 23,
24, 26
Presbyterian Church, USA · 148,
149, 182
Protestant churches · xiii, 63, 147,
153, 160, 253, 305, 308
Pruessen, Ronald W. · 23, 25, 92,
128, 133, 177, 178, 208, 215, 247
public opinion · xiii, 1, 9, 10, 12, 13,
28, 42, 49, 52, 64, 69, 79, 100,
105, 106, 114, 121, 193, 202,
208, 209, 212-214, 226, 227, 229,
231, 233, 243, 250, 253, 254,
257, 262, 263, 265, 267, 268,
271, 283, 297-299, 308, 309, 313

# R

reparations · 6-8, 23-26, 243

Rhodes Trust · 19, 20, 45, 46, 49, 70,
231
Roosevelt, President Franklin · 66,
91, 95, 130, 139, 149, 153, 158-
162, 166, 168, 169, 171, 174,
180, 183, 185, 186, 211, 212,
214, 216, 249, 252, 267, 275,
278, 291, 307, 309, 312
Round Table Group · 1, 10, 20, 39,
40-42, 48-52, 56, 60, 64, 66, 69,
70, 72, 78, 107, 111, 221, 228,
231, 234, 285, 302, 303, 308, 312
175 Piccadilly · 50
Blickling Hall · 50
Cliveden · 50
Royal Institute of International
Affairs, *see also* Council on
Foreign Relations, Institute of
International Affairs · 2, 14, 15,
17, 20, 24, 27, 28, 40, 54, 77, 79,
97, 103, 108, 131, 227, 230, 245,
282, 284, 301
*International Affairs* · 16, 17, 77
*Survey of International Affairs* ·
13, 16
*Yearbook of International Law* ·
16
Ruskin, John · 20, 35-37, 70
*A Knight's Faith* (1885) · 36
Slade Professor of Fine Art · 35
St. George's Guild · 36

# S

San Francisco United Nations
Conference · 267
Schrobanco · 91-93, 127, 128
Second World War · xiii, 1, 88, 89,
94, 199, 201, 216, 224, 230, 247,
278, 292, 310, 311, 313
Sermon on the Mount · ix, 57, 59,
61, 66, 116, 303, 304
Shepardson, Whitney H. · 1, 11, 13,
17, 18, 27, 28, 30-32
social gospel · 122, 123, 131, 137,
152, 154-157, 168, 197, 307
socialism · 40, 41, 71, 306

South Africa · 17, 38, 39, 43-49, 51,
62, 235, 312
sovereign nation-states · 68, 107,
108, 308
sovereignty system, *see also* national
sovereignty system · 113, 114,
121, 198, 199, 206, 210, 216,
234, 312
sovereignty-war system · 85, 124
Streit, Clarence K. · 222, 231-239,
284, 285-288, 303, 312
Sullivan & Cromwell · 2, 3, 89, 90-
92, 96, 125

# T

Taft, Charles P. · 101, 197, 198, 291
Temple, William · 101, 221, 222,
226-229, 246, 256, 283
*Towards a Christian Britain*
(1940) · 228
Tiarks, Frank C. · 92, 93
*Time magazine* · 142, 166, 243, 311
totalitarianism · 89, 90, 122, 158,
162, 174, 235, 309, 310
Toynbee, Arnold · 36, 39, 40, 71,
226
*Lectures on the Industrial
Revolution* · 40
Toynbee, Arnold J. · 6, 16, 30, 50,
52, 56, 59, 61, 76, 86, 103, 112,
221, 229, 230, 235, 245, 256,
282, 284
Treaty of Versailles, *see also* Paris
Peace Treaty · 8, 25, 43

# U

*Union Now* (1939) · 222, 231-235,
237, 239, 285, 303, 312
*Union Now with Britain* (1941) ·
231, 237
United Nations (Organisation) · xiii,
1, 2, 10, 69, 120, 133, 142, 199,
200, 213-216, 225, 229, 230, 246,
249, 252, 253, 255, 259, 261,

# Z

2638451R00201

Printed in Great Britain
by Amazon.co.uk, Ltd.,
Marston Gate.